Political Theory
and
Public Policy

Robert E. Goodin

Political Theory
and
Public Policy

The University of Chicago Press
Chicago and London

The University of Chicago Press, Chicago 60637
The University of Chicago Press, Ltd, London

01 00 99 98 97 96 95 94 93 92   3 4 5 6 7 8 9

Library of Congress Cataloging in Publication Data

Goodin, Robert E.
  Political theory and public policy.

  Bibliography: p.
  Includes index.
  1. Policy sciences.   2. Political ethics.   3. Social
values.   I. Title.
H97.G66   361.6'1   81-23120
                                    AACR2
ISBN 0-226-30297-0 (paper)

To Charles S. Hyneman
who tried to teach me better

Contents

Preface

Portions of this text profited enormously from discussions in diverse settings: Oslo and Leiden, Washington and Paris, New York and London, Norwich and Ghent, Jakarta and Manila, Florence and Dubrovnik. I am grateful to all those who commented so usefully at that stage, and to Brian Barry, Jon Elster, and Russell Hardin for assistance and encouragement all along the way. Many of these ideas can be traced, directly or indirectly, to my time among the remarkable group that Dave Bobrow and Mancur Olson gathered together at the University of Maryland. We learned a lot about public policymaking together—and, in the end, a fair bit about village-pump politics. Pleased though I may be with my present sanctuary, my thoughts continually hark back to that department that might have been.

Wivenhoe, Essex
August 1981

What intellectuals chiefly bring to policy debates, and what chiefly accounts for their influence, is not knowledge but theory . . . . There is little point in denouncing theory as an inadequate substitute for experience, knowledge, or prudence (which it is); it will be propounded, it will affect policy, and those skilled at formulating it will rise in influence. Moreover, theorizing is not the same as empty talk. Good theory calls attention to obvious truths that were previously overlooked, finds crucial flaws in existing theories, and reinterprets solid evidence in a new light. And some theories, if adopted, will make us better-off. The problem is to know which ones.

James Q. Wilson
"'Policy Intellectuals' and Public Policy"

The Need
for Theory

1 Theoretical Foundations for Policy Analysis

The proudest boast of "the policy sciences" always has been the blending of theory and practice. They aspired to "relevance" without suggesting that "social scientists ought to desert science and engage full time in practical politics." Emphasis was to be "upon the most fundamental problems of man in society"—those "most pregnant with theoretical significance"—"rather than upon the topical issues of the moment" (Lerner and Lasswell 1951, 7; Kecskemeti 1951, 527). Maybe the policy sciences were just "old public administration in a refurbished wardrobe" (Eulau 1977, 419), but institutional minutia was to be set in a larger theoretical context and the omnipresent case study was to pack a new theoretical punch (Heclo 1972). Maybe policy science was merely operational research and econometrics masquerading behind another name; still, the emphasis was to be on empirical validation of theoretical models with practical payoffs, rather than on displays of sheer technical virtuosity (Leontief 1971). Above all, the policy sciences were to bring values back into the relentlessly positivistic disciplines from which they sprang (Heclo 1972). All of these goals—especially the last—remain only partially fulfilled. That shortfall between aspiration and accomplishment provides the impetus for this book.

What has gone wrong? First of all, methodological tendencies and simple oversights combine to make moral philosophy less useful than it might be and policy analysis less rigorous than it should be. Those are exposed in this introductory chapter. Ultimately, however, the atheoretical cast of policy studies probably owes much to the influence of incrementalism. This is a doctrine which, in its boldest form, maintains that theoretical understanding of the social system is unnecessary and probably even undesirable for policymaking—both empirical relationships and moral values are, it claims, best discovered by trial and error. These claims are countered systematically in the next two chapters. Incrementalism is shown to be an unwise strategy for ascertaining empirical truths (chapter 2) and an unduly restrictive method of obtaining moral guidance (chapter 3).

The bulk of this book is dedicated to the more constructive task of helping the policy sciences realize their early evaluative promise. This requires systematic connections between empirical and evaluative propositions on *all* levels of analysis. Theoretically informed analyses of particular policy problems—e.g., energy policy as in chapter 10 and defense policy as in chapter 11—are obviously needed. But these are not enough in themselves. They must be supplemented, as in chapters 7 through 9, by critical reflection upon the sorts of excuses that politicians typically offer for the inadequacies of their policies. And all of this must eventually rest on some more general understanding (once again, well grounded both empirically and evaluatively) of the principles underlying and the institutions shaping these policies. Such foundations are here laid in chapters 4 through 6.

Comprehensiveness in such matters is clearly impossible. There are more policies, excuses, institutions, and principles than any one author could possibly hope to cover. Neither is there any standard subset that all agree must be included in such discussions. No doubt others would choose different emphases. But no matter. Mostly this should be seen as a "sampler" illustrating the sort of analysis that can and should be undertaken by those of us truly committed to the joint practice of both the social and the moral sciences. Even if facts and values could be separated—and there is much in policy debates to put pay to the myth that they can (Rein 1976)—this book argues strongly that they should not be. Empirical and ethical theory ought both to be used, and used in tandem, to guide public policymaking.

1.1. Empirical Theory for Policymaking

The case for some sort of empirical theory informing policy choices is intuitively obvious. We choose policies hoping to produce certain kinds of results, and we must know how the system is wired in order to know which lever to pull. But this understanding must be theoretical, not just the product of accumulated practical experience or random hunches, if we are to be able to anticipate all the side effects of the policy and say how the system will respond under altered conditions or in the long term, of which we have no experience.

To illustrate this argument, consider the long-standing dispute over "incentive effects" in welfare and tax policy. As early as 1787, reforms in the English Poor Laws were being opposed by the Reverend Joseph Townsend on the grounds that they would constitute a disincentive to labor: "to promote industry and economy it is necessary that the relief given to the poor be limited and precarious," he claimed (Cowherd 1977, 7). President Nixon similarly scorned public welfare recipients as "welfare bums" who would not undertake gainful employment as long as the public supported them. Were this true, perhaps welfare payments should be made conditional upon the recipient's proving that he has tried to find work. Or perhaps income taxes for higher wage-earners should be reduced if, as Prime Minister Thatcher imagines, people will work harder, the more of their extra earnings they can pocket. But before embarking on either course it is crucial to know what the facts really are. It would be inhumane to deny poor people public welfare if nothing would be gained by a "tough" attitude, and it would be irresponsibly generous of the Tories to cut rich people's taxes unless the lost revenue would in fact be replaced through increased productivity.

Empirical political theories can go wrong in either of two ways. First, they may fail the empirical test—failing *when put* to the test or, more commonly, failing *to be put* to the empirical test (Leontief 1971). Advocates of the "welfare bum" and "tax disincentive" hypotheses typically treat them as articles of faith rather than as empirical propositions to be subjected to systematic testing, but when the "welfare bum" hypothesis was finally put to the test—in negative income tax experiments in New Jersey and then elsewhere—it turned out to be largely incorrect: it was found that unconditional guarantees of public assistance seem to reduce labor force supply by only about 5 percent among white male heads of households, while actually increasing it slightly among black males in New Jersey and among female heads of particularly poor households in Gary, Indiana (Brown 1980, chap. 6; cf. Ferber and Hirsch 1978; Pechman and Timpane 1975). A flaw in the study design badly exaggerated the dropoff in work effort of a family's second and third wage-earners (Greenberg, et al. 1981). Some such dropoff would, however, be both reasonable and desirable, given wives' and dependent children's other responsibilities at home or at school.[1] At the

---

1. Upon emancipation, former slaves in the American South similarly reduced their work hours by 28 percent to 37 percent. Ransom and Sutch (1977, 6) find that, "as slaves, blacks were compelled to work long hours with few days off. Women, adolescents, and the aged were all expected—and forced—to work as long and as often as the men. When free to set their own hours of work, the ex-slaves, quite predictably,

opposite end of the income spectrum, empirical examination reveals that "tax disincentives" to the rich are equally weak. The evidence suggests that "high-income people are more motivated by the 'scores' they make—their pretax income—than by the actual disposable income they receive" (Lindblom 1977, 44). One survey of high-income Americans, for example, finds that "seven-eighths...explicitly stated that they had not curtailed their work effort on account of the income tax" (Bronfenbrenner 1971, 150; cf. Break 1957; Brown 1980, chap. 4; Barlow, et al. 1966, chap. 10).

Empirical political theories may fail, second, because they are inadequate as theories. Sometimes policymakers do not even attempt to find theoretical explanations for empirical regularities. They act on the basis of rules that just seem to work, without knowing why. More commonly, theories predict the direction but not the magnitudes of policy effects. Then we have no choice but to estimate the parameters by experimenting with the policies themselves (Ferber and Hirsch 1978). But this too can be dangerous. Where the thinness of theory forces us to derive parameters empirically, the theory is often also insufficient to warn us of the conditions under which the parameters will change. For instance, the Phillips Curve, relating inflation and unemployment, has needed recalibrating for virtually every period; and, as if such wild shifting were not bad enough, it now even threatens to slope positively (Friedman 1977).

Moreover, theoretical explanations offered are often simply incoherent. When the conclusions do not follow logically from premises, we must reject the theory, however well it may fit the empirical data. Some arguments for promoting economic development by curtailing human rights fall into this category. Three World Bank economists (Averch, et al. 1971) analyzed the "lurching" of the Philippine economy in terms of a classic "political business cycle," with the government of the day heating up the economy in anticipation of every election and cooling it down afterward. Supporters of President Marcos claim that martial law should, therefore, aid stable economic development, i.e., suspending democratic competition should end this destructive cycle. But that theory is fatally flawed. However destabilizing a political business cycle may be, at least it is

---

chose to exchange a fraction of their potential income for 'free' time . . . . They duplicated . . . the work-leisure patterns of other free Americans. Adolescents in their early teens, women with children, and elderly men and women all worked significantly fewer hours per day and fewer days per year than had been the standard under the oppression of slavery . . . . Too often this perfectly normal response to emancipation has been taken as 'evidence' to support racist characterizations of blacks as lazy, incompetent, and unwilling to work without compulsion." Surely we should take an equally sympathetic view of the remarkably similar response of those freed by a guaranteed income from the ravages of poverty.

a cycle: after the elections, politicians have a chance to cool the economy down again; and, whereas democratic politicians need drum up support only during the runup to elections, tyrants constantly need propping up, with potentially far worse consequences for the economy (Goodin 1979).

Thus, sound policies must be based on an analysis of the situation that is both empirically well grounded and theoretically defensible. Threats come not only from atheoretical number-crunchers but also from model-builders impervious to empirical realities. Notice, in this connection, Leontief's (1971, 3) criticism of tendencies in econometric modeling:

> Continued preoccupation with imaginary, hypothetical, rather than with observable reality has gradually led to a distortion of the informal valuation scale used in our academic community.... Empirical analysis, according to this scale, gets a lower rating than formal mathematical reasoning. Devising a new statistical procedure, however tenuous, that makes it possible to squeeze out one more unknown parameter from a given set of data is judged a greater scientific achievement than the successful search for additional information that would permit us to measure the magnitude of the same parameter in a less ingenious, but more realistic way.

This complaint hauntingly recurs in only slightly different form in my criticisms of bizarre hypotheticals in moral modeling, discussed below.

1.2. Ethical Theory for Policymaking

The need for some sort of normative theory to guide policy choices is also, in some sense, intuitively obvious. We need to know not only which results follow from which policies but also which results we should prefer and strive to achieve. No evaluation is possible without some sort of theory of value. This need not be very sophisticated. In policy studies, it tends not to be. It is painful to hear a well-trained policy scientist "turn to the normative implications" of his analysis, which usually will amount to nothing more than supplementing his efficiency calculations with some considerations of distributive impacts. Many otherwise highly sophisticated policy analysts still seem very much stuck in nineteenth-century moral ruts, regarding "equality and efficiency" as the "big" tradeoff if not quite the only one with moral significance (Okun 1975; Anderson 1979; Wolf 1981).

With the advent in 1971 of *Philosophy & Public Affairs*, explicitly devoted to forging links between these two areas, it should have become easier to bring modern moral philosophy to bear on policy choices. In fact, it has become more difficult. That journal has stamped on the whole subdiscipline a "house style" incorporating methodological and doctrinal implications that are counter-productive to effective moral argumentation on genuine policy issues. The best brief description I can give of the sorts of ethical arguments I shall be advancing is to say that they conform in neither style nor substance to this orthodoxy.

1.2.1. Moral Methodology

The methodological hallmark of *Philosophy & Public Affairs* is the "thought experiment." First we are invited to reflect on a few hypothetical examples—the more preposterous, the better, apparently. Then, with very little further argument or analysis, general moral principles are quickly inferred from our intuitive responses to these "crazy cases." Even philosophers sometimes get impatient with that way of arguing (Anscombe 1957, 267; Warnock 1960, 206–7; Barry 1979c, 3). Whatever their role in settling deeper philosophical issues, bizarre hypotheticals are of little help in resolving real dilemmas of public policy. Crazy cases can be inappropriate for policy analysis for a variety of reasons:

1. Often contrived examples are gratuitous. I share Onora Nell's (1975) dismay over the fact that some on this earth enjoy the high life while others starve. Like her, I would regard it as similarly perverse to provide "first-class cabins" on a lifeboat. But talk of lifeboats adds nothing here. Our objections to some luxuriating while others starve apply equally to the mother ship (first-class passengers feasting while hundreds die below decks) or to the real world directly (Americans overeating while Somalis starve). Or, again, Thomas Nagel (1972) argues that the slaughter of innocent civilians during war is wrong because it is "inappropriate" to military goals in the same way that it would be inappropriate, when arguing with a taxi driver over an exorbitant fare, to let the air out of his tires or to stick chewing gum on his windshield. But my intuitions about the wrongness of gunning down noncombatants or obliteration bombing are just a lot stronger than my intuitions about the wrongness of "inappropriate" action against the crook behind the wheel.

2. Often the examples are too stripped down to be of any real policy guidance. Robert Nozick's (1974, 160–64) famous "Wilt Chamberlain example" falls into this category. Suppose a tremendously gifted athlete offers to play an exhibition game, provided everyone pays twenty-five cents to watch; and suppose that many people gladly pay up and thoroughly enjoy the

game. The net effect is to make many people poorer, if only slightly, and one (Chamberlain) much richer. This upsets patterns of equality, but who is to say that spectators were wrong to pay or that Chamberlain was wrong to accept their voluntary offerings? Nozick's conclusion is that "capitalist acts between consenting adults" must be morally permissible. But this follows only from underspecification of the case. We find nothing wrong with Chamberlain's new-found wealth merely because we have not considered all the things that he might do with it. What if he could use that stack of quarters to acquire some of the spectators as his slaves? Or buy their houses out from under them, or all the food off their tables? Without objecting to the transfer of cash per se, we might object strongly to some of the consequences that follow from it. And, on balance, we might suppose that the best way to prevent them would be to prevent or restrict certain forms of voluntary transfers.

3. Often clean cases obscure those interactions between several moral considerations that are so typical of the complex cases in the real world. This is particularly apparent in the problem of punishment. Retributivists use the "innocent man" example to refute utilitarian principles of punishment: suppose a recent run of murders could be ended by hanging the murderer's wife, although she took no part in the crimes, and further suppose that victimizing her would not undermine general confidence in the judicial system. Do we really suppose, as utilitarians must, that she should be put to death (Mabbott 1939)? Utilitarians reply by asking us to imagine a criminal who is quite certainly guilty of hideous crimes but whose punishment would, for one reason or another, have absolutely no effect on the future crime rate. Surely it would be perverse to punish him nevertheless, as retributivists demand (Glover 1977, 33–34). Since each case seems compelling, the conclusion appears to be that neither deterrence nor retribution is adequate justification for punishment. Actually we have proven that both are, but only in conjunction. Guilt and deterrence are individually necessary and jointly sufficient conditions of morally justified punishment. But since the justification depends on the interaction between the two, dropping each condition one at a time and asking "what would you say then?" naturally leads us to mistaken conclusions.[2]

4. Clean cases fail to tell us how to trade off one moral consideration for another. They can only prove, disprove, or cir-

2. Nozick (1974, 205) makes great play of the fact that moral principles which are "individually compelling . . . may yield surprising results when combined together." No doubt this is true, as the spate of Arrow-style impossibility theorems shows. But the fact that principles can and do interact in surprising ways is a powerful argument for studying the interaction per se—for examining the macro situation where several principles are in play—rather than focusing narrowly, as Nozick does, upon micro situations represented by antiseptically clean cases.

cumscribe moral absolutes (Bennett 1966). That is a marginal service at best.[3] Hard policy choices are required where absolutes fail and tradeoffs are required. Shue (1978) persuasively argues that torturing a prisoner with nothing left to offer his tormentors constitutes gratuitous cruelty which should be prohibited absolutely. But Shue concedes that it may be permissible to torture a terrorist to learn where he has planted a bomb that will kill many innocent people. How are we to trade these two moral values off for one another? How many people must be at risk before we may pull out the rubber hose? The thumbscrews? The rack? Clean cases simply cannot say.

5. Often crazy cases are cluttered with too much unrealistic or inappropriate detail. Judith Jarvis Thompson (1971) argues against prohibiting abortion, saying that it would be analogous to allowing a gang of music lovers to kidnap someone and force him to donate blood to a brilliant violinist who would otherwise die. That analogy, however, builds in a crucial feature—the original kidnaping—that is usually missing in the case of pregnant women. The only ones among them in a position strictly analogous to the kidnap victim are those pregnant through rape, and even pronatalists usually agree that those pregnancies may properly be terminated. All the hard cases, where the kidnaping analogy is inapposite, remain unresolved by this example. Similarly, Thompson (1973) argues for preferential hiring of women and blacks in universities by analogy to a dining club. Since every member is equally entitled to be served, we should make special efforts to accommodate anyone who had to be excluded at the last sitting. By analogy, we should give equally qualified blacks and women preference over white males in university hiring. But, of course, the real argument revolves around hiring less-qualified minority candidates in preference to those white males who are, on meritocratic grounds, more entitled to the position. In these ways, hypothetical cases can contain stipulations making them inapplicable to the actual policy issue.[4]

3. It may actually be a dissservice to disprove absolute principles using crazy cases. Maybe we can imagine some extraordinary circumstances in which slavery might be permissible; but, assuming our society is (and will continue) operating very far from those extremes, it would be wrong to soothe the consciences of slaveholders with talk of hypotheticals. Similarly, we can imagine extraordinary cases where we might be tempted to excuse a rapist on the grounds that he believed, sincerely but wrongly, that the victim consented (Curley 1976). But relaxing the absolute ban on rape in this way opens pernicious possibilities of disingenuous excuses (Pateman 1980).

4. Barry (1965, 312) originally argued for the "naturalness" of majority rule by reference to the example of "five people in a railway compartment which the railway operator has omitted to label either 'smoking' or 'no smoking' .... Is there any reason ... three out of five should *not* be a sufficient majority to decide?" But Barry (1979b, 162–72) now concedes that this conclusion "is contingent on the presence of a number of highly restrictive conditions," e.g., that the issue is not "of vital impor-

6. Often crazy cases contain so much preposterous detail that they stretch our intuitions too far. Bizarre hypotheticals can go so far beyond our ordinary range of experience that we cease to have any faith in our intuitive responses to them. To show that rights and duties are not reducible to utility maximization, Sir David Ross (1930, 39) asks us to imagine a desert island inhabited only by two old men, both of whom are dying. "Do we think that the duty ... to fulfill a promise one has made to the other would be extinguished by the fact that neither act would have any effect on the general confidence" in the institution of promising? Ross wants us to say that it would not—that we should keep the promise anyway—and I am inclined to agree. But why? Perhaps just because my intuitions about promising were not shaped on a desert island with a dying companion. What socioeconomic principles would I advocate if wealth were not created by human labor but rather fell from the sky as manna from heaven? Offhand, I cannot say. All I know is that my intuitions, having been shaped by very different circumstances, would serve me in that situation about as poorly as lessons learned in a lifetime of walking serve me when on skis.[5]

All these objections lead to the conclusion that crazy cases such as those that characterize *Philosophy & Public Affairs* cannot directly inform policy choices. Either they are too thin or else they are overly rich in unrealistic detail. Their indirect impact on policy through their contribution to moral theory-building is equally limited. Certainly moral intuitions and moral theories stand in "reflective equilibrium"; theories build on data points supplied by intuitions, and on intuitions revised in light of the theories (Sidgwick 1874, bk. 4, chaps. 3–5; Ross 1930, 40–41; Rawls 1957; 1972). Crazy

---

tance for the long-term well-being of any of those involved." If, in contrast, "one of the passengers suffers from severe asthma ... , and being subjected to tobacco smoke is liable to precipitate a dangerous attack, [he] would be behaving with an almost insane disregard for his ... interests in accepting a majority decision to allow smoking. ... The political parallels hardly need to be filled in. No minority can be, or should be, expected to acquiesce in the majority's trampling on its vital interests."

5. Feinberg (1980, 106), arguing for legal protection of public sensibilities, is confronted with the bizarre counterexample: "What if something perfectly innocuous and inoffensive to any reasonable person, say, ... eating chocolate candy in public, were to affect onlookers in some hypothetical society in precisely the way the public eating of excrement affects onlookers in our society?" Feinberg replies that "this sort of example usually disturbs me for a moment until I fully grasp what the imagined circumstances would actually be like, and then invariably, the example begins to lose its intuitive persuasiveness. ... If the sight of a person eating chocolate affects all onlookers in that society in *precisely the same way* as the sight of a person eating excrement affects all onlookers in our society, then why should one want the hypothetical law to treat that hypothetical case any differently from the way in which the actual law treats the actual case? The example derives its initial plausibility from the difficulty of imagining that chocolate *could* be as revolting as excrement; but that difficulty, of course, is logically irrelevant."

cases, however, have little role to play in this process. Cases too rich in unrealistic detail are the most obviously useless. Rawls (1957, sec. 2.5) is firm on this: "All judgments on hypothetical cases are excluded. In addition, it is preferable that the case not be especially difficult and one that is likely to arise in ordinary life. These restrictions are desirable in order that the judgments in question be made in the effort to settle problems with which men are familiar and whereupon they have had an opportunity to reflect." Or, to pursue the data analysis analogy, we want our data points to cluster in the center of our graph: outliers are not very welcome, whether you are trying to fit lines or moral philosophies. Much the same is true of overly clean cases. Easy cases such as these make bad law—or, more precisely, make no law at all. Clean cases merely map the boundaries of the moral universe, whereas the real action takes place in midfield, where all the principles mix it up together. Clean cases cannot help in establishing what we most need from a moral theory, namely, principles for combining competing moral considerations, weighting them, trading them off for one another, and so on.

This is not to deny hypothetical cases any role at all in applied moral philosophy. They can contribute quite usefully to the more modest preanalytic task of stimulating new theories or raising doubts about old ones. My point is simply that our intuitive responses to hypotheticals—especially to bizarre ones—neither prove any policy lessons directly nor provide any very firmly fixed points (as intuitions about actual, standard cases might) that moral theories must accommodate. While we may legitimately look to contrived examples for theoretical inspiration, we must treat their ostensible "lessons" very skeptically indeed. Trying to decide why we respond as we do to these cases may lead us to discover interesting new moral propositions. But these propositions must stand or fall, not on the strength of our intuitive responses to the handful of contrived cases that might be offered to illustrate them, but rather on the strength of the independent arguments that can be adduced for them.

1.2.2. Moral Dogma

The substantive side of the *Philosophy & Public Affairs* orthodoxy against which I rebel is its callous disregard for consequences. There is a narcissistic fixation on "moral character" and its tainting. *What* happens is deemed morally far less significant than *how* it happens and *who* causes it to happen. This is to present morality as essentially a matter of "not getting one's hands dirty" (Bennett 1966; Williams 1973; Walzer 1973; Hampshire 1978). Certainly I do not deny the importance of protecting people's moral integrity and self-conceptions—on the contrary, that is the whole theme of chapter 5 below. But surely it is a parody of this principle to insist, as some writers of this school seem to, that we should protect one person's integrity even if that entails sacrificing another person's life and, with it, any chance *he* might have of leading a dignified existence.[6]

One effect of this curious orientation is to restrict drastically the sorts of ethical issues that public life is thought to pose. There is a preoccupation with classic "conscience" issues—most conspicuously war, discrimination and abortion (Cohen, et al. 1974a; 1974b; 1977).[7] And even this narrowly delimited set of issues is treated in a characteristically dainty way. Discussions of abortion focus entirely upon the woman's moral dilemma, utterly ignoring larger social consequences, such as overpopulation. Discussions of discrimination tend to focus on conscience-soothing remedial measures, such as reverse discrimination, which may get a handful of women or blacks jobs or better education but do little to end ongoing patterns of racial and sexual prejudice with far greater real impact. In discussions of the ethics of war, we hear altogether too much of peripheral "personal conscience" issues, such as exempting conscientious objectors from military service or protecting noncombatants, and altogether too little about the obligations of politicians to strive to avoid war in the first place (Barry 1979c; cf. Walzer 1971).

There is undeniable intuitive appeal to the nonconsequentialist claim that some things are right or wrong whatever their consequences. Anscombe (1970) offers as an example of one such absolute wrong the obliteration bombing of population centers; Nagel (1972) suggests extending her argument to include any massacre of innocent civilians; and Nozick (1974) tries to put the violation of property rights on the same plane. But upon closer inspection, it seems that our intuitions here might mislead us. The things we clearly should not do, whatever their consequences—such as killing masses of innocent civilians—are things we should not do *because*

6. Barry (1979a, 644–45), reviewing Fried (1978), discusses the classic case where "by telling a lie you can save a man's life," and concludes: "If I were the man who was fleeing death, I should not think much of the 'moral nature' or 'moral status' of somebody who was agonizing about whether to pollute his precious 'integrity' to save my life . . . . The question Fried would have us keep in the forefront of our minds is always 'How do I come out of this looking?' I know people like this, but the idea that I should be expected to admire them seems to me bizarre."

7. Even those broadly committed to the utilitarian program have come to embrace this limited agenda. Singer (1979), for example, devotes as much space to the niceties of abortion, euthanasia, and animal rights as to the larger social problems of famine and equality.

of their consequences. The misery of the victims, combined with the long-term and unpredictable consequences of the "dangerous precedent," are surely enough to rule out war crimes on ordinary consequentialistic premises (Bennett 1966; Brandt 1972; Hare 1972). Where it really does seem likely that the dictates of consequentialism and nonconsequentialism might diverge—as, perhaps, in the case of property rights—it is not at all obvious that the nonconsequentialistic considerations should trump the others.

Much the same is true of the distinction between "acts" and "omissions," which is so crucial to the case against consequentialism. For the consequentialist, an outcome is an outcome—it should not matter whether it was produced by our acting or by our failing to act. But, intuitively, we feel it is far worse if a baby dies because we passively omit to contribute to famine relief. The sentiment that we should "do no direct harm" shapes our political as well as our philosophical responses to policy puzzles (Schultze 1977, 23, 70–72; Howard, et al. 1972). Upon closer examination, however, we find that the act/omission doctrine has no independent appeal. Rather, it merely conflates "a cluster of reasons which seem more impressive before they are separated out than after critical examination" (Glover 1977, 94; cf. Davis 1980).

1. Immoral acts usually violate obligations not to harm others, whereas omissions usually are failures to perform actions above and beyond the call of moral duty.[8] Insofar as this is true, acts clearly are worse than omissions. But occasionally we are under an obligation to act in aid of others. Defaulting on that obligation certainly renders us liable to moral—and legal— blame. Parents omitting to feed their children, bodyguards omitting to protect their employers, or sleeping sentries omitting to sound the alarm are not off the moral hook just because theirs were omissions rather than acts (Hart and Honoré 1959, 31, 35–36; Hughes 1958; Brand 1971; Fitzgerald 1967, 135–36; Green 1980; Foot 1978, 50–51).

2. Victims of immoral acts are usually worse off than they were before, whereas victims of omissions have usually only missed a chance to gain more. Given diminishing marginal utility, it would be less pleasurable to gain a certain amount more of a good than it would be painful to lose the same increment from our present stock (Mosteller and Nogee 1951; Rapaport and Wallsten 1972). While this lends general support to our preference for omissions over harmful actions, there are instances wherein it points in the opposite direction. Omissions can result in substantial harms—if a sleeping sentry or a careless airplane inspector neglects his duties, many lives might be lost. Then it is

8. Significantly, this class of "supererogatory" actions can itself be analyzed in consequentialistic and, indeed, utilitarian terms (Urmson 1958).

far from clear that the "mere" omission is morally favored (Foot 1978, 26; Hart and Honoré 1959, 34–35).

3. Immoral acts might seem worse than omissions because there seems to be a firmer causal connection with the evil consequences in view (Morillo 1976; Honderich 1980).[9] Letting unwanted infants die of exposure on a mountainside might be better than killing them outright because, "after all, even exposed children have *some* chance of surviving—for example, if picked up by honest shepherds" (O'Neill 1979, 28). Omitting to perform an abortion on a woman likely to die in childbirth might be preferable on the grounds "that if the operation is not performed the woman still has *some* chance of survival while if it is performed the child has *none*" (Bennett 1966). Again, however, this bears out the act/omission doctrine only in a rough-and-ready way since "some omissions create just as strong a probability of death as their corresponding acts" (Glover 1977, 98).

Consequentialistic moral reasoning thus seems safe from the challenge posed by the act/omission doctrine. Just as there are not acts that are obviously right or wrong, whatever their consequences, so too are there no grounds for looking more favorably upon omissions than upon acts with similar consequences. Such intuitive plausibility as the doctrine possesses is derived from a combination of other moral considerations. When disentangling them, we find that omissions are not always preferable to acts. Furthermore, and more important for present purposes, we find that the moral considerations underlying the act/omission doctrine are themselves broadly consequentialistic in character.

The evaluative principles I shall be urging not only assess policies according to their consequences, but go on to assess those consequences in broadly utilitarian terms. Until recently, this position was so orthodox as to require neither explanation nor apology. Perhaps among welfare economists and policy scientists it still is. But the philosophical world is in the midst of a transition, away "from a once widely accepted old faith that some form of utilitarianism ... *must* capture the essence of political morality," and toward a new deontological faith trading heavily on notions of absolute right and wrong (Hart 1979, 77). I am, therefore, fighting a fundamentally rearguard action.

Unlike Hart (1979, 98), I *do* believe that a satisfactory solution to

9. This helps explain the "vital difference" Williams (1973, 94) sees between outcomes that are wholly the product of my own behavior and those where "a vital link in the production of the outcome is provided by *someone else's* doing something." The reason the distinction seems so important is not, as Williams supposes, that our moral integrity is more at stake in one case than the other. Rather, the reason is that the outcome is inevitable (being wholly determined by your action) in one case and not the other (cf. Davis 1980, 205–6).

the problems of political morality can be found "in the shadow of utilitarianism." Saying "the shadow" is important, and not just a stylistic affectation. There can be no question of embracing any form of "universal hedonism" without qualifications. We must not, for example, read "hedonism" as the satisfaction of narrowly material interests. Dignity and self-respect might be incorporeal but they are hardly immaterial to the concerns of the morally sensitive policymaker. Indeed, protecting them is implicit in the utilitarian principle itself, as I argue at length in chapter 5.

Similarly, notions of "universalism" will probably also have to be watered down, at least for purposes of assessing individual moral responsibility.[10] Making each individual responsible for pleasures and pains the world over would impose psychologically debilitating burdens. Our moral code must be realistically tailored to what we can reasonably expect of people. Just as it is necessary to limit the sorts of duty-bound performances our morality can demand of us (Urmson 1958), so too is it necessary to limit those persons on whose behalf demands may be made of us (Hume 1777, sec. 5, pt. 2). This is not to endorse the excessively restrictive boundaries of our present moral community or the niggardly level of aid offered across those boundaries. Certainly, the prosperous should be expected to offer more than they do; equally certainly, there have to be some limits. Philosophers having only recently returned to the problem of where such boundaries should be drawn and how strong they should be, it is premature to try to anticipate what principle will ultimately look most attractive (Beitz 1979; Walzer 1980; Brown and Shue 1981; Barry 1983). What is most important in the present context, however, is that there might well be utilitarian grounds for setting some such limits.

Once such qualifications have been entered, the major remaining stumbling block to utilitarian policy evaluation centers on the putative impossibility of interpersonal utility comparisons. Before policymakers can decide which option promises to produce the most net happiness, they need some common metric for comparing one person's pleasures with another's pains. If, as it is alleged, "every mind is inscrutable to every other mind, ... no common denominator of feeling is possible" (Jevons 1911, 14; cf. Robbins 1932, 122–25; 1938). Early reaction to this allegation was one of annoyed impatience: "Nobody can prove that anybody besides himself exists, but, nevertheless, everybody is quite sure of it" (Pigou 1951, 292; cf. Little 1957, chap. 4, and Barry 1965, 44–47). After several failed attempts to put interpersonal comparisons on a re-

10. "Universalism" might still be appropriate in assessing our collective moral responsibilities as discharged by and through government.

spectable scientific footing, and after seeing the perverse consequences of trying to do without them altogether, opinion seems to be
swinging back to that earlier position.[11] Davidson (1983), for example, offers an analogy to the philosophy of language. We can no
more see into other minds to read off meanings of other people's
utterances than we can to read off their pleasures and pains. That,
however, does not prevent us from attributing meaning to their utterances. We merely use a "principle of charity," assuming that
they (like us) try to speak sense, and interpret their utterance accordingly. Similarly, we can make sense of interpersonal comparisons of pleasures and pains by assuming that others are very much
like us.

Sometimes fairly precise interpersonal utility comparisons are required. When necessary, we can provide them by building on the
ethical postulate that "each person counts for one and none counts
for more than one." Assume that each person has an equal "capacity for happiness," meaning that at their bliss points one person
would be as happy as the next. Their happiness in subbliss states can
then be compared by measuring how near or far they are, subjectively, from their bliss points (Goodin 1975).[12] For most policy
purposes, however, such refinements are unnecessary. "Negative
utilitarianism" takes us an awfully long way with its enormously
plausible assumption that, much as individuals differ in their tastes
for goods, they all share roughly similar perceptions of and aver-
sions to those things that cause them misery (Moore 1970; Popper
1945, vol. 1, pp. 284–85; Acton 1963; Watkins 1963).[13]

11. For a discussion of the problems, see Goodin (1975). The utilitarian counter-
attack is led by Harsanyi (1977) among economists, and MacRae (1976, chap. 5)
among policy scientists. The strongest ethical argument in favor of interpersonal
utility comparisons comes from Hare (1981, 118): "Only a theory which allowed no
place at all to beneficence or to respect for the interests of others could escape this
demand. Anybody, therefore, who is tempted to bring up this objection against
utilitarians should ask himself whether he is himself attracted by a theory which
leaves out such considerations entirely."

12. A similar procedure is mentioned, in another context, by Arrow (1963, 32). It is
repudiated by Sen (1970, 91, 98) and Rawls (1972, 323) on grounds of nonuniqueness:
they say there is no reason to prefer this procedure to a number of others with "equal
symmetry." Instead of setting an individual's worst state of affairs equal to zero and
his best equal to one, Sen and Rawls say we might equally well "assign the value zero
to the worst alternative and the value one to the sum of the utilities from all
alternatives." The difference, however, is more apparent than real. In the latter
procedure, what is being evaluated is surely particular commodities one by one,
whereas in the former what is being evaluated is an entire state of the world. (It
simply makes no sense to sum up all the utilities an individual might have enjoyed in
all possible states of the world, when only one of them can be actualized.) Thus, the
latter is just an alternative formulation of the former procedure. And it is an inferior
one, at that, because it trades on outmoded notions of additive utility functions
which, for example, would not allow for diminishing marginal utility.

13. Even as regards "positive" goods, tastes may be less variable than commonly
supposed. Stigler and Becker (1977) postulate that people really have much the same

For an especially impressive example of this minimal sort of inter-personal comparison at work, consider Bruce Russett's (1978) cal-culation of "the marginal utility of income transfers to the Third World." He finds a statistically significant, curvilinear relationship between a nation's per capita income on the one hand and its infant mortality and average life expectancy rates on the other. This curve indicates, for example, that collecting $150 from each person in the rich countries and distributing the sum thereby generated equally among everyone in the poor countries would decrease average life expectancy in rich countries by only a month, but would increase it in poor countries by one and a half years. We may refuse to make such transfers for practical reasons: given most Third World gov-ernments, for example, we doubt that those most in need would see any (much less an equal share) of our contributions; and so on. But I cannot imagine anyone not contaminated by the microeconomic metaphysic seriously rejecting Russett's conclusion on the grounds that it makes unreasonable interpersonal utility comparisons. Surely it is right and reasonable to assume that a poor person's life is just as valuable to him as a rich person's is to him.

Perhaps there is some deeper unity underlying both the *Philos-ophy & Public Affairs* methodology and its dogma. Maybe crazy cases naturally lend themselves to nonconsequentialistic and non-utilitarian principles. It would hardly be surprising to find that bizarre generalities flow from bizarre particulars. If, in contrast, we focus upon more realistic policy dilemmas—as methodologically we must—a modified form of utilitarianism seems by far the more plausible general theory.[14]

"bedrock" preference orderings. Such differences in "tastes" as they appear to have can, for Stigler and Becker, be explained by the fact that people's different personal histories and circumstances have given them different amounts of "consumption capital" for converting the goods into pleasurable experiences (cf. Scanlon 1975).

14. Some may suppose that conceding the need for any modifications at all in utilitarianism sets us on a slippery slope, whereby we ultimately end up the same place we would have done starting from starkly nonutilitarian premises. While this is in principle possible, "in practice it tends to make a big difference which cases you take as clear and central and which as difficult and exceptional." We must never underestimate what Barry (1979a, 630) calls "the importance of where you start."

2 Anticipating Outcomes: Overcoming the Errors of Incrementalism

The lack of a proper theoretical base for policy studies is probably due less to methodological error than to the perverse and pervasive doctrine of incrementalism. That doctrine is an undeniable success, in purely descriptive terms. Most policymaking surely does proceed incrementally, if only because the power relations and organizational routines underlying it themselves vary slightly from one period to the next. But advocates of incrementalism—Lindblom, Wildavsky, & Co.—want to claim more than descriptive success. For them, incrementalism is not only inevitable in practice but also desirable on principle. Policy, they say, *should* be made through a series of small changes, with each successive step based on an evaluation of the observed results of the last.

The prescriptive case for incrementalism rests on twin foundations. First is the claim, challenged in this chapter, that we cannot anticipate the real effects of social interventions prior to actually experiencing them. Second is the claim, challenged in the next chapter, that even if we could anticipate the outcomes we could not anticipate our evaluative response prior to actually experiencing those outcomes. Underlying all this is a more fundamental presupposition concerning the possibility and necessity of theory for policymaking: "analytical problem-solving" ("intellectual cognition") is shunned because our social theories are too infirm to form the basis for policymaking; and incrementalism ("social interaction") is championed as a

This chapter is reprinted, with substantial revisions, from Robert E. Goodin and Ilmar Waldner, "Thinking Big, Thinking Small, and Not Thinking at All," *Public Policy* 27, no. 1 (1979): 1–24.

reliable method of policymaking in the absence of such theories (Lindblom and Cohen 1979; Wildavsky 1979). If either half of this proposition fails, the case for incrementalism fails with it. The burden of these two chapters is to argue that both are substantially flawed.

2.1. Incrementalism$_1$:
Muddling through Black Boxes

There is, in fact, not a single form of incrementalism. Instead there are three, each with distinctive goals, strategic imperatives, and rationales. Each, however, employs basic procedures sufficiently similar to produce a family resemblance among all the varieties. The most standard form of incrementalism, which I shall call "incrementalism$_1$", is a "strategy of decision" strictly speaking. It calls for us to continue the type of incremental intervention that is perceived to have yielded desirable results previously. This might be described as a willful man's behavioralism: people *decide* to repeat what is reinforced; but reinforcement is still the mechanism dictating future behavior. The core of this strategy of decision might be described, uncharitably but not inaccurately, as unreflective reaction. The decision maker undertakes slow, small changes. If he likes the results he then continues with more of the same, where "same" is defined in terms of what he thinks the essential character of his previous action to have been.[1] If he does not like the results, he tries something else. Whereas the ordinary decision maker who is confronted with new data feels obliged to try to understand them, the incrementalist$_1$ needs only to react to them. An incrementalist$_1$ in the role of central banker might, for example, learn to raise taxes slightly every time the inflation rate creeps upward without ever bothering to try to discover what was causing the inflation; so long as the remedy seems to work, he will keep using it. By "thinking small" in this way, the incrementalist$_1$ does not have to think at all. As Lindblom writes in *A Strategy of Decision*, incrementalism$_1$ "can adapt itself to the absence of theories—it is a way of getting along without theory when necessary."[2]

1. Thus, I am speaking of the "intentional description" a person gives of his actions. Apparently similar acts can be described differently by different people. What one person sees as "hiring another employee" might be seen by another as "hiring an electronics expert." One Congressman might describe his vote to cut food stamps as "balancing the budget" whereas another describes the same vote as "curtailing creeping socialism." What counts as the "same" incremental step next time around is that which the agent sees as fitting this same description once again.

2. Braybrooke and Lindblom (1963, 118). Braybrooke (personal correspondence) would like to treat this as a hyperbolic remark deviating from the general thrust of the book. Unfortunately, a close reading of the text does not bear out this interpretation. Notice, for example, that the theme of one whole chapter (chap. 4) is that "disjointed

Suppose policymakers really are operating without the benefit of any theory whatsoever; i.e., they have no empirical generalizations structured into any coherent theoretical package. Pursuing the incrementalist₁ strategy, they forswear research that would attempt to construct such theories in favor of simple reaction to policy outputs. In so doing, they treat the world as a black box: they feed in policy inputs at one end and see what results come out the other. The *goal* of incrementalism₁ is to produce utility-maximizing results directly. The bare bones of the incrementalist₁ *strategy* are as follows:

1. Arbitrarily select an incremental intervention.
2. If the results are positive, repeat it on a slightly larger scale.
3. If the results are negative, switch to some other arbitrarily selected intervention that thus far has not produced any significant negative results overall.

The *rationale* for making and increasing interventions by small increments is that they are likely to result in similarly small increments of output, allowing decision-makers subsequent opportunities to adjust policies accordingly. The great fear of the incrementalist₁ is that, by twisting too many knobs on the black box too wildly, he may cause it to explode in his face.

Having renounced pursuit of theoretical understanding of what goes on inside the black box, incrementalists₁ of course do not necessarily have any idea of how inputs translate into outputs. They argue, however, that they need not understand how the system works, useful though such understanding might be were they blest with it. They need only know how to make the system work for them, which they can do merely by observing which inputs produce the most satisfactory outcomes. A Social Science Research Council advisory group discussing educational innovations writes, "One may be quite willing to pay for the cost of learning whether performance contracting works or not without, at the same time, learning why it does or does not work" (Riecken and Boruch 1974, 33).

Any policy generates feedback, to be sure. But it does not necessarily get widely reported. No one likes to confess failure, either to superiors or to peers. Thus, the world is deprived of whatever lessons might be learned from the largest nuclear accident to date simply because the Soviets are embarrassed to report the details (Trabalka, et al. 1980).

---

incrementalism" is uniquely suited to situations characterized by small change on one dimension and *"low understanding"* on the other. There is, of course, a difference between "low" and "no" understanding. This suggests that the authors want to equivocate between what I call incrementalism₁ (no theoretical understanding of the system at all) and incrementalism₂ (refining the limited theoretical understanding we already have).

Furthermore, and more fundamentally, black box incrementalists₁ cannot possibly know how to interpret the feedback. It is not enough to know that you did something at t_1 and that at t_2 something good or bad happened. You also need to know what would have happened at t_2 without your intervention. To specify such counterfactuals, we really need the aid of theoretical understanding of the system. On a simple-minded standard, we might call an alcoholic treatment center a success if 67 percent of its clients are "in remission," and an arthritis treatment a failure if patients continue getting worse. But what would we say if we discovered that the same percentage of alcoholics would have dried out after a year anyway with or without treatment, or if patients' arthritis would have been even worse without treatment (Hatry 1980, 167–68)? To borrow Coddington's (1974, 438) pointed phrase, "Nothing fails like the appearance of success." Even champions of technological short cuts concede that, with them, we are "accepting fundamentally unascertainable risks" because "we do not really know what we are doing; we only know that one of the immediate, overt results is desirable" (Etzioni and Remp 1973, 198). As Merton (1973, 96) emphasizes, "Unless the crucial theoretical variable . . . can be identified, there is no basis for assuming that the same results will be obtained on other occasions."

Without any theoretical understanding at all, we do not even know what counts as an incremental intervention. Braybrooke and Lindblom (1963, 62–65) define an incremental change as one that will have only marginal impact on the other variables in the system. But incrementalists₁ have no way of knowing how big the reactions will be to a change until they have tried it. No one would seriously consider it an "incremental" step to drop just one little bomb on the suburbs of Leningrad to test Russian reactions. The reason, however, is that we are sufficiently confident of our theories about what motivates Russian foreign policy to know that this action would be regarded as a fundamental violation of their sovereignty and that they would react accordingly. Had we no such theory, we would have no way of knowing whether this would be an incremental step or not.

Furthermore, the incrementalist₁ who merely monitors the outputs and ignores the internal workings of the black box has no way of knowing which outputs are his and which are someone else's. He does not know how long to wait for his inputs to work their way through the box: if he reads the policy output too early, he picks up results from the activities of his predecessors; if too late, he misses his own data. To complicate matters more, any policy typically generates both short-term and long-term effects, so an incrementalist₁ will always be presented with output that is only partially his own. Even with a well-elaborated theory it is difficult to sort these things out. Working with a black box, it is impossible. The upshot is that learning by trial and error is necessarily slow and uncertain. The errors will lie in both directions: some policy innovations will be adjudged failures prematurely and on the basis of an inadequate demonstration (Rein and Miller 1970, 146–47); in other cases, false optimism will persist unduly long, as apparently happens with surgical innovations judged merely on the basis of impressionistic case history demonstrations (Barnes 1977; Wortman 1981). Either way, however, the errors are bound to exist.

The precipitous decline of the once-powerful British economy, and the failure of successive governments to halt it, might be attributed to the flaws in this form of incrementalism. Governments, of course, did not lack theories about the economy. Rather, they had too many. Faced with profound disagreement among economic advisers and heavy pressure for quick results, British governments approached the decision problem in a highly incremental₁ manner. A wide range of policy alternatives were tried in quick succession—attacking the balance of payments deficit, wage-price restraints and controls, cuts in government spending, and so on—and each was rejected as it failed to produce dramatic results quickly. Bacon and Eltis (1976) offer good reasons for believing that any of these strategies would have proven successful if only it had been given more time. But governments, operating in an extremely atheoretical way, had no clear idea how long to ask insistent citizens and Zurich gnomes to wait for results.[3]

Incrementalists₁ typically decide when to conduct the final evaluation by setting an arbitrary cutoff date.[4] Decision-makers using other strategies might, of course, justify the use of a time horizon or payout period by saying that, given their theoretical understanding of the processes involved, they have reason to believe that most of the results will be in by that time. But the incrementalist₁ disclaims any such understanding; for him the choice of a cutoff point is arbitrary in the extreme. The only way he can avoid this charge is by asserting that the choice of points does not matter.

3. Braybrooke (personal correspondence) rightly replies that incrementalists never claim that their strategy will never lead to error—they claim only that it was the best that could be done under the circumstances. Yet had British governments employed the sort of theory Bacon and Eltis (1976) offer—and could well have offered without the benefit of hindsight—they might arguably have halted the decline by sticking with any of the policy instruments long enough for its influence to have been felt.

4. For a critical discussion of these practices, see Little and Mirrlees (1974, secs. 1.6 and 15.7). Braybrooke and Lindblom (1963, 64) mention, in a slightly different context, the arbitrary figure of five years.

For an incrementalist₁ this must necessarily be mere assertion. He must just *assume* that the results will come promptly and completely within the specified period.

The assumption is not only unexamined but also often unwarranted. Incremental changes in one factor generally do not produce immediate and correspondingly incremental changes in other variables. Even when they seem to, appearances can deceive. Response functions which are smooth over large ranges can, without warning, display very dramatic discontinuities at one or more points (Zeeman 1976; cf. Kolta 1977). Nonincremental responses come from "threshold" and "sleeper" effects (Kahn 1966; Rose 1974; Schulman 1980). Rivers cleanse themselves naturally of certain quantities of sewage, but above some threshold they can remove no more. Social systems display analogous properties as in, for example, the neighborhood "tipping" phenomenon: when the proportion of black families or overcrowded dwellings passes some crucial threshold, the present residents flee en masse, leaving the neighborhood to become all black or all slum. Sleeper effects are equally common. Black lung disease and cancer take time to appear. Burning coal and oil produces increases in atmospheric CO_2 which, in the long run, threaten to change the global climate; but in the short term this effect may be masked by ocean absorption (Siegenthaler and Oeschager 1978). The really beneficial effects of preschool education show up, apparently, only when the children reach secondary school (Schweinhart and Weikart 1980). Similarly, the New Deal resettlement program—regarded as a failure at the time—had beneficial long-term effects in creating a landed black middle class that formed the backbone of the 1960s civil rights movement in the South (Salamon 1979).

Either threshold or sleeper effects make the knee jerk reaction of incrementalists₁ to policy outputs grossly inappropriate. Threshold effects mislead incrementalists₁ by showing up suddenly. Incremental changes in inputs may produce incremental changes in outputs until the threshold is crossed, at which point the change in outputs is markedly nonincremental.[5] Sleeper effects mislead incrementalists₁ by appearing late. If the goods of a policy come im-

5. Braybrooke (personal correspondence) correctly observes that this causes problems only for policies crossing the threshold. But without theoretical understanding there is no way of knowing where the threshold is until you have crossed it. Incrementalists₁ cannot *plan* to avoid crossing thresholds. Once they realize that thresholds have been crossed, or once sleeper effects start appearing, incrementalists₁ of course respond to them. Once a few lakes or a few miners have been killed, incrementalists₁ curtail activities that would have killed many more in future. But such delayed reaction is far from optimal. It comes too late to save many who are already dead or dying and who could have been saved had policy been theoretically well grounded from the outset.

mediately but there is a hundred-year time lag between a program and its ill effects, incrementalists[1] will be expanding a program every year for a century before feeling the unwelcome consequences of the first year's intervention; and even if they then halt the program immediately they will reap the increasingly grievous fruits of a hundred years of misguided intervention.

For an example of policy disasters attributable to such sleeper effects, consider the problems related to licensing new drugs. The original American "Poison Squad" was a case of pure black box incrementalism[1]. It consisted of a "dozen robust young men who received all of their meals at the Bureau of Chemistry, where they were fed daily cocktails of such chemicals as borax or formaldehyde" and monitored for any ill effects (Friedel and Servos 1977). Testing has obviously become more sophisticated since then. But it is still largely an atheoretical matter of trying out drugs on mice, monkeys, and men and waiting to see what happens. Here sleeper effects are a special danger. The deformities of thalidomide children and cancers in daughters of DES-takers, for example, were unanticipated because testing procedures bore too strong a resemblance to incrementalism[1]. These drugs were approved for general use when they displayed no harmful effects on those actually ingesting them. Only after they had been used widely were their sleeper effects—harm to the next generation—discovered (Pringle and Fiddes 1970; Hubbart 1973).

Once again, incrementalists[1] can cope with such a problem only by building time lags into their response pattern. Pushing back the cutoff date for evaluation will, to some extent, overcome the problem. Americans were spared the thalidomide tragedy, after all, by the foot-dragging of bureaucratic regulators. Two serious objections may be raised, however, to any such strategy. First, given the black box methodology of incrementalists[1] they must build in time lags without benefit of any theoretical understanding of why the lags should be there or how long they should be. The danger on one side is that the lags will not be long enough to detect all the effects of a policy. The danger on the other side is the sort of abuse Anderson (1964, 246) describes in *The Federal Bulldozer:* "Some say that it is too early to judge the federal urban renewal program; they say, 'The program is only 15 years old.' . . . This line of argument holds that government programs should not be judged unless they are finished or unless they are proceeding as planned . . . . To postpone evaluation is simply to advocate implicitly the continuance of a program without knowing why." The logic of the incrementalist[1] strategy does not commit them to permitting such a long time lag, but neither does it offer any grounds for preventing it. The second objection to the time lags incrementalism$_1$ requires to cope with sleeper effects is that there is, after all, a legitimate demand for prompt action. New drugs, if safe and effective, should be rushed to the public (Peltzman 1973). With time-lagged incrementalism$_1$ we would necessarily be waiting, possibly a very long time, to see if the new drugs were safe and effective. Were we to seek theoretical understanding of the potential dangers, we might well resolve our doubts more promptly.

It is important to see that there are genuine alternatives to just waiting to see what happens. What we really need in order to anticipate threshold or sleeper effects is a fairly full set of theoretically integrated empirical generalizations. We might build toward these in a variety of ways. One method is to construct models simulating the system and then observe how they behave. Pentagon decision-makers conduct "war games," looking for clues to the prospective behavior of Soviet leaders in the behavior of those assigned to play their roles. On a more sophisticated level, computer models of the national economy help national planners judge the effects of alternative interventions. Another method is experimentation on analogous systems. For example, Food and Drug Administration experimenters infer the effects of new drugs on man by observing their effects on laboratory animals. Of course, we must have good theoretical reasons for believing the systems to be truly analogous. False analogies can lead to catastrophic errors, as when in the 1950s researchers tested thalidomide on rats (whose offspring show no ill effects) rather than on rabbits or monkeys (whose offspring display deformities similar to those found in humans). But provided the analogy is a good one, backed by theory, it can be extremely useful (McLean 1981). So too can historical analogies, subject to the same caveat. A third method is to employ a set of logically connected propositions, as used by mathematical economists for example. If we have good theoretical reasons to believe that the propositions do actually mirror something of empirical significance, we can use such systems to deduce the effects of our interventions.

For a simple example of the difference the quest for theoretically informed decisions would make, consider the American decision whether to grant or withhold landing rights for the Concorde SST. Transportation Secretary William Coleman, acting rather like an incrementalist$_1$, proposed to decide on the basis of results from a sixteen-month demonstration period. The choice of this cutoff date was not quite arbitrary—Coleman had theoretical reasons for supposing that he needed at least as long as that. But he had no grounds for asserting that "a 16-month demonstration period will be sufficiently long" to acquire and assess data concerning the noise of the airplane during takeoff and landing and its impact on people living near airports (Coleman 1976a, 61). There is some evidence suggesting that psychological effects of aircraft noise on humans are cumulative, so tendencies that may not show up in a brief experiment may well become very strong after long exposure.[6] Incrementalism₁ would be forced to build incredibly long time lags into the decision process, forcing the French and British to wait unreasonably long for a decision. A theoretically oriented inquiry would reexamine the evidence from workers on aircraft carriers and people living near airports for some theoretically unified explanation of the contradictory results.

So far I have been offering examples of how the lack of theoretical understanding can lead to policy failures. Perhaps an even stronger reductio ad absurdum of the incrementalist₁ claim that it can work without theory can be achieved by starting from the opposite end. Let us now focus on policies about which we possess comparatively full theoretical understanding of how they work and why. One such example is the space program. Theory clearly tells us to expect sleeper effects—much had to be done before a man could walk on the moon. Had Congressmen treated the program as an absolutely black box, deciding next year's appropriation for NASA on the basis of the tangible results flowing from last year's expenditure, the program would never have been renewed. No man stood on the moon after the first year, or the second or the third. Congressmen, of course, appreciated the crucial thresholds involved in NASA's task and agreed to provide the massive infusion of funds needed to carry it across that threshold (Schulman 1980, chap. 2). But Congressmen avoided the obviously absurd results of incrementalism₁—terminating the program prematurely—only by falling back on theoretical understanding of the processes involved in a space launch.[7]

6. Kryter (1966) summarizes evidence that, "following an initial adjustment to and learning the nature of one's noise environment, people become less, rather than more, tolerant of continued exposure to aircraft noise." On the question of whether this is mere annoyance or real damage, the evidence is mixed: Project Anehin, a study of men working on aircraft carriers, found no connection between noise and mental illness (Rodda 1967, 59 ff.); but British doctors find that a disproportionate number of admissions to mental hospitals come from populations living around Heathrow Airport (Abey-Wickrama, et al. 1969).

7. Schulman (1975) had earlier seen the space program as an example of Etzioni's (1967) model of "mixed scanning," which recommends that rationalistic-synoptic procedures be used to choose broad policy outlines, with incrementalist procedures being used to fill in the details. But there are no grounds for such a recommendation: when the proposed policy is known to be perfectly divisible and the system into which it intervenes smoothly responsive, it is safe enough to use piecemeal strategies to choose broad policy outlines as well; and when this is not known, or when it is known not to be true, incrementalism cannot be trusted even to fill in the details. The history of the space program itself belies Etzioni's analysis: it started from incrementalist experiments (e.g., launching Sputnik with a bunch of World War II vintage rockets strapped together) and built up to large-scale planning, whereas "mixed scanning" would have predicted a synoptic decision first followed by incrementalist tinkering.

Often we know enough about the nature of the system to be confident that a proposed change is too small to make any real difference (Rein and Miller 1970, 142; Marris and Rein 1967, 89). For a rather mundane example, consider an experimental smallpox vaccination program that administers a minuscule amount of vaccine to subjects: scientists can predict with confidence that such amounts of vaccine will not produce a sufficiently strong reaction in subjects to generate immunity. Likewise, Marx and Engels (1848), drawing upon their theoretical understanding of the necessity of class struggle for the radical alteration of society, reached the conclusion that the "small experiments" of Saint-Simon, Fourier, Owen and other Utopian Socialists were "necessarily doomed to failure" because they were too modest.

Lange (1936–37, 134) similarly offers arguments derived from formal economic theory to show that the transition to his market socialist ideal cannot come about through a policy of gradualism: "A socialist government really intent upon socialism has to decide to carry out its socialisation programme at a stroke, or give it up altogether." In such ways, theories can often tell us that some policies fail not because they are fundamentally misguided but merely because they are too modest or somehow incomplete.

Thus we must reject the bold claim that incrementalism$_1$, unaided by theoretical understanding of the system, can constitute an acceptable strategy of decision. Some theory is required for decision-makers: (1) to know what would count as an incremental intervention; (2) to interpret and act upon the results of their incremental tinkering; and (3) to know when it would be safe for them so to intervene. The first—and, indeed, the only—responsible course for a decision-maker presented with a black box is to pry open a corner of it.

2.2. Incrementalism$_2$:
The Epistemic Rationale

Incrementalism$_1$ claims to be able to get by without any theoretical understanding whatsoever of the system into which we intervene. I have now shown that some theory is always required. Any theory, however poorly worked out, satisfies that simple requirement. Yet the nature of the incrementalism is changed once we introduce any theory at all. Whereas incrementalism$_1$ reacts unreflectively to policy outputs, incrementalism$_2$ acknowledges its reliance on theories of how a system works and utilizes incremental procedures for perfecting such theories.

Defenses of incrementalism$_2$ explicitly treat it as a research strategy using the policy arena itself as a laboratory. Advocates of this approach readily concede that incrementalism$_2$ cannot substitute for theoretical understanding. They assert instead that it might usefully contribute to it. Based on a sketchy theory and tentative hypotheses, incremental changes provide feedback against which hypotheses can be tested and theories refined. "We know relatively little about the relationship of inputs to outputs in social problems," writes Goldfarb (1975, 283), "and a priori theorizing at best provides first hints of actual results. Such theorizing must be supplemented by 'learning by doing' to get full appreciation of the costs and outputs" (cf. Webb and Webb 1932, 220–27; Popper 1957; Campbell 1969; Rivlin 1971, chap. 5; 1974; Ginzburg and Solow 1974, 211–20; Riecken and Boruch 1974). The *goal* of incrementalism$_2$ is to produce theoretical models that we can use to manipulate the system to our maximum advantage. The essence of the *strategy* of incrementalism$_2$ is as follows:

1. Start with a theoretically informed hypothesis about the system.
2. On that basis, nonarbitrarily select an incremental intervention chosen both for its practical and epistemic utility.[8]
3. Observe the results of the intervention.
4. Revise the hypothesis, or change it if necessary.
5. Repeat the experimental procedure.

In this hypothesis-testing context, incrementalism$_2$ has a very special epistemic *rationale:* by making only small changes in a few variables at a time, causal chains may more easily be traced. "The piecemeal engineer," Popper (1957, 67) observes approvingly, "will avoid undertaking reforms of a complexity and scope which make it impossible for him to disentangle causes and effects, and to know what he is really doing" (cf. Phillips 1976).

There are two ways this incrementalist$_2$ research program might be marred. The first possibility is that the experiment itself might be

8. The interventions an incrementalist$_2$ policymaker selects are "in no case . . . exactly the experiments that the scientific investigator would have chosen to test his own hypotheses" (Webb and Webb 1932, 225). Sometimes the "crucial experiment" has utterly unacceptable consequences when implemented as policy, such as wiping out a species or a city (Häfele 1974; Weinberg 1972a). But the policymaker cannot simply say, as Coleman (1975) seems to suggest, that hypothesis-testing and theory construction are academic tasks, whereas he is obliged simply to get results. Without well-tested theories, we can have no confidence in our results. Thus, even if they are concerned just to "get results," policymakers should be willing to divert resources from "current consumption" of policy outputs into policy research, including incrementalist$_2$ experiments they would not have chosen for their practical utility alone (Goldfarb 1975).

contaminated. Sometimes, with the aid of our theoretical understanding of the system, we may be able to correct for this contamination; other times we cannot, even with the aid of theory. The
second possibility is that, although the integrity of the experiment
itself is not compromised, the situation into which we intervene has
changed so much as to render the results of the experiment irrelevant for future action.

The incrementalist$_2$ proceeds by small steps in hopes of thereby
holding constant all variables except the one he is intending to alter.
With large-scale and broad-aim demonstration projects, we are
always left wondering "exactly what is being demonstrated" (Rein
and Miller 1970, 146; cf. Weiss and Rein 1970, and Campbell 1970).
But the same question often arises with even small-scale experiments. There are other environmental sources of variation quite
apart from anything the experimenter does, especially when he uses
the policy arena itself as his laboratory. The world simply will not
stand still for the duration of the policy experiment, producing an
"intermixture of effects" that prevents interpretation of experimental results (Webb and Webb 1932, 226). Merton (1973, 91) observes that

> in applied research, ceteris paribus is often an embarrassing
> obstacle—for what if the "other factors" do not remain con-
> stant? . . . If action is to be based on his findings, he [the analyst]
> must indicate whether relevant "other factors" *will* remain con-
> stant. And since they typically will not, he has the further large
> task of assessing the changes in these factors and their effect
> upon contemplated action.

A well-researched case in point is Governor Ribicoff's severe
crackdown on Connecticut speeding in 1955. At the end of the year,
traffic fatalities had dropped 12 percent from the previous year, and
Ribicoff proclaimed the experiment a success. That experiment had,
however, failed to "control for the effects of other potential change
agents. For instance, 1956 might have been a particularly dry year,
with fewer accidents due to rain or snow" (Campbell 1969, 413).
Examining an extended time series, Campbell concludes that "the
great pretreatment instability . . . makes the treatment effect look
relatively trivial. The 1955–56 shift is less than the gains of both
1954–55 and 1952–53. It is the largest drop in the series, but it exceeds the drops of 1951–52, 1953–54 and 1957–58 by trivial amounts.
Thus, the unexplained instabilities of the series are such as to make
the 1955–56 drop understandable as more of the same." Similarly,
education experimenters confess that they simply do not know what

to control for when studying performance contracting: "The initial hope of this project was that the introduction of some combination of learning technology from private industry and short-run economic incentives were the missing ingredients in previous programs to improve compensatory education.... [I]t is now obvious that many other ingredients are missing as well. One can only speculate on what they are.... Whatever the most promising approaches turn out to be, however, it will take more careful and intensive examination than this experiment provides to find them" (Gramlich and Koshel 1975, 76).

Perhaps there are ways to factor out these contaminating influences without actually understanding how and why they upset the experiment. Rivlin (1971, 114) suggests that "if some factors cannot be controlled, the experiment must be repeated a sufficient number of times to average out the effects of the uncontrolled elements" (cf. Riecken and Boruch 1974, chap. 4). But that approach will work only under rather special conditions. One requirement that worries Rivlin is the need to repeat the experiment in exactly the same form each time. In practice, policymakers (e.g., in the Community Action Program) try to adapt the experiment in light of past experience; they are unwilling to repeat the same experiment, and the same perceived "mistakes," time and again (Brooks 1965; Weiss and Rein 1970). Another possibility is that the extraneous variables will influence the experiment in the same way each time it is repeated, so their effects do not really cancel each other and "average out" as Rivlin hopes. The strategy misfires when the extraneous variables have the property of being "public" goods or evils, affecting each instantiation of the experiment equally (Olson 1977). Imagine, for instance, a program designed to train youths to make them more employable. Were the experiment being conducted in the midst of a persistent nationwide recession, repeating the experiment at several sites or several times would do little to average out the effects of a continuing lack of jobs nationwide. Incrementalist$_2$ experimenters would be led to conclude that job-training programs are a failure, while the more appropriate conclusion is simply that youth employment depends upon both training and the availability of jobs. Hence, I am skeptical of the possibility of "averaging out" extraneous effects through multiple experiments.

Policymakers may find ways to correct for these contaminating influences, but that presupposes a large body of theory about the system in which they intervene. First, they must know about the nature and permeability of the boundary between the policy arena and the larger environment. Not all uncontrolled changes in the environmental setting of a policy experiment necessarily threaten the integrity of the experiment. A drought in the West will do little to compromise an experimental preschool program in the East. But the incrementalist$_2$ experimenter needs theoretical understanding of the system to know which changes in the environment will contaminate the experiment and which will be irrelevant.[9] Second, to correct for these contaminating influences, incrementalists$_2$ need theoretical understanding of how these influences behave and how they contaminate his policy experiment.

On the basis of such theories, incrementalists$_2$ will sometimes be able to anticipate these contaminating influences and to correct in advance for them. In arranging a demonstration period for testing the noise of the Concorde SST and its impact on people living near American airports, it was stipulated that data collection should continue for twelve months, "during all four seasons."[10] Seasonal variations clearly interfere with the experiment—people will surely mind the noise much more during the summer, when windows are open and they spend more time out of doors, than during the winter. Yet a balanced assessment of impact is easily obtained simply by extending the period of the experiment.

At other times policymakers will not be able to anticipate the contamination, and they may not even be able to correct for it after the fact. Consider the New Jersey negative income tax experiment. While the experiment was under way, the state made drastic changes in the laws governing welfare payments. Since the microeconomic theory underlying the experiment was well worked out and well tested empirically, the economists conducting the experiment could say without doubt that the changes would have a profound impact on their results. Shifting incentives for welfare families created by those complex changes in the law constitute serious contamination of the experiment, and there is no simple way to correct for it. Perhaps, using economic theory and data from else-

9. Discussing decision-making within the Chicago Housing Authority, Myerson and Banfield (1955, 282) remark: "What was needed was not research but experiment, or, better yet, 'pilot' operations of various alternatives." Without some prior knowledge of what variables were relevant, however, the Authority could not know how to set up the experiment and how to protect it from contamination by outside influences.

10. Coleman (1976, 3). Significantly, the demonstration was justified on experimental-incrementalist grounds of minimizing variance in other respects. New York State, requesting a court injunction to block the demonstration, argued that an American demonstration was unnecessary since the same noise data are being collected in Bahrain. Judge Robb echoed the logic underlying the demonstration in denying that petition: "They aren't the same people . . . . Isn't it rather obvious that if you want to test a Palm Beach suit you don't test it on an Eskimo?" (Feaver 1976).

where, interpreters might be able to make the necessary adjustments, but it would be no simple task, and we cannot place any great confidence in the results.[11]

In both these cases, incrementalist$_2$ policy experiments went ahead. Since contaminating influences could be anticipated, the Concorde experiment was redesigned to avoid them. Where experimenters could neither anticipate nor correct for contamination (as may be the case with the New Jersey negative income tax experiment), they will be forced to treat the results with great caution. What should a policymaker do when theory warns him to expect contaminating influences but cautions that there is no way to correct for them? Then it would be folly to set out on the experimental incrementalist$_2$ course at all. Policymakers have no alternative but to plan as best they can with such information and theory as are available to them at the time. This category of cases is of tremendous importance, since the policy environment is typically highly volatile.

For a particularly dramatic instance in which policymakers rightly regarded research-oriented incrementalism$_2$ as inappropriate, consider the situation of the British Labour Government elected in 1945. Many of the reforms launched at that time could clearly have profited from the experience of pilot projects. In the midst of demobilization and the gross economic dislocations necessarily attending that process, however, the results of those experiments would surely have been masked by much stronger influences unrelated to the experiment at hand. The only tenable course of action was to plan as best the government could on the basis of existing theory and data.[12]

Until now I have been discussing ways in which the integrity of an incrementalist$_2$ policy experiment may be threatened. Even if the experiment is a sound one, however, its usefulness as a guide for future policy may be minimal. Often the system itself, and the causal connections within it, will be in a state of flux. "People and circumstances are always changing, even whilst the experiments are actually in progress" (Webb and Webb 1932, 226), often reflexively in consequence of the policy itself (Schulman 1980, 53–59; Deutsch 1972). When the changes in the system are slow, there might be some hope of capturing them in incrementalist experiments (Rivlin 1971, 119). When they are not, experiments which accurately reveal

11. Aaron (1975). Subsequent replications of this experiment are discussed in Brown (1980, chap. 6) and Ferber and Hirsch (1978).

12. Even if pilot projects had made sense, the Labour ministers, opposed to piecemeal tinkering as a matter of high socialist principle, might not have agreed to them. Here prejudice and prudence might have been mutually reinforcing.

causal connections as they existed at the moment of experimentation serve as poor policy guides, because the connections themselves have changed in the meanwhile. To know when the results of policy experiments are applicable to future decisions, still more theory—this time about the stability of the system itself—is required.

The epistemic defense of incrementalism$_2$, then, is not absolutely in error, as is the incrementalist$_1$ claim. But it is problematical in several ways. First, it works only when one of two conditions is satisfied: either the environment must not be volatile in ways that matter to the experiment, or we must be able to correct for these contaminating influences. Second, it presupposes a fairly full theory embracing information about: how the policy arena relates to its environment, so we can recognize contaminating influences; how to control for these contaminating influences; and how stable the system is, so we can know when the lessons of one experiment cease to be relevant to future policy considerations. When these preconditions are missing, we may once again have to fall back upon theoretically based techniques (simulations, analogues, mathematical models, etc.) for guidance.

To recapitulate: logic alone requires instrumentalists to use *some* sort of theory. Without *any* theory there can be *no* interpretation of the results of incremental interventions. It does not take much of a theory to get around this logical obstacle to incrementalism$_1$—any theory, slipshod though it may be, will suffice. But then practical pressures begin to force improvement of the theoretical base, through careful assessment of and reflection upon incrementalist$_2$ experiments whenever feasible. An incrementalist's policy prescriptions can be no more reliable than the theory he uses in interpreting the past experience upon which his recommendations are based.

2.3. Incrementalism$_3$: The Adaptation Rationale

A third minor theme in the prescriptive case for incrementalism is that, by proceeding slowly and cautiously, we can correct mistakes and adapt future moves in light of past experiences. Braybrooke and Lindblom (1963, 120–27), like Popper (1945, vol. 1, 160) before them, praise incrementalism for its adaptive capacities. The general point is best put by Caiden and Wildavsky (1974, 309): "It is a mistake to encase probable errors in concrete.... The scope for error is large but the margin for maneuver is small." They invite us to "consider, by contrast, the virtues of thinking small. A large number of small projects with short time horizons greatly increase the prospects of learning, adaptation and correction'' (cf. Wildavsky 1979, 393, 63–67). The great fear is that nonincremental decision-making might produce irreversible effects, encasing errors in concrete. Indeed, mathematical economists have proven that ordinary expected utility calculations (long the predominant mode of non-incremental analysis) favor irreversible courses of action more often than would be socially optimal, and they suggest that we explicitly build our aversion to such outcomes into a revised utility function (Arrow and Fisher 1974; Henry 1974).

The distinctive *goal* of incrementalism$_3$, then, is to prevent potentially desirable options from being foreclosed. The essence of the incrementalist$_3$ *strategy* is as follows:

1. Start with a theoretically informed hypothesis about the system.
2. On that basis, nonarbitrarily select the incremental intervention that is expected to maximize utility subject to the constraint that whichever course of action is pursued must be reversible.[13]
3. Observe the results of the interventions to obtain data regarding the comparative advantages of alternative courses of action.
4. Revise the hypothesis, or change it if necessary.
5. Repeat the procedure, backtracking and pursuing an alternative course of action if the revised theory so indicates.

The *rationale* for confining the interventions to merely incremental alterations is the empirical hypothesis that such a modest alteration is less likely to foreclose future options.

Incrementalism$_3$ bears a strong and clear resemblance to incrementalism$_2$. Both frankly admit the need for a theoretical understanding of the system, and both view incremental interventions as essentially research tools. Theoretical understanding is needed in incrementalism$_3$ at various points. Mostly, we need theories to tell us which paths *are* reversible and to indicate which among these promise (perhaps falsely) to maximize expected utility. Such a large role for theory is wholly appropriate, as my critique of incrementalism$_1$ has demonstrated.

While incrementalism$_3$ secures for us the option of reversing course, it is rarely crucial itself in helping us decide whether to take up that option. More typically, we decide to change course simply as the result of things that happen with the passage of time and the

13. This is, of course, subject to the inescapable constraint that time itself is irreversible.

fruition of research programs. With the other two forms of incrementalism, the advantages in view came from *doing* something incrementally. With incrementalism$_3$, in contrast, the advantage in view comes not from anything we do, incrementally or otherwise, but merely from waiting. Little and Mirrlees (1974, 320), for example, suggest we "postpone the irreversible aspects of the project for, say, five years...because...information about people's tastes or technical developments...may become available in the meanwhile." But that information does not become available *because* we have proceeded incrementally. At most, we can credit incrementalism$_3$ with preserving the opportunity for utilizing information that arises independently.[14]

The linchpin of the incrementalist$_3$ argument, obviously, is the empirical hypothesis that the smaller the change the more likely it is to be reversible. This, after all, is why incrementalists$_3$ are incrementalists at all; this is why they recommend we pursue policies incrementally rather than just insisting, more straightforwardly, that we strive to avoid irreversible outcomes. This hypothesis may be plausible as a general rule, but the correlation between the size of the intervention and its reversibility is far from perfect. In part, this is because irreversibility often involves the crossing of thresholds: overfishing, for example, may entail the irreversible extinction of blue whales if, but only if, the catch regularly exceeds the maximum sustainable yield; no irreversible effects follow from catches, even very large ones, that leave enough whales to breed. Occasionally, the reversibility of an intervention is absolutely unrelated to its size. Consider the disposal of radioactive wastes from nuclear power plants or atomic bomb-building. Since these materials will continue to be lethal for millions of years, and since no storage system could be guaranteed for such extended periods, it is often thought desirable that stored wastes should be retrievable should anything go wrong. Insisting upon reversibility—that what we store we can retrieve—argues for certain storage methods, such as salt mines, over others, such as letting wastes melt their way into polar ice or settle into deep sea trenches (Kubo and Rose 1973; Angino 1977; Rochlin 1978). But reversibility in this case has nothing to do with the rate at which (or amounts in which) wastes were deposited. A few thousand cubic feet of wastes deposited all at once are no less

14. For another example, Coleman (1976, 58) justified the sixteen-month demonstration period for the Concorde partially on the grounds that "during this period there will be the opportunity to undertake additional tests and measurements, to seek additional scientific consensus at international conferences already scheduled or proposed, and to conduct the FAA-sponsored High Altitude Pollution Program" in order to determine the impact of the SST on the ozone layer.

retrievable than a few hundred cubic feet deposited slowly and in small batches. In cases such as this, the reversibility criterion does not argue for incremental interventions per se.

A final objection to incrementalism$_3$ centers on its suppressed premise that irreversibility is always undesirable. Surely it is wrong to destroy irreplaceable goods or to commit ourselves irreversibly to a policy with disastrous consequences—it is, as Caiden and Wildavsky say, wrong to encase errors in concrete. But by the same token, it is enormously desirable to eradicate evils once and for all. "Smallpox was no doubt in some sense irreplaceable, but its eradication was a great good. Most of us would probably feel the same way about mosquitoes. Various regimes and eyesores, including even some natural landscapes like the original Marais of Paris, are all in some way unique, but the world is probably better off without them" (Martin 1979, 31). Similarly, suppose we find a way of shooting nuclear wastes into space on a trajectory that guarantees they will not return while still radioactive, without risk of leaking wastes en route to the launch site or during launch. The more strongly we can guarantee the irreversibility of such an orbit the more attractive this alternative becomes, although we may of course still object to the pollution of space it would entail. Thus, irreversibility might be positively desirable where the eradication of evil is concerned.

For a more politically charged account of the advantages of irreversibility, recall Schelling's (1963) discussion of the strategic advantages of irrevocably committing yourself to a certain course of action. If you are locked into a course—even one you would yourself find distasteful—your opponent will back down far more and far more quickly than he might otherwise have done. Such irreversibility not only is of strategic advantage to those who get themselves locked into a course of action but can also benefit everyone else by stabilizing the system. One of the better ways of preventing a nuclear holocaust, for example, is to guarantee that anyone launching a first strike would set in motion an automatic and irreversible chain of events that would certainly lead to "Mutually Assured Destruction." Introducing a more "flexible" response makes the process more reversible—but more likely, for that very reason. By making it easier to stop such a war, the "flexible response" doctrine makes it easier to start one. Thus, the irreversibility of the MAD doctrine might have been one of its larger virtues.

2.4. Conclusion

Two basic conclusions emerge from this survey of the three "ideal types" of incrementalism. The first is that any responsible policy must be based on some theoretical understanding of the system into which it intervenes. Some are inclined to say that, where theory is available, policymakers should of course use it, but that they can and should pursue incrementalist strategies when no theory is available. This chapter has shown, contrary to those claims, that some theory is always required if incrementalism is to make any sense at all. On the basis of that theory, of course, either hesitant incremental interventions or sweeping synoptic ones might be recommended. But in the absence of theory, neither can be. Second, there is no optimal size for a policy intervention in perfectly general terms. Incrementalists claim that there are certain sorts of circumstances which call for small changes exclusively. Here I have argued that, based on our theoretical understanding of the particular system concerned, it is sometimes appropriate to think big and sometimes appropriate to think small. Clearly the most dangerous course, however, is to deny the need for theory and refuse to think at all.

3 Anticipating Evaluations: Saving People from Their Former Selves

Some of the most conclusive cases for state action have been built by exposing the ways in which liberal theorists have exaggerated the competence of the individual. Perhaps each man would be the best judge of his own interests, had he perfect information. But people always act partly in ignorance, obliging the state to protect them through all sorts of regulatory actions (Arrow 1973a; Dworkin 1971; Ten 1971; Hodson 1977; Cornell, et al. 1976; Nichols and Zeckhauser 1977). Perhaps state intervention would not be required were people perfectly capable of pursuing their own interests, either individually or in voluntary cooperation with others. But a great many "public goods," ranging from pollution control to road-building and from national defense to economic stability, can be pursued best (if not quite only) with the aid of coercive state power (Olson 1965; Feinberg 1973, chap. 3).

All these exceptions were, of course, acknowledged in the great liberal texts (Mill 1848, bk. 5, chaps. 1, 11; Sidgwick 1897, chaps. 9, 10). Where classical liberals hoped to minimize them as being rare and of peripheral concern, however, modern social theory has shown such exceptions to be the rule. In this case, frequencies clearly do matter: if individuals were only occasionally inept then liberals might still argue for a basically laissez-faire state, but if they are often incompetent then an activist state is indicated.

In this chapter I shall pursue yet another liberal concession to what once again will prove to be rather illiberal

This chapter is reprinted, with minor revisions, from Robert E. Goodin, "Retrospective Rationality: Saving People from Their Former Selves," *Social Science Information* 18, no. 6 (1979): 967–90, by permission of the publisher, Sage Publications Ltd., London.

conclusions. Liberals agree that people are not always fully rational. J. S. Mill (1859), phrasing the point particularly conservatively, allows that children and idiots cannot be expected to look after themselves. But even mature and stable people sometimes suffer lapses of rationality. Liberals simply must admit this fact when the individual concerned actually anticipated his moment of weakness, as did Ulysses with the Sirens. They would dearly hope to confine their theory of "imperfect rationality" to people who actually admit their failings (Elster 1977 and 1979b, chap. 2). But knowing that self-confessedly weak men exist and deciding what to do with them, we are led to a more general repudiation of the orthodox liberal model of interests.

Ultimately the problem is that liberals ignore the passage of time and what it does to people. Their model is meant for people with well-formed preferences and a firm mind, who can choose a course and stick to it. Real people, of course, are otherwise. They change and grow, largely as a result of their experiences in pursuing what they previously thought they wanted.

Incrementalists, to their eternal credit, realize more clearly than most that "we discover our objectives and the intensity that we assign to them only in the process of considering particular programs or policies. We articulate 'ends' as we evaluate 'means'" (Schultze 1968, 38). But from this valid and valuable insight, incrementalists improperly proceed to the conclusion that it is impossible to make social policy in such a way as to anticipate those changing values. Since "not even the chooser himself knows his preferences until he is confronted with an actual choice," Lindblom (1977, 103) deems any attempt by anyone else at forward planning on his behalf to be doomed to failure. "The trouble," as Wildavsky (1979, 139, 135) sees it, "is that . . . people can't be trusted to be predictable. . . . How can we be goal-directed if we don't know what our goal is until we get there?" Such uncertainties, incrementalists argue, paralyze intellectual efforts at social planning. Policy, if it is to respond to people's ever-changing and fundamentally unpredictable preferences, simply *must* proceed incrementally (Braybrooke and Lindblom 1963).

Occasionally these uncertainties may be just as serious as incrementalists make out. Often, however, it seems that preference changes can be reasonably well predicted—but, crucially, that the person himself is the least able to do so. Policymakers who appreciate the way people's preferences will change need not slavishly follow their present preferences, and may instead pursue more enlightened policies of which people will ultimately approve. Recall the early history of the National Health Service in Britain:

> Many doctors who resisted and attacked the Health Insurance
> Act when it was first proposed and who worked its provisions in
> a spirit of hostile and grudging acquiescence, would now admit
> that they were quickly convinced that the results were wholly
> good, and that they now carry out those regulations with no
> more feeling of enslavement than they have towards their
> stethoscopes ... or any other tried and trusted tool of their
> trade. [Mabbott 1967, 66]

It certainly would have been a pity to scrap the scheme because, ahead of time, doctors mistakenly thought they would dislike it. Similarly, it would be unfortunate in the extreme to let the natural environment continue to deteriorate or toxic wastes accumulate in leaky dumps or heavy metals in the ocean just because ecology suffers ups and downs in public opinion polls (cf. Downs 1972).

Classical liberalism commits us to those unfortunate results through its overly robust model of rationality, which fails to notice that people change their minds. Incrementalism commits us to the same results through its overly flaccid model of rationality, which fails to recognize that people have good grounds for changing their minds in one direction rather than another. These absurdities can be avoided using an alternative analysis of "retrospective rationality," which is suggested by the case of people who are admittedly weak and susceptible to temptation. Instead of worrying whether a policy has consistently strong support throughout its life, this standard advises us to proceed with it so long as there are good grounds for believing that at the end of the day it will be agreed to have been a good thing. This, presumably, is a test both the National Health Service and environmental protection could pass. No one with a full and vivid awareness of all the options could seriously deny that a reasonably effective system of each is vastly preferable to its real alternatives.

3.1. Overcoming Private Temptations

Liberals loudly insist that each individual be regarded as the best judge of his own interests. But sometimes the man confesses he is not—and, to the liberal's way of thinking, he should know. The situation is structurally parallel to that discussed by moral psychologists under the heading of "weakness of will": an individual at t_1 foresees that at some later time t_2 he will be unable to resist doing something he anticipates with disdain and, at a still later t_3, will come to regret; knowing this, he binds himself ahead of time so as to prevent his t_2 self from betraying the values his t_1 and t_3 selves share. My focus here—unlike that in traditional moral philosophy (Mortimore 1971)—will be on the confessed inadequacy of the t_2 self as a judge of the individual's true interests.

In deciding what to do with individuals who confess their own inadequacies, a slightly "crazy" case might help. Of course, it is crucial to generalize up from such bizarre examples, as section 1.2.1 emphasized. But the example does seem useful, both in motivating and illustrating the subsequent discussion.

Imagine Ian, a Glaswegian dockworker of times past. Ordinarily a reliable fellow saving faithfully to marry his childhood sweetheart, Ian nevertheless is weak and knows it. He realizes that if he receives his pay along with everyone else on Friday afternoon, he will be unable to resist the temptation to join his mates in the pub and drink away his week's wages. So he arranges for his supervisor, Alistair, to collect his pay and not to give it to him until teatime Sunday. Alistair's task is a difficult one, for every Friday Ian comes begging to be given his pay packet. But it is not a thankless one, for every Sunday Ian proves grateful.

Knowing Ian as he does, Alistair refuses his requests every Friday. But how does he justify this action? Two alternatives are available to him. One points to Ian's earlier request, and Alistair's promise, that Ian's Friday plea for the pay be ignored. A second points to the fact that Ian will be grateful when he comes around on Sunday. The first alternative seems far the more natural. Alistair, in helping Ian bind himself, seems merely to be following the liberal principle of letting Ian choose for himself. On this account, the fact that Ian will prove grateful matters only insofar as Ian has consented to "the practice of relying on future consent in such situations" (Haksar 1979, 249). And, since requests for such assistance and consent to such interference come only infrequently, the peripheral role liberal theory accords "imperfect rationality" seems appropriate. Here, however, I shall discuss two reasons for finding that justification of Alistair's interference untenable. In so doing, I shall argue for the second alternative and the more fundamental revision of liberal theory and political practice that it entails.

Two objections combine against the argument for respecting Ian's earlier request. First is the problem of choosing *which* Ian to obey. After all, there are two of them—one who demands his pay every Friday and another who is grateful the rest of the week for having it withheld. What sort of argument can Alistair give for favoring one over the other, assisting the sober Ian in binding the thirsty Ian?

The two Ians seem to have symmetrical claims. The thirsty Ian appears just as regularly—every Friday, like clockwork. The fact that the sober Ian came first or occupies the body longer surely cannot matter. Were their situations reversed, and Ian an alcoholic who occasionally tries to dry out, we would hardly think it proper for Alistair to collaborate with Ian's ordinary (drunk) self in binding Ian against the excesses of sobriety occasionally threatened by Ian's "better" self.

Alistair might argue that the sober Ian deserves more respect because he is more rational. But in what sense? Ordinarily, the hallmark of rationality is taken to be prudential planning. Where individuals change in ways under discussion here, this criterion seems inappropriate.[1] In any case, however, the planning criterion cannot distinguish between the two Ians. Just as the sober Ian has a coherent plan for his life (steady work, marriage, a family, etc.), so too does the thirsty Ian have something of a plan (good fellowship every weekend and all that goes with it). Furthermore, neither of these plans is clearly subordinate to the other, in the sense of the one's being a "partial" plan embedded in another which is more "comprehensive."[2] Thus, favoring one Ian over the other seems to be based on nothing more than our own preference for the one Ian's lifestyle over the other's. And it is, of course, a fundamental violation of liberal principles to impose such preferences on others.

Finally, Alistair might try to defend favoring the sober Ian on the grounds of the irreversible damage done to Ian's body by his weekend drinking bouts. Even J. S. Mill (1859, chap. 5) would approve of paternalistic measures aimed at preventing a person from irreversibly alienating his freedom by selling himself into slavery. The more general principle that that suggests is one justifying paternalistic interferences designed to prevent people from taking decisions "which are far-reaching, potentially dangerous and irreversible" (Dworkin 1971, 123).

While irreversible acts certainly should be considered very carefully, however, their irreversibility alone does not argue conclusively against an individual's pursuing them. Even consumption

1. The problem is not that a man who changes and anticipates changing cannot have a coherent life plan. People often do devise long-range plans for their lives even though they know that they themselves will change, scrapping the plan when they do; not knowing when or how they will change, people plan as if they will not. The problem, rather, is why people who know they will change must plan as if they will not in order to be called "rational." The six-year-old who "plans" to be a doctor is cute but, I submit, not necessarily any more rational than one choosing to maximize current consumption of candy. Even Nagel (1970, chap. 8), who is otherwise strongly attached to this definition of rationality, concedes this point.

2. Presumably the plans of thirsty Ian to obtain drink are not just a subset of sober Ian's larger life plan, nor are the schemes of sober Ian to avoid drink embedded in drunk Ian's plans. On the contrary, sober Ian's plans include stratagems for avoiding the drunk Ian, and thirsty Ian similarly deploys strategies to foil sober Ian's attempts at enforcing abstention.

acts are irreversible, insofar as resources devoted to consuming one commodity are irrevocably lost to other uses.[3] And "most deaths are suicides" (Becker 1976b, 10), insofar as life could have been prolonged had more resources been devoted to that goal and fewer to others which are more dangerous but more fun. The liberal, of course, has no business telling a man that he should prefer a longer life without the pleasures of drink to a shorter life with them. As Dworkin (1971, 121) himself acknowledges, "it may be more important" for a Christian Scientist "to reject 'impure substances' [i.e., a blood transfusion] than to go on living," in which case the liberal is obliged to let him die.

Hence, there seem to be no objective bases for Alistair's choice of which Ian to obey, causing the "he asked, I promised" argument to flounder. Originally it appeared as if Alistair merely helps Ian to bind himself. Now we see that Ian has multiple selves between which Alistair must choose. In making that choice, Alistair must go well beyond the simple liberal principle of letting Ian choose for himself which at first appeared to guide him.

A second problem with the "he asked, I promised" argument also grows out of the fact that Ian is constantly changing. For Alistair to hold Ian at t_2 (Friday afternoon) to the words of Ian at t_1 (earlier in the week), he must expect that at t_3 (Sunday teatime) the same old Ian of t_1 will reappear with all the same preferences, unaffected by his intervening experiences and temptations. But only the most radically divided personality would be utterly unaffected by his ordeals. Perhaps when Mr. Hyde takes leave of the body, Dr. Jekyll reappears just as before, with no recollection of Hyde's adventures. Ordinarily, however, an individual displays "mental continuity or connectedness," which is what enables us to identify and reidentify him as the same individual through time (Rorty 1976). People not only recollect past experiences but also allow them to shape their present desires and characters. Even economists have come to appreciate that "the preference system in existence at one moment is the consequence of actual purchases in the past" (Duesenberry 1949, 14, 24), and their models increasingly reflect this fact (Peston

3. True, we can be restored to the same position as before our last consumption act with the infusion of new capital. But once we allow such a deus ex machina, nothing is irreversible—we could postulate a "miracle healer" restoring lost health as readily as a "miracle financier" restoring depleted capital. For a philosophical analysis of the parallel notion of "irreplaceability," see Martin (1979). Economists, following the generally unacknowledged lead of Mill (1848, bk. 5, chap. 11, sec. 10), object to irreversible acts because they close off future options which, while not high among our present priorities, we may later come to prefer. But far from prohibiting irreversible acts, those arguments imply only that they should carry a surcharge of something on the order of, say, 13 percent (Henry 1974; Arrow and Fisher 1974).

1967; Georgescu-Roegen 1967; 1971; Weiszäcker 1971; Stigler and Becker 1977).

The extent of Alistair's obligation to keep his promise depends, under these circumstances, on the nature of the change that will be produced in Ian by his intervening experiences. If the Ian of next Sunday will differ only marginally from the Ian who wrung the promise from Alistair last week, he may be said to have an obligation to keep his promise to what is essentially the same person now as before. If Ian changes radically, however, very different problems arise in justifying Alistair's intervention. A promise is still involved, but it is a promise to an Ian-who-is-no-longer that Alistair proposes using to excuse denying Ian-as-he-now-is his pay. Rather than just helping Ian bind himself, Alistair would be collaborating with one person in binding another (Parfit 1973, 145–46). Ordinarily promises count for little in mitigating the immorality of such actions: the fact that I promised to help a kidnapper hardly excuses my complicity in his crime.

From Alistair's point of view, the central question must be how much the preferences of the new Ian will differ from those of the old. More specifically, would the new Ian have wanted Alistair to keep the promise he made to the old Ian? If so, then Alistair clearly should deny the thirsty Ian his pay packet. If not, then it is not at all clear that he should; and it is at least arguable that he should not, on the grounds that one person must not interfere with the self-regarding acts of another without special warrant (permission, etc.), which Alistair lacks. The problem of a changing Ian thus forces Alistair to fall back on the second argument for denying Ian's temptations: the best reason he can give is that, come Sunday, Ian will prove grateful.

These two arguments, if roughly correct, suggest that Alistair cannot safely adopt the backward-looking liberal standard of "you asked, I promised" but must instead rely on the forward-looking standard of "you will be grateful." Ian's earlier request to be bound need not be entirely irrelevant. We might regard it as a prediction of how he will feel about the matter come Sunday. Sometimes people might make reliable predictions about the nature and preferences of their future selves. But Ian's earlier request is, on this analysis, no more than a prediction. As such, it is on a par with any other "informed" prediction. And since the individual concerned has no monopoly on information relevant to these predictions, his judgment is nowise privileged. While the practical implications of "he will be grateful" models might often mirror those of "he asked, I promised," where they diverge the former are to be preferred.

Although the "he will be grateful" standard repudiates important particulars of the liberal orthodoxy, it adheres closely to its spirit. To say that "he will be grateful" in this context is merely to say that *his future preferences warrant my present behavior.*[4] Here, just as in the liberal orthodoxy, the justification for Alistair's interference is couched very crucially in terms of Ian's preferences. But while the liberal insists that we always leave Ian to the mercies of his former self, the "he will be grateful" standard allows us to make better provision for an Ian with capacities to change and grow.

Incrementalists rightly emphasize that it is not easy for Alistair to apply the "he will be grateful" standard. It requires him to look deeply into the minds of all the possible Ians. Simply saying that the sober Ian will be grateful when he comes to collect his pay envelope on Sunday is not enough to justify Alistair's decision, since the thirsty Ian would himself have been grateful had he been given the pay packet when he asked for it on Friday. The mere fact of gratitude is insufficient to distinguish between the two cases. Alistair must judge the magnitude of the gratitude the two Ians would feel for the two acts, withholding the pay if and only if he judges that Ian (with the preferences of his sober self) would be more grateful for that act than Ian (with the preferences of his thirsty self) would be were Alistair to do otherwise. This is, fundamentally, an interpersonal comparison of utility (Sen 1979, 14–16). These are never easy but, as section 1.2.2 above has argued, neither are they impossible.

Alistair would naturally like to shrink from such a difficult task, leaving such decisions to Ian himself and merely helping enforce whatever Ian decides. That would be quite the right strategy, provided Ian were capable of an informed and impartial assessment of the pleasures and pains of all his various selves. Usually, however, people in Ian's position will be ill informed of the alternatives and

4. I take "prudence" to be a matter of planning to promote future (or, at most, present and future) want satisfaction—bygones are bygone forever (cf. Bricker 1980). The possibility of "future-oriented consent" as a justification for apparently paternalistic actions is floated by Dworkin (1971, 119 ff.) and Gert and Culver (1976). Various minor complications in this model must be noted. (1) What if Ian were to die unexpectedly (in a traffic accident, say) on Saturday night, and hence never come to be grateful for Alistair's interference (Husak 1981, 33)? I think we would still say that Alistair was justified, so long as he had good grounds for expecting the preference change and no grounds for anticipating Ian's death in the interim. (2) What if Ian never actually *expresses* gratitude? That is irrelevant. All that matters is that Alistair correctly anticipates Ian's future preferences. (3) What if Alistair predicts Ian's future preferences correctly but botches unforgivably the selection of methods for securing those ends? Then we would say that Alistair was justified in *substituting his judgment* for Ian's but not in actually *acting* on his behalf. I concentrate here on the problem of substituting judgment, since liberals (Mill 1859; Feinberg 1973) already concede in their discussions of "provisional paternalism" that interfering with another's choice of means might be justified.

will assess their past and future experiences in terms of their present preferences. Thus, their reports on the pains and pleasures of alternative selves will be unjustifiably biased in favor of the particular self making the report. In that case, people like Alistair could easily be a better judge of the quantity of gratitude of the various Ians. It is, of course, something of a "wager," since Alistair can never be certain he has predicted Ian's future preferences correctly. But he also has plenty of room for error. For his intervention to be justified, Alistair need not, after all, make the absolutely optimal choice on Ian's behalf, but need only do better than Ian would have done for himself.

3.2. Extensions and Implications of Retrospective Rationality

Liberals would welcome the "craziness" of my story of a schizophrenic Glaswegian docker as reinforcing their claim that models of imperfect rationality can be confined to special and somewhat extraordinary cases. Their theories crucially presuppose that most people most of the time are fully rational and perfectly capable of handling their own affairs. The "imperfect rationality subroutine" truly does deserve a modest role so long as it can be triggered only by an actual admission of weakness and a request for assistance. These, after all, are rare. Secton 3.1 has, however, shown that an interference with others is warranted not by their requests but rather by their future gratitude. It is justified wherever we can foresee that an individual's preferences will change in such a way as to cause him to regret actions which, from his present perspective, he supposes will prove optimal.

This expands the role of imperfect rationality tremendously. People ask for help only occasionally; they need to be defended against their former preferences much more often. For example, social welfare legislation is often initially resisted in ways and for reasons that can barely be believed only a few years later. The example of the British National Health Service has already been mentioned. Another concerns the American Social Security Act. This was hardly an unpopular measure even at its inception. But in light of its ultimately rapturous acceptance, it is surprising that the program was favored by only 68 percent of those polled in 1936. Within eight years, that had risen to 96 percent (Schiltz 1970, 36). Apparently, early doubts were easily put to rest by just a little experience of the program's operation. Of course, surveys alone cannot tell us to what extent this amounted to a change of preferences, as opposed to mere reassurance about the mechanical operations of the program. It seems safe to assume, however, that there was a little of each involved.

An inverse case might involve the operations of multinational corporations in the Third World. At the outset, there is often considerable enthusiasm in a country for inviting foreign investment in order to stimulate economic development. This enthusiasm soon wanes as people see the multinationals siphoning off natural resources and leaving behind little more than polluted landscapes and ties of technological dependence. The long history of Third World nationalization of foreign enterprises abounds with cases of people who changed their minds—who once thought of multinationals as being on balance beneficial and who came to see them instead as leeches. On the other hand, host countries may sometimes not have known the true facts about how badly multinationals could misbehave, or they may have intended their confiscations from the first. But at least sometimes host countries invite in multinationals with their eyes open and intentions honorable, and their subsequent reversals really are due to a change in preferences. They simply came to mind corporate misbehavior much more than they initially thought they would.

Contrary to the claims of incrementalists, it seems that policymakers would not have needed all that much insight to have anticipated these preference changes. Even if they had anticipated the changes, however, classical liberalism would have committed them to the myopic course of satisfying the preferences of people which are certain to change. Just as in section 3.1 we would allow Alistair to deny Ian his pay if he is certain that Ian will ultimately prove grateful for that act, so too do we here want to allow policymakers to frustrate current desires in order to serve preferences which are soon sure to emerge. Thus, a model of retrospective rationality would allow policymakers to impose social welfare programs or ban multinationals over public protest, provided those actions are warranted by people's future preferences.[5]

Besides these interesting implications for particular policies, this model also demands important alterations in political institutions and practices more generally. Without attempting to be exhaustive, I will indicate something of its range by drawing examples from legal,

5. Retrospective rationality justifies two rather different types of intervention: in Case A, we impose a policy which people currently resist but eventually come to like; in Case B, we refuse to adopt a policy which people currently desire but would eventually come to loathe. Both cases require that the policymaker correctly predict people's future preferences. But, politically, Case A is much easier. There people actually experience the policy—their preferences change in consequence, and they congratulate the policymaker for his foresight. In Case B, people never know how miserable they might have been—so the policymaker gets no political credit for his service.

economic, and political theory. Each of these discussions has a long history of its own, of course; but at a deeper level all are intimately related, together comprising the core of liberal social theory. Surveying the revisions required by the model of retrospective rationality suggests something of the scope of the reorientation it demands of the liberal orthodoxy.

3.2.1. Legal Paternalism

The most obvious application of this doctrine is in the area of legal paternalism. Liberals regard each man as the sole judge of his own welfare, leaving no room for the possibility that his interests might be better served if some external agency (legal or otherwise) were to compel him to do something against his will (Mill 1859, chap. 1). The model of retrospective rationality, in contrast, foresees many occasions on which the individual concerned might mistake his future interests and, hence, on which legal compulsion could help protect a person from himself. Not only do individuals err by choosing wrong instruments to realize their goals, which even orthodox liberals concede justifies some external intervention (advice surely, and perhaps more). The model of retrospective rationality goes much further, justifying interference on the grounds that the individuals concerned cannot adequately anticipate their future preferences. People often efficiently pursue goals which, once realized, they come to detest. Retrospective rationality saves them from this fate.

Consider the case of cigarette smokers. Over 90 percent do now know the risks of lung cancer. Nevertheless, the fact that they continue smoking constitutes, for liberals, ironclad proof that the pleasures outweigh the risks of pain in their minds. But the psychological evidence makes us wonder (Tamerin and Resnick 1972; Kunreuther, et al. 1978, 14–15). Smokers tend to discount the probabilities psychologically, thinking "it could never happen to me." And, psychologically, they lack a full and vivid awareness of the pleasures and pains of the alternative outcomes, exaggerating tobacco's joys and underestimating cancer's miseries. As Dworkin (1971, 121) remarks of the parallel problem of seat belt use, "Although I know in some intellectual sense what the probabilities and risks are I do not fully appreciate them in an emotionally genuine manner." Similarly with the smoker. While he may antecedently suppose that the pleasures of tobacco outweigh the risks of pain, there is every reason to suppose he would think otherwise should he contract cancer—not just in the sense that anyone who gambles and loses wishes he had never gambled at all, but more importantly in the sense that he had badly underestimated the pains associated with losing the gamble.

Policymakers who foresee this preference shift would, following retrospective rationality, be perfectly justified in prohibiting, limiting, or discouraging smoking.

The best examples here seem to involve catastrophes against which people fail to protect themselves adequately, such as car crashes, lung cancer, floods, earthquakes, and so on (Kunreuther, et al. 1978; chapter 8 below). The argument can also be used, however, against all sorts of illusory goods that lose their appeal the closer we approach them. For example, an automobile, mountain hut, or suburban home is useful if and only if not too many others also have one. If we can obtain these goods for ourselves only by allowing others to obtain them too, then we cannot expect any net gain in welfare from joint pursuit of those goods (Hirsch 1976). Prohibiting the pursuit of such "positional" or "status" goods is paternalistic in the strong sense—legislators substitute their judgment for that of the people most directly involved. But this is justified ultimately in terms of the (hypothetical) preferences of the very individuals with whom legislators interfere.

3.2.2.   Consumer Sovereignty and Social Planning

Were individuals the exclusive judges of their own interests, as in liberal orthodoxy, productive endeavors should be rigidly linked to those judgments. "Consumer sovereignty implies that the pattern of production should be determined by the actual choices that the consumer makes amongst the goods that are offered to him for sale" (Wootton 1945, 55–56). The great attraction of ideal markets for the liberal is that they make the individual consumer sovereign in this sense.

The great fallacy of planning on this basis is that it figures future satisfactions according to present preferences. Were we really trying to maximize want satisfaction we should plan on the basis of the increment of satisfaction that would actually be experienced at the moment the plan comes to fruition and delivers the promised goods. As Sen (1957, 746; cf. 1975, 53–54) rightly insists, "We are interested in tomorrow's satisfaction as such, not in today's assessment of tomorrow's satisfaction." But by making consumers sovereign we necessarily link productive decisions to present anticipations of future pleasures.[6] These, as we have seen, may be considerably

6. This becomes particularly important with respect to risk preferences, discussed in chapter 8 below. Broome (1978, 95) argues that especially where risks are concerned "the *ex post* valuation is the correct one . . . because it is the valuation of the actual project, whereas the other is really a valuation of the expectations created by the project."

wide of the mark. "We therefore have to ask," with Weiszäcker (1971, 371), "whether it is reasonable for a society to build its decisions on its present preferences.... If present preferences are strongly influenced by myopic thinking, by lack of imagination how a different world would look, we should not accept these preferences as the last word." The retrospective rationality standard cuts planners free of their absolute subservience to the present will of the people they serve. If planners can predict with reasonable confidence how future preferences will differ from present ones, this principle justifies them in planning on that basis instead.

Incrementalists would emphasize the difficulty of making any precise predictions along these lines. Certainly planners can never expect to predict future preferences perfectly. But neither do they need to do so. All that is required is that their predictions be more accurate than those of the citizens themselves, for which planners' predictions are being substituted. This does not seem nearly so arduous a task, especially where macro decisions about the structure of the economy (as opposed to micro decisions about particular products) are concerned.

3.2.3. Democratic Responsibility

The liberal case for popular sovereignty parallels that for consumer sovereignty: people being the best judge of their own interests, democracy is the utility-maximizing form of government (Mill 1828). Even if people are incompetent to judge technical details, and specialized elites are required, liberals insist they be democratically selected through a competitive process (Mill 1861, chap. 12; Schumpeter 1950, chap. 22). Once again, however, the liberal model has voters choosing on the basis of their present preferences. If these will change in ways voters themselves cannot (or do not) foresee, then they will come to regret the earlier decision, however democratic it might have been. The retrospective rationality model would ask elites to override the popular will not only to correct misperceptions of technical facts but also to anticipate changes in citizen preferences. Pitkin (1972, 204–5) claims less originality than is her due for the observation that "a man's true interest is what gives him pleasure . . . when he experiences it . . . . But most men do not know how to get what will really give them pleasure (at least in politics) . . . . Hence a representative can often promote their true interest (separate and common) by disobeying their wishes."

But while retrospective rationality repudiates any form of knee-jerk democratic responsiveness, it is reassuringly consistent with "democratic responsibility" understood as a post hoc check. After the fact, citizens are of course in a position to say whether rulers anticipated preference changes correctly or not. In designing democratic institutions, retrospective rationality puts far more emphasis on citizens dismissing a government on the basis of its past record than on electing it on the basis of its prior promises (Downs 1957; Fiorina 1981). One model might be the mechanisms used in several American states to ensure accountability of judges. The governor initially appoints people to the bench, with the advice and consent of the legislature but without any popular vote. After a judge has been serving for a fixed period, he must be confirmed in office by the voters. But in this election he simply runs against his own record rather than against any opposing candidate—voters have only the choice of letting the judge continue to serve or not. If they turn him out, the governor appoints a successor on the same terms.

3.3. The "Seduction" Objection

Such models of retrospective rationality have been accused of santioning "seduction," in that they seem to justify coercing someone to do something disagreeable now on the grounds that he will later come to like it.[7] This objection might rest on any of four distinct grounds. First is the coercion involved. Models of "future consent" are sometimes accused of justifying the use of "paternalistic *force*" and of "*forcibly* doing things" to people (Haksar 1979, 249, emphasis added). Retrospective rationality, however, would allow no more violence against people than would characteristically be approved by models predicated on prior consent. How much force people would—either ex ante or ex post—consent to having used against them depends on how important the stakes are (or will be) to them. Where vital interests are involved, a fair bit of force might be warranted. Ulysses, recall, agreed to being bound to his mast. But Ulysses could hardly have been thought to consent to the use of deadly force to keep him aboard—death was the most he had to fear from answering the Sirens' call, after all. Similar limits apply to the force that can legitimately be used against someone in the service of his future preferences.

A second strand of the "seduction" objection is to the circularity involved: my intervention causes your preferences to change in such a way as to justify (on the "you will be grateful" standard) my actions. There is something self-serving about the justification that makes us uneasy. But notice that with the element of coercion re-

7. Elster (1977, 500; 1979b, chap. 2.6). "Seduction" is something of a misnomer. It is more like a case of a woman's falling in love with her rapist. One ordinarily succumbs to a seducer voluntarily and only later comes to regret it, which is the opposite pattern of preference change from that Elster envisages.

moved, "seduction" is no worse than "persuasion." That, too, is a self-serving interference with the preferences and beliefs of others, but we ordinarily regard persuasion as an ethically acceptable form of social influence (Goodin 1980, chap. 1). Perhaps this is because we suppose persuasion leaves its object subjectively better off than he was before being persuaded. But if seduction is to be justified on the "he will be grateful" standard, it must do likewise. Thus, if we approve of persuasion we must also approve of "seduction."[8]

A third strand in the "seduction" objection is to deception. For Elster, as for many before him (cf. Goodin 1980, chap. 1), what distinguishes impermissible seduction from morally permissible persuasion is that in seduction "the persuasion is not accompanied by a statement of intention informing the individual that he is about to be manipulated." The model of retrospective rationality, however, neither justifies deception nor depends on it for its efficient functioning. It is perfectly possible for Alistair to *tell* Ian on Friday that he is withholding his pay on the grounds that he will be grateful later, just as it is possible for British politicians to admit openly that they are enacting National Health legislation expecting that citizens and even physicians will eventually come to like it.[9]

A final strand of the "seduction" objection focuses upon the fact that retrospective rationality plays on people's psychological frail-

8. Elster (1977, 83) agrees that "persuasion is more similar to seduction than to voluntary choice," but he concludes from that that persuasion must therefore be evil rather than that seduction might be permissible. Our prejudice against self-serving interventions is predicated on a contingent and imperfect connection with harming someone else in the process of serving oneself (Goodin 1980, 16–17). In any case, retrospective rationality rarely sanctions self-serving interventions. Section 3.4 below argues that involvement subverts foresight. As this tendency affects seducers and seduced alike, a seducer who stands to benefit from his actions is unlikely to have the kind of superior foresight that would justify his intervention.

9. Since people's resenting the interference is all that matters, some might suggest saving people from themselves behind their backs: people will be pleased with the results and, provided the illusion of choice is preserved for them, no resentment will diminish their satisfaction (Barry 1965, 70–71; Haksar 1979, 249). But this depends upon an unacceptably narrow understanding of "gratitude." For one to be "grateful" in the sense that can excuse another's interference, one's gratitude (actual, if ex post; anticipated, if ex ante) must be predicated on full knowledge of what the other has done. Suppose Alistair collects Ian's Friday pay and bets it on the Saturday races, luckily winning enough to give Ian his due on Sunday. Ian, unaware of the risks taken with his money, expresses profound gratitude for Alistair's assistance. The fact that Ian, acting partially in ignorance, thanked him surely cannot excuse Alistair's behavior. Analogously, it is not enough that people under the illusion that they are making real choices are pleased that things are going well. For behind-the-scenes interference to be justified, it must be true that they would be grateful if they knew *all* about it. The counterfactual formulation, however, might still cause problems. Justifying interference requires only that they *would* be grateful if they knew; but, not knowing, they might be even happier. Manipulators might point to this added increment of happiness to justify their secrecy, thereby preventing their assertion that the interference is justified (because people *would* be grateful) from ever being put to the test.

ties. Elster (1977, 83) argues that "exploiting intrapsychic mechanisms that are unknown to the individual can never be justified .... Planning other people's experience is unethical." What seems so evil about "exploiting" those mechanisms and "seducing" people, however, is the implication that we are taking unfair advantage of their weaknesses. In fact, retrospective rationality models do just the opposite. The goal is to help people to overcome those weaknesses—to save them from their former selves—rather than to take undue advantage of them. When these four strands of the "seduction" objection are disentangled and examined separately, they appear really rather weak.

3.4. Preconditions

Incrementalists fully appreciate that people's preferences change in a way that classical liberals rarely acknowledged. They end up with the same laissez-faire recommendations, however, because of their deep doubt about the most crucial precondition for making the model of retrospective rationality operational. A policymaker must be able to predict people's future preferences better than they can themselves. At first blush, that seems impossible (Wildavsky 1979, 179–81; Culyer 1971). Upon reflection, it seems easy. Involvement and foresight often are inversely related, an actor's perceptions and judgment being subverted by his very proximity to the activity at hand. Independent observers with only modest insight often can, through their very detachment, achieve a better perspective on long-term consequences and the actor's ultimate evaluation of them. There are various reasons for this. People who are intimately involved typically lack the "strength of mind, which might enable them to resist the temptation of present ease or pleasure, and carry them forward in search of more distant profit and enjoyment" (Hume 1977, sec. 6, pt. 1). Furthermore, people who are deeply involved usually face such a heavy burden of pressing decisions as to leave them little opportunity for calm reflection on the implications for their own want satisfaction of their actions in the long term and across the full range of possible outcomes (Kahneman and Tversky 1979). All of this suggests that there may well be people in a position to predict a person's future preferences better than the person himself.[10]

10. Maybe that is just the sort of imperfect rationality that orthodox liberals would agree justifies paternalistic interference, but the point is that examples of it are so frequent as to constitute the rule rather than the exception. Even if no one can anticipate other people's future preferences, the model of retrospective rationality would still imply that people should buy "insurance" against the risk that their preferences might change, i.e., should keep more options open than they would

Another precondition of retrospective rationality models which may prove more of an obstacle to their application is that, for one man to be justified in acting on another's behalf, the other must be willing to accept his help. This goes far toward preventing retrospective rationality from justifying wholesale meddling. Other things being equal, most people prefer to make their own choices. Their gratitude to meddlesome benefactors is always reduced by some increment corresponding to the strength of this preference. In marginal cases—and, if the preference is a strong one, perhaps not so marginal ones—they may prove ungrateful even though conceding that the interference produced tangible results superior to those they could (or would) have achieved for themselves. In such a situation, the "he will be grateful" standard obviously does not approve the intervention. How severely this curtails application of the retrospective rationality model depends, of course, upon how strong the preference for doing it oneself is in any particular individual or population. For radical individualists who rank "doing it themselves" lexicographically above the quality of the results produced, resentment at interference would always render such interventions unjustifiable. Most people, however, seem considerably less stubborn. That leaves plenty of room for the retrospective rationality model to operate.[11]

3.5. Conclusion

Liberal orthodoxy presupposes perfectly rational individuals capable of fantastic feats of anticipation and evaluation. Its concessions to the flawed reality of social life come in the form of a theory of imperfect or intermittent rationality: the trick is to catch a person in his rational moments, get a statement of his "settled" preferences, and hold him to them in moments of madness. The critique of this as a solution to the problem of weakness of will suggests that the flaws in this liberal analysis are more general. The problem is nowise confined to Ulysses and the Sirens or drunken dockworkers. Very many of us very often fail to anticipate the ways in which our character and preferences will change over time. The preferences of a person at one moment—even if they reflect his

---

otherwise be inclined to do (Zeckhauser 1969). And they are unlikely to be very good judges of how much insurance they will need, so paternalism once again may be justified.

11. If someone were to rank "keeping the preferences I presently have" lexicographically above all else, that too would limit the applicability of the model: it would still approve interventions justified in terms of preference changes that occur independently of the policymaker's intervention; but it would disapprove interventions justified in terms of preference changes induced by the intervention itself. But this lexicographical ordering, too, seems implausible.

"calm" judgment—are likely to differ dramatically from his future ones. Pursuing those desires may produce results he intended but no longer desires. The same can be said for a society at large: if preferences are ever-changing, a plan which promises to pursue priority goals at the time it was instituted may be promoting goals no one cares about by the time it actually delivers the goods; and other goals which originally found few champions may now be all the rage. In such situations, a model of retrospective rationality is needed. Instead of trying to maximize satisfaction of current preferences as if they were permanent fixtures, this model anticipates preference changes. A plan of action is rational on that model if and only if at the time of its fruition it maximizes the satisfaction of those pursuing it. Incrementalists mount a last-ditch battle for the laissez-faire liberal conclusion by conceding that people are poor judges of their future preferences but denying that anyone else could predict them any better. While that might occasionally prove correct, it seems rather implausible as a general rule.

With this I conclude my protracted attack upon incrementalism, the predominant mode of atheoretical policymaking. It claims that unreflective trial-and-error is the best and, indeed, the only way to know what the effects of a policy will be and how people will evaluate those outcomes. The first half of that claim has been undermined by the previous chapter. There it was shown that incrementalism itself requires some theoretical understanding of the system into which we intervene, and that the selfsame theories that underwrite incremental interventions might also be used to guide non-incremental ones. The second half of the incrementalist claim has been challenged in this chapter. Certainly it would be folly for social planners to count upon people's values remaining fixed forever. They are constantly changing, just as incrementalists insist. But they do not change in such radically unpredictable ways as to force us to fall back upon incremental adaptation. Policymakers can and should use their theoretical understanding of where preferences come from and how they change to save people from their former selves. Thus, on both empirical and evaluative grounds, theory is urgently required for policymaking. The balance of this book is devoted to tracing out precisely what contributions it can make.

Principles and
Institutions

4 Institutional Framework: Loose Laws

The previous chapters conclude that well-grounded empirical and ethical theories can and should be used to guide public policymaking. There, incrementalists' principled objections have been met. Having defended the general principle, we must now give it some practical substance. This chapter discusses the institutional framework appropriate to this kind of policymaking. The next discusses moral principles that should underlie it. Chapter 6 discusses how people might be motivated to act upon them.

Some of the strongest objections to my proposal turn upon the sorts of social institutions it seems, in practice, to require. Theoretically informed policymaking appears inevitably to entail "social planning," and planners' edicts seem inevitably to be cast in the form of rigid legal mandates. Commentators with a practical cast of mind protest that these are inherently ill suited for the governance of any complex social system. Students of regulatory policy especially find command-and-control techniques unsatisfactory (Schultze 1977; Breyer 1979; Morrison, et al. 1980). The problem is that "rules that are reasonable for one subclass of regulated organizations will be unreasonable for another. Normally an agency (or a legislature) tries to take such variations into account in developing the rules, but there are distinct limits on how much differentiation is possible." Bardach (1978, 370, 369) concludes that we should leave such judgments less structured so "it is possible to act in-

This chapter is reprinted, with substantial revisions, from Robert E. Goodin, "Loose Laws: The Ethics of Vagueness vs. the Politics of Precision," *Philosophica* 23, no. 1 (1979): 79–96.

formally and with sensitivity to the local context."[1] And this is a serious criticism both morally and pragmatically. It is unequitable as well as inefficient to overlook significant differences between two different cases. Yet in "following a rule" we necessarily turn "away from consideration of the particular merits of particular cases" (Warnock 1971, 66. Cf. Singer 1958; Lyons 1965; Richards 1971; Hare 1972; Mew 1975; Raz 1975).

There is no denying that legal rules often do display these faults. The crucial question for present purposes, however, is whether they must necessarily do so. There is a popular and superficially plausible argument saying they must. The legal system is characterized by formally codified "rules," if we are to believe the positivists (Hart 1961). Morality consists of "principles" or "reasons for action" of a looser sort which by their nature are not "exhaustively codifiable" (Mew 1975, 304). Since these two systems possess distinct and incompatible structures, the argument goes, legal rules always miss morally significant nuances to a greater or lesser extent. Here I shall resist that claim. The contrast between rules of law and principles of morality is too stark; a system of "loose laws" can adequately allow for all the moral nuances we like. Admittedly, there are political obstacles to installing and maintaining such a system, as section 4.5 shows. But these need not be insurmountable.

4.1. Collapsing the Rule-Principle
Distinction

The fullest exposition of the distinction between rules and principles comes in Ronald Dworkin's (1977, chap. 2) critique, "The Model of Rules." His discussion focuses on rules and principles in their pure forms. Many "principles" are misleadingly phrased in the form of rules, in a way that serves only to confuse what he sees as two distinct categories. More misleadingly, many rules look much like principles because they are fragmentary, incomplete specifications of the rule and its exceptions. "Of course a rule may have exceptions," Dworkin (1977, 24–25) allows. "However, an accurate statement of the rule would take this exception into account, and any that did not would be incomplete. If the list of exceptions is very large, it would be too clumsy to repeat them each time the rule is

1. Schultze (1977, 52) illustrates the point: "There are 62,000 point sources of water pollution in the United States, of which 9,000 are major sources, with huge variation in them.... Any given situation usually presents a broad range of possibilities for pollution reduction.... Selecting the appropriate effluent limitation for each firm, in a way that will produce an efficient and effective overall strategy, depends on balancing these possibilities against their respective costs, taking into account the economic circumstances confronting each firm. To do this for 62,000 point sources of pollution demands omniscience" from the Environmental Protection Agency.

cited; there is, however, no reason in theory why they could not all be added on, and the more that are, the more accurate is the statement of the rule" (cf. Rees 1953).

Rules, filled out in this way, are "applicable in an all-or-nothing fashion. If the facts a rule stipulates are given, then either the rule is valid, in which case the answer it supplies must be accepted, or it is not, in which case it contributes nothing to the decision" (Dworkin 1977, 24; cf. von Wright 1963, 135, 148–49, 205). A principle, in contrast, "does not even purport to set out conditions that make its application necessary. Rather it states a reason that argues in one direction, but does not necessitate a particular decision.... There may be other principles or policies arguing in the other direction.... If so, our principle may not prevail, but that does not mean that it is not a principle of our... system, because in the next case, when these contravening considerations are absent or less weighty, the principle may be decisive" (Dworkin 1977, 25–26). Moral philosophers similarly maintain that rules "cannot be overriden, but only altered or qualified to admit of some exceptions" (Hare 1963, 169), whereas "moral principles *may* point in opposite directions" and there is "no ground on which one could ever pronounce in general which, in such a case, is to predominate over another" (Warnock 1971, 88–89).[2]

The second criterion for distinguishing rules from principles follows logically from the first. "Principles have a dimension that rules do not—the dimension of weight or importance. When principles intersect..., one who must resolve the conflict has to take into account the relative weight of each.... Rules do not have this dimension.... We cannot say that one rule is more important than another within the system of rules, so that when two rules conflict one supersedes the other by virtue of greater weight. If two rules conflict, one of them cannot be a valid rule" (Dworkin 1977, 26–27). Those "conflicts of law" that characterize so much actual litigation result, Dworkin would argue, from incomplete specificatons of the rules: had all the exceptions been specified in the original rule statement, such conflicts would never have occurred; the reason they do occur is simply that the rules fail to qualify fully as complete rules. Again, moral philosophers make substantially the same point. Warnock (1971, 93), for example, holds that "the exercise of moral judgment involves the taking notice, and due weighting, of all pertinent moral reasons," which clearly implies that several conflicting moral reasons (i.e., princples) can be simultaneously operative.

Both criteria rely heavily upon the list of exceptions Dworkin

2. The distinction is more standard than the labels. Notice, for example, that Hare's statement refers to "universalizable prescriptions," which Dworkin would call "rules" but which Hare calls "moral principles."

would have us append to all rule statements. The strategy I shall pursue in partially collapsing Dworkin's rule-principle distinction is to show that the list of exceptions is the functional equivalent of a principle's weight. In this way, I will have shown that the two modes of regulating conduct are isomorphic rather than structurally distinct.

Consider first the "weight" which principles are alleged to possess and rules to lack. Abstractly, this must (according to the *Oxford English Dictionary*) be a reference to their "persuasive or convincing power." That, however, implies a substantial element of private introspection. Since the aim of moral or legal principles is the *social* prescription of behavior, emphasis must fall on the weight of principles in operational form. Operationally, the relative weight of two principles might be measured simply as the extent to which one has predominated over the other in our past deliberations. The more often one principle has overridden the other, the weightier it is (Hare 1981, chap. 3). Weight, thus surmised, can then be used as a shorthand guide to future tradeoffs between the principles.

In exactly like fashion one might produce a measure of the relative weight of rules. If we follow Dworkin's admonition to incorporate all exceptions and qualifications into the statement of the rule itself, the relative weight of a rule can simply be read off the list of exceptions. The less qualified the rule, the greater its weight.[3] The parallels between rules and principles do not end with the procedure for assessing their relative weight. They also extend to the abstract level: a rule's weight (defined as its "persuasiveness") is what formed the basis for adjudging competing claims of rules and for thereby deciding which exceptions to allow and which to disallow in the first place.

Of course, weights are crucial to principles in a way they are not to rules. That is merely because weights are used to decide between competing principles, whereas with rules all possible conflicts have been decided in advance and the resolution recorded in the list of exceptions. Once that list is at hand, we may dispense with the list of relative weights, just as a bridge-builder can forget all he knows about civil engineering once he has a detailed blueprint. But to explain what he is doing now or to do it again elsewhere, he must recall the principles of engineering that went into the design. So too must the social engineer.

Analogous arguments can be deployed against Dworkin's assertion that rules apply in an all-or-nothing fashion, whereas principles have a mysterious "on-again, off-again" property. Upon reflection,

3. We need some principle of individuation before we can begin counting up the exceptions to each rule, of course. But it does not matter what one we use, provided we apply the same one consistently in counting exceptions to all rules.

there is nothing at all mysterious or unusual about this, however. When applying abstract principles to particular cases, we must bear two considerations in mind. One is their weight, already discussed. The other is the centrality of the principle to the case at hand. Depending on the facts of the case, a principle P_1 might be centrally implicated and another P_2 only marginally involved. Were the two principles of equal weight, the more central principle P should clearly govern. Centrality might also counteract the effects of weight upon occasion: a lightweight but centrally implicated principle can, in some cases, overrule a weightier but more tangentially involved one. The joint effects of weight and centrality can, then, account for the peculiar pattern of choices among principles—P_1 winning out over P_2 sometimes and sometimes losing out to it.

Considerations of centrality naturally figure just as largely in resolving conflicts between rules and in generating lists of their exceptions. Indeed, many of the exceptions will be little more than descriptions of circumstances in which one rule will have to yield to another which is more centrally implicated. Again, considerations of centrality which characterize the application of principles also characterize the application of rules, only at one remove. They are used to construct a list of exceptions which, once constructed, obviates the need for further reference back.[4]

The implication of this analysis is that the rule/principle distinction can be largely collapsed. There are differences, but more of degree than of kind. Principles are just inchoate rules. This conclusion is borne out, incidentally, by analysis of ordinary language. The *Oxford English Dictionary* defines a *rule* as "a *principle*, regulation or maxim governing individual conduct" (emphasis added). And, on the other side, lawyers commonly characterize "principles" as "fundamental rules" (Wechsler 1959; Hughes 1968). Such distinctions as ordinary language does suggest are between relatively more precise "rules" and relatively less precise "principles." "Principle" is to "rule" as "plan" is to "blueprint," the latter being merely a more detailed form of the former in each case (Rawls 1955; Singer 1958; Black 1958; Hare 1981, chaps. 2, 3).

4.2.   How Precise Ought a Good Law to Be?

The previous section has refuted the strong thesis that legal rules are structurally incapable of capturing moral principles. The rule/principle distinction points to a continuum rather than to any stark

4. Examining the way in which judges apply legal rules to particular cases, we find that these rules are used in much the same way as Dworkin suggests principles would be (Hodgson 1967, 133–41; Bayles 1971). Indeed, Christie (1968) shows that the cases Dworkin uses to illustrate legal principles at work actually just apply general rules.

dichotomy. The question is merely where on that continuum legal prescriptions ought to be located: how precise ought a good law to be?

Ordinarily it is said that a law's precision should be governed by two competing criteria. On the one hand, the need for certainty in the application of law argues for a fully specified system of rules. On the other hand, the need for flexibility argues for the opposite—an absolutely open-ended set of principles. Conventional wisdom holds that here (as in any situation where competing criteria pull in opposite directions) the decision should be a·compromise, in this case, a partially specified system of legal rules (Blackstone 1785, vol. 1, 62; Hart 1961, 127; Fuller 1964, 212–14; Hodgson 1967, chap. 2).

Such a compromise, however, flies in the face of the "general theory of second best" (Lipsey and Lancaster 1956). Where there are multiple dimensions involved in the "good behavior" to be prompted, the rules must capture all the dimensions if they attempt to capture any in detail. Otherwise suboptimization is sure to occur as actors cut corners on those dimensions rule-makers have neglected to make mandatory. This is precisely the reason Alexander Hamilton (1788) and James Jackson (1789) opposed attaching a Bill of Rights to the U.S. Constitution: the very act of enumerating rights implies that the government is free to misbehave in any way not explicitly prohibited; so, since Constitutional draftsmen cannot hope to list all rights they would like to see protected, they ought not to attempt to list any.

In light of such considerations, lawmakers must refrain from the ordinary practice of compromising between competing criteria. They must make the hard choice between two very different strategies available for promoting good behavior. One is to issue very detailed directives capturing in full all the desirable characteristics of behavior. The other is to outline in vague and general terms the types of behavior they desire, without going into particulars on any point. Here lawmakers would confine themselves to setting social goals and allow administrators and private individuals considerable leeway in choosing how to implement them. There may be some after-the-fact determination of how well citizens have done, with rewards or penalties attached; but in the first instance, anyway, they would be allowed substantial discretion.[5]

5. The second strategy has many advocates. Hayek (1944, 75), arguing that private individuals should enjoy substantial discretion, suggests that "the state should confine itself to establishing rules applying to general types of situations and should allow individuals freedom in everything which depends on the circumstances of time and place, because only the individuals concerned in each instance can fully know these circumstances and adapt their actions to them." As concerns public administration, Ackerman and Hassler (1981, 122) argue that the best remedy for "agency

In principle, lawmakers are free to opt for either of these two approaches. All that the theory of second best says is that they must face up to the choice, or else frustrate their own goals. In practice, however, the nature of the principles which lawmakers hope to capture militates against the rigidly rule-based strategy. Principles of practical reason in general are such that they cannot all be listed with any confidence in the completeness of the list. Hare (1972–73, 8–9) offers a trivial example:

> a person who is devoted to golf and has played it from his youth . . . will go on until he can hardly shuffle around the course, getting all the time more and more canny; he, we might say, is learning all the time how to play better, and is in some sense acquiring ever more sophisticated principles. No doubt, well before he reached middle age, his principles got sufficiently complex for it to be no longer possible for him to express them in words.

For a less trivial example, consider the findings of the President's Commission on the Accident at Three Mile Island (Kemeny 1979, 9, 10, 49). It found "the training of TMI operators was greatly deficient" and complained of a "preoccupation with regulations . . . . It is, of course, the responsibility of the Nuclear Regulatory Commission to issue regulations to assure the safety of nuclear power plants. However, we are convinced that regulations alone cannot assure safety." Reactor operators were taught to go by the rule book, which is fine during ordinary operations. But "the training program gave insufficient emphasis to principles" underlying those rules. Consequently, operators lacked any "depth of understanding" and were left "unprepared to deal with something as confusing as the circumstances in which they found themselves" during the Three Mile Island accident. Just as the principles of golf resist codification in any manual, so too do those of nuclear reactor safety resist codification in formal rules and regulations.

What is true of principles of practical reason in general is equally true of moral principles. Mew, for example, remarks that "if someone were to ask me what were my moral principles, I should be unable to state them. I suspect that this would be true of many people who are nevertheless indisputably moral agents" (1975, 290; cf. Hayek 1973). This being the case, the strategy of enjoining good behavior through specific rules runs intolerable risks of leaving out important provisions, thereby producing suboptimal results. The strategy of vagueness wins by default.

---

inaction" is an "ends-oriented agency forcing statute" which, unlike its "means-oriented" alternative, "does not require Congress to indulge in instrumental judgments beyond its capacity."

The efficiencies available by making "public use of private interest" (Schultze 1977) argue for the same conclusion. Economists have grown increasingly critical of regulation-and-enforcement styles of social policymaking. Often achieving the mandated standard costs more than it is worth to society. Commentators on environmental pollution suggest that, instead of imposing rigid standards of cleanliness and enforcing compliance, we should simply charge polluters an "emissions tax" fully reflecting the social costs of their discharges. Then, if they still found it profitable to pollute, they could—and, indeed, it is socially optimal for them to do so (Schultze 1970; Kneese and Schultze 1975). Besides, it is folly to dictate the precise steps polluters must take to curtail their emissions, demanding that coal-burning power plants install "scrubbers," when shifting to low-sulfur coal might be both cheaper and more effective (Ackerman and Hassler 1981). Similarly, occupational safety might be better promoted if, instead of mandating precise steps for employers to take, government instead merely imposed a "hazard tax" on the basis of the injuries experienced in the firm each year, leaving it to the firm to discover the most efficient method of reducing injuries and taxes (Nichols and Zeckhauser 1977; Bardach 1978). Loose laws, specifying goals but not specifying any particular mechanism for achieving them, offer opportunities for realizing efficiencies impossible with rigid rules.[6]

4.3. Objections to Loose Laws

Any proposal for very loose laws will automatically be met with two standard objections. The first protests that the "progressive introduction of vague formulas" will result in "the increasing arbitrariness and uncertainty of law" (Hayek 1944, 78). Good outcomes often depend upon being able to predict with confidence what others will do (Hodgson 1967). Governing one's conduct by rules contributes much to the creation of these stable expectations. Thus, lawyers speak of "the need for certain rules which can, over great areas of conduct, safely be applied by private individuals to themselves without fresh official guidance or weighing up of social issues" (Hart 1961, 127). And even moralists concede a "special need, in the case of public, legal or political institutions, for uniformity and predictability of operation" (Warnock 1971, 67). Indeed, very vague laws so badly interfere with the certain and predictable application of law that American courts consider them an unconstitutional denial of due process (Aigler 1922).

6. This merely echoes Bentham's (1787) remedy for the brutality of prison guards: instead of trying to monitor and prevent brutal actions themselves, simply charge Panopticon contractors for a high death rate and reward them for a low one.

This objection is at best a partial one, however. Beyond some point, the specificity strategy must backfire. Detailed lists of exceptions and qualifications to the rules can themselves be a source of confusion. The Civil Procedure of the Punjab, which "had originally been exceedingly simple," had by Maine's (1871, 213) time "become so overlaid by explanations and modifications conveyed in Circular orders, that I do not hesitate to pronounce it as uncertain and difficult a body of rules as I ever attempted to study." Furthermore, more detailed rules are more difficult to communicate fully or to remember in detail (Hare 1972–73; 1981, 35–38; Raz 1970, chaps. 5, 6). The President's Commission on the Accident at Three Mile Island, for example, concludes that "once regulations have become as voluminous and complex as those regulations now in place, they can serve as a negative factor in nuclear safety" (Kemeny 1979, 9). Thus specificity, taken to extremes, defeats its own purpose, confusing people rather than clarifying what is expected of them.

There is yet another reason to oppose certain kinds of certainty and predictability in the law. Where reducing mutual interference is concerned—as with promises, contracts, and so on—there are undeniable advantages to precise rules rendering behavior predictable (Freund 1921; Hodgson 1967). However, were a police patrolman to govern his conduct by precise and unchanging rules, always walking his beat in just the same path and at just the same pace, his behavior would indeed be predictable; but that would be a gain to the criminal rather than to the community at large. More generally, rendering public regulatory practices predictable holds benefits mostly for those anxious to know how badly they may misbehave without penalty. There are real advantages to keeping scoundrels guessing. Not knowing how far they can safely go before incurring legal liability, and being somewhat averse to taking the risk, many prospective criminals would err on the side of caution and behave better than they would do under a regime of precise and predictable rules.

The second broad objection to vague laws protests at the injustice of their arbitrary application. Detailed rules of law are needed "to lessen the chance of improper discrimination" and in order to introduce "some measure of uniformity in the way they operate" (Warnock 1971, 66–67). If identical cases are decided differently, then certainly injustice has been done. But no two cases are absolutely identical in every respect, and most of these differences will carry some ethical significance. The focus is then on equity—treating cases differently only in proportion to the ethically significant difference between them—rather than upon justice and injustice narrowly construed. And, as section 4.4 shows, equity is better served by the application of flexible principles than by rigid rules of law.

4.4. Loose Laws in Practice

The best examples of the sort of vague, principled law for which I have been arguing come from studies of "primitive" societies. There judges "manipulate the flexibility of concepts—what is often denigrated as their 'ambiguity'—as they do the multiplicity of laws, to achieve justice" (Gluckman 1955, 364). It is a pattern more "developed" legal systems could do well to emulate.

Of primary importance are peculiar properties of the concepts characterizing loose primitive laws. They are "*flexible,* in that they are *elastic,* capable of being stretched to cover various circumstances and/or in that they are *multiple,* in having several referents or definitions." Furthermore, they are "*absorbent* in that they can absorb the raw facts of evidence into their categories."[7] Under these conditions, judicial decision-making becomes a process of "fitting facts into absorbent legal concepts" in a way that "gives flexibility and scope for development to the legal system" as a whole (Gluckman 1955, 364, 293–94, 319, 305). Similarly among the Cheyenne, judicial rationales "run in terms of semi-open points or areas . . . so that however one detail might take shape, some other detail would provide much of whatever corrective might be needed. Throughout, all patterns retained around their normative or imperative cores a joyous range of flexible adaptivity, called on repeatedly" (Llewellyn and Hoebel 1941, 323).

The flexible application of loose legal concepts is facilitated largely through the absence of constraining *precedents*. There is a kind of " 'social amnesia' which operates in an unrecorded system of law so that unpalatable legal rules or edicts are forgotten" (Gluckman 1955, 261). Where precedents are ignored, the possibilities for deciding each case on its merits are obviously expanded.

A further feature contributing to the impressive power of primitive law to reach just verdicts on particular cases is the relatively unstructured character of judicial proceedings. "There are no restrictive 'pleadings' in the form of the preparation and sifting of facts by professional lawyers to bring them within some form of action or some defined legal grounds . . . . Each litigant and each witness tells his tale without restraint so that the court is given from the outset a view of all the circumstances of the dispute, and often of its past history." Since "hard cases" in primitive societies typically involve litigants laboring under conflicting role demands, the open-ended nature of judicial proceedings allows judges to "achieve justice in

---

7. Of course, concepts in any legal system necessarily have a "penumbra of uncertainty" (Williams 1945–46). But the flexibility and uncertainty surrounding Lozi and Cheyenne legal concepts seem to go far beyond what is minimally necessary.

with clients on a mass basis." Thus, "rigid and unresponsive patterns of behavior result from street-level bureaucrats' substantial discretion, exercised in a particular work context" (Lipsky 1980, xii, 29, 27).

Equally often, however, the undermining of loose, principled law is far from unintentional. This was clearly true of the recent effort to return to "traditional" law in India. The scheme obviously threatened the power base of lawyers, who formed a frankly political—and enormously successful—coalition to foil the plan (Galanter 1974; Randolph and Randolph 1965).

The way principled law becomes increasingly precedent-bound suggests similar political forces are at work even where the rhetoric indicates otherwise. Power is the essence of politics, and the essence of power lies in restricting the choices available to others. (See chapter 7 below.) A system of loose, principled law asks those in positions of power—legislators, judges, administrators, and so on—to pass up opportunities for binding their inferiors and successors to precise rules and precedents. This really amounts to asking them to forgo opportunities to exercise power.[9] Thus it is not surprising that attempts at reintroducing loose, principled law prove abortive.

Although these political pressures are undeniably present, they are far from irresistible. Societies have various ways for holding power-hungry politicians in check. Once we recognize the rigid codification of social rules for the power play it is, and see that self-aggrandizement for the politician comes at a high social cost, we can deploy all these familiar devices for curtailing his abuse of power. That is not to say that the task is always easy, but neither is it totally unfamiliar or obviously hopeless. Mostly it is just a matter of recognizing where the public interest really lies—with loose, principled laws rather than with rigid, precise formulations.

4.6. Conclusion

The inefficiencies and immoralities that result from overly rigid legal rules can now been seen to be a political artifact rather than a structural necessity. The *rules* of law are, indeed, structurally isomorphic with the *principles* of morality. Far from pointing to funda-

9. The sort of loose law for which I am arguing would allow discretion to those applying it, so they can respond to the particular circumstances of the case at hand (cf. Shapiro 1965). This is in stark contrast to the Public Welfare Amendments of 1962, for example, which bind administrators "to match whatever state governments spend...for 'social services.'" Derthick (1975, 2–3) calls this a "loose law" on the grounds that it contains an open-ended commitment. But in my terms it would be quite a rigid one, since it explicitly denies administrators discretion.

mentally different kinds of social regulation, these two concepts merely identify the endpoints of a continuum. Where along it legal enactments should fall is, formally, an open question. Practically, the "general theory of second best," combined with the difficulty of listing in detail all morally desirable performances, means that a system of relatively loose laws is best able to capture our moral concerns. At the same time, loose laws mandating ends but leaving the choice of means for attaining them to the people most directly involved will also be the most efficient methods of obtaining compliance.

5 Moral Foundations: Choice and Dignity

In practice, public policy is usually predicated upon a crude, implicit utilitarianism or contractarianism of one form or another. However different these forms may be in other respects, they all share the common premise that we must respect the choices people make for themselves. This premise, in turn, has direct and really quite disagreeable policy implications. Yet it is basic to both philosophies. Neither can deny this premise without denying its own basic logic.

That does not mean that we must abandon such philosophies and flee to the absolutist camp criticized in chapter 1, however. We need only look more deeply into those philosophies and realize that we respect people's choices because of a more fundamental premise, that we must respect people and their dignity. This premise, being the most fundamental of all, can often excuse us in overriding the more direct and disagreeable implications of respecting people's choices *tout court*. Thus, what we find "in the shadow of utilitarianism" is a theory of human dignity capable of saving utilitarianism from its most notorious excesses.

5.1. The Role of Choice

Conventional complaints against the liberal contract (e.g., "possessive individualism") object to little more than its gestalt. The focus of my criticism will be an ordinarily

This chapter is reprinted, with substantial revisions, from Robert E. Goodin, "The Political Theories of Choice and Dignity," *American Philosophical Quarterly* 18, no. 2 (1981): 91–100, by permission of The American Philosophical Quarterly, the copyrightholder.

unexamined presumption which is fundamental to the theory in a way that those criticized by others are not. The presupposition that we should respect people's choices is logically required for the argument ever to get off the ground. All that the fable of the contract can by itself prove is that men would voluntarily choose to live in civil society. That provides a justification for civil society only insofar as we implicitly assume that we should respect people's choices. Anyone refusing to make such an assumption could read through the entire contractarian tale and at the end say, quite rightly, So what?

This assumption is required equally by contemporary and historical theorists. Hobbes and Locke talk as if the choices were ones people actually made; Rawls talks explicitly about hypothetical choices people would have made. Neither matters unless we suppose that choices and their consequences command respect. Likewise, this is a premise Rousseau requires in common with his more liberal counterparts. "There is one law which by its nature requires unanimous consent, that is, the social compact" (Rousseau 1762b, bk. 4, chap. 2). People can be "forced to be free" only after they have chosen to accept the general will of the community in the first place. For Rousseau, just as surely as for Hobbes or Locke or Hume or Rawls, people have good reasons for choosing to agree. But it is their agreement rather than the good reasons underlying it which makes the compact binding.[1]

Among utilitarians, choice figures even more prominently. Their injunction to make people happy is constantly conjoined with an injunction to let people choose for themselves what will make them happy. Sometimes this extends only to the choice of ends. Sometimes utilitarians suppose that people should also be allowed to choose their own means, either because being more interested they are likely to make better choices or so they can learn from their own mistakes. Many utilitarians, finding these claims empirically implausible, balk at letting people choose their own means. But all are committed at least to letting people choose their own ends, as my discussion of liberalism more generally (chapter 3 above) has shown.

Indicative of the utilitarian preoccupation with choice is the way in which John Stuart Mill reduces "higher pleasures" to a form of hypothetical choice. Whereas later ideal utilitarians really did let an abstract theory of the good specify their ideals, Mill left it to the

1. Or so they say. Both Rawls and Rousseau, however, want to restrict the conditions under which these choices are made, and this undermines the choice rationale in ways neither adequately appreciates. They must move outside the choice rationale to justify restrictions on the conditions of choice (Haksar 1979, chap. 11). This renders the contractarian rationale "spurious": "Since the initial situation is selected to ensure the 'correct' choice, the act of choice is evidently neither necessary nor sufficient to justify the legitimating principle" (Gauthier 1977, 139).

choice of people "competently acquainted with both" higher and lower pleasures. "Of two pleasures, if there be one to which all or almost all who have experience of both give a decided preference, ... that is the more desirable pleasure" (Mill 1863, chap. 2; Connolly 1974, chap. 2). Ideal preferences are thus just those which people would choose, had they the requisite experiences.

The current preoccupation with models of choice—rational, social, public, collective, or whatever—should be seen in this historical context. Among New Welfare Economists whose work underlies all such models, "the criterion used for an increase in an individual's welfare means that he is in a chosen position" (Little 1957, 37). New Political Economists similarly attempt to link social decisions more generally to the choices of individual citizens. If the mathematical sophistication is new, the enterprise is not. Current choice models merely make explicit our long-standing commitment to respecting choices people have made for themselves.

5.2. The Implications of Respecting Choices

"Respecting" a person's choice means, inter alia and ceteris paribus, allowing him opportunities to choose and to act upon choices he makes. This in turn implies something about the nature and limits of government instituted between men whose choices we should respect: it must further their opportunities for choice and respond to choices they make. This is just as contractarians and utilitarians suggest. The danger is not one of inconsistency between implications of their suppressed premises and their explicit assertions. Rather, it is just the opposite. If the argument requires an assumption which is itself capable of generating all the results the argument hopes to establish, there is hardly any reason to bother with the rest of the argument—all the results were built in right from the start. Such is particularly the case with contractarianism: the same sorts of reciprocal constraints on choices which would be agreed to in contractualist negotiations are, broadly speaking, already implicit in the presupposition that we should insofar as possible respect all choices equally. Utilitarian conclusions about optimal social institutions could similarly be deduced more directly from utiliarianism's first principle, viz., that we should respect people's choices.

The assumption that we must respect people's choices not only preempts the fable of the social contract and utilitarian calculations. It also implies further and more specific principles of its own. Exploring these reveals the sort of society to which contractarians and utilitarians, along with their heirs among rational choice theorists, must logically be committed.

First, respecting choices entails a particular standard of distributive justice, viz., "from each as they choose, to each as they are chosen" (Nozick 1974, 160; Hayek 1976). Any gift, exchange, or bequest must be honored. To do otherwise would be to deny someone's choice. Compulsory redistribution is similarly prohibited. Taking anything from a person which he chooses to keep for himself is blocked, prima facie, by the injunction to respect people's choices. Nozick may have been the first mainstream philosopher to formulate this principle so brutally and face up to its consequences so unblinkingly. But this libertarian premise has long regulated social life, perhaps all the more powerfully for having remained unstated. The principle of "the justice of allocation according to choice" is, according to Honoré (1962), "so obvious that it is generally overlooked." Hart and Sacks (1958, 183 ff.) see much of the "legal process" as simply ratifying "private orderings," mutually agreeable arrangements private citizens have chosen for themselves, such as marriages, contracts, banks, trade unions, and so forth. That justice consists in giving people what they choose is, then, well entrenched in social practice if not in social philosophy.

Second, respecting choices entails a model of rights as "protected choices." Hobbes (1651, chap. 14) supposes that it is the nature of a right that we may either demand or lay down our claim to that which is, by right, our own. On this model, a right is a subspecies of entitlement whose distinctive feature is that it can be waived. The essence of a right is that it secures such a choice for the right-holder. One important corollary of this is that people can have no rights if they are incapable of exercising the choices the rights secure for them. As Flathman (1976, 167) remarks, rights construed in this way "postulate agents who have interests, desires, intentions, objectives, and other types of reasons for acting in certain ways." A further corollary is that people can have no rights which are inalienable, i.e., no rights to things so important (either morally or practically) that they cannot be done without.[2]

Third, respecting choices presupposes actors possessing freedom of choice. This is required to activate the injunction at all. We respect choices only insofar as they really *were* choices, only insofar as it was within an agent's power to decide differently. The actions of people incapable of doing otherwise command no respect under this principle. Furthermore, the model of rights as "special war-

2. Modern choice theorists typically echo Bentham's dismissal of "inalienable" rights as "nonsense on stilts," although earlier choice theorists sometimes took a more sympathetic view of them.

rants" for interfering with others, binding them by your choices, makes sense only against a moral/legal background in which people are ordinarily free to make such choices for themselves. Otherwise no special warrant would be required (Hart 1955).

These points are nicely illustrated in choice theorists' analysis of citizenship (Bickel 1975). Chief Justice Earl Warren (1957) calls citizenship "a man's basic right, for it is nothing less than the right to have rights. Remove this priceless possession and . . . he has no lawful claim to protection from any nation, and no nation may assert rights on his behalf. His very existence is at the sufferance of the state within whose borders he happens to be." Yet the sad fact remains that "neither the law nor the accepted morality of societies need extend their minimal protections and benefits to all within their scope" (Hart 1961, 196). Analysis of who gets included and why can tell us much about a political theory.

On the choice model, there are three reasons for denying someone citizenship: (1) he chose, or would have chosen, to opt out of the club; (2) other members of the society chose, or would have chosen, not to allow him in; or (3) he is incapable of choice and hence unfit for the status of citizen. The first ground is unobjectionable and the focus of most explicit discussions of the problem. Even Rousseau (1972b, bk. 4, chap. 2), otherwise keen on equal rights of citizenship, allows that "if, at the time of the social compact, there are opponents of it, their opposition does not invalidate the contract but only prevents them from being included in it; they are foreigners among citizens."

The flip side of the rule of distributive justice—awarding rights of citizenship "to each as he is chosen"—is far more pernicious. If, as choice theorists suppose, political society is organized for mutual advantage, then rational actors would choose partners who would be useful if included or dangerous if not. There are, of course, many whose participation would contribute nothing (or even constitute a net liability) to the partnership; and they are naturally left outside the protection of any government organized by rational self-interested agents. Imagine, with Hume (1777, sec. 3, pt. 1),

> a species of creatures intermingled with men, which, though rational, were possessed of such inferior strength, both of body and mind, that they were incapable of all resistance, and could never, upon the highest provocation, make us feel the effects of their resentment; the necessary consequence, I think, is that we should be bound by the laws of humanity to give gentle usage to these creatures, but should not, properly speaking, lie under any restraint of justice with regard to them. . . . Whatever we covet, they must instantly resign: Our permission is the only

tenure, by which they hold their possessions: Our compassion and kindness the only check by which they curb our lawless will. [Cf. Barry 1978, 220–23]

Historically, positions almost this precarious have been occupied by various groups—American Indians and women (as Hume acknowledges) along with slaves, colonials, and so on. When choosing fellow citizens, rational actors naturally exclude as "superfluous" those who are so weak that no one ever needs them or has anything to fear from them.[3]

Denying rights of citizenship to those who want them was traditionally excused most explicitly on the third ground that they were incapable of making meaningful choices. Richer Enlightenment notions of citizenship had, by the time of choice theorists, degenerated into "a voluntaristic notion.... The term 'citizenship' was thought to refer to the behaviour of individuals that expressed their individual, subjective, arbitrary 'will' or 'choice'" (van Gunsteren 1978, 17; cf. Pateman 1979). Those incapable of choice (children, idiots, etc.), along with those subject to the will of another (women, Catholics, the propertyless, etc.), were all deemed unsuited to the duties and rights of citizenship. Some of the sinners on this score are predictable: Locke (1690, sec. 60), Hume (1739, bk. 3, sec. 7), James Mill (1828, sec. 8), John Stuart Mill (1861, chap. 8), James Madison (1787), and so forth. They are joined, somewhat surprisingly, by Rousseau (1762a), who gives Émile an education fit for an active citizen while giving Sophie an education fit only for a subservient being incapable of free choice or active participation in community affairs (Pateman 1980).

To this day, philosophers linking citizenship to free will tend to focus just on the implications for the franchise (Dahl 1979). Practical men have fewer scruples in following the proposition to its logical conclusion, restricting rights of citizenship quite generally. When finding that under the American Constitution Negroes were "con-

3. In Riker's (1962) terms, they strive for "minimal winning coalitions," although what they are trying to "win" and how many are minimally required to do so are open questions. The rules for excluding others from a club are rarely discussed within the choice model. Respecting choices imposes something of a presumption that anyone who so chooses should be allowed to join; but the presumption can be overcome if his membership is opposed by sufficiently many other people, whose choices also command respect. (In market transactions, after all, your unilateral choice to possess my merchandise cannot be decisive in effecting a trade unless I also choose to let you have it, for an agreed price.) How many opposing choices suffice to blackball an applicant for membership in the club or citizenship in the state is uncertain. Nozick (1974, pt. 3) surely goes too far in allowing a single black ball to exclude anyone from his Utopia; it is equally ludicrous to allow anyone in on a single member's say-so. On the assumption that we are to respect equally the choices of all existing members of the club, it would seem that a majority vote among existing members should suffice to admit new ones.

sidered as a subordinate and inferior class of beings" lacking moral freedom and incapable of citizenship, the Supreme Court concluded that slaves such as Dred Scott "had no rights or privileges but such as those who held the power and the Government might choose to grant them" (Taney 1857, 404–5). If the government chose to enslave them, the Court could see no Constitutional objection.

The notion of "nationality" performs a parallel function in international transactions. "Without Country," Mazzini (1912, 53–54) advised Italians, "you have neither name, token, voice nor rights. . . . Do not beguile yourselves with the hope of emancipation from unjust social conditions if you do not first conquer a Country for yourselves." Not only do choice theorists allow people to set boundaries to their political system and to deny "foreigners" its benefits. They also allow people to draw the boundaries anywhere they choose—they recognize no "natural" boundaries. In Hobbes's (1651, chap. 16) famous phrase, "A multitude of men are made *one* person when they are by one man or person represented. . . . *Unity* cannot otherwise be understood in multitude" (cf. Mill 1861, chap. 16). Thus, when sorting themselves into nations, people are entirely at liberty to choose or refuse to join together with whomsoever they please. Rich nations and poor are thus born of unconstrained choices as the rich and powerful naturally club together, leaving the rest to their own devices.

5.3. Respecting People versus Respecting Choices

Any theory requires some logical primitives, some elementary building blocks. Different sets are of course available, and starting with different logical primitives you can build very different theories. Arguments over the choice of logical primitives—between individualists and communitarians, for example—are difficult to resolve. More conclusive challenges to a theory come from showing that it misapplies the logical primitives with which it chooses to deal.

This is the protest I shall lodge against choice theory in all its various forms. It treats the principle "respect people's choices" as a logical primitive when it is not really one at all within our individualistic moral system. It is itself derived from another more fundamental principle. Choice theories thus build upon a mere corollary following from, but not fully capturing, this more basic principle. Insofar as their implications contradict other aspects of that principle, choice theories are dangerously misleading. But where there is no contradiction, choice-based arguments can be decisive. The argument here is not that choice theories are *wrong* but only that they are *incomplete*. The effect of my argument is not to repudiate the results of choice theories altogether, but rather to justify us in simultaneously embracing and modifying them.[4]

The first step in making this case is to identify the more fundamental moral principle from which the injunction to "respect people's choices" can be derived. It is, quite simply, the principle that we should "respect people." We respect people's choices because we respect people, not the other way around.

In philosophical circles, this sentiment finds clearest expression in the resentment felt at the way in which the utilitarian calculus loses all track of individual people when summing up utilities or preferences or choices (Findlay 1961, 235–36; Rawls 1972, secs. 5, 29, 30; Williams 1973, 108–18; 1976a; Hart 1979). In part, the objection is motivated by distributive concerns—overlooking the "separateness" of people is bound up with neglecting the division of benefits and burdens between them. But, more fundamentally, the resentment seems directed at the way in which individual people drop out entirely when utilitarians are doing their sums. Their calculations work instead with disembodied choices and preferences. The procedure is embarrassingly consistent with the injunction to respect choices *simpliciter*. If it rankles, it does so because we feel that we should respect people rather than just their choices.

The sentiment is even more firmly entrenched in ordinary than in philosophical discourse. The very way we phrase the principle "respect people's choices" reveals that respecting people is somehow central. Why is it necessary to interpose the word "people's" between "respect" and "choices"? Perhaps the word really does qualify the type of choice we should respect—not an animal's or a computer's but rather a person's—but that would be to concede that nonhumans make choices just as do humans. Advocates of the principle are then obliged to explain why we should respect some choices (those of humans) but not others (those of dogs, digital computers, etc.). Since what distinguishes the favored class of choices is that they are those of *people,* such advocates will be

4. Most choice theorists seem, in principle, prepared to respect *any* genuine choices. Notice, in this connection, their differing treatments of the problems posed by selling oneself into slavery. Hobbes (1651, chap. 14) declines to respect that choice just because it is such a bad bargain that he doubts anyone could ever really have meant to agree. Rousseau (1762b, bk. 1, chap. 4) declines to respect the choice on the grounds that it is such a reckless bargain that "he who performs it is not in his right mind" and "madness does not confer rights." Both Hobbes and Rousseau refuse to respect the choice to enslave oneself merely because they doubt that it was a *genuine* choice. Only Locke (1690, sec. 23) among choice theorists would impose constraints on the sorts of choices he is prepared to respect: constraints of natural law prevent one from selling oneself into slavery even if one genuinely chose to do so. These natural law constraints are, of course, very different from those constraints on choice I shall derive below.

driven toward an argument that we should respect people as such.

Some may avoid this trap by denying that animals or computers or, indeed, anything except humans can make *real* choices. But then they are at a loss to explain the phrase "respect people's choices." If only people can make choices, the word "people's" cannot qualify what type of choice is to be respected—all choices are of this type. Grammatically, the word "people's" occupies the place of a modifier; logically it cannot act as one. The word has no place in the phrase. Including it amounts to a sort of logical stuttering.

My interpretation is that the principle refers, perhaps redundantly, to *people's* choices as a way of emphasizing what is morally important. Whether or not the word also functions as an actual modifier—whether or not animals can make real choices—the primary reason we talk in terms of respecting *people's* choices is to remind ourselves of the *reason* for respecting those choices. The reason is not that they are choices but rather that they are the choices of *people*. Such moral claim as choices have to our respect is derived, simply and exhaustively, from the more basic claim that persons have to our respect.

5.4. The Bases of Human Dignity

The important question of why to respect people, of what to respect about them, remains open. The phrase should, I suggest, be filled out by referring to their *dignity*. This is a slippery notion used in contradictory ways in both ordinary and philosophical discourse (Spiegelberg 1970). Insofar as there is a philosophical conventional wisdom on the topic at all, however, it seems badly in error in tracing an individual's dignity to his capacity for choice. Renaissance philosopher Pico della Mirandola's (1948) *Oration on the Dignity of Man* set the tone when portraying God as boasting to Adam,

> I have given you, Adam, neither a predetermined place nor a
> particular aspect nor any special prerogatives in order that you
> may take and possess these through your own decision and
> choice. The limitations on the nature of other creatures are
> contained within my prescribed laws. You shall determine your
> own nature without constraint from any barrier, by means of the
> freedom to whose power I have entrusted you . . . . I have made
> you neither heavenly nor earthly, neither mortal nor immortal,
> so that like a free and sovereign artificer you might mould and
> fashion yourself into that form you yourself shall have chosen.

Kant (1785, sec. 2), tightening this ancient link between "dignity" and "autonomy," holds that a man leads a dignified existence worthy of moral respect because (and only insofar as) he is self-legislating, overcoming natural necessity and willing his own actions. This analysis largely dominates contemporary discussions of "human dignity" and the "respect for persons" it requires. Unpacking that phrase, Benn (1971, 8–9) makes "capacity for choice" central:

> To *conceive* someone as a person is to see him as actually or potentially a chooser, as one attempting to steer his course through the world, adjusting his behavior as his appreciation of the world changes, and correcting course as he perceives his errors.... To *respect* someone as a person is to concede that one ought to take account of the way in which his enterprise might be affected by one's own decision.

Bernard Williams persistently pursues a similar line, equating "self-respect" with identifying with "what one is doing, [being] able to realize purposes of one's own" (1962, 114); "integrity" with identifying with one's own "projects and attitudes" (1973, 116–17); and "character" with identifying with one's own "desires, concerns, ... or projects" (1976a, 201).

Perhaps such restatements vulgarize Kant's conception of dignity. Maybe he meant to say more than that men deserve respect just because they are "actually or potentially choosers" with "projects, purposes, desires, and concerns" of their own. Or he may have meant something less and more precise—that men are capable of one crucial choice (succumbing to the requirements of the categorical imperative), and that their capacity for this one fundamental choice confers dignity. But notice how Nozick (1974, 30–33), like Hospers (1961, 405) before him, derives the distributive principle "from each as they choose, to each as they are chosen" from the Kantian injunction to "treat people as ends, never only as means." If this is a misinterpretation, Kant himself must bear much of the blame. "Means" and "ends" are notions borrowed from the logic of choice. The point in distinguishing absolute, intrinsic value ("dignity") from instrumental value is ordinarily to make sure that the instruments serve the ends rather than vice versa, i.e., the point is to choose wisely.

Be Kant's intentions as they may, it has now become commonplace to substitute "capacity for choice" for "dignity." This makes the injunction to "respect the dignity of people" perilously close to the injunction to "respect the choices of people." The point of the former principle was just the opposite, that we should respect people *rather* than their choices. If the capacity to choose is what we respect about people, the two principles become virtually equivalent.

This conventional account of human dignity is incomplete rather than wrong. Surely it is undignified to be pushed around by causal forces beyond one's control. In everyday affairs, we suppose loss of bladder control an undignified accompaniment to senility or slipping on a banana peel an undignified way for a debutante to make her entrance; and the reason they are undignified is that those concerned are not "in control" of themselves. Similarly, when we are consciously trying to strip people of their individual dignity—e.g., as part of the "mortification process" accompanying entry into prisons, asylums, boarding schools, armies, convents, and so on—we start by conspicuously depriving people of their capacity for autonomous action (Goffman 1968, chap. 1).

Standing outside causal chains cannot, however, constitute the *whole* of a person's dignity. If it did, someone whose actions were completely dictated by forces beyond his control would totally and necessarily lack dignity—he would be "beyond freedom and dignity," as Skinner (1971, chap. 2) concludes. Now, we can all agree with Skinner that people without freedom of choice deserve no credit or blame for doing what they could not help doing. But that has little to do with their dignity. Skinner's analysis makes a person's dignity depend upon how much credit he can claim for his freely chosen actions. People "prove their dignity by demonstrations of personal ability" and worth (Sennett and Cobb 1972, 220). The more drowning children someone saves, the more "dignified" he would be on this analysis. That is simply not how we use the word. The man who saves drowning children by the score may be "heroic" but he is not necessarily "dignified" or "noble." Dignity refers to what one *is* rather than what one *does*.[5]

For people lacking freedom of choice, the difference is crucial. If dignity is a matter of what one is rather than does, then someone with little free choice could still enjoy dignity or suffer indignities. A prisoner of war, although having few opportunities for autonomous action, can nevertheless carry himself with great dignity. (That, recall, was what the *Bridge on the River Kwai* was all about.) And a paraplegic, utterly at the mercy of natural necessity, still suffers an "indignity" when the nurse examines him in the public ward of the hospital without drawing the curtain.

Autonomy is neither the only nor even the most important element of dignity. What *is* central is indicated by another Kantian aphorism (quoted in Spiegelberg 1970, 60): "The fact that man can have the idea of an 'I' elevates him immeasurably above all other

5. Rawls (1972, sec. 67) similarly errs in linking dignity with accomplishments, successfully implementing plans, completing projects, and so on. He makes it a definitional point that "self-respect implies a confidence in one's ability . . . to fulfil one's intentions."

living beings on this earth. This is what makes him a person.'' Man is, at least potentially, a self-conscious being capable of possessing a self-image and self-respect. The fact that man can respect himself provides a reason for us to respect him in turn. Philosophers have long supposed that one's self-respect can be sustained best (and perhaps only) with the aid of others. Rawls (1972, sec. 67), for example, writes that self-respect—primary among his primary goods—depends upon our "finding our person and deeds appreciated and confirmed by others, who are likewise esteemed and their association enjoyed by us" in turn.[6] Extensive psychological studies confirm this hypothesis, at least in broad outline.[7]

Thus analyzed, the phrase "respect the dignity of people" is rather unusual. Ordinarily in such phrases ("respect your father" or "respect Ali's left jab"), the thing we are to respect (father, Ali's punch) exists independently of and prior to our respecting it. Likewise with political principles: when we are told to "respect the Queen's authority" or to "respect the equality of man," the things to be respected must have already been established or the argument is fatally flawed. Respecting human dignity is different because the thing to be respected is created by the act of respecting it. Thus it may seem that the principle amounts to little more than question-begging—following it provides the reason for following it. Such a finding would usually lead us to reject the principle altogether. In the case of respecting people's dignity, however, I would urge a different conclusion: that we cannot argue for the principle in terms of anything else indicates that the principle is a logical primitive, a fundamental axiom in our individualistic ethical system.[8]

6. In a way, this still has us respecting choices—it merely elevates one special choice (of self-conception) above all others. There may be good, objective reasons for choosing one self-conception rather than another (Haksar 1979). But those reasons do not, in themselves, command our respect. Rawls (1975) argues that we are worried about justice to persons rather than to ways of life in the abstract. Analogously, I would argue that we are worried about offending *people* (by defying their self-conceptions) rather than abstract "good reasons." We might hope that any divergence will soon be eliminated as people come to appreciate the good reasons and revise their self-perceptions accordingly. Sometimes, as in the cases of hierarchical societies (Williams 1962, 119–20), this seems so inevitable as to justify anticipatory social action of the sort discussed in chapter 3 above. But it is always choices or anticipated choices, rather than abstract good reasons, that must justify our action.

7. Shrauger and Schoeneman (1979, 549), surveying over one hundred fifty other studies, conclude that "people's self-perceptions agree substantially with the way they perceive themselves as being viewed by others." These perceptions are often in error—"there is no consistent agreement between people's self-perceptions and how they are actually viewed by others"—suggesting that feedback from others is ambiguous in naturally occurring situations. However, "when feedback from others is manipulated experimentally, self-perceptions are usually changed," just as the hypothesis suggests.

8. This is not to sanction self-indulgence, in the form of excessive concern for

5.5. The Demands of Dignity

Respecting a person's dignity commits us to respecting his choices, ceteris paribus. But what must be held equal for this principle to apply is the impact of his choices upon the dignity of others. Whereas one person's choice is only one among many, subject always to being overridden by sufficiently strong or numerous countervailing choices, his dignity must never be sacrificed to the mere whims of others, however numerous or strong the demands. Perhaps in desperate circumstances one person's dignity can be protected only if another's is denied: dignity then has to be traded off for dignity.[9] In more ordinary circumstances, however, the demands of dignity impose a minimum standard of decent treatment for every individual not to be sacrificed for any less weighty considerations.

The divergence between the two principles is best demonstrated by comparing the implications of respecting dignity with the three implications of respecting choices *simpliciter* derived in section 5.2. One contrast has already been discussed. Respecting choices presupposes individuals with freedom of choice and enjoins us to organize political systems to protect and further that freedom. But people retain dignity, understood as self-respect, even when totally deprived of such freedom—recall the "dignified" prisoner of war or the paraplegic—and we should respect their dignity even if they make no choices for us to respect. More importantly, respecting people's dignity does not commit us to protecting their freedom of choice at any cost. Constraints on one's freedom are justified not

---

protecting one's self-image. Williams (1976b) is right to say that we find this offensive. But the reason is not, as Williams supposes, that it involves "reflexive motivation"—that action is undertaken to protect one's own self-image rather than for its own sake. Instead, what offends us is the *excessive* concern for one's own self-image, at the expense of due regard for the claims and interests and self-images of others. Unlike the narcissistic theories criticized in section 1.2.2 above, my argument for respecting people's dignity requires everyone to be concerned with everyone's dignity, rather than each merely protecting his own.

9. To borrow Feinberg's (1980, 88) example, we would not want to prohibit an interracial couple from walking hand-in-hand down a southern street just because onlookers would take offense. The reason is not, *pace* Feinberg, that the larger national community would find nothing offensive in it. Rather, it is that the dignity of the couple would be more badly injured by prohibiting them from holding hands than that of onlookers is by allowing them to do so. Indeed, the dignity—as opposed to the sensitivities—of onlookers hardly seems involved at all. Thomas (1980) argues that the self-image of whites is not contingent upon humiliating blacks; and, contrary to his claims, I do not think that of males depends upon degrading women, either. In general, it seems rare that one group's dignity depends upon inflicting indignities upon another's. Dignity, like honor, is usually subject to an absolute rather than comparative standard (Pitt-Rivers 1968).

only to protect freedom itself but also to protect the dignity of people in any way it might be threatened, including through the unconstrained exercise of another's free choice.

Secondly, respecting choices commits us to the distributive rule "from each as they choose, to each as they are chosen." Someone not chosen to receive others' favors might be reduced to absolute squalor, limited only by our obligation to respect his choice to evade it. He has no *claim* on anyone else: his only relief can come from begging them for assistance; and if they choose to be uncharitable he has no further recourse. All this might—and all too often does—happen when we respect choices above all else. None of it would be permitted were we respecting people's dignity. There would be some social minimum, corresponding to what is required to lead a dignified existence, below which no one would be allowed to fall. And everyone would be entitled to that level of support as a matter of moral right, without any undignified begging.

The choice model might generate analogous protections, but only for those chosen as members of the club. People agree to join the club only on condition that it assure them of some bare minimum and, if others accept them on these conditions, they might enjoy protections similar to those required for everyone by the dignity model. These, however, are courtesies extended only to members of the club. People remaining outside the club—either by their choice or through the choices of others—have no opportunity to impose conditions and, therefore, have no claim to the protections the club provides for its members.[10]

The third contrast is between the kinds of rights generated by the two principles. Respecting choices entails a conception of rights as protected choices, implying that only people who can choose can have rights; and that they can have rights only insofar as they can choose, i.e., only to those things they are practically and morally free to forgo. The more important a thing the less one can afford to forgo it, and hence the less of a right one can have to it. Respecting a person's dignity, in contrast, not only allows us to protect claims too important to waive—it actually demands that we do so, at least in certain respects. A person must, at an absolute minimum, have a right to "respect as a person" which he cannot alienate or waive. He also has a further unqualified claim (a right, if you will) to those

10. Neither do they have any obligation to respect others' claims or, for that matter, any other rules of a club they never joined. But Hobbes (1651, chap. 14), Locke (1690, secs. 22–24), and Rousseau (1762b, bk. 1, chap. 4) offer little consolation when saying to slaves that they are morally free to rebel when they are, in practical terms, so utterly incapable of doing so.

social and economic advantages which are somehow central to his leading a dignified existence.[11]

Thus it is wholly appropriate that arguments for respecting "inalienable human rights" have long been couched in terms of dignity. Consider women's rights. Characteristic of choice theorists, J. S. Mill (1869) had to resolve his opposition to the "subjection of women" into an essentially empirical claim: women are *not* innately lacking in free will; any observed weakness reflects their adaptation to the way society treats them. Wollstonecraft (1790) argues for rights of women much more powerfully in terms of the indignities visited upon the "weaker" sex.[12] Demands for civil and political rights—from the nineteenth-century British working class as well as contemporary American blacks—are couched in terms of the indignity and loss of self-respect resulting from second-class citizenship (Carlyle 1890; de Man 1928, chap. 2; King 1964, 86; Bendix 1964). Legal documents conferring such rights—the U.N. Charter and Declaration of Human Rights, and bills of rights and constitutions of nations as diverse as the Federal Republic of Germany and the Republic of the Philippines—justify them in terms of human dignity. Even novelists make the connection. In Roth's (1971, 21) satire *Our Gang,* President Tricky Dixon argues for voting rights for foetuses saying, "I can tell you, they have really impressed me with their silent dignity and politeness."

Whereas choice models tolerate a very restrictive allocation of citizenship rights, models based on human dignity enter universal claims. They create a "single-status" moral community. Everyone is included automatically—people need do nothing special to qualify for membership. Neither can anything they do justify their being cast out of the community. "The moral community is not a club from which members may be dropped for delinquency. Our morality does not provide for moral outcasts or half-castes."[13] By including

11. "No matter how willing a person is to submit to humiliation by others, they ought to show him some respect as a person .... To the extent that a person gives even tacit consent to humiliations incompatible with this equal respect, he will be acting as if he waives a right which he cannot in fact give up" (Hill 1973, 101–2).

12. In the Introduction to her *Vindication of the Rights of Women,* Wollstonecraft (1790) writes, "I earnestly wish to point out in what true dignity and human happiness consists. I wish to persuade women to endeavour to acquire strength, both of mind and body, and to convince them that the soft phrases, susceptibility of heart, delicacy of sentiment, and refinement of tastes are almost synonymous with epithets of weakness, and that those beings who are only the objects of pity and that kind of love which has been termed its sister, will soon become objects of contempt."

13. "Punishment takes place *within* the moral community and under its rules. It is for this reason that, for example, one has no right to be cruel to a cruel person. His offense against the moral law has not put him outside the law .... Capital punishment, if we believe in it, is no exception. The fact that a man has been condemned to

everyone in the moral community, the model of dignity avoids the abuses licensed by choice models in sanctioning citizenship cliques.

While membership in the club is universal, the particular entitlements arising out of it may vary somewhat with time and place. Dignity consists in self-respect, which is largely if not wholly a function of the respect shown you by others. Consequently, what they *mean* by their actions is crucial, and performances intended to humiliate in one culture or one context might be intended to honor in another. Hobbes (1651, chap. 10) offers the example of a king who honored one man by having him carried through the streets wearing one of the king's cloaks; when an upstart demanded a similar honor, the king agreed that he should be similarly carried through the streets but directed that all should laugh at him. Thus, there are real difficulties in deciding in any general way what showing people respect requires.

Some leverage on the problem can be obtained through an analogy to the way language communicates intentions. The meaning of an action can be understood, as can the meaning of a word, by reference to "conventional intentions." Some people have idiosyncratic ways of using words and gestures, and others have idiosyncratic ways of understanding them; but we understand *public* language or gestures only by reference to the intentions conventionally associated with the words or gestures in our larger social and linguistic community. What we must do if we are to treat a person respectfully is, therefore, largely governed by convention.

Conventional intentions are, however, only half the story. We must also allow for conventional understandings. The rationale for respecting people's dignity was, after all, couched in terms of *self-respect*. The strong empirical link between respecting oneself and being respected by others makes us concerned that others' actions display respectful intentions. But more important than their view of you is your own view of yourself. Others' standards of respectful conduct may diverge from your own: something they mean as an honor may embarrass you; or something may humiliate you even though they "meant nothing by it." White Americans, raised in an earlier era, meant to be polite when calling Stokely Carmichael "colored." His pride and self-respect were nevertheless injured, even if they intended no disrespect. This must be guarded against if people's dignity is to be respected. It is not enough that people mean well—they must also be sensitive to how others will *take* their words

---

death does not license his jailors to beat him or virtuous citizens to lynch him" (Vlastos 1962, 47–48).

and gestures.[14] Of course, neither individuals nor especially the society at large can be expected to know and respond to each individual's idiosyncrasies in this regard. Insofar as such sensitivities are widely shared among members of some identifiable group, however, a system of "conventional understandings" (strictly analogous to "conventional intentions") will have grown up, and the society is responsible for responding appropriately.

5.6. Putting the Principle into Practice

Some practical instruments for showing people respect have been mentioned in passing. Here, in concluding this discussion, a more systematic survey is in order. Respecting people's dignity requires not only the formal legal rights which are so often discussed in this connection, but also socioeconomic and political guarantees of a sort that tend to get far less attention.

5.6.1. Formal Legal Rights

Traditionally, the practical upshot of a concern with people's self-respect has been thought to amount to little more than guaranteeing a few formal legal rights. Rawls (1972, sec. 82), for example, claims that "self-respect is secured by public affirmation of the status of equal citizenship for all," by which he means, roughly, those civil and political rights embodied in the U.S. Bill of Rights. (The quotation from Rawls finishes by saying, "The distribution of material means is left to take care of itself in accordance with the idea of pure procedural justice.") This focus upon purely procedural due process as the primary guarantor of dignity is widespread. The arbitrary behavior of public officials who refuse to explain their decisions to people affected by them "clashes unbearably with a preferred conception of social and political life, in which self-respect is recognized as the fundamental human good that social life affects" (Michelman 1977, 148; cf. Kadish 1957).

Formal legal rights and procedural safeguards doubtless are important components of a social scheme for protecting people's

14. Conventional understandings also help overcome the sorts of uncertainties mentioned by Mazrui (1979, 656): "Surely the most exasperating humiliation of all is when you are not sure whether you are, in fact, being humiliated. If I pass through customs in Europe and I'm stopped when none of the white passengers is, can I be sure that this is simply the luck of the draw on that particular day? Or was the customs man influenced in his choice by the fact that I was not white?" The customs agent should realize that, given conventional understandings, collaring the only black man coming off the plane would be seen as discrimination whatever his actual intentions.

dignity. One of the more mortifying aspects of inmates' lives in Goffman's (1968) asylums is that no one will listen to them. Political persecution might be marginally less degrading if people are at least given a chance to make their voices heard. Kirchheimer (1961, 430), no friend of the "political trial," nevertheless sees this minimal advantage in it: "Most people, if they have to be hanged, enjoy being able to protest against it." For the American black, Jim Crow laws designed "to ostracize him, humiliate him, and rob him of elemental human dignity" began by stripping him of basic Constitutional rights (Woodward 1955, 28).

Crucial though these formal rights are to a person's self-respect, however, it would be folly to suppose that they are sufficient in themselves. "Proper" procedures can, after all, be pursued to perverse, degrading ends. Dworkin (1977, 273) commendably demands that governments treat people "with equal concern and respect." Then he spoils it by saying, "This is the right, not to an equal distribution of some good or opportunity, but the right to equal concern and respect in the political decision about how these goods and opportunities are to be distributed." All that Dworkin—or any other champion of pure procedural justice—could guarantee is that people's demands will be "duly noted." For most people, that is not enough. They also take it as a personal affront when some public official listens attentively, but then promptly ignores everything they have just said when making his decision.[15] Showing people respect entails more than merely giving people a hearing ("recognition respect"); it also entails giving them something of the results they wanted ("appraisal respect") (Darwell 1977). Guaranteeing people's formal legal status is not enough to secure their self-respect. We must also stipulate something about substantive outcomes.

5.6.2. Socioeconomic Guarantees

The second practical implication of respecting dignity, then, is that people must be guaranteed some decent share of their society's social and economic resources. There are, of course, many arguments leading to similar conclusions: one is quasi-logical, finding "subsistence rights" implicit in any other rights guarantees (H. Shue 1980); another is frankly utilitarian, justifying equality on the basis of

15. The fact that they do make such demands is, perhaps, testimony to the power of formal rights in boosting people's self-respect. No symbolic act is devoid of tangible implications (Goodin 1980, chap. 5), but perhaps people actually demand the material rewards that are their due only because their self-conceptions have been altered by the symbolism (Marshall 1963; Scheingold 1974). Be that as it may, once people start making such demands it is clearly degrading to deny that which the symbols of their dignity clearly promise.

"diminishing marginal utility." Arguments in terms of human dignity powerfully reinforce such conclusions. "The assurance of dignity for every member of society requires a right to a decent existence—to some minimum standard of nutrition, health care, and other essentials of life. Starvation and dignity do not mix well" (Okun 1975, 17).

Dignity probably requires merely a minimum standard rather than an absolutely equal allocation. "Dignity," after all, is not predominantly a comparative notion: in this, it is more like "honor" (Pitt-Rivers 1968) than "status" (Hirsch 1976). My dignity is undiminished when a heroic soldier receives an award or when my neighbor is named in the Queen's Honours List. Both "dignity" and "honor" are largely absolutes characterized by thresholds, bare minima below which people suffer indignity and dishonor but above which their dignity and honor are secure.

Precisely what socioeconomic rights should be guaranteed, and at what levels, will doubtless vary from one society to the next. Certainly "subsistence" levels of the standard trio—food, shelter, and clothing—will always be required. Equally certainly, the social guarantee should stop short of underwriting all claims whatsoever. Dignity, after all, is a matter of what one is rather than what one does: interests connected to one's "essence" should be protected as rights; those connected merely to one's various life projects need not be, if protecting one's dignity is the goal.[16]

In modern industrial societies at least (and perhaps much more broadly as well), meaningful employment is one of the most important elements in a dignified existence. From his study of blacks hanging out on Tally's Corner, Liebow (1967, 210) concludes,

> One of the major points of articulation between the inside world and the larger society surrounding it is in the area of employment. The way in which the man makes a living and the kind of living he makes have important consequences for how the man sees himself and is seen by others; and these, in turn, importantly shape his relationships with family members, lovers, friends and neighbors.

In modern industrial societies, this vital component of self-esteem is best assured by a "full employment" policy, conjoined with a program of "worker participation" which can turn otherwise menial

16. This explains the puzzle, set out by Flathman (1976, chap. 10), of why the "Great Rights" embodied in national constitutions—free speech, assembly, association, and so forth—tend to protect "symbolic" rather than "real" interests. My argument here is that a few "real interests" carry such overwhelmingly powerful symbolic connotations as to deserve similar treatment, in a way that is rare in classical (but not in modern) enumerations.

jobs into meaningful ones.[17] Both goals require substantial departures from the classic liberal "free market," the former obviously so and the latter only slightly less obviously. Some say that
even capitalists will introduce shop floor participation if it leads to
greater job satisfaction, fewer work stoppages, and higher productivity (Nozick 1974, 250–53). But there is, in truth, an "inherent
contradiction" between respecting the desires of workers and respecting the demands of market forces and the consumer preferences they embody: there will inevitably arise circumstances in
which workers want to organize their tasks in a manner which is less
efficient (and hence less profitable) but more satisfying (Hayek 1960,
277; Bergson 1967). Market socialism on the Yugoslav model seems
to constitute the most promising strategy for reconciling these conflicting demands. There workers are allocated a certain stock of
capital, which they pool with that of other workers to form pro-
ducers' cooperatives. Their products are sold in ordinary markets
where they must compete with those of other cooperatives, so that
workers must respond at least minimally to consumer demand or
else go bankrupt. But the cooperative arrangement allows workers
to trade off job satisfaction for pecuniary rewards ("profits") just as
they please (Lange 1936–37; Lindblom 1977, chap. 24).

It must, of course, be conceded that how far a country can go
toward providing its people with the employment that is crucial to
their self-respect depends upon the country's economic circumstances. But it must also be emphasized that even poor countries,
desperate to develop, can still often do more than they do. Typically, they promote capital-intensive development projects which
result in a "dual economy." These are characterized by "modern
islands in unmodern seas," with

> a restricted group of nationals of each New State rather thor-
> oughly integrated into the most advanced sectors of the modern
> world economy, and becoming more so all the time, while the
> mass of the people are even less directly touched by it than they
> were in the Colonial Period when labor-intensive plantations,
> mines, and infrastructural constructions were the main product
> of contact between the developed world and the undeveloped.
> [Geertz 1977, 256–57]

17. "There is hardly a study in the entire literature which fails to demonstrate that
satisfaction in work is enhanced or that other generally acknowledged beneficial
consequences accrue from a general increase in workers' decision-making power.
Such consistency of findings, I submit, is rare in social research" (Blumberg 1968,
chap. 6; see also Pateman 1970, and Vanek 1975).

Labor-intensive development plans are much more successful in involving the masses in the effort and spreading its products to them (Myrdal 1968, chap. 20; Sen 1960).

5.6.3. Political Guarantees

There is yet another way in which formal legal rights prove inadequate to protect people's dignity. Prohibiting certain classes of policy *outcomes,* which is all rights traditionally do, is not enough. People show each other respect or disrespect predominantly through their attitudes and motives and intentions, whether or not these culminate in action; and people's self-esteem depends far more "upon the attitudes and intentions of other human beings" than upon their actions pure and simple. As Strawson (1974, 5) points out, "If someone treads on my hand accidentally, while trying to help me, the pain may be no less acute than if he treads on it in contemptuous disregard of my existence or with a malevolent wish to injure me. But I shall generally feel in the second case a kind and degree of resentment that I shall not feel in the first." The basic insight is very old. Rousseau (1755, pt. 2), for example, remarks upon how, with the growth of civil society, "every voluntary injury became an affront, as besides the hurt which resulted from it as an injury, the offended party was sure to find in it a contempt for his person often more intolerable than the hurt itself."

While rights guarantee that public actions show citizens no disrespect, something more is required if we are to prevent the sort of humiliation that comes from socially sanctioning mean motives. Respecting people's dignity thus requires us to filter the *inputs* into the social decision machinery as well as the outputs. Ordinarily we would count all preferences without prejudice—humiliating and degrading ones included—in coming to a social decision. Only at the very last moment might we say, "Alas, the socially preferred outcome is not within the feasible set; it violates someone's rights." The state would thereby be saved from *doing* anything that shows its citizens disrespect. But by counting degrading preferences in the first place, it has already shown them disrespect.[18] Only by censoring the sorts of demands of which society will even take

18. We show people respect or disrespect less in what we do than in how we do it, as Cameron (1981, 238–39) argues. Dworkin (1977, 277), who finds "external preferences" objectionable (albeit for the wrong reasons—see Raz 1978), erroneously supposes that "rights" are an adequate remedy for "the philosophical defects of a utilitarianism that counts external preferences and the practical impossibility of a utilitarianism that does not." Contrary to Dworkin's claim, rights do not "protect the fundamental right of citizens to equal concern and respect." Agreed, they succeed in

cognizance—only by refusing even to consider certain sorts of choices and preferences, much less to act upon them—can we spare people the sort of humiliation that comes from the mean motives of others (Arrow 1963, 18; Harsanyi 1977, 62; Goodin 1983).

Here, as in saving people from their former preferences (section 3.2.3 above), the political institutions that are required are ones allowing policymakers a certain amount of leeway for ignoring citizen demands.[19] Just as some aspects of our friends' characters are better ignored, so too are some of our fellow citizens' preferences. And that can be squared with democratic principles in roughly the same way as J. S. Mill (1859, chap. 5) squares his refusal to let people sell themselves into slavery with his liberty principle. Mill writes, "The principle of freedom cannot require that he should be free not to be free. It is not freedom to be allowed to alienate his freedom." We might similarly justify censoring people's preferences by referring to our motives for establishing democratic institutions in the first place. The reason we want policy to respond to people's preferences is "human sympathy." But, Harsanyi (1977, 62) notes, "Human sympathy can hardly impose . . . the obligation to respect . . . preferences . . . in clear conflict with human sympathy. For example, human sympathy can hardly require that [policymakers] should help sadists to cause unnecessary human suffering." Policymakers' refusal even to listen to certain sorts of peculiarly degrading demands is thus consistent with our deeper motivation for embracing democratic principles in the first place.

"prohibiting decisions that seem, antecedently, likely to have been reached by virtue of the external components of the preferences democracy reveals." But merely counting degrading preferences—much less acting on them—is an affront to people.

19. There may be no institutional technique for distinguishing *perfectly* between preferences predicated on worthy and unworthy intentions, as Dworkin (1977, 276–77) argues. But the above argument suggests that dishonorable intentions can have such a devastating impact upon other people's self-respect that policymakers should try to make some such discriminations, however imperfect they may have to be.

6 Motivational Framework: Moral Incentives

There are not many fundamentally different ways of motivating people to perform socially useful and morally desirable behavior. Basically, we must choose among three: "coercion"; "self-interest incentives" offering to make them better off materially; or appealing to " 'emotional' forces" such as moral principle or social solidarity (Schultze 1977, 17–18). Offering the latter sorts of "moral incentives" obviously has much to recommend it. Pragmatically, that is a cheap and effective way to secure voluntary compliance with policies whose heavy burdens might otherwise make them intolerable. Ethically, it is highly desirable that public policies should conform as closely to citizens' deepest moral sentiments as the moral incentive strategy requires.

Hence, moral incentives have held continuing fascination for social theorists. Lindsay (1924), inspired by the altruism displayed in the British Army during World War I, wrote to the *Economic Journal* suggesting lessons to be drawn for the organization of labor in the civilian economy. In the midst of the Great Depression, Jevons (1933) wrote longingly of a "cooperative commonwealth" governed by altruism and self-sacrifice rather than by coercion and self-aggrandizement. In our own day, Sen (1966) has carefully detailed the moral dynamics governing labor allocation in Chinese communes, hoping that similar incentives can be used elsewhere (Sen 1973, chap. 4).

This chapter is reprinted, with substantial additions, from Robert E. Goodin, "Making Moral Incentives Pay," *Policy Sciences* 12 (1981): 131–45, by permission of the publisher, Elsevier Scientific Publishing Company, Amsterdam.

Tempting as moral incentives might seem for the social engineer, however, most hard-headed analysts "do not want to rely too heavily on substituting ethics for self-interest" (Arrow 1972, 354). They fear that sentiments such as "compassion, brotherly love, and patriotism are in too short supply to serve as substitutes" for more ordinary material incentives (Schultze 1977, 18; cf. Lindblom 1977, 284–90). To their way of thinking, "harnessing the 'base' motive of material self-interest to promote the common good is perhaps *the* most important invention mankind has yet achieved. Turning silk into a silk purse is no great trick, but turning a sow's ear into a silk purse does indeed partake of the miraculous" (Schultze 1977, 18).

Here I shall show that playing on people's moral sentiments requires considerably more finesse than that suggests. Indeed, the only reason moral sentiments seem to form such a slender basis for social control is that our appeals to them tend to be too clumsy. Before we can design social policies to play on people's better instincts, we must first understand how moral principles figure in ordinary people's decision calculi. This chapter surveys three models, one representing morality as enlightened self-interest, another depicting it as internalized norms, and a third focusing upon formally distinct "seriously held" moral principles. Policymakers would most like to evoke the very strong principles of this third category. But to do so they must respect the formalisms that give these principles their strength; and, in particular, they must avoid mixing moral and material incentives, lest people be put off their principles altogether.

6.1. Prudential Morality

First I shall discuss "moral behavior" among individuals lacking any internalized moral principles as such. For them, the sort of socially useful behavior we would ordinarily call "moral" is motivated instead by simple prudence and enlightened self-interest. From their own point of view, there is nothing distinctively "moral" about their intentions or conduct (Arrow 1967). This prudential morality constitutes a minimum standard, not in Hart's (1961, chap. 9) sense of being a core of principles that any fuller standard must contain, but rather in the sense of being a standard which minimally moral men must rationally respect.

The demands of prudence depend, of course, upon the details of the situation. Here I shall sketch how one sort of situation, which is arguably common, could lead a prudential actor to embrace most of the tenets of liberal political morality. Let us suppose that most people most of the time are very uncertain of their relative standings in the power hierarchy within their society. Were they dealing with people demonstrably weaker than themselves they might be tempted to try to dominate and exploit them. But they can never be altogether certain that there are not (or will not be) others stronger than themselves who will subsequently turn the tables. In the limiting case—absolute certainty about power relations—one would reckon any outcome equally likely.

Under such conditions, enlightened self-interest commends two principles of rational action. First, as an aggregative principle, a rational egoist prefers to maximize the total stock of goods available in the society as a whole. He is equally likely to find himself in any position in society, so he maximizes his own expected utility by maximizing the utility of society as a whole. Second, as a distributive principle, a rational egoist prefers to reward each individual according to his works and to rectify departures from that. (That is, those who profit from A's works should be required to repay A; and A would be required to compensate those who suffer from A's activities.) This rule offers each individual the most he can, given his uncertain power, reasonably expect to obtain over the long run. Had he certain knowledge that he is more powerful than anyone else in the community, he might try an exploitative strategy of taking the preponderance of goods for himself. Lacking that, however, it is reasonable for him to let such opportunities pass. Basically, it is a matter of insurance: by forgoing an opportunity to exploit others, the individual secures similar forbearance from others should the situation seem to be reversed.

As I have shown elsewhere (Goodin 1976), the corpus of liberal political morality can be derived from this pair of principles. A citizen's political obligation, for instance, is explained as fair recompense for benefits conferred upon him by others' sacrifices in obeying the law themselves; but the obligation is easily overridden and civil disobedience justified if the law imposes unbalanced burdens and benefits. Similarly, justice, equity, and equality, seen as strictly formal principles, simply require that a society make and act consistently upon rules distinguishing between individuals on bases instrumentally related to social goals—which is, of course, required merely for the efficient utilization of social resources. Equality of opportunity is justifiable in the same terms of making the most of scarce talents, as are equalization of results and affirmative action against a historical background of unequal opportunities. Freedom here (as in liberal orthodoxy) is of capital, if only instrumental, importance insofar as doing as one pleases presupposes being free to do so; and rights are valued as guarantees of freedom of choice. In these many ways, even an unprincipled egoist might be led by careful reflection upon his true interests to behave in ways we would commonly call "moral."

6.2. The Morality of Men of Principle

Much of what liberals would describe as moral behavior might, therefore, be motivated by nothing more than simple prudence. But there is more to morality than liberals would recognize or than political economists could explain in narrowly prudential terms (Benn 1978). Some people actually internalize certain moral principles. For them, acting well is its own reward and badly its own penalty, quite apart from considerations of the external payoffs.

Traditionally, this is formally represented by entering "moral principles" as another type of consumption good in an ordinary utility function. For those who internalize moral sentiments, aggregate utility U is a function not only of rewards derived from egoistic goods e but also of rewards from moralistic goods m. That is to say, $U = U(e, m)$. This is the model clearly implied by casual comments—from Hume (1739, bk. 3; 1977), Adam Smith (1790), and Bentham (1789, chap. 5), through Harsanyi (1955; 1969, 521–22; 1977, chap. 4.1) and Sen (1977)—that individuals act on both self-interest and moral "sympathies" whose claims are enforced internally through conscience.

In terms of modern utility theory, this might be translated as an assertion that individuals make choices on the basis of indifference maps over multiple dimensions, some representing egoistic evaluations and others moralistic ones. More often, it is written in the old-fashioned and technically misleading terms of additive utility functions: whereas the egoist maximizes the sum $U(e_1) + U(e_2) + \ldots + U(e_n)$, the moralist is said to maximize the sum $U(e_1) + U(e_2) + \ldots + U(e_n) + U(m_1) + U(m_2) + \ldots + U(m_r)$. In other words, morality is taken into account simply by tacking another set of arguments onto the individual's utility function. Some such equation is strongly suggested by the way in which specific moral principles are represented in political economic models. Consider the following cases.

1. Civic duty in the voting calculus. Riker and Ordeshook, in their "Theory of the Calculus of Voting" (1968, 36–40) and again in their *Introduction to Positive Political Theory* (1973, 62–65), offer an equation expressing the reward "R, in utiles, that an individual voter receives from his act of voting," which reads

$$R = PB - C + D,$$

where

B = the "differential benefit, in utiles, that an individual voter receives from the success of his more preferred candidate over his less preferred one";

P = the "probability that the citizen will, by voting, bring about the benefit B";

C = the "cost to the individual of the act of voting"; and

D = the private benefit accruing directly to the individual from the act of voting itself.

The principal component of D is said to be "the satisfaction from compliance with the ethic of voting, which if the citizen is at all socialized into the democratic tradition is positive when he votes and negative (from guilt) when he does not." Significantly, in the operationalization of their model other components of D drop away entirely, leaving only "civic duty" as measured in SRC survey questionnaires.

2. *Lying and a guilty conscience.* In *Toward a Mathematics of Politics,* Gordon Tullock (1967, chap. 9) offers an analysis of the "economics of lying."

Its payoff P_1 is shown as

$$P_1 = BLP - C_c - (1 - L)(C_p L_p + C_r L_r),$$

where

B = the "benefit expected to be derived from the action being urged";

L = the "likelihood that the lie will be believed";

P = the "persuasive effect of the lie; probability that the lie, if believed, will bring about the desired action";

C_c = the cost of "conscience; internal cost of lying";

C_p = "costs of punishment";

L_p = the "likelihood of punishment if the lie is not believed";

C_r = the "injury to reputation through other's knowledge that an individual has lied"; and

L_r = the "likelihood that injury to reputation will occur if lie is not believed."

Of the crucial cost C_c, Tullock writes: this "is the 'pain' of doing something which you think you should not do. It presumably results from indoctrination in various socially approved ethical principles, primarily in childhood."

3. *Altruism.* Recently economists have come to see interdependencies among people's utility functions. One person internalizes the pains and pleasures of certain other people in certain circumstances. For decision-makers governed (even occasionally) by this ethic of benevolence, the utility function must be rewritten. Each economist has his own notation.

(Compare Valavanis 1958; Sawyer 1966; Lieberman 1969; Hochman and Rogers 1969; Scott 1972; Culyer 1973; Becker 1974; 1976a; Taylor 1976.) The basic point, however, is the same: altruists are happy because (certain) others are happy. Accordingly, the utility function of the altruist U_a must be reformulated along these lines:

$$U_a = \sum_{i=1}^{n} \sum_{j=1}^{m} U_a(g_i) + q_j[U_j(g_j)] , \quad j \neq a$$

where

$(g_1, g_2, \ldots, g_n)$ = the set of goods to be distributed;
$U_1, U_2, \ldots, U_m$ = the utilities enjoyed by individuals $1, 2, \ldots,$
          m, whose pains and pleasures actor A
          internalizes; and
$q_1, q_2, \ldots, q_m$ = the weights actor A assigns to the pains
          and pleasures of individuals $1, 2, \ldots, m$
          respectively relative to his own.

The more formal point is, for present purposes, the more important one. All these examples point to a general consensus that the proper way to account for moral principles is simply to tack another argument onto an ordinary utility function. The general implication of this way of representing moral preferences is that individuals will consider all goods, egoistic or moralistic, simultaneously in coming to a decision in any particular instance.

6.3. Taking Morality Seriously

Moral principles are by their very nature ones which, if internalized at all, tend to be taken very seriously. Learning the difference between right and wrong "includes an inculcated caring, a habit of taking certain sorts of things seriously" (Ryle 1958, 156). But we have not bothered to investigate at all carefully what it means to take a principle of action seriously. For Dworkin (1977, 186), "taking rights seriously" requires merely that governments "follow a coherent theory of what these rights are, and act consistently with its own professions." Surely there is more to it than that.

At first blush, we are inclined to suppose that "James takes X seriously" means merely that "James attaches great importance to X," which can be translated into economic parlance as "James assigns high utility to X." To say that "James takes his cricket seriously," for example, might indicate no more than that James appears punctually and regularly for matches, concentrates on the tasks at hand, takes great pride in his accomplishments and shame in his errors, and so on. As applied to moral principles, this would suggest that taking morality seriously means simply that we attach great weight to moralistic elements in our utility functions. That is to say, we would demand a high price in terms of egoistic goods to forsake principles. In any particular case, the price may be prohibitive and the principles indeed rule the decision. But on this model, we are always juggling both egoistic and moralistic considerations, and there is always a price (albeit a very high one, perhaps) for which we would cash in our moral principles.

This model badly misrepresents what it is to take a principle of action seriously. Typically, when we take something seriously we differentiate it from run-of-the-mill endeavors according to certain formal criteria. We do not simply accord it greater weight in an ordinary decision calculus. Rather, we formally set it apart.[1] The following examples illustrate the generality of this pattern.

1. Dress. We typically require distinct attire for serious occasions. Engraved invitations phrase this as a demand for "formal" dress. Sartorial distinctions are employed to acknowledge the differential seriousness of political occasions as well. An illustrative anecdote comes from *The Final Days*. Senator Goldwater, scheduled to meet with President Nixon to convey the Republican leadership's plea for resignation, was to have lunch with Dean Burch to discuss strategy. "Goldwater spent the morning in his large apartment on Cathedral Avenue, surrounded with his ham-radio equipment and model cars. Burch called to set the time—twelve-thirty—and tell him that [General Alexander] Haig would be there. 'Are you going to wear a suit?' Burch asked. Goldwater generally showed up at his house in Levis and cowboy boots. 'Shit, what do you expect me to wear?' Goldwater responded; it was a serious occasion" (Woodward and Bernstein 1976, 405–6).

2. Language. On serious occasions or in serious settings, we employ a linguistic code which is formally distinct from that which we employ in everyday affairs. For example, the Chirachaua Apache, who took their martial endeavors very seriously indeed, had a special "warpath" language far more elaborate and formal than their ordinary speech (Opler and Hoijer 1940). "Traditional societies" more generally require orators to use a specialized mode of address, formally distinct from their workaday discourse, when addressing assemblies on the ceremonial "speaking ground" (Bloch 1975).

3. Currency. Certain transactions are taken more seriously

1. It may also be true that the values of serious and mundane objects are, objectively, incommensurable. The point here is that, even if unit comparability could be established, taking something seriously entails a refusal to engage in such comparisons.

than others. In traditional societies especially, these are distinguished from more mundane ones by being conducted in a special currency. In the Caroline Islands, for example, "strict norms . . . reserved certain kinds of money exclusively for important or ceremonial transactions" such as "acquisition of a wife, membership in the local state," and so on (Simmel 1907, 366). In this connection, recall with Galbraith (1975, 7) that "it has always been thought derogatory that Judas delivered up Jesus for 30 pieces of silver. That it was silver suggests that it was a normal commercial transaction; had it been three pieces of gold, a plausible early ratio, the deal would have been somewhat exceptional."

Insofar as individuals take their moral principles seriously, we should expect them to employ some similar device for differentiating them from the more mundane considerations impinging on their decisions.

Among Western philosophers, the most widely discussed method of setting seriously held moral principles formally apart from more mundane objects of desire is to repudiate the use of instrumental rationality altogether in morally charged situations. That certainly sets the moral realm off from the ordinary world. Instrumental rationality is now very much the norm, both in the statistical sense of being the principle most often followed and in the normative sense of being the precept by which people self-consciously strive to guide their behavior. But, on this account, its very success as an explanation of social behavior is self-limiting: since instrumental rationality constitutes the background against which modern man frames his actions, what he takes seriously must be guided by other precepts entirely if it is to stand out against that background. Thus, insofar as instrumental rationality offers a good account of what people typically do, to the same extent it is incapable of explaining those aspects of their behavior which they take most seriously.[2]

This analysis has some warrant in the comments of contemporary philosophers, who decry the sort of scheming behavior required to fit means to ends efficiently as being antithetical to truly moral behavior. One of the first rejoinders of such a philosopher to a utilitarian critic would, significantly, be that the utilitarian simply fails to appreciate the *seriousness* of moral duties and obligations. Were he

2. This model appeals to the ironical side of Saul Bellow (1970, chap. 3): "To perform higher actions, to serve the imagination with special distinction, it seems essential to be histrionic. This, too, is a brand of madness. Madness has always been a favorable choice of the civilized man who prepares himself for a noble achievement. It is often the simplest state of availability to ideals. Most of us are satisfied with that: signifying by a kind of madness devotion to, availability for, higher purposes. Higher purposes do not necessarily come."

to take morality seriously, the argument would go, the utilitarian would have to forsake his tortuous attempts to tease duties and obligations out of pleasures and pains.

Although it attracts much philosophical attention, I suspect that his way of distinguishing moral from mundane endeavors has little support among the population at large. Perhaps one of the more important reasons is as utilitarians suggest: where instrumental rationality is banned, we are deprived of the only mechanism for choosing means to translate our morally laudable intentions into morally desirable outcomes. Even those who deny that the consequences of our actions are everything, ethically speaking, would usually not go so far as to assert that the consequences are utterly devoid of moral significance (Williams 1973, 82–93). For this reason, the repudiation of instrumental rationality as the basis for seriously held moral principles is simply implausible.

A second way in which people might formally signal their moral seriousness is by refusing to consider mundane goals alongside moralistic ones. The more radical strategy just dismissed repudiated means-ends reasoning and, with it, *any* reference to one's utility function in deciding moral questions. This second strategy, while allowing reference to utility functions, nevertheless departs fundamentally from the orthodox model (developed in section 6.2) of how moral principles fit together with ordinary egoistic desires. On that model, an individual who internalizes moral principles simply maximizes a utility function incorporating rewards from both egoistic and moralistic goods. Saying that he takes his principles seriously just means that he weighs them more heavily than other reasons for action. But, as we have seen, taking a principle of action seriously seems to entail more than merely according it a little extra weight in our decision calculus. "Sacred forces are not to be distinguished from profane ones simply by their greater intensity, they are different—they have special qualities which the others do not have," Durkheim (1915, 85) emphasizes. Bernard Williams (1973, 116), replying to crude utilitarians, says similarly that "the point is not . . . that if the project or attitude is that central to his life, then to abandon it would be very disagreeable to him and a great loss of utility would be involved . . . . Once he is prepared to look at it like that, the argument in any serious case is over anyway." Taking something seriously seems, instead, to entail distinguishing it in some formal way from our everyday world. On the present account, this is done by refusing to allow seriously held moral principles to be contaminated by association with more mundane (and especially egoistic) concerns. If so, the orthodox model is dramatically in error when representing moral principles as just another argument tacked onto an ordinary utility function. People whose moral seriousness is manifested in this way either make decisions exclusively on the basis of moral considerations or else they make decisions exclusively on the basis of ordinary considerations of efficiency, advantage, and so forth. Under no circumstances do they allow their moral principles to be tainted by juxtaposition with more mundane concerns.[3]

For examples of the way in which seriously held moral values are kept formally distinct from mundane, and especially egoistic, values, consider the following cases:

1. Morality and personal relations. Moral principles governing the personal relationships people take especially seriously are often marked off in this way. Marx (1844, 83) insists, "Assume *man* to be *man* and his relationship to the world to be a human one: then you can exchange love only for love, trust for trust, etc." This sentiment is institutionalized among primitive peoples in the form of distinct "spheres of exchange." Among the Tiv, for example, brides are not bought but must be swapped: "A man could not get a wife without being allowed by the lineage head to offer one of the lineage girls as an exchange" (Bohannan 1955; Bohannan and Dalton 1962). Maine (1871, 195–96) concludes more generally that people in organic village communities "do not trade together on commercial principles. ... It is not creditable to drive a hard bargain with a near relative or friend." And even in our own societies there is an "operative boundary between two kinds of services: professional, paid with money . . . , and personal, recompensed in kind and in no other way . . . . It is all right to send flowers to your aunt in the hospital, but never right to send the cash they are worth with a message to 'get yourself some flowers'; all right to offer lunch or drinks, but not to offer the price of a lunch or a drink. Hosts may go to extravagant lengths to attract and please guests—short of offering them money to come to the party" (Douglas and Isherwood 1978, 58–59). Hirsch (1976, chap. 6) offers the parallel observation that "bought sex is not the same."

2. Morality and social relations: the gift relationship. Where people take the moral principles of solidarity and collective welfare seriously, they signal this by insisting on "gift" rather than "exchange" relationships. The two may well be functional equivalents; but such a description misses what the participants

---

3. Among contemporary philosophers, the only recognition of this need for formal partitioning of things we take seriously is a chance footnote from Bernard Williams (1978, 64): "I have known a politician, now dead, who used to say 'that is not a serious political argument' to mean, more or less, 'that is an argument about what to do in politics which mentions a non-political consideration.' "

themselves take to be the most important features of the gift. For those involved, it is crucial to "pretend to put the law of self-interest into abeyance," which they accomplish by impos- ing a time lag between gift and counter-gift. "A rational contract would telescope into an instant a transaction which gift ex- change disguises by stretching it out in time" (Bourdieu 1977, 171). Obscuring the element of self-interest in the gift trans- action is important precisely because the participants take the social relationships and the associated moral principles seri- ously and, accordingly, mark them off formally by refusing (ostensibly, at least) to let them mix with selfish considerations. Notice, for example, how the British Blood Transfusion Service refuses to allow donors to specify who (family, friends, mem- bers of certain groups, etc.) should get the blood they have given (Titmuss 1971, chap. 14). By institutionalizing in this way the refusal of those who take their community seriously to allow selfish considerations to contaminate their principles, the Na- tional Health Service "may strengthen feelings of community and mutual interdependence" (Singer 1973, 317).

   3. Patriotic duty. Merton's 1946 study, *Mass Persuasion: The Social Psychology of a War Bond Drive,* suggests that people similarly demonstrate that they take their patriotic duty seri- ously by refusing to put a price on it. In some war bond drives there had been a "conflict between the 'sacred' area of patrio- tism and the 'profane' area of private gain." In the drive Merton studied, however, Kate Smith pointedly omitted mention of the materialistic reasons (good investments, etc.) for buying bonds, much to the approval of her audience. A sample survey showed that fully half of the listeners were "opposed in princi- ple to premiums, bonuses or other such inducements to per- suade people to buy bonds"; and "many of the remainder thought it a good idea only for 'other people' who might not buy otherwise." These results, combined with responses to other open-ended questions, led Merton (1946, 47) to conclude, "For many people, the buying of war bonds is not like buying goods and services, or even like buying railroad bonds or preferred stocks. It is, rather, more nearly analogous to the monetary collections made in church which are thought of not as the wherewithal for the bread and butter of the minister but rather as an 'offering.' To tinge such contributions with commer- cialism would profane the sentiments centered about war bonds, which have been termed 'sacred' as compared with the more secular attitudes involved in the purchase of material goods for one's self. Patriotic feelings, like religious feelings, are usually, to those experiencing them, beyond the realm of the controversial, and any exhortation to contribute money in either of these fields would be tainted were it spoken of in terms of material advantage accruing to the contributor."

6.4. Responses to Moral Pollution

Similar conclusions about the nature of seriously held moral principles can be reached by approaching the problem from the opposite
end. What puts people off their most cherished principles is typically
phrased in terms of "moral pollution." And "pollution" is essentially a matter of boundary-crossing. Pollutants straddle categories.
In them are mixed elements of two or more different classes of
things (Douglas 1966; 1968; Douglas and Isherwood 1978).[4] This
analysis is rooted in Durkheimian sociology, which holds that
"the sacred thing is par excellence that which the profane should
not touch, and cannot touch with impunity..... We picture a
sort of logical chasm between the two" (Durkheim 1915, 40). But it
is by now so conventional as to have found its way into the *Oxford
English Dictionary* definition of *pollute* as "to destroy the purity or
sanctity of," where *pure* is defined in turn as "unmixed, un-
adulterated."

When complaining of "moral pollution," then, we implicitly dis-
close the structure of our value judgments. Such talk suggests we try
to fence off those things we regard as especially important through
the use of rigid boundaries, rather as the *purdah* affords at least
"symbolic shelter" to South Asian women (Papanek 1973). Not
every value or moral principle is susceptible to pollution, of course.
But the ones that are, and that therefore must be protected in this
way, are necessarily the ones we cherish most.

The notion of "moral pollution," like that of "taking morality
seriously," therefore seems to entail barriers to set morality off from
mundane affairs. Where, as in modern society, day-to-day affairs are
governed largely by calculations of self-interest, this will amount to
refusing to allow moral principles to be contaminated by being juxtaposed alongside ordinary considerations of private gain. The formal barrier will be between moral principles and egoistic reckoning.
Moral principles can be seen as something special only so long as

---

4. Boundary-crossing is a necessary but not sufficient condition of pollution. Not
every anomaly is an instance of pollution. When pure copper and pure tin are mixed
to form brass, it is certainly true that their original "purity" has been lost. It would,
however, be odd to phrase the point as a complaint about the "pollution" of the
original elements. This is partially because "pollution" *is* a complaint, unlike the
more strictly descriptive term "impure"—and since the resulting alloy is more useful
than either pure element alone, there is simply no cause for complaint. But, more
fundamentally, we hesitate to speak of "pollution" there because that is a term we
reserve for the transgression of boundaries we consider vitally important, and the
boundaries between copper and tin are (in our culture, at least) simply too trivial to
warrant the term. When we complain of something as "moral pollution," then, we are
implicitly saying that the boundaries protecting our moral principles are important
ones to us.

these boundaries are maintained—only so long as people refuse to trade them off for egoistic advantage.

Once the boundaries have been breached, how will people react? Assuming the nature and cause of moral pollution are as described above, there are basically four possibilities: denial of the contamination; upgrading the pollutant; downgrading the moral principle; and withdrawing the moral principle. These are surveyed below.

6.4.1. Denial

The most immediate response to moral pollution is, no doubt, merely to turn one's head. Although the breaching of boundaries is an objective phenomenon, its impact on moral principles is necessarily subjective. Someone's principles are compromised only when, and only insofar as, he perceives them to be. So long as he can maintain for himself the fiction of purity, his moral principles will be secure. Basically, this amounts to pure self-deception. But it would be wrong to minimize people's capacity for deceiving themselves, at least in the short term. Consider the following illustrations:

1. V S. Naipaul (quoted in Thompson 1979, 3–4), upon first visiting his Indian homeland, observed that "Indians defecate everywhere . . . . They never look for cover . . . . These squatting figures—to the visitor, after a time, as eternal and emblematic as Rodin's Thinker—are never spoken of; they are never written about; they are not mentioned in novels or stories; they do not appear in feature films or documentaries . . . . The truth is that *Indians do not see these squatters* and might even, with complete sincerity, deny that they exist. A collective blindness [arises] out of the Indian fear of pollution and the resulting conviction that Indians are the cleanest people in the world. They are required by their religion to take a bath every day. This is crucial and they have devised minute rules to protect themselves from every conceivable contamination . . . . It has all been regulated and purified. To observe the squatters is therefore distorting."

2. Zeckhauser (1973, 164) discusses the myth that "if medical expenditures can save a man's life, we will spare no expense to do so . . . . A variety of subterfuges can be tried to attempt to preserve this myth. If we get another kidney machine, we can save some more patients suffering from renal failure. If we believe it uneconomic to save everyone, the best we can do to maintain the notion that inadequate funds are never a barrier to the saving of life is to restrict the supply of machines from the start. This confronts us with the difficult problem of allocating people to machines. But we have managed to change the prob-

lem. The shortage is not one of funds, but rather of life-saving machinery.''

3. Similar subterfuges are often employed to purchase indirectly things not officially obtainable for money. Simmel (1907, 373) offers the example of the Laplanders, who ''give their daughters away in return for presents but . . . consider it improper to take money for them.'' Similarly ''in Dafur labor cannot be exchanged for millet directly; but you can use millet to brew beer, and beer can then be exchanged for labor'' (Barth 1967). Even in contemporary America, ''money can buy a great many things'' ranging from political influence to legal justice ''that are not supposed to be for sale in our democracy. . . . Even though money generally cannot buy extra helpings of rights directly, it can buy services that, in effect, produce more or better rights'' (Okun 1975, 22). The indirectness of the connection helps us deny, even to ourselves, that it exists at all.

Such self-deception is facilitated, first, by its being so difficult to distinguish (even within one's own mind) between high moral motives and base egoistic ones which would contaminate them. Our social actions—venal ones as well as noble ones—bear alternative interpretations. This ambiguity enables us to overlook much that might otherwise have compromised our morals (MacIntyre 1968, 466; Collard 1978, ix; Cameron 1981). Second, collective self-deception is facilitated by the use of social choice mechanisms that obscure the fact that any choices (and, hence, any prohibited tradeoffs) are being made at all.[5] This is supplemented by constant shifting back and forth between various techniques, each being abandoned as soon as its role in making the prohibited tradeoffs is exposed. In such a pea-and-shell game the fact that a tradeoff is being made is easily kept hidden (Calabresi and Bobbitt 1978).

6.4.2.   Upgrading the Pollutant

Once we admit to ourselves that the barriers have been breached, pollution is presumably a real worry. One mechanism for coping is to upgrade the pollutants through some sort of ''ritual transformation'' by which that which once would have been a contaminant is

5. Reflect upon the horrendous example of American Indian removal. ''The Creek, Choctaw and Chickasaw removal treaties gave individual plots of land to thousands of Indians. Each was then free to sell his plot and cross the Mississippi, or remain under state law [which was heavily biased against the Indians]. Since the government had left each Indian free to make his own decision, it was not implicated in the extraordinary fraud, thievery and violence which followed . . . . The principle was to structure the environment so that the dice were loaded strongly in favor of a single alternative, and then give the target of social planning the onus of choice'' (Rogin 1971, 306–7).

magically made over into something sacred (Durkheim 1915, 39). This sort of thing seems to underlie the shifting American attitude toward life insurance in the nineteenth century: originally, fixing a monetary equivalent for human life was thought to profane something sacred; but eventually the purchase and payment of life insurance were incorporated as part of the ritual surrounding death in America (Zelizer 1978). More prosaically, we concede that boundaries have been crossed and merely redraw the boundaries so as to include what once would have counted as a pollutant when found on the sacred side of the divide. This, some say, is the classic American response to the dilemma under discussion: if money threatens to pollute sacred values, then simply include the pursuit of wealth as part of the sacred quest. But that highlights the weakness of the whole approach. If the pollution is pervasive—if everything would have to be made sacred (i.e., included among those things "taken seriously") to avoid pollution—then the category of the sacred ceases to be special. The category of the sacred has meaning and behavioral significance only in contrast to that of the profane. If all of the profane has to be incorporated into the sacred for that category to be preserved, then in the act of preserving it we will have destroyed it.

6.4.3. Downgrading the Principle

Where the pollution is undeniable and pollutants are too pervasive to upgrade, we face the threat of having our seriously held moral principles downgraded. Our seriously held moral principles must be kept formally distinct from our mundane world—which, in societies governed by the commercial spirit, means being protected from contamination by self-interest. Such principles inevitably cease to be anything special once they start figuring regularly in everyday affairs, being traded off for any and all other values.

Downgrading our principles does not mean abandoning them. It just means that they have less hold over us than they once had. Formerly, we would have refused even to consider trading them off for ordinary advantages—that would violate the formalisms that allow us to take the principles seriously. Now, we are admitting that we do trade off moral principles for ordinary goods, i.e., that they are just second-tier principles of the sort described in section 6.2. Perhaps we put a high price on our principles, so they are only occasionally sacrificed in pursuit of ordinary self-interest. But putting a price on our principles at all in effect reduces their price. Principles whose value is *above* pricing will clearly decide moral issues much more decisively than principles which carry a price, however high it might be.[6]

6.4.4. Withdrawing the Principle

Suppose the contamination can no longer be ignored, that pollutants are too pervasive to be upgraded, but that you still are deeply attached to your principles and refuse to see them downgraded. The only remaining alternative is to withdraw your principles. This deprives you of the opportunity to use the principles, but at least it protects them from pollution. Principles get polluted, recall, only when they are juxtaposed alongside ordinary considerations in making a decision. They can be protected from such pollution by being "set aside," by an individual's refusing to take them into consideration when making a decision he knows must involve mundane reckonings. Thus, Montezuma's men stashed away their sacred relics instead of letting them fall to Cortez—they could no longer use them to appeal to the gods, but at least they avoided the sacrilege of having the relics fall into the hands of infidels. A similar phenomenon is found in one of the most common vignettes of modern cinema: during discussions of some squalid business, a thug angrily demands, "Keep my kids out of this!"; in such disgusting affairs, he refuses even to think about someone he cherishes, often to his (and their) considerable disadvantage.

Initially, we might have been tempted to describe the attitude of morally serious people toward their principles by saying that they rank their principles as lexicographically prior to more mundane reasons for action. But that would be to say that moral principles always prevail over any other considerations in a head-on clash. The principles of morally serious people are, I hope to have shown, more precarious than that. If other (e.g., egoistic) considerations are in play at all, then the opportunity for taking a moral stand is lost: where all motives mix, the formal distinctions associated with taking

6. Paradoxically, this subordinate tier of principles-with-a-price commands most of our moral attention. Such principles demand careful calculation and balancing of a sort which is unnecessary with "seriously held" moral principles, which by their nature exclude the whole range of competing considerations. They also admit of degrees—and hence require refinement—in ways seriously held moral principles do not. Furthermore, where principles-with-a-price are involved, exercises in moral character-building (understood as getting people to increase their price) make sense in a way they do not where seriously held principles beyond pricing are concerned. The fact that, for all these reasons, we spend less time contemplating our seriously held moral principles is, however, testimony to their strength and centrality. We naturally devote most attention to borderline cases and marginal, "hard" judgments. Bedrock values tend to be taken for granted.

moral principles seriously must be missing. Far from always prevailing over other more mundane motives, as a lexicographical ordering would suggest, moral principles drop out altogether (or at least are reduced to the status of those described in section 6.2) when more ordinary motives are evoked.

This notion of a motivational flip-flop has been popularized, although inadequately explained, by Titmuss's *Gift Relationship* (1971). A far more adequate analysis, whose conclusions parallel my own, can be found in Georg Simmel's long-forgotten *Philosophy of Money*. Simmel (1907, 365–66, 393, 391) recounts how, in primitive societies, people could use money to purchase absolution for serious sins, such as murder and perjury; in modern societies, however, money can no longer "be used as an equivalent in very special and uncommon conditions where the innermost and most basic aspects of the person are concerned. This is not in spite of the fact that one can obtain almost anything for money, rather, it is precisely for this reason that money was no longer used to settle moral-religious demands upon which religious penance rested." More generally, in a money economy "the individual significance of different objects" is "degraded through their exchangeability.... All things are connected by means of money as through a central station, all float with the same specific gravity in the constantly moving current of money." Money contaminates sacred values by breaking down the barriers by which we define and protect that which we take seriously. Okun (1975, 13) offers a similar analysis of how the market "can destroy every other value in sight": "All tradable goods and services are assigned their prices, and their values become dimensionally comparable: a book is ten loaves of bread or two dozen bottles of beer. The imperialism of the market's valuation accounts for its contribution, and for its threat to other institutions." And Lane (1978, 19) goes on to explain how the market leads to an "erosion of a sense of purpose" by causing us to live "in a culture subtly facilitating a sense that the dailyness of life is all there is to it." Without the barriers, we can take nothing particularly seriously.

The most conclusive evidence for a motivational flip-flop comes from social-psychological experiments investigating the impact of extrinsic rewards upon intrinsic motivation. Introducing a monetary reward for a task which subjects originally regarded as intrinsically enjoyable reduced the intrinsic pleasure subjects reported deriving from the task and, furthermore, reduced their rate of volunteering to repeat the experiment (Deci 1975; Notz 1975; Staw 1975). What is true of intrinsically satisfying tasks in general also applies to morally satisfying ones in particular. Batson, et al. (1978) confirm that "buying kindness"—the offer of monetary rewards for helping others with a task—reduces the subjects' self-reported altruism.[7] Thus, a Gresham's Law of sentiments really does seem to be at work, with base motives driving out noble ones.[8]

6.5. Institutional Implications

This analysis has institutional implications on various levels. Here I shall discuss its lessons for social incentive systems, the political process, and the economic system.

6.5.1. Implications for Incentive Systems

Even if the internalization of moral principles does not make it any easier for us to reach social decisions (Frohlich 1974), it certainly might make it easier to enforce them. Marxists have been most conspicuous in championing "moral" rather than "material" incentives (Clecak 1969; Bernardo 1971). But the promise of moral appeals clearly transcends ideological boundaries, as indicated by sympathetic liberal discussions of "moral suasion" and "moral causation" effected by appealing to people's "sense of justice" (Mill 1859, chap. 4; Rawls 1963; 1972, chap. 8; Fried 1964; Carens 1981). Enforcing social claims through moral rather than material incentives is not only cheaper but also more reliable. Studies of voluntary blood donorship, following from Titmuss (1971), find that "when the initial impetus arises externally, the individual is significantly less likely to become involved on a continuing basis. On the other hand, those for whom the initial action has been motivated by the strongest statement of moral obligation to the community are significantly less likely to drop by the wayside" (Lightman 1981, 70).

---

7. Social psychologists themselves explain these results implausibly in terms of "attribution theory." Where altruism carries extrinsic as well as intrinsic rewards, subjects simply attribute their behavior to the baser motive. The introduction of monetary rewards has not made people worse, really; it has only confused them about their own true motives (Batson, et al. 1978). But why, when there are both altruistic and egoistic reasons for an action, should subjects always attribute their action to the baser motive? Surely Kant (1785, 407) is right that generally "we like to flatter ourselves with a pretended nobler motive" when offered such a choice. The more reasonable interpretation of these results, it seems to me, is that people are accurately reporting the fact that they *have* been made worse, that the introduction of a monetary reward has actually driven out their natural altruism. Even if it has not, however, there is something to be said in terms of self-respect for allowing people the opportunity for taking a clear moral stand, as section 6.5.2 argues.

8. Someone setting aside seriously held moral principles is not left without any principles at all, of course. The second tier of principles, described in section 6.2, remains to guide him.

We must conclude that the most strongly held principles, which we would most like to tap, are the most difficult to blend just as we please into an overall enforcement strategy. Prudential morality of the sort discussed in section 6.1 fits easily into any larger scheme, but it exercises only a rather weak hold on people. The sort of barely principled morality discussed in section 6.2 fits equally well alongside more ordinary sanctions and incentives. It might exercise a strong hold on people—but only if they weight moral principles heavily in their decision calculi. And it seems likely that, instead of just assigning morality great weight, people would "take morality seriously" and consequently try to shield their principles as described in section 6.3. If so, barely principled morality will offer incentives only slightly stronger than those of prudential morality. What we would really like to tap are the seriously held principles discussed in section 6.3. These are truly compelling—they can get people to do lots of things they would not otherwise do—but they are also terribly precarious. They are highly susceptible to "pollution" from less pure motives, in which case a motivational flip-flop will occur. If we are to enforce social policies by playing on seriously held moral principles, we must design our schemes so as to avoid this pollution and the motivational flip-flop it entails.[9]

What exactly this implies for policy design depends on precisely how morally serious people choose to differentiate their sacred principles from their profane general environment. All that taking a principle seriously entails is that it be set apart according to some formal criterion. Which formalisms are employed will vary from society to society and, to some extent, from individual to individual. But if we assume that the account offered in section 6.3 is broadly accurate for most people in modern industrial societies, at least, then one common type of pollution must be anticipated: *material incentives destroy rather than supplement moral incentives.*

This contradicts one of the most popular principles of social engineering from Hume's (1739, bk. 3; 1760) time forward. His famous and influential advice is to "design institutions for knaves." That is not to deny the existence or reliability of benevolent impulses. Rather, Hume suggests we take such impulses for granted. Good men will be good regardless; it is evil men with whom constitutional engineers must be concerned. Designing institutions for knaves is a

---

9. Moral pollution would also occur under conditions of severe scarcity, forcing us to trade off our seriously held principles for more mundane considerations (Braybrooke 1978, 24). There, too, the motivational flip-flop would occur and seriously held principles be driven out of consideration. "Moderate scarcity" is, therefore, a condition not only for justice (Hume 1777) but also for utilizing seriously held moral principles to enforce social policies: superabundance renders such policies irrelevant; extreme scarcity renders such sanctions ineffective.

fail-safe strategy. If everyone is kindly disposed anyway, then no harm will have been done. But if some people are inclined to behave badly, we will be glad for institutions capable of dealing with them.

Such an approach, however, crucially presupposes that good men *will* be good regardless—that benevolent motives *will* continue to operate undiminished by the addition of extrinsic incentives. This proposition has enjoyed a long run of popularity. The economist Wicksteed (1933, 203–5), asserting that economic forces can sensibly be studied in isolation from the larger context of altruistic relations in which they are set, suggests an analogy to physical forces: "Any force which, acting on a body, would produce a certain result, were that body at rest and were no other forces acting upon it, will actually produce its full effect (that is to say, will tell in exactly the same direction and to the same extent), whatever may be the motion of the body at the moment and however many other forces may be acting on the body at the same time." Through this analogy, Wicksteed wants to deny any interaction effect between economic and altruistic motives. Two centuries before, Francis Hutcheson (1738, 319) had employed a strikingly similar analogy to suggest similarly that the strength of a person's benevolent motive is undiminished by the superimposition of a selfish one. And Sen (1966), in his modern formalization of the experience of Chinese communes, omits to provide any term to take account of the possibility that the offer of private, material incentives might undermine people's natural benevolence.

This is plausible enough within a model depicting morals as just another argument tacked onto ordinary utility functions. It is palpably false for people who take their moral principles seriously. They can do so only by formally partitioning them off from mundane considerations. Hume's institutions designed for knaves, by offering material sanctions and incentives for good behavior, break down those partitions. In classic cases of institutions designed for knaves, this breaching of the barriers is so conspicuous and pervasive that morally serious people can hardly ignore it or upgrade the pollutants. Thus they are forced either to downgrade their principles or, at the very least, to withdraw them in the present circumstances. Among morally serious people, then, Hume's strategy is bound to backfire. What was meant merely to back up natural benevolence ends by undercutting it instead. The material sanctions and incentives might be sufficiently large to overcome the damage, in the sense of preventing any net increase in bad behavior. But in another sense, the damage remains. Although we can still secure the same performances as before, the good works which were formerly produced out of the goodness of people's hearts must now be compelled through more expensive and inefficient external mechanisms of social control.

Obviously we cannot avoid this pollution of people's moral principles simply by designing social policies in such a way that they have no material consequences whatsoever. That would defeat our purpose in trying to play on moral principles in the first place. Fortunately, that is also unnecessary. A great many seriously held moral principles, when put into practice, carry practical consequences without being polluted by them: devoutly placing an "offering" in the church collection plate results in the priest's getting fed; patriotically purchasing war bonds results in the investor's receiving dividends; high-mindedly allowing "freedom of choice" of birth control techniques results in a reduction in overpopulation; and so on.

The question is not how, in playing on people's seriously held moral principles, to design a policy which has no material consequences at all. It is, instead, how to prevent such consequences from polluting their principles. This, essentially, is a matter of setting up the incentive structure in such a way as to avoid the implication that participation in socially useful activities is typically prompted by base, material motives. This means, for example, not offering cash premiums for donating blood or for looking in on an elderly neighbor, not offering umbrellas for contributing to the Public Broadcasting System, and so forth. The strongest form of moral sentiments can be tapped for enforcing social policy, but only if incentives are designed in such a way as to protect their purity.

6.5.2. Implications for
the Electoral Process

The electoral process in a mass democracy might provide an especially important forum for seriously held moral principles. The key to this argument lies with the famous "paradox of voting" (Downs 1957, chap. 14). A person may have all sorts of private, material interests at stake in an election; but his is only one vote among millions. Were he rationally calculating how to further his material interests, he would never bother voting at all. The chance of his ballot's deciding the election is so infinitesimal that its expected utility for him will easily be outweighed by the cost of getting to the poll booth.

To explain why people bother going to the polls at all, much less how they vote once they get there, we must move beyond narrow calculations of material self-interest. The explanation must be in terms of "ethical" or "social" or "community-oriented" components of people's utility functions rather than private, egoistic ones. These would dominate the voting decision even if they were only the weaker sorts of principles described in section 6.2. Since there is nothing an individual can do through his single vote to further his own material self-interest, he will vote instead on the basis of his ethical and community-oriented values, however weak they may be (Goodin and Roberts 1975; Margolis 1981; Goodin 1983). But voting offers an especially dramatic opportunity for acting on seriously held moral principles. No mundane, material motives can be involved, because each individual's vote, in itself, carries no larger social consequences. Hence individuals are free to activate their seriously held moral principles without fear of pollution.[10]

It is important to emphasize that taking a moral stand in this way is almost entirely a symbolic act. Virtually no consequences follow from the vote of each person, taken individually. Nevertheless, the act can be crucial in confirming his self-image. Benn argues forcefully that

> political activity may be a form of moral self-expression, necessary not for achieving any objective beyond itself . . . , nor yet for the satisfaction of knowing that one had let everyone else know that one was on the side of the right, but because one could not seriously claim, even to oneself, to be on that side without expressing the attitude by the action most appropriate to it in the paradigm situation. [1979, 310; cf. Cameron 1981, 232–34, and Hill 1979]

Protecting people's self-images, in turn, is one of the most fundamental moral tasks before the state. Thus, when empirical researchers report that people's policy positions and presidential votes reflect "symbolic values" far more than "self-interest," that should be cause for celebration rather than dismay (Sears, et al. 1980).

6.5.3.   Implications for the Economic System

Finally, we might consider how alternative economic institutions affect moral motivation. Here I shall survey very briefly the pos-

10. Again, of course, this depends upon the particular formalisms people choose for partitioning their moral principles off from the mundane world. On some standards, even altruism might be thought to be contaminated, because it contains essential references to the mundane, material components of welfare, albeit other people's welfare. The ethical community-oriented values underlying the voting decision will typically contain equally crucial references to mundane, material components of social life. But this is surely an extreme standard. In our own societies, the background expectation against which seriously held moral principles must stand out is one of people acting in their *own* material self-interest; and actions furthering the

sibilities of moral motives operating uncontaminated in the liberal market, under communal socialism, and under market socialism.

Liberal markets are often accused of having a tendency to corrupt and deprave. As increasingly large areas of human experience pass under the measuring rod of money, they are tainted by it: we bemoan the commercialization of Christmas; we smirk at a *grande dame* hiring a "companion," as if friendship were a service to be contracted for in the same way as trash removal; and so on. Even more important, however, the market is accused of corrupting public morals and "depleting the moral legacy" (Hirsch 1976). This has been a continuing theme. "Political arguments for capitalism before its triumph" in the seventeenth and eighteenth centuries focused upon the tendency of commerce to gentle all passions, virtuous as well as vicious (Hirschman 1977). Montesquieu (1748, bk. 20, chaps. 1, 2), for example, concedes,

> Commercial laws . . . improve manners for the same reason that they destroy them. They corrupt the purest morals . . . . We see that in countries where the people move only by the spirit of commerce, they make traffic of all the humane, all the moral virtues; the most trifling things, those which humanity would demand, are there done, or there given, only for money.

And Montesquieu himself claims no originality for the observation, attributing it to Caesar's *Gallic War*.

The corrosive effects of markets on public morals—or community spirit, friendship, Christmas, and so forth—are best understood as reflecting the pollution of seriously held moral principles. Anything we take seriously—be it morality or friendship—must be set apart from ordinary life. Markets destroy all those cherished values by breaking down the barriers, trivializing values by bringing them up against the workaday world. Recall Simmel's (1907, 393) observation, quoted above, that in a money economy "the individual significance of different objects" is "degraded through their exchangeability," and Lane's (1978, 19, 22) parallel complaint that the market creates "a culture subtly facilitating a sense that the dailyness of life is all there is to it . . . . The market has desanctified place, commercialized time, certainly altered and weakened the concept of the sacred, and created doubts about the larger purposes which informed daily living."

Socialists sometimes suggest that these failings of the market be remedied through collective consumption arrangements. They hope that shared consumption experiences will induce shared values in

---

material interests of others certainly do stand out sharply against this background. Feeding people may be mundane, if the people concerned are yourself and your family. It is far from mundane if the people concerned are starving strangers.

the community, which can then be governed merely by appeals to those shared moral sentiments. This theme runs through the "Utopian socialists" from Rousseau, Saint-Simon, Comte, and Durkheim to Morris, Tawney, and Titmuss. With everyone living in public housing, being educated at state schools, riding public transportation, and so on, communal spirit will be generated; and, at the same time, market contamination of those noble sentiments is avoided.[11]

However, it is one thing to say—with Rousseau—that all citizens must play common games together, and quite another to say what game that should be. In making this decision, narrowly egoistic sentiments are certain to be aroused. In ordinary economic markets, people can choose to consume any goods they please in any amounts they please. Under a regime of communal socialism, everyone must enjoy identical goods. But, as economists (Olson 1976) are quick to emphasize, not all people derive identical pleasures from identical goods: some want more of it, some less; some want one good, some another. Nevertheless, it is in the nature of public goods—and it is essential to the communal socialist's strategy—that all enjoy identical consumption experiences, so a single public determination of how much to produce must be made. This naturally evokes narrowly egoistic demands from people, not because they expect their votes to be any more decisive on this issue than on any other, but merely because there is unlikely to be any principled basis for making detailed determinations of the appropriate level and composition of public services. These egoistic demands, in turn, naturally contaminate systems designed to generate and evoke strong moral sentiments, driving seriously held moral principles underground.[12] Much as we would like the state to embody our highest moral ideals, it is hard to take such pretensions seriously when it also tries to serve our most base material desires. Collective consumption, then, pro-

11. "The better constituted the State, the more public affairs dominate private ones in the minds of the citizens. There is even less private business, because since the sum of common happiness furnishes a larger portion of each individual's happiness, the individual has less to seek through private efforts" (Rousseau 1762b, bk. 3, chap. 15).

12. Di Quattro (1978, 881) similarly worries that "the step-by-step substitution of public for private goods could very well exacerbate the spirit of egoism and envy. . . . Whether there is a market in goods *or* goods are publicly provided, their distribution proceeds under circumstances of scarcity that lay the basis for a competitive scramble." The text formulates the problem with reference to a vaguely democratic policy which invites citizens to make demands. Those, being predicated upon mundane egoistic desires, will tend to act as moral pollutants. But the problem is only slightly mitigated in authoritarian polities—ordinary egoistic sentiments are aroused and conveyed to planners, even if there are few formal channels for citizen input. The only way to avoid moral pollution here is for mundane demands to be automatically sanctified by the very fact that they have been fed into the social decision machine. This, clearly, is plausible only in the few polities practicing a particularly strong form of "civil religion."

duces just as much moral pollution as does the market and undercuts seriously held moral principles just as badly.[13]

To be set above ordinary reasons for action, moral pollution must first be set apart from them. This may be consistent with using moral incentives to secure compliance with particularly important social policies from time to time. But in governing the full range of day-to-day social affairs, through either markets or collective choice of public goods, mundane considerations inevitably intrude. The remaining possibility is to use moral principles merely to decide the basic structure of society. Rawls (1972; 1977) has accustomed us to regarding "basic structures" as the appropriate subjects for judgments of justice. He comments approvingly upon the impartiality produced when people are asked to make choices so basic that none can foresee how his particular interests might be affected. In a theory of justice, of course, impartiality itself is of importance. In connection with moral pollution, what matters more is that self-interest—and mundane details more generally—must necessarily be set aside in rendering judgments on basic structures. There is no telling what the ramifications of alternative choices might be for your own particular situation; and, besides, each of us has only one vote and is therefore virtually powerless to alter the outcome even if he could calculate his interests precisely. Together, these facts free an individual to choose among basic structures without any narrow, mundane reckoning of their consequences for his everyday life. Those very considerations which would cause moral pollution are eliminated by the very abstract nature of the choice being made.

The trick, obviously, is to create a two-tier decision structure, with the competing claims of material interests being settled on one level and kept out of higher-level discussions of moral principle, which they would contaminate. This is a trick performed particularly well by market socialist arrangements (Lange 1936–37). Ordinary consumer demands, which would pollute any seriously held moral principles with which they came into contact, are channeled through the market. This frees the public (political) arena of contaminants, and people are able to activate their most-prized moral principles without fear of pollution.[14]

13. This seems consistent with experience in the two most famous attempts at using moral incentives, in China and Cuba. The Chinese case (Riskin 1975; V. Shue 1980) involved an appeal to prudential rather than moral motivations. Perhaps the incentives were structured the way they were—toward collective rather than private gratification—as a means of inculcating moral sentiments. But in the first instance, anyway, the appeal was to private rather than public interests. The Cuban case is even more easily dismissed: right from the start, the moralistic rhetoric was accompanied by some pretty strong-arm tactics; and in 1973 Castro abandoned even the rhetoric, conceding "idealistic excesses" (Bernardo 1971; MacEwan 1975ab).

14. The same motivational duality appears, in a slightly different context, in Di Quattro's (1978, 878–79) defense of market socialism.

6.6. Policy Implications:
Protecting the Priceless

This analysis of the structure of moral reasoning, when combined with the analysis of human dignity in chapter 5, yields one particularly important practical precept for policymaking. That is, quite simply, that there is a firm logical foundation underlying the "superstitious" refusal to put a price on everything. It is clearly humiliating for someone to be told explicitly that his life or his rights are "not worth preserving" (cf. Schelling 1981, 44). To spare people such degradation, we establish boundaries fencing off as "priceless" those things which are crucial to a person's leading a dignified existence. This partitioning is crucial for expressing due respect for the "moral worth" of people (Douglas and Isherwood 1978, 59).

Economists sometimes see this point.[15] But more often they curtly dismiss the category of "the priceless" as nonsense. After all, we implicitly impute a value to such "priceless" commodities every time we trade one off for another or for anything else. And such tradeoffs are inevitable, since no sphere of life is totally isolated from every other: kidney machines are for sale, even if lives per se are not; television time is for sale, even if votes per se are not. Thus, economists usually conclude that we are simply fooling ourselves when we claim to regard some goods as "priceless," and that only good can come from getting these implicit value judgments out into the open.[16]

Certainly economists are right to emphasize that the notion of anything's being truly priceless is little more than a polite fiction. What they miss, however, is the importance of such fictions in preserving people's dignity and self-respect. In personal life, we show grandfather respect by allowing him to pretend he is the patriarch to be consulted in all matters, even if we consistently decline to put his advice into practice; and we show our maiden aunt respect by allowing her to pretend she is still the gay young debutante she has long ceased to be. Similarly in social life, we show people respect by refraining from putting an explicit price on their heads, even if we

15. Okun (1975, 19), for example, comments insightfully, "Once political and civil rights are seen as integral to human dignity, it becomes clear why they shouldn't be bought or sold for money. If someone can buy your vote, or favorable draft number, or a contract for your indentured service, he can buy part of your dignity.... By prohibiting your sale of rights, society is [guaranteeing]...your creditors cannot make you part with your dignity."

16. This is, for example, the whole thrust of cost effectiveness studies. It is manifestly unjust and inefficient to refuse to spend more than $0.1 million to prevent a traffic fatality when we are willing to spend $2 to $5 million to prevent premature death from other causes (Okrent 1981, 143; Weinstein and Stason 1977).

cannot help doing so implicitly. Obviously, the reality is far better than the illusion, and should be pursued wherever possible. But where it is not possible, the polite fiction might just be enough to protect people's self-respect.

Excuses

7 Impossibility as an Excuse for Inaction

Public officials start out proudly championing bold new policy initiatives. They end up, as often as not, sheepishly apologizing for their or their policy's failures. A debate inevitably follows. But it typically focuses on narrow questions of whether, in the circumstances, those excuses are appropriate, acceptable, and adequate. There is surprisingly little general critical discussion querying the forms and limits of political excuses as a whole.

The real limits of that genre of debate become most apparent once we transcend the details of specific cases. Three of the most important excuses seem to be couched in terms of impossibility, risk, and uncertainty. The latter two are taken up in subsequent chapters. This chapter considers the most fundamental constraint of all, impossibility, and the excuses to which it gives rise. I shall, in due course, largely dismiss all of these excuses; but it is important to emphasize at the outset that each contains the kernel of a valid plea. They would pose no danger unless they did. The task of these chapters is, therefore, to identify this valid core and to isolate it from the multitude of impermissible extensions.

7.1. Rigging the Feasible Set

"The plea of impossibility offers itself at every step, in justification of injustice in all its forms," complains Bentham (1827, vol. 7, 285). Yet it is easy to see why the plea works. As moral philosophers say, "ought implies can." There is no point in antecedently exhorting someone to perform impossible feats, or in retrospectively blaming him for failing to do so (Hare 1951; Montefiore 1958). In policy analysis, the analogous principle holds that "politics is the art of the possible" (Wildavsky 1966; Huitt 1968; Meltsner 1972; Moynihan 1973; Majone 1975; MacRae and Wilde 1979, chap. 6). Perhaps we should describe the optimum, even if it is unattainable, just so policymakers will recognize it if they ever see it (Morley 1974, 116; Pigou 1935, 10; Friedman 1953, 264; Philbrook 1953). And perhaps we should engage in a little "technology-forcing" *à la* the Clean Air Amendments of 1970, setting goals slightly beyond our reach just so we do not, "from want of energy, or of self-reliance, or of imaginative power, underrate our own capacity and overestimate the difficulties" (Lewis 1852, vol. 2, chap. 22, sec. 25; cf. Flathman 1972, chap. 2, and Heal 1973, 20). But basically all agree that policymakers are not to be held responsible for outcomes outside their power to control.

The trouble is that the impossible and the inevitable do not come prelabeled in our social world. We can never know what really was possible, except in the trivial sense that whatever actually happened must ipso facto have fallen within the feasible set. Without some understanding of what might have been, however, we are incapable of evaluating the social order as it is. "People do not know whether to congratulate themselves for what they have achieved given the obstacles they have faced or condemn themselves for having squandered the possibilities they have had" (Geertz 1977, 245). Those contemplating political action, not knowing what is possible, do not know what to expect or demand. It is a mark of realism, perhaps of sanity itself, not to resist the inevitable or to insist upon the impossible—but only if what is said to be inevitable really is inevitable, and what is said to be impossible really is impossible. Often they are not. One of the more pernicious political stratagems consists in the manipulation of perceptions of possibilities, thereby artificially constraining social choices.

A particularly good illustration of the manipulation of perceptions of possibility for political advantage came during planning of the American reaction to the 1962 Cuban missile crisis. Initially, the president and his advisers all favored a "surgical" air strike, attacking only the Soviet missile installations. "What effectively foreclosed that option was the Air Force's assertion that the air strike the leaders wanted could not be carried out with high confidence of success." The Air Force claimed it could guarantee only 90 percent effectiveness. That made a "surgical" air strike too risky to contemplate. But, as Allison (1971, 124) states bluntly, "That 'fact' was false."

Were we being charitable, this false report of Air Force

capabilities might be attributed to a simple misreading of handbooks, leading to the belief that Soviet MRBMs were more "mobile" than they actually were. But a more sinister interpretation is equally plausible. On this account, military leaders deliberately lied to the president, hoping to cast his options in such a way as to force him to choose their most-preferred alternative, viz., massive military action to overthrow Castro.[1] The scheme backfired. When forced to choose, the president opted for a modest blockade rather than a massive air attack. But the nature of the scheme seems clear. The Joint Chiefs hoped that, by artificially limiting the president's perceptions of his feasible alternatives, they could force him into a more dramatic military adventure than he would have chosen had he perceived his options correctly.

Here as elsewhere, the effect of declaring some option impossible is to remove it from consideration. Hobbes (1651, chap. 6) tells us "There is no *deliberation* . . . of things known to be impossible, or thought so, because men know or think such deliberation vain." Inspection of the U.S. Senate agenda confirms this. "There are many problems—such as decay of central city housing stocks—that can be documented easily but attract little serious debate for years because no . . . feasible solution is thought to exist" (Walker 1977, 431). Most politicians and most citizens implicitly accept the advice of Joseph Heller's (1979, 198) thinly disguised Texas governor: "The first time I left our dirt farm for the great big city of Austin . . . my momma, bless her heart, instructed me, 'Don't make personal remarks, never tell a hostess you enjoyed yourself, don't force anything mechanical, never kick anything inanimate, and don't fart around with the inevitable'" (cf. Wildavsky 1979, 42). The inevitable and the impossible must be taken as given. What lies in between constitutes the appropriate scope for choice and efforts at change.

Possibilistic reasoning limits not only our range of choices but even our desires themselves. As Wildavsky (1979, 216) observes, "feasibility is part of desirability." It is not just a matter of keeping our choices within the possibility frontier, while casting wistful glances at all the lovely options unfortunately falling on the other side. Rather, objectives beyond the possibility frontier are forgotten

1. "From the perspective of the military planners, the issue was straightforward: elimination of the Communist Cuban thorn. Their problem was to guarantee that the job would be done successfully. The Services had prepared and coordinated a contingency plan for military action against Castro . . . that . . . deeply reflected the lesson that these organizations had learned from the Bay of Pigs: the Kennedy administration could not be trusted to do what was required in the heat of military action. When *these* leaders wanted military action, they would have to sign on to a plan that called for massive military force . . . . Thus, the 'air strike' option served up by the Air Force called for extensive bombardment of all storage depots, airports, and . . . the artillery batteries opposite the naval base at Guantanamo" (Allison 1971, 124–25).

altogether. "What one wants, or is capable of wanting, ... importantly rests on a sense of what is possible" (Williams 1973, 147). This is the basis of Arrow's (1963, 73) Independence of Irrelevant Alternatives condition: "Tastes for unattainable alternatives should have nothing to do with the decision among the attainable ones; desires in conflict with reality are not entitled to consideration." And, in practice, they are rarely given much, if any.[2]

Keeping aspirations pretty well in line with possibilities is reasonable enough where the possibility constraints are objective and unalterable features of the world. Sometimes they truly are both. More often they are neither. What is now impossible could have been otherwise with prudent action. We are not impressed by the plea of American auto manufacturers for exemption from emission control standards which, after years of refusing to research alternative engine designs, they now find impossible to meet.[3] Constraints of an actor's own creation can hardly count as genuine limits on his possibilities because they are not, in a broader dynamic sense, unalterable (Bentham 1827, vol. 7, 285; Geertz 1977, 247; Goodin 1977). Much the same is true of the many nonobjective constraints to which pleas of mere political (as opposed to genuine technical) impossibility typically refer.[4]

2. "What we establish as policy objectives we derive in large part from an inspection of our means. It was once an American policy objective to be able to fight any war without serious damage to life and property within the continental United States; it is no longer an objective. The objective shifted with the shift in possible means . . . . We can aspire to fly without mechanical aids, to eliminate boredom, to prevent pain and the occasions for it, to bring democracy to the Soviet Union next year, or to safeguard the atmosphere while simultaneously testing nuclear weapons. None of these is our policy objective, however, because we have neither means to its achievement nor any likely prospect of finding them" (Braybrooke and Lindblom 1963, 93).

3. The Clean Air Amendments of 1970, which set the emission standards, provide in Section 202 that the administrator of the Environmental Protection Agency "shall grant . . . suspension [of the standards] only if he declares that . . . all good faith efforts have been made to meet the standards established." In reluctantly granting such a suspension in April 1973, William Ruckleshaus remarked, "If Congress had provided me with some sanctions short of . . . , in effect, closing down that major corporation [Chrysler], my finding on good faith may have been otherwise" (Lynn 1980, 332).

4. Walker's (1977) study of three pieces of innovative safety legislation in America finds that only one—auto safety—was preceded by recent technical breakthroughs. Passage of mine and occupational safety legislation is better explained in straightforwardly political terms. When economists talk of "scarce resources," they are usually talking of material resources (Little and Mirrlees 1974, chap. 3). But even they sometimes defer to political obstacles. Discussing project evaluation in developing countries, Sen (1972, 486) remarks sympathetically that "the planner . . . is part of a political machinery and is constrained by a complex structure within which he has to operate . . . . The limits of a planner's effective control depend on his position *vis-à-vis* the rest of the Government as well as on the nature of the political, social and economic forces operating in the economy." Samuelson (1950) is willing to go so far as to adjust his calculations of real national income to take account of the political impossibility of certain redistributions of income in some countries.

Options that are deemed politically impossible drop off the agenda in just the same way as do technically impossible ones. This is particularly clear in Schilling's (1962, 96–98) discussion of U.S. defense budgeting. "The area of... choice is," he writes, "closely limited by the prevailing climate of opinion regarding desirable and possible defense budgets. All figures outside these limits, in either direction, are rejected out of hand as manifestly undesirable, infeasible, or just plain inconceivable." The perceived impossibilities that constrain choice here, however, are political rather than technical. The "climate of opinion" which circumscribes possibilities merely "defines... the areas of agreement and the areas of possible agreement and therefore of fruitful conflict.... It is here that the effort can be made to argue, fight, and bargain for particular goals and programs with some prospect of success." Objectives falling outside this range of politically respectable opinion are treated just as those falling beyond the "real" possibility frontier. "Outside of these limits... voices may be raised in support of goals and programs. But these will be voices in the policy wilderness. As in the case of the Alsop brothers with their December 1948 columns urging higher taxes and a larger defense budget, they will be advocating alternatives in support of which no effective political consensus is possible," and hence they will be disregarded (Schilling 1962, 96–98).

This case is unusual insofar as the source of the impossibilities was clearly specified and blatantly political. More typically, "impossibility" is rendered as a summary judgment with little explanation of the reason why.[5] Such sketchy explanations as are offered usually aim at deceiving people into believing that the constraints are objective ones. The word *impossibility* itself somehow suggests that the constraints lie in the fabric of the universe. Logically, "unwilling" is sharply distinct from "unable." Insistently using the latter term when we really mean the former is a crass attempt at shifting responsibility from people onto things.

One of the more devious methods of conjuring up illusions of objective impossibility is to talk of the "timeliness" of particular political reforms. It is understandable that people fall for the ruse. References to the demands of time seem to point to an objective natural ordering: time marches on, relentlessly and at its own pace; and accepting that constitutes the "reality principle" par excellence. Ali, refusing to surrender the heavyweight crown although at age

5. In his *Handbook of Political Fallacies,* Bentham (1824, chap. 3) identifies the Procrastinator's Argument—"Wait a little, this is not the time"—and observes that typically it "is made without any proof being offered of its truth, such as, for instance, the lack of information, or the need of some preparatory measures."

thirty-six his "time" had clearly passed, is seen to be living an illusion that is sure soon to be shattered. The flow of time must be taken as an objective given, it would seem. Its constraints truly and objectively restrict our options.[6]

That, anyway, is the image politicians hope to conjure up when saying that "the time is not right" for some reform. Actually, all notions of "timeliness" are, of necessity, socially constructed and socially manipulated. Sorokin and Merton (1937) emphasize this in their early analysis of "social time." Roth (1963) provides vivid illustrations from his study of tuberculosis hospitals. Patients there use temporal benchmarks as "signposts of progress" to gauge how near they are to eventual discharge. Usually the whole process takes about a year, with various intermediate steps coming at standard points along the way. But when a member of staff falls ill and is processed out in approximately half the normal time, it becomes clear that there are no objective medical bases for the prevailing timetable norms. Instead, they merely reflect "hospital routines . . . organized primarily for the convenience of staff, and the urgencies of the patients must be worked into staff-oriented schedules" (Roth 1963, 31–33). So too in politics, notions of "timeliness" typically reflect little more than the political bargaining routines organized for the convenience of politicians.[7]

The crucial difference between objective, technical impossibility and political impossibility is just this. Options falling outside the technical possibility frontier truly do not bear discussing—desirable though they may be, there is nothing we can do to achieve them. Options that are merely politically infeasible, in contrast, certainly do bear discussing. We have the technical capability to implement such choices—all we lack is the will to do so. And if these options really are optimal then we should invest considerable effort in trying to muster the will to do what is right. Basically, this just amounts to recognizing the possibility that "political leadership"—a much-neglected notion in policy studies (Axelrod 1977, 432)—"can create new environments of acceptability" (Rein 1976, 163). If leaders do not exercise this possibility, then the political constraints on them are ones of their own making, and can no more excuse their inaction

6. The same is true of talk of the "political climate" constraining action (Schilling 1962, 96; Heclo and Wildavsky 1974, chap. 1). That, too, alludes metaphorically to an objective, natural constraint: we have to take the weather as given; nobody can change the climate. (Or so we always thought!) But, of course, political climates are human contrivances very much within people's power to change.

7. Whereas in the TB hospital the manipulation of time only delays action, in politics it can kill it completely. "Time," Cornford (1908, 16) writes in his guide for young academic politicians, "is like the medlar; it has a trick of going rotten before it is ripe." For examples from Britain and America, see Goodin (1982).

than can Chrysler's refusal to undertake research into alternative automotive design excuse its failure to comply with emission standards.[8]

Braybrooke and Lindblom (1963, 93–94) observe that "'Impossible' often means no more than 'prohibitively costly.' When, for example, we say that it is impossible to eliminate automobile accidents, we mean that most people would view the elimination of automobiles, which is the best possible method of eliminating automobile accidents, as too great a sacrifice or cost." But, of course, there is no objective standard of what is "too great a sacrifice." The putative impossibility here resides merely in the preferences and values of people who judge the convenience of the private automobile to be worth quite a few lives. Here, unlike the case of technical impossibility, there is something to argue about. There is a clear, practical purpose to be served by demanding road safety, and by shaming those unwilling to bear reasonable costs to assure it. The "impossibility" can be lifted simply by persuading others that they have assigned a perversely low value to lives lost on the roads.

The conclusion is, therefore, that we must distinguish various sorts of impossibilities. There are *real* constraints, which are objective and unalterable, and which we must respect. Then there are self-imposed and political constraints, which merely reflect a failure of will or of planning to create future opportunities. These can hardly excuse inaction. But manipulative politicians do their best to blur the distinction, passing off self-imposed impossibilities for real ones. Those taken in by the ruse drop demands for policies which are both desirable and objectively feasible. They succumb to another's will without ever realizing it, which is the essence of political manipulation (Goodin 1980).

7.2. Objections to Possibility-Rigging

There are many reasons to object to this manipulation of people by rigging their perceptions of possibilities. The most fundamental protests its effect upon people's freedom and rationality and, ultimately, upon their self-image and self-respect.

8. Political leaders who have tried and failed to persuade others might be partially excused. But "it has always to be remembered that few excuses get us out of it *completely:* the average excuse, in a poor situation, gets us out of the fire into the frying pan" (Austin 1956–57, 4). In the case of the political leader, his failure is excused completely only if he continues to take advantage of whatever opportunities that arise to persuade people of the proper course of action. Continually haranguing people is not required—that is probably not the most effective persuasive strategy— but neither is he permitted to let the matter drop altogether.

Someone whose range of available options is artificially restricted obviously suffers a loss of freedom in some sense. Partridge (1968, 222–23), for example, regards "knowing what alternatives there are and . . . knowing that some of them might be capable or worthy of being pursued" as a crucial aspect of the "positive side of liberty." And Abell (1977, 10) considers someone more "autonomous" the wider the set of feasible options he sees himself as having. Here I shall argue that manipulating perceptions of possibility infringe a person's freedom not just in *some* sense but in the most important sense.

Traditionally, we are offered two alternative models of "freedom." The first model views man as, in essence, a *powerful* creature. His freedom consists in his capacity to act in and upon the world; and unfreedom for him consists in constraints upon his actions. The second model views man as, in essence, a *willful* creature. His freedom consists in willing and working his will upon the world; and unfreedom for him consists principally in interferences, most often of a psychological nature, with his will. A third model, which I prefer, views man as, in essence, a *rational* creature. His freedom consists in reflection and choice; and for him unfreedom consists basically in interferences with his rational choices.[9]

This third model best captures those aspects of freedom which are most tightly bound up with a person's self-image and self-respect which, as chapter 5 above has shown, are of prime ethical importance. What the third model identifies as the paradigm case of unfreedom looks, on this criterion, clearly worse than the paradigm cases identified by the other two models. When we compare the third model with the first, the question is simple: which is worse, force or fraud? The individual himself may well mind force more—it, by definition, must be painfully apparent whereas fraud, if done well, is never noticed. But from the viewpoint of the omniscient observer or of the individual himself once the fraudulent dealings become apparent, I think it would be clearly worse to be tricked than to be overpowered. Having my rational capacities circumvented seems clearly more humiliating than merely having my physical capacities overwhelmed, although the material consequences might be the same in each case. Resentful though I may be if a gang of

---

9. The differences between these models may just be differences in emphasis. No doubt each model could, with sufficient twisting and turning, be made to render conclusions similar to those of every other. Saying "it is just a difference in emphasis," however, is not to suggest that the difference does not matter. In practice, all good things rarely go together—we are forced to trade off one desirable goal for another—and it is the "emphasis" in our theory that helps us distinguish lesser freedoms which should be sacrificed from greater freedoms which should be retained. Thus, "getting the emphasis right" is no trivial matter.

crooks seized my property forcibly, I would be more resentful still if they had tricked me out of it in a crooked card game. Notice, in this connection, that even the law of war legitimates the outcome of a fair contest of force while prohibiting sneaky dealings (surprise attacks, etc.) in the course of such a contest. Thus it seems that circumventing people's rational powers—the paradigm case of unfreedom on the third account—is clearly worse than the first model's paradigm case of simply overpowering them (Goodin 1980, chap. 1).

To establish the superiority of this third model over the second, consider what (if any) objection we might have to manipulating someone whose will is never backed up by rational reflection. Imagine someone who is just a bundle of compulsions. He wills a great many things, but as a result of intrapsychic "switches" thrown by external stimuli rather than as a result of any rational reflection upon the alternatives. He is absolutely at the mercy of his compulsions. Certainly we would rather avoid being responsible for throwing his intrapsychic switches if we could. But this is almost a superstitious reaction, rather like not wanting to step on someone's grave. Since *ex hypothesi* the person concerned is incapable of rational reflection, he is no more capable of "taking offense" at our action than is the cadaver below our feet. Of course, few real people are so utterly at the mercy of their compulsions. The real reason we object to playing on the compulsions of real people is precisely that they are capable of reflecting rationally upon and feeling humiliated by what we have done to them.

Freedom thus seems intimately bound up with rationality. That, in turn, presupposes "first, self-knowledge . . . ; and, second, sufficient knowledge of the world to perceive what alternatives are open to you and which of them are favourable to your true interests" (Santayana 1953, 179). If false perceptions of impossibility have been created, and an individual maximizes over an artificially and unnecessarily truncated feasible set, irrational choices inevitable result. First, and most obviously, an individual misses important opportunities to pursue some of his goals because he (mistakenly) regards them as "impossible." From his own (distorted) perspective, the person is of course behaving perfectly rationally—it would be the height of folly for him to demand what he himself saw was impossible to deliver. But if his perceptions of the feasible set were in error—if some goals he passed over as impossible were in fact within his grasp—he will (from the perspective of the omniscient observer) be guilty of suboptimization. He will have settled for an outcome which he himself regards as worse than some other outcome he could actually have achieved instead.

This mistake has the secondary and probably more important effect of skewing all those goals he continues to pursue. Dropping one goal which he regards (albeit mistakenly) as impossible, he is usually forced to reorder all his other goals. Not only does he fail to pursue one goal he could and should have been able to realize; he also adjusts his other goals accordingly and pursues them differently than he would have done had he correctly assessed the possibility of the first. This follows from the economic theory of second best, mentioned in another connection in chapter 4 above (Lipsey and Lancaster 1956). The second-best state of affairs usually departs in several respects from the first best, rather than being defined by exactly the same characteristics save one. If, for example, my ideal auto is a new silver Rolls, it is more likely that my second choice will depart from that description in all respects (being an antique black Duesenberg) rather than in only one (e.g., a new silver Ford). Whenever we rule out one goal as impossible—mistakenly or otherwise—we usually readjust all our other goals as well.

7.3. Expanding Notions of the Feasible

Expanding and refining our understanding of the possibilities before us is no easy matter. Basically, what is required for overcoming manipulated perceptions is some sort of frame-breaking activity (Goodin 1980, chaps. 2, 3). This can come in any of several forms.

The most dramatic sort of frame-breaking is, of course, a revolution. Routine power struggles are distinguished from revolutionary ones precisely by the range of possibilities they envisage. "In the former the fight, by common agreement, takes place within the borders of the possible; in the latter the fight concerns how these borders should be drawn" (Elster 1978, 50). Even rather routine political squabbles, however, can have revolutionary impacts upon perceptions of possibilities. Mundane "turf disputes" between rival government agencies sometimes open up new policy options whose impossibility we had previously taken for granted (Goodin 1982).

A rather more interesting technique of discovering neglected possibilities involves politicians exercising a "fanciful imagination" (Novitz 1980). The key to March's strategy of "sensible foolishness" is deliberately adopting an attitude of "playfulness," defined as "the deliberate, temporary relaxation of rules in order to explore the possibilities of alternative rules." This, according to March (1972, 426–29), "is a natural outgrowth of our standard view of reason. A strict insistence on purpose, consistency, and rationality limits our ability to find new purposes" or innovative methods of achieving old ones.

Actually, this is a relatively familiar phenomenon. A great many of our more attractive political leaders have been valued for their "creativity" and their ability to produce "novel combinations" through the exercise of a fairly "fanciful imagination." Who, before Franklin Roosevelt, could have conceived of a political coalition embracing southerners, blacks, Jews, and union bosses? Who, before Lincoln, could have united negrophobes and abolitionists in opposition to slavery?[10]

This tradition of creative political eccentrics carries into our own time. The limiting case might be Governor Jerry Brown of California: he opens his cabinet meetings by chanting Buddhist mantras, negotiates his own foreign trade deals independently of the State Department, hopes for California to launch its own spacecraft, and combines countercultural causes such as opposition to nuclear power with suburbanite favorites like property tax relief. Perhaps that is carrying things a bit far. Still, his playfulness seems to be the source of his strength.[11] And that is arguably the same sort of charm that Jimmy Carter exerted in 1976. His appeal lay in the fact that he was an "outsider" uncorrupted by the conventional wisdoms of Washington— he just did not seem to have the ordinary ideas of what things went together in a political program, and the same thing that made him hard to label made him a promising presidential prospect. Inevitably, some promises go unfulfilled—so it was with Carter's. Ultimately, however, such playfulness looks like the most promising path to expanding our notions of the feasible set.[12]

10. This is how Hofstadter (1948, chap. 5) describes the problem facing the Republican Party in the 1850s: "If the Republicans were to succeed in the strategic Northwest, how were they to win the support of both Negrophobes and antislavery men? Merely to insist that slavery was an evil would sound like abolitionism and offend the Negrophobes. Yet pitching their opposition to slavery extension on too low a moral level might lose the valued support of the humanitarians." Lincoln hit upon a formula that would appeal to both: "If freedom should be broken down they might themselves have to compete with the labor of slaves in the then free states—or might even be reduced to bondage along with the blacks! Here was an argument that could strike a responsive chord in the nervous system of every Northern man, farmer or worker, abolitionist or racist: if a stop was not put somewhere to the spread of slavery, the institution would become nation-wide."

11. Broder (1980, 27) explains the success of Jerry Brown in the words of William Scranton III: "He had credibility when he was doing incredible things. When he is trying to be credible, he loses credibility . . . . His first term, he flew in the face of traditional political thinking and forced a kind of new-age outlook . . . . He ran well against Carter [in 1976 primaries] because . . . people saw the boundary being expanded somewhat, and they ran to that. Not because Jerry Brown had the answer, but because they saw an opening . . . . I think a lot of politics is intuitive . . . . A lot of it is off the wall . . . . The times are putting a premium on that, putting a premium on boldness and experiment, and that will continue while these old forces of politics are breaking up and until the new patterns recombine. How they will recombine I don't know. I think for a time, there's going to be very much of that flow that Jerry Brown likes to go with."

12. Of course, "at some point either the playful behavior will be stopped or it will be integrated into the structure of intelligence in some way that makes sense. The suspension of the rules [of ordinary reason] is temporary" (March 1972, 426).

This is, of course, something of a mixed blessing. There are parallel dangers in *over*-estimating the feasible set. Revolutions, especially, are *too* successful in expanding people's sense of the possible. Typically, revolutions are followed by "moments of madness." People suppose that, if overthrowing the old regime was possible, then *anything* must be possible (Zolberg 1972; Geertz 1977, 245). The effects of other mechanisms for increasing our perceived feasible set will doubtless be less dramatic, but all surely run similar risks of an exaggerated sense of the possible.

Perhaps some will say this is a better presumption, to suppose everything is possible until proven otherwise. But this is far from clear. Overestimating possibilities can lead to the same sorts of irrationality as underestimating them. Indeed, the same sorts of political maneuvers might underlie (and the same sorts of political advantages flow from) an exaggerated possibility set as an impoverished one. The most extreme form is, of course, the erroneous assumption that something is not only possible but also inevitable. People are often conned into accepting disagreeable outcomes on the grounds that they are inevitable—i.e., impossible to prevent.

A rather craftier ploy is to suggest that things which are actually quite impossible could really be accomplished. Elster (1978, 51) offers an example:

> Until quite recently no political party in Western Europe could state openly that full employment, economic growth, and stable prices were ends that could not be realized simultaneously within the framework of a modern capitalist economy. All political parties . . . had to state economic impossibilities as political possibilities . . . . Similar problems face the newly liberated countries where political development is more advanced than the state of the economy; here, too, it may be a political necessity to proclaim rates of growth or to promise levels of consumption that are plainly impossible at that stage.

These false claims might just reflect wishful thinking or bad economics. They might equally well form part of a clever manipulative scheme. Often we accept some disagreeable outcomes only as part of a larger package—had we seen that the more desirable components of the package were unattainable, we never would have agreed. By instilling false beliefs about the feasibility of all components of the package, devious politicians might be able to persuade people to bear otherwise intolerable burdens. Thus, increasing people's perceptions of what is possible is a mixed blessing. It is an advantage only if those perceptions are accurate ones. But where unactualized possibilities are concerned, it is always very hard to tell.

8 Risk as an Excuse for Maldistribution

Modern social theory tends to treat risk as a friend to justice. A person who is uncertain of which social position he will eventually occupy is forced to reflect impartially upon the allocation to each, and that assures the fairness of the social institutions he chooses. Of course, if the allocation of people to places really is random, no one *deserves* the fortune or misfortune that ultimately befalls him.[1] The operation of chance is, as Rawls (1972, 32) rightly remarks, "arbitrary from a moral point of view"; distributions dictated by dumb luck are beyond the bounds of moral assessment, neither moral nor immoral.[2] If "competitions of skill ... contain an element of ineluctable mischance" then philosophers advise that "when one encounters such misadventures, he should not complain but should rather suffer them nobly as what they truly are, the slings and arrows of outrageous Fortune" (Day 1977, 83).

1. This might have been thought otherwise in earlier days, when "luck" was described as "providence," as the "beneficent care of God" (Viner 1972; Aubert 1959). Perhaps, as a kind of subliminal carryover from these earlier days, that is why we still tend to regard chance events respectfully.

2. Nozick (1974, 227) effectively sets Rawls (1972, 15) right on this score. Notice how, in both law and morals, chance and luck mitigate if not eliminate responsibility. Sometimes good luck saves people from their own evil intentions, as when a bird strays into the path of a bullet the would-be murderer intends for his victim. Other times bad luck exacerbates intentions that are only slightly nasty, as when you slap the face of someone you did not realize was a hemophiliac, killing him when you meant only to assault him (Feinberg 1970). Bad luck can thus lumber you with some responsibility for outcomes worse than those you intended. But the fact that it was bad luck—that an element of chance intervened—prevents you from bearing as much responsibility as you would otherwise have done for producing that outcome. Had you slapped the face of a known hemophiliac you would stand accused of murder rather than merely of manslaughter.

Perceptions of randomness work, in practice as well as in philosophy, to remove much of the moral pressure from individuals and institutions.[3] Psychologists report that people feel disproportionately more responsible for results that are certain than for those that are just probable consequences of their actions (Tversky and Kahneman 1981). And anthropologists (e.g., Douglas and Isherwood 1978, 41) concur with Merton (1949, 139) that,

> In sociological terms, the doctrine of luck serves the dual function of explaining the frequent discrepancy between merit and reward while keeping immune from criticism a social structure which allows this discrepancy to become frequent. For if success is primarily a matter of luck, if it is just in the blind nature of things, ... then surely it is beyond control and will occur in the same measure whatever the social structure.

This was how the findings of the Jencks (1972) study were received. Its showing that "the causes of inequality in America include a large, irreducible factor of luck ... produced a sociological sigh of relief" (Perelman 1980, 398), because no serious redistribution or institutional reform is required to remedy what is merely the result of the workings of chance.

In another way, however, this analysis of risk and luck goes some distance toward providing a positive justification for existing distributions. While "there is no form of activity ... that does not involve some risks," people often do "have a choice between more and less risky actions" (Feinberg 1980, 114). Naturally, people's tastes for risk-bearing (as for everything else) vary. Some will choose to gamble, while others play safe. Among those who gamble, some win big while others lose heavily. But, in the absence of any strong moral counterarguments, it seems both efficient (Buchanan 1970) and just (Dworkin 1981, 292–304) to let people pursue their preferences and live with the consequences of having done so.

The upshot of his argument is that people *do*, in some sense, deserve their fate. Entrepreneurs who owe their fortunes to inspired

---

Likewise, how much we blame a truck driver for running down a child when his brakes fail depends upon how unexpected the failure of the brakes and the appearance of the child in his path were. If the mechanical flaw were a freak one, undetected in a routine inspection only last week, or if all of his driving were done in an industrial park where he rarely has to brake hard for anything, much less children, he would not be deemed particularly negligent. In law, "a defendant is responsible for and only for such harm as he could reasonably have foreseen and prevented" (Hart and Honoré 1959, 231).

3. Perhaps Merton (1949, 139) is also right that "the doctrine of luck serves the psychological function of enabling [people] to preserve their self-esteem in the face of failure." But such polite fictions are permissible, in the terms of section 6.6, only if that is the best we can do. This chapter argues we can do far better.

risk-taking have more of a claim to their good fortunes than those
who refused to gamble at all (Baumol 1968; Kirzner 1973, 82 ff.).
Conversely, the "hard luck stories" of those who have taken fair
bets and lost evoke far less sympathy than the suffering that comes
to a person through absolutely no fault of his own (Sugden 1982;
Stone 1978). Thus, Kunreuther (1968, 161) concludes that it has been
"inequitable" for the U.S. government to offer blanket assistance to
disaster victims regardless of whatever risks or precautions they
may have taken ex ante; and Veatch (1980, 54) argues that it is both
fair and just "if persons in need of health services resulting
from . . . voluntary risks are treated differently from those in need of
the same services for other reasons."[4]

This has some important implications for how policymakers approach the regulation of risky activities. It suggests that laws should
be framed in such a way as to facilitate the taking of risks by those
who want to do so, while protecting those who do not. The latter are
insulated from the consequences of others' risky behavior by the law
of torts, and from the caprice of fortune by insurance schemes. For
the rest, the legal doctrine of the "assumption of risk" permits
"those who like risk to trade on their taste" (Posner 1972, 73).

Such, I shall argue, is an inadequate response to the real problems
posed by social risk. The first and most obvious objection is, of
course, that pure luck does not play nearly as large a role in social
life as this suggests.[5] But even if it did, letting people take whatever
risks they want invites errors in judgment and biases in distributions.
Furthermore, the protections notionally available to the risk-averse
are both inadequate and biased. Notions of risk thus fail to excuse
the existing maldistribution of social resources and rewards. In the
course of this chapter, I shall suggest a more satisfactory strategy for
the thoroughgoing regulation of social risks which may help remedy
those iniquities.

8.1. Errors in Individual Risk Judgments

When saying we will respect people's risk preferences and the
choices to which they give rise, we are implicitly counting on people
to make proper assessments of (1) the probabilities, and (2) the pains

4. The bulk of Veatch's (1980) paper is, however, devoted to demonstrating how
few risks are truly voluntary, and that the "different treatment" in view is usually just
charging risk-takers higher fees for treatment or insurance.

5. Notice, for example, that in the study of Jencks, et al. (1972) "luck" is just the
residual variation that cannot be accounted for by any other factor in the analysis.
Since the study contains no measures of such immensely important factors as "effort" and "motivation," the impact of luck is certain to be very considerably over-
stated.

and pleasures of all the various possible outcomes of the gamble. There are reasons for doubting their ability to determine either to a tolerable degree of accuracy.

8.1.1. Errors in Assessing Probabilities

People are undeniably poor probability assessors, wildly exaggerating some risks while recklessly downplaying others (Slovic, et al. 1981). These errors, furthermore, demonstrably lead them to compromise their interests in risky choices. Although seat belts have been conclusively shown to prevent a great many traffic fatalities, for example, few people voluntarily use them regularly. And the reason seems to be that they grossly underestimate their chances of crashing, in most cases by a factor of ten or more (Arnould and Grabowski 1981, 34).

These errors arise from limitations in the techniques people have available for assessing probabilities. They can acquire information about hazards through either experience or study. For the most part, people tend to act as intuitive probability assessors, relying upon experience to guide them. That may work well enough where small and frequently recurring choices are concerned—as, for example, in ordinary consumer purchases. But it fails even for guiding purchases of consumer durables, which are replaced infrequently—you have spent so much money on your new car that, even if it is a lemon, you are probably stuck with it for some time (Arrow 1973a). Similarly where risks of grievous injury are concerned, "experience is a costly teacher" on which we would not want to rely (Cornell, et al. 1976, 465).

Where low-probability events are concerned, experience is a particularly unreliable teacher. Few of us are intimately acquainted with the medical histories and lifestyles of the thousands of people it would take to infer with confidence the risks of even a rather substantial health hazard, such as smoking. It is "no wonder that a hurricane-zone shopkeeper who has seen only one severe hurricane in 20 years has difficulty making an estimate of the likely future occurrence of damaging winds" (Burton, et al. 1978, 97).

The alternative to trusting experience is formally studying the information on hazards. But it must be recalled that information is costly, and people's resources for acquiring and processing it are limited. Thus it is perfectly understandable that, even when governments or consumer associations make safety information freely available, people make less use of it than they might (Cornell, et al. 1976, 465–67). This tendency is especially apparent with respect to low-probability outcomes. People may choose to ignore these altogether simply "because they have more pressing things on their minds. The many decisions that have to be made during their daily routine tend to push these low-probability events near the bottom of a long list where they are not likely to receive any attention" (Kunreuther, et al. 1978, 239; cf. Kahneman and Tversky 1979).

Given the limited time, attention, and resources people can afford to devote to assessing the probabilities of all the hazards facing them, they must adopt various decisional short cuts. It should be emphasized that it is perfectly rational for people to do so, in light of the constraints under which they are operating.[6] But it must also be emphasized that using such short cuts inevitably leads to systematic errors with sometimes serious consequences.

Tversky and Kahneman (1974) categorize these "heuristics" ordinary people use for coping with uncertainty and discuss the "biases" to which they give rise. Their evidence for these generalizations comes predominantly from social-psychological laboratory experiments. The same conclusions are also borne out by examination of geographers' descriptions of how people in various parts of the world cope with the risks of diverse natural disasters. Some of the more important of these are as follows:

1. Gambler's fallacy. Most hazards actually are random, independent events. The probability of their occurring at any time is the same, regardless of the pattern of their past occurrence. Thus, for example, "two floods estimated to have a probability of once in a century took place on the Housatonic River [New England] during the same summer of 1955" (Burton, et al. 1978, 97). Sometimes, however, people try to cope with the uncertainty of hazards by denying this indeterminacy: they try to trace patterns in their recurrence; or, even more often, they think that recent past suffering makes them immune to recurrence in the near future. This fallacy is rather more common in preindustrial societies, being committed by 44 percent of respondents in Malawi discussing flood risks and by 30 percent of Brazilians and 47 percent of Mexicans contemplating drought

6. For example, an omniscient expected utility maximizer would never ignore low-probability events altogether, since even a very low-probability event can (if the costs attached are very high) carry a high expected disutility (Slovic, et al. 1974; Kunreuther, et al. 1978). But, in practice, people can never know which low-probability events carry those very high costs without investigating; and the costs of investigating every unlikely possibility might be extraordinarily high. Thus it could be perfectly rational for expected utility maximizers, as a short cut, to examine only those possibilities with probabilities over a certain threshold. They thereby run the risk of a nasty surprise from a low-probability/high-cost outcome; but they also thereby avoid having all their resources eaten up in the process of acquiring costly and possibly useless information. See more generally Smith (1978).

risks. But even in prosperous communities the gambler's fallacy is often committed in discussing risks of floods (15% on the Rock River in Illinois), earthquakes (15% in San Francisco), drought (17% in Australia), high winds (30% in Boulder), and coastal erosion (53% in Bolinas, California) (Burton, et al. 1978, 99).

2. Availability bias. People tend to judge the probability of an event by the ease with which they can recall some similar event's having occurred in the past. Sometimes this leads to an overestimation of probabilities of sensational hazards. Thus people overstate the risk of dying of snake bite or a grizzly bear attack (Slovic and Fischhoff 1980, 123–24), and they buy flight insurance at rates much less advantageous than they pass up when offered regular life insurance (Eisner and Strotz 1961). Other times, the availability bias leads to underestimation of probabilities of hazards that are hard to envisage because they recur only infrequently. "Men on floodplains," for example, "appear to be very much prisoners of their experience" insofar as "recently experienced floods appear to set an upward bound to the size of loss with which managers believe they ought to be concerned" (Slovic, et al. 1974, 194). Similarly, San Franciscans make a "suboptimal level of adjustment to the earthquake hazard" because most of them had not recently "experienced intense and damaging earthquakes, and thus dismissed the hazard as unworthy of consideration" (Jackson and Mukerjee 1974, 165–66).

3. Anchoring and overconfidence. People tend to fix an initial probability estimate too firmly on the basis of inadequate information, and to cling to it too tenaciously in the face of conflicting evidence. Even trained statisticians often jump to unwarranted conclusions on the basis of small samples, Tversky and Kahneman (1971) show. These estimates then act as "anchors" which are moved only marginally by subsequent experience. Consequently, people persist in their initial errors. This tendency is especially evident in laboratory experiments. A subject is asked an "almanac" question (e.g., how many cars were imported into the U.S. in 1968?). Then he is asked to specify a pair of high and low estimates "such that he believes there is a 98 percent chance that the true answer will fall within the interval." If he perceived his uncertainty correctly, only 2 percent of the true values would fall outside that interval. In fact, 40 to 50 percent of them do so (Slovic, et al. 1974, 195). Replicating this experiment by asking geotechnical engineers questions about dam failures shows that "experts seem as prone to overconfidence as lay people" (Slovic and Fischhoff 1980, 125). Conclusive naturalistic experiments are difficult to devise, but a similar tendency might be reflected in the unrealistically low estimates Florida and Utah fruit farmers persistently offer for the probability of late frosts (Burton, et al. 1978, 98).

8.1.2. Errors in Evaluating Outcomes

Estimating the probabilities of each of the hazards, difficult though that is, is only half the struggle. People must also somehow assess the pains and pleasures they would experience under each possible outcome. This task is, if anything, the more difficult. As chapter 3 has shown, people are just not very good generally at anticipating what their preferences will be far in the future or under radically different circumstances.

This is especially apparent when people are choosing risks. They underestimate the pains they might suffer because they simply cannot imagine the accident's happening *to them*. Subconsciously, people tend to assume that "such things always happen to 'the other guy,'" and they cannot imagine themselves in his shoes. Thus, "even if individuals had adequate data for evaluating the risk, they would be psychologically unable to do so" (Calabresi 1970, 56). The most dramatic demonstration of this tendency comes in an informal poll of Chicago shoppers: they "estimated that if an atomic bomb landed in the 'Loop' it would kill 97% of the residents of Chicago; yet when it came to predicting what they might be doing three days after the bomb fell, more than 90 percent figured that they would be helping to bury the dead or taking care of themselves, only 2% believing that they would have died in the blast" (Burton, et al. 1978, 106). Such refusal to face up to disagreeable possibilities is common. In San Francisco, 78 percent refused even to talk to interviewers about the risks of an earthquake—but "the tone of most such refusals suggested that many people *are* worried about the earthquake hazard but do not allow themselves to think about it" (Jackson and Mukerjee 1974, 163). Deep down, each of us expects to be the one to walk away from a serious auto accident, as proved by the fact that "people are much more likely to carry liability insurance (for injuries 'the other guy' may receive) than personal accident insurance (for injuries they may receive)" (Calabresi 1970, 56).

Ordinarily we are prepared to respect people's preferences if—but only if—they are predicated on a full and vivid awareness of all the alternatives. It is not enough that people know, in some intellectual sense, all the relevant facts. It is also necessary that they *feel* them, that they be able to imagine clearly and vividly what it would be like to live with each of the alternative possibilities. This is precisely what people lack in choosing risks: subliminally, they always assume the worse consequences are reserved for "the other guy"; they never imagine clearly and vividly what it would be like to experience those consequences themselves. Failing to do so, they badly underrate the possible horrors that might come from the risks they choose to run.[7]

There are various tricks for trying to give people an empathetic understanding of what disasters are like. The Tennessee Valley Authority tries "plotting flood heights on photographs of familiar buildings" (Kunreuther, et al. 1968, 250), and the Greater London Council conspicuously displays maps of the city's flood plain in particularly claustrophobic corners of the Underground. But, ultimately, people have no vivid image of a disaster until they or someone they know has lived through one.[8]

Kunreuther's (1978) study of federal disaster insurance is particularly instructive in this connection. By any objective measure, such schemes are wildly undersubscribed: only about half of Americans at risk from earthquakes or floods carry insurance against those hazards, in the latter case despite the fact that rates are subsidized to the tune of 90 percent by the federal government. Kunreuther undertook an extensive survey to find out why the uptake was so low. His principal finding is that knowing someone who suffered earthquake or flood losses is by far the strongest determinant of the decision to purchase insurance. It is, indeed, more than twice as powerful a factor as the next most important one—the level of future damage the respondent expects to suffer (Kunreuther, et al. 1978, 145, 147, 152–53). This suggests that knowing someone who has suffered that kind of loss does not just increase your perception of the probability of loss. It has some further effect—best analyzed, I suggest, as increased awareness of what it would be like should the same (unlikely) event occur to you.

A further anomaly in the analysis of risky choices can be explained in much the same way. The theory of diminishing marginal

7. Economists stubbornly refuse to take this point. Schelling (1981, 47), for example, remarks that "you may have put too low a value on your life, but I don't know why I should feel guilty about that." And Mishan (1969, 172) insists upon pretending that "each person knows his own interest best," even if, "owing either to deficient information, or congenital optimism, a person consistently overestimates his chance of survival." Perhaps it is also difficult to imagine winning very big, just as it is to imagine losing very big. But a brief daydream will give us a pretty vivid picture of at least some of the things we might do with our winnings from the Irish Sweepstakes, whereas a similar exercise gives virtually no insight into what life in a wheelchair might be like. Thus, the perceptual biases are far from symmetrical.

8. This may also explain the risks we seem to believe "a person is entitled to take with his life." Dworkin (1971, 125) nominates "mountain-climbing, bull-fighting, sports-car racing, etc." Notice that in all those cases, the serious enthusiast will have inevitably seen one or two close friends killed by the sport, so he can be presumed to have a vivid awareness of the risks he is running.

utility says a person's utility function should be concave throughout its range: the marginal utility of each increment of gain should be less than the last; or, working in the other direction, the marginal utility of each increment of loss should be more than the last. Experimental psychologists find that this expectation is fully satisfied as far as gains are concerned but, contrary to expectations, people's utility functions are "commonly convex for losses" (Kahneman and Tversky 1979, 263; Swalm 1966). Psychologically, this is understandable: "well-substantiated principles of perception and judgment" suggest that "sensitivity to changes decreases as one moves away" from the familiar status quo (Kunreuther 1978, 182; Kahneman and Tversky 1979). But, understandable though it may be psychologically, this tendency is utterly irrational. It is simply one more manifestation of people's psychological incapacity to judge their own interests accurately in risky situations.

8.1.3. Implications for Policy Analysis

In modern policy analysis, risk preferences figure crucially in attempts at putting a price on otherwise invaluable commodities. The best example is that of human life. "To ourselves and our loved ones, we are precious and irreplaceable and priceless" (Wildavsky 1980, 33). If a person is asked how much benefit a social project would have to produce to justify its causing his own certain death, the sum is likely to be almost infinite. And this is not mere bluff: placed in life-threatening situations, a person often will engage in "desperation bidding," offering "to throw in all he owns" in exchange for scarce medical resources that might save him (Calabresi and Bobbitt 1978, 121).

Policy analysts try to make the problem more tractable by casting the question in probabilistic terms. Instead of asking how much is required to justify an identifiable person's certain death, they ask how much benefit B is required to justify an increase of X percent in a person's mortality risks (Schelling 1968; 1981, 45–46; Mishan 1969; 1971). Multiplying B times X gives us a measure of the value the person imputes to his own life in risk situations. And it is generally a much more "realistic" (i.e., lower) value than he sets when faced with the prospect of certain death.[9]

9. This procedure assumes, quite unreasonably, a linear function for the disutility of increasing probabilities of death. Much observed behavior that seems irrational on that model can be explained perfectly adequately by shifting to a curvilinear model. Parallel with our expectations about diminishing marginal utility in general, it is perfectly reasonable to assume that "the value per life saved depends on the level of the mortality probability being changed, and not just on the increment: the higher the level, the higher the value" (Weinstein, et al. 1980, 393).

In one way, this can be seen as a crass attempt at playing on people's ignorance. If a project is certain to take one statistical life, then whoever that eventually turns out to be will, ex post, have had an interest in demanding an infinite price for his life. He was simply wrong in agreeing ex ante to run the risk for a lower price, although of course he had no way of knowing this until after the uncertainty played itself out (Broome 1978). In another way, however, ignorance of who is to die simply forces a morally laudable impartiality upon our judgments. From this perspective, casting life-and-death questions in probabilistic terms merely performs the same function as Rawls's (1972) "veil of ignorance."

This strategy for pricing the priceless looks far more dubious, however, once we see all the ways in which people's risk judgments can err. What can we infer from the fact that some people are willing to run more risks than others, or that people are willing to run some risks but not others? If it truly meant that people attach different values to the goods at risk (e.g., their lives), then it would be efficient, fair, and just for social decisions to be predicated on "risk markets" evoking those diverse preferences. But notice what else such a difference might mean:

1. it might mean just that people attach different values to the act of gambling;
2. it might mean just that people err to greater or lesser extents in their perceptions of the magnitudes of the risks involved; or
3. it might mean just that people have greater or lesser difficulties in imagining themselves suffering different calamities.

In the latter two cases, it is obviously neither efficient nor fair nor just to let final distributions be determined by such differences. Yet this seems to be precisely how introducing probabilistic considerations works to reduce the price of a statistical death: the less certain people are of who will suffer it, the less easy it is for them to imagine clearly and vividly anyone's suffering it.[10]

Even where the first factor—the differential thrill of gambling—is

10. This also explains the more general tendency to undervalue statistical lives relative to identifiable ones. We are prepared to spend vast sums to rescue the trapped miner, compared with the amount we spend to prevent the marginal traffic fatality next year (Fried 1969). The difference, I suggest, is merely that "on-the-scene reporters" provide painfully vivid details concerning the trapped miner's family, friends, and life situation, whereas traffic victims' identities (and, hence, their life situations) are unknown to us. Thus, we can easily imagine what it must be like for the miner but not for the road casualty.

concerned, it is doubtful how far it should influence our decisions.[11] What is crucial to recognize is that the risk-lover would not actually love for the accident to befall him. If I am willing to run more risks when driving, that may mean only that I worry less ahead of time about the prospect of crashing—it does not necessarily mean that I would feel any less pain in the ensuing crunch of flesh and metal. Traditional decision theory evades this issue by assuming that "all lotteries are resolved instantaneously" (Zeckhauser 1975, 442–43); but in the real world, where they are not, it often seems that precisely this differential evaluation of anxiety and suspense is what marks risk-lovers off from risk-haters. This is still a "difference of tastes" which we might want to take into account, but it would usually be only a marginal consideration. If we assume that the pains and pleasures of suspense are slight in comparison with those of the actual outcomes of the hazardous activities (e.g., the car's crashing), this slight difference between people should shade into insignificance in our overall decision. If we leave the decision to the interplay of people's preferences in risk markets, however, it will inevitably loom large.

8.2. Distributive Biases of Risk Markets

The case for risk markets, as for markets in general, is cast in terms of freedom of choice. In truth, the differences between people in the risks they bear is rarely just the product of their own free choice. Socioeconomic as well as psychological forces impinge (Veatch 1980). Probably the most powerful objection to risk markets is the distributive one: some people are driven by economic necessity to bear bad risks, while others can pick and choose which (if any) risks they will run.

Notice, for example, how workers seem to be prepared to engage in very dangerous activities for relatively little extra remuneration. The average annual bonus for Americans working in hazardous jobs in 1969 was calculated at around $400, implying that workers treat the average industrial injury as being equivalent to a certain loss of between $13,000 and $14,000 (Viscusi 1978). If that sum seems ludicrously low—if it seems incredible that anyone should really be indifferent between the money and the accident—the proper conclusion is not that these workers lack the ordinary fondness for their

11. As Calabresi and Bobbitt (1978, 120–21) observe, "In a risks market, the resource being sold is not the scarce resource itself but a package deal, the scarce resource plus the willingness to gamble. Since the object of the market is to allocate the scarce resource, one may well ask whether . . . this is best accomplished by an allocation according to willingness to buy the package deal."

arms or their lives, or even that they are insensitive to the gamble of losing them.[12] The proper conclusion is, I submit, simply that they need the money very badly. We enact minimum wage and safety laws on the assumption "that anyone who takes an absurdly underpaid or extremely risky job must be acting out of desperation" and that such desperation bidding "should be kept out of the marketplace" (Okun 1975, 21). But we allow slightly more modest forms of it every time we allow someone to be induced to take risks others shun, not because he minds them less but because he needs the money more.

Certainly it is true that the poor run worse risks than the rich and, furthermore, they would prefer to continue living with those risks rather than to divert scarce resources away from their many other urgent requirements (Wildavsky 1980; Schelling 1981, 47–50). But that does not mean that they have thicker skins than the rich—that they are less sensitive to the risks, at some deep level of their preference functions. It means only that their desperate socioeconomic position forces those with even very ordinary preferences regarding risk-bearing to react in some rather peculiar ways.

Being nearer the "disaster" threshold skews the risk behavior of poor people in two ways. First, they can ill afford to take some risks that are objectively "good" ones, i.e., ones promising them relatively secure and high payoffs in the long run and on average. The reason is that the very poor cannot sustain the occasional loss that would be required to let things average out—it would push them below the disaster threshold (Lipton 1968, 332–35). The extreme case of this is, perhaps, the Southeast Asian peasant who insists on continuing to cultivate traditional strains of rice instead of shifting to newer varieties. Although the average yield of the new strain is higher, so too may be the variation from year to year; and if one year's crop is ever insufficient to sustain the peasant family, it will not be around next year to let things average out (Scott 1976; Roumasset 1976, chaps. 1–3). For another example nearer home, reflect upon the fact that "in much of England from the earliest times to the 19th century, peasants held their land in many little scattered plots." This seems "most peculiar": "it appears to reduce output" by 10 to 13 percent; and that is "a strange burden for a community near starvation to assume." Yet such a scattered pattern of land

12. Neither, in this case, does the explanation lie in misperceptions of accident probabilities: "A large number of workers . . . viewed their jobs as being hazardous" (Viscusi 1978, 415). There is also evidence of a correlation, precisely as my explanation would predict, between workers' willingness to take risks and their assets, "although the effect was not as large as we would expect if more appropriate data were available to evaluate the magnitude of this relationship." (Cf. Viscusi 1979.)

holdings can be explained perfectly adequately if we look upon it as an attempt at insuring against disaster. "Within a single English village there was enough variability of yield of land in different locations and under different crops to make it desirable to hold a diversified portfolio of plots" (McCloskey 1976). English peasants could, on average, expect to increase their output substantially by consolidating their fields, just as their Southeast Asian counterparts could do by cultivating "wonder" rice. But, being on the brink of disaster, neither dares take the risk.

Just as being near the disaster threshold causes the poor to pass up good risks, it also sometimes inclines them to accept bad ones. Poor people with a slight surplus tend to risk it on improbable long shots rather than on objectively "better" investments.[13] Whyte (1943, 141) found in "street corner society" during the Great Depression that people shunned reliable returns of savings accounts in favor of the numbers racket, where the odds were heavily stacked against them. The reason he offers is that "the small change [i.e., bank interest payments] would have been dissipated in one way or another, whereas the large amounts occasionally won [on the numbers] have real meaning for the corner boy," who thereby lifts himself out of poverty. Similarly reckless gambling occurs in peasant societies "when a small loss would mean little and a win would move the peasant up one level" (Popkin 1979, 21).

The point is not that the poor run too few risks or too many. Rather it is that, by reason of economic circumstance, they are forced to run *bad* risks. The rich can be more selective about their risks. Since they can afford to sustain a few setbacks in the course of winning big, they will bear risks that look likely to pay off handsomely in the long term; the poor can ill afford losses, however minimal, and must let such opportunities pass them by. When they can afford to gamble at all, poverty drives people to play long shots, hoping against all the odds that a really big win will lift them out of their desperate circumstances.

That the poor endure inferior risks should come as no surprise. Poverty forces people to make do with inferior goods across the board, risks being one among so many others. As Schelling (1981, 48) says to the poor, "You cannot afford to pay as much for anything, including personal safety, as I can, precisely because you are

13. What happens in the third possible case, i.e., if the safety-first strategy is certain to yield a payoff well below the threshold of disaster? Then people grasp desperately at any chance they are offered. Usually this means playing unfavorable odds. Occasionally, however, people in this situation might be forced against their will to take "good" risks they would otherwise have shunned in favor of safety first. Roumasset (1976) finds this is the case with Southeast Asian peasants and "wonder" rice.

poorer." Hence, protesting that the poor bear inferior risks is nothing more, and nothing less, than "a complaint against the social system that some people have harder times in life, reflected in risk, than do others more fortunate" (Wildavsky 1980, 37). That established, economists then go on to suggest that such distributional objections are separable issues, resolvable through the infamous "lump sum transfer."

In a way, that is quite the right response. Objecting to the risks the poor are forced to bear is, essentially, arguing for a redistribution of basic resources. But in another way, that glib response from economists overlooks the way in which notions of risk and luck work (implicitly, and sometimes even explicitly) to sustain our faith in the fairness of whatever outcomes the "distributional lottery" might have thrown up. In truth, of course, everything depends upon just how fair the odds in that lottery are. And objecting that the poor run systematically worse risks than the rich is, in this context, just a way of reminding ourselves that the odds are very far from fair.

8.3. Inadequate Protections

The previous sections have demonstrated the folly of respecting people's risk preferences. That just produces erroneous judgments and distributive biases. Next I shall demonstrate the shortcomings of the two mechanisms traditionally offered to safeguard those who prefer to avoid risks. Neither tort liability nor insurance schemes really provide adequate protection.

8.3.1. Tort Liability

The classic alternative to the caveat emptor doctrine of "letting accident costs lie where they fall" is a doctrine of tort liability, which assigns people responsiblity for the harms they have caused to others. In the old days, the standard was one of strict liability: you were responsible for whatsoever followed from your actions. With the "moralizing" of tort law in the nineteenth century, more sophisticated notions of "fault" were introduced, and under various conditions (compulsion, unavoidable ignorance, etc.) people were excused from responsibility for the consequences of their actions.

Tort remedies are often inadequate because people can evade judgments rendered against them. As individuals, we live in fear of the recklessness of "judgment-proof drivers" who, through bankruptcy or diplomatic immunity, avoid paying for the damage they have done (Calabresi 1970, 58). As societies, we worry similarly about the recklessness of limited liability corporations, since they too can declare bankruptcy when presented with claims for the damage they have done. This problem is only exacerbated by laws further limiting their liability. Perhaps the most notorious is the Price-Anderson Act limiting operator liability for an accident at a nuclear power plant to $560 million, which is only 3 percent of the $17 billion property damage the U.S. Atomic Energy Commission (as it then was) estimated might result from such an accident (Shrader-Frechette 1980, 78–79; Green 1973; Cornell, et al. 1976, 470–75; Okrent and Whipple 1977).

A second reason for doubting that the victim will necessarily collect what is due him under a regime of tort liability concerns the burden and standard of proof ordinarily required to win a judgment. In ordinary civil proceedings, the burden is upon the plaintiff to prove "that a preponderance of evidence substantiates the claim that the damage was the *direct* result of a hazard that the defendant could *reasonably* have prevented" (Cornell, et al. 1976, 471, emphasis added). For some risks, this is easy. The workman injured by a factory machine in a poor state of repair will have little difficulty in proving that he suffered directly from the factory owner's unreasonable negligence. But many cases are less straightforward. Clear, direct causation is difficult to establish where damage is probabilistic rather than certain and several factors contribute to producing the same effect. Cancers, for example, carry no certificates of origin: a worker's lung cancer might have been caused by exposure to carcinogens at works; but it might also have been due to his smoking or his genetic endowment. Under such circumstances of confused causation, damages are not unambiguously attributable to any particular source and hence are often uncollectable (Anon. 1981, 592). Furthermore, negligence is hard to prove if, ex ante, probabilities of harm were either low or uncertain. A defendant will ordinarily be liable for unintentional torts only if he behaved "unreasonably," which means among other things that the harm was not only "foreseeable" but also sufficiently likely for it to have been (on a cost-benefit calculation) worth guarding against (Posner 1972, chap. 4). With many hazards, such as toxic chemicals or low-level radiation, probabilities of harm are typically unknown and, indeed, virtually unknowable from current research techniques. At best, there might be conflicting preliminary reports, some suggesting there is no cause for concern while others warn of real dangers (Cornell, et al. 1976, 471–75; Schultze 1977, 38–39; Cornfield 1977; Nemetz and Vining 1981). But even when there have been some tentative warning signals, tort law would ordinarily deem people not liable for harms unless there had been fairly conclusive evidence ex ante that they would arise.[14]

8.3.2. Insurance

Insurance schemes would seem to be the obvious solution to such problems. With them, there is no need to prove causation, much less responsibility. Victims need prove only that they have suffered losses covered by the terms of their insurance. A victim's reimbursement comes not from those responsible for his losses but rather from others running similar risks who have agreed to pool them with his own. An "insurance fund" is basically just a way for "a large group of people to convert an occasional, large financial loss into a regular, certain, small cost—the insurance premium" (Cornell, et al. 475).

The effectiveness of this as a protection against risk is compromised, however, by the voluntariness of standard insurance schemes. Whether a person insures at all, and how much coverage he purchases, are ordinarily left entirely for him to determine. Section 8.1 has argued that it is folly to rely upon people's risk preferences in this way. Kunreuther's (1978) study of disaster insurance confirms the fears voiced there by showing that people do indeed tend to underinsure, especially against low-probability hazards, even where the possible losses are very large.

Furthermore, insurance is appropriate only to certain sorts of hazards. Their probabilities have to be relatively determinate. The insurance fund would be bankrupted by claims against it unless underwriters could estimate risk probabilities accurately and assess premiums accordingly. Likewise, the risk-spreading logic underlying insurance schemes presupposes that some members of the risk pool are doing well while others sustain losses. Where the risk is of a really widespread disaster, this logic breaks down. There is little point for all the inhabitants of a single river valley to pool their flood risks, since if the dam breaks they are all losers. Some of the most frightening risks we face are fundamentally uninsurable precisely

14. There might be various ways to overcome these problems. One is to ease the standard of proof that the plaintiff must meet; another is to reallocate the burden of proof, making the defendant prove his activities are safe (or that it was reasonable ex ante to suppose they were) rather than making the plaintiff prove they were dangerous. But it may still be difficult to collect in cases of ambiguous causation, as experience with workmen's compensation laws (the model for this approach) suggests (Anon. 1980). Another seldom-discussed option is to rely upon the law of equity rather than the law of torts (Cornell, et al. 1976, 473–74). My own solution is offered in section 8.4 below.

because they pose unknown (and perhaps unknowable) probabilities of really widespread disasters.[15]

Even if insurance could protect us adequately against risks, there would be further questions about the distribution of the protection thus offered. People will naturally be pretty particular about who is admitted to their risk pool. The whole point of joining the pool is to reduce your own risks, which is best accomplished by pooling risks with others running fewer (or, at most, the same) risks as yourself. Those organizing risk pools therefore make fine distinctions between individuals according to the magnitude of the risks they run, and separate pools are set up for each category. "Good drivers" and nondrinkers get cheaper automobile insurance, nonsmokers get cheaper home fire coverage, and so on. Conversely, those who are "bad risks"—who have a family history of cancer, for example— either get no insurance or must pay exorbitant premiums for it. In short, those most at risk, and most in need of protection, are least likely to find insurance available or affordable on the private market.[16]

Indeed, very bad risks may not organize a pool at all. They are, by definition, those who are uncomfortably likely to incur very large losses. They are often also—hardly by coincidence—those who can least afford to sustain such losses. Any one of them would be utterly ruined should disaster strike. Hence he is tempted to insure against it. But if his only option is to pool risks with others equally likely to incur similarly large losses, there may be little point—paying his share of their very large losses may ruin him just as certainly. All that he has accomplished by pooling his risks with theirs is to make this fate more likely, since now it happens not only when disaster strikes him but also whenever it strikes anyone else in his risk pool (Liebow 1967, 216–17).

8.3.3. The Problem of Compensatability

Both tort and insurance schemes try to protect people from unwanted risks by offering to compensate victims for their losses. The

15. The partial remedies suggested by Kunreuther, et al. (1978, chap. 10) and Lave (1968, 521–22), such as mandatory insurance and government reinsurance, can be easily blended into the overall solution I propose in section 8.4 below.

16. This might be partially overcome through a policy of "assigned risks," legally compelling insurance companies to offer coverage to individuals who would be unable to find protection on the open market, as now happens with "bad drivers." But the premiums charged for this coverage by private underwriters would typically be very high, reflecting the high probability of having to pay out on the policy.

only difference comes in who makes the payment, the tort-feasor or the underwriter. There are serious doubts, raised above, over whether either scheme can really guarantee that payments would actually be forthcoming in all cases. There remains a more fundamental question, however: even if the payments are made, can they completely put right the victims' losses? Sometimes, at least, it seems that they cannot. There are some things which not only are irreplaceable but for which also no close substitutes exist.[17] Neither tort nor insurance schemes can offer adequate protection against the wide range of risks—of loss of life or limb, genetic damage, or environmental deterioration—for which there can be no adequate compensation, either in cash or in kind.

Economists concede that "theory is lacking for the large class of commodities that are essentially unique or irreplaceable (commodities for which there are no market substitutes) such as family snapshots, the family pet, good health, the life of a beloved spouse or child, etc." Preliminary inquiries, however, suggest that insurance markets will operate very differently for those goods, that for example "a rational individual, risk-averse with respect to lotteries on wealth, will typically not fully insure an irreplaceable commodity and may even choose to bet *against* losing it" (Cook and Graham 1977, 143). Zeckhauser (1975, 454) powerfully develops a similar point by reference to the example of a woman facing the risk of breast cancer. Suppose she is willing to spend $5,000 for medical treatment to reduce the risk of cancer from 10 percent to 5 percent. Following the methodology described (and criticized) in section 8.1.3, we can infer from this that the value of a healthy breast to her is $100,000. Suppose now that she is offered actuarially fair insurance, each premium dollar buying $20 of coverage. Does it necessarily follow that she should pay another $5,000 for coverage worth the full $100,000 value of the breast? Certainly not, because the money will not restore the breast. Zeckhauser concludes that "it would be quite rational for her to insure no more than the medical expenses" of the mastectomy. Where monetary compensation cannot fully put losses right, insurance cannot completely ameliorate risks.

The same is true of tort actions. When the widow of an auto accident victim secures judgment against a negligent auto manufacturer, the monetary damages—however large—hardly constitute

17. The existence of close substitutes makes us indifferent to the loss of goods that are themselves irreplaceable. Cummings and Norton (1974), for example, argue that we need not worry overly much about irreversible damage to a unique natural landmark because we can always build new recreation areas that serve the same function. To argue against such destruction, Fisher, et al. (1974) must reply that man-made parks are not really a close substitute for natural landscapes.

complete compensation for her loss. She is compensated as fully as she can be with money—for her husband's lost earnings, and so forth—just as the breast cancer victim arranges to collect medical expenses from her insurance company. Neither, however, is truly full compensation for the loss, so neither insurance nor tort schemes have succeeded in fully ameliorating the risks.[18]

8.4. Collective Control of Social Hazards

All these arguments combine to undermine the conventional wisdom on the question of risk. We cannot, as this wisdom seems to suggest, simply let people take their own chances, and put whatever distributive anomalies that arise down to plain bad luck. Doing so would play on people's risk preferences, which are likely to be mistaken. Furthermore, we must recognize that *letting* some people run risks amounts to *making* others do likewise, on less advantageous odds. Those already advantaged get to take good risks which will, in all probability, compound their good fortunes. The destitute are forced to take chances which will, in all probability, only compound their misery. And these effects are, if anything, exaggerated rather than ameliorated by traditional strategies for protecting against risk. What is clearly needed is some collective intervention to restrict the risks themselves. In deciding how best to accomplish this goal, we must distinguish risks threatening damage that cannot be put right from those whose harms are compensatable.

8.4.1. Risk Tax for
Compensatable Harms

The easier case is, obviously, where people actually can be compensated for their losses. Then the only problem for policy is to make sure that all the externalities are internalized, i.e., that costs are brought home to those who create them. That is basically what tort law tries to do. But, as section 8.3.1 has shown, it is not altogether successful where causal connections are unclear and harm is merely probabilistic. Schultze (1977, 39) offers an example:

18. This explains Nozick's (1974, 66) seemingly paradoxical observation that there are "some things we would fear, even knowing we shall be compensated fully for their happening." If we really were *fully* compensated, and if compensation were swift and certain, this would make no sense: by definition, "full" compensation leaves us as well off after the event as we would have been had it never occurred, so there is nothing to fear from it. As I have argued before, "The only way to make sense of intuitions that such cases might arise is to say that those are occurrences for which one can never be fully compensated" (Goodin 1976, 81).

Spending twenty-five years exposed to asbestos fibers at the workplace . . . might raise the probability of lung cancer from 0.03 to 0.04, an increase of 33 percent. Ideally, . . . the employer should be liable to pay every worker contracting lung cancer one-quarter the value of the damages thereby incurred. But in the courts one is either liable or not liable. Legal findings of liability are not suited to probabilistic situations.

Both justice and efficiency can be produced in such situations through the device of a "risk tax." The first step is to determine how much would be required to compensate victims for such harms, should they occur.[19] The second is to determine the marginal increase in the probabilities of such harms that is attributable to the activities of each agent.[20] On the basis of these two factors, a "risk tax" is then assessed against those who create hazards equivalent to the full expected value of the social costs of their activities.[21] This provides an incentive—and, assuming we have done the sums correctly, an optimal one—for them to reduce their risks and thereby their taxes. But contrasted with the more orthodox regulation-and-enforcement technique, it does so through an admirably "loose law" leaving those most directly involved to choose precisely how they will reduce their hazards. It is perfectly conceivable that, even within the same industry, worker injuries might be best reduced through better machinery in one factory, through better lighting and ventilation in another, and through better employee training in still another (Smith 1974; Schultze 1977, 56; Nichols and Zeckhauser 1977; Okrent and Whipple 1977).

Half the problem of justice, construed as internalizing externalities, is solved by taxing people according to the risks of harm they create. The other half—compensating those who suffer as a result of those risks—remains. Where the harms are directly attributable, as in the case of industrial accidents, this is a simple matter of paying compensation directly to those who are harmed as a result of the risky activities being taxed. Where the risks are statisti-

19. If we recall the discussions in chapter 3 and section 8.1.2 above, this must be a sum that reflects what their post-harm preferences would actually be rather than just their ex ante anticipations of them.

20. Where these probabilities are uncertain, as they often are, it seems prudent to err on the high side. Even then, we may underestimate them and find ourselves paying out more in compensation than was paid in through the risk tax. At that point, it is the job of the government as ultimate underwriter to make up the difference, through general fund financing in the first instance but recouping the losses wherever possible through surcharges on those who created the risks.

21. The alternative to taxing people on the risks as they create them is to assign everyone involved "joint and several, strict and continuing liability" for harms that eventually result, as a *Harvard Law Review* note suggests for chemical waste disposal (Anon. 1981). The trouble with that is that by the time the damage appears the individuals or firms may no longer exist.

cal ones only, and we cannot identify particular agents as the causes of harms suffered by particular other individuals, the task is more difficult. We want to use the risk tax to benefit those who suffer the risks, rather than merely treating it as general fund revenue (cf. Okrent and Whipple 1977, 25). Furthermore, we do not want just to divide the funds equally among all those at risk who have suffered—in the case of the lung cancer victims who inhaled asbestos at work, for example, we do not want to give all of them one-quarter compensation (cf. Anon. 1981, 600–601). That overcompensates those who would have contracted cancer anyway, and undercompensates those who would not. In individual cases, of course, it is impossible to tell which is which. But the distinction is clear enough in aggregate statistics, and we would like our compensation system to be sensitive to it. One way to assure full, just compensation in such circumstances might be this: everyone eligible to draw compensation from the risk tax pool would be required also to carry mandatory insurance, through the government, against their normal "background risk" of suffering similar harms. This supplemented by the risk tax paid by those have added to that background level of risk, would enable us to compensate everyone for his full losses.

8.4.2. Prohibition of Noncompensatable Harms

The risk tax strategy works by removing all doubts that people will receive adequate compensation for the consequences of others' risky behavior. But that crucially presupposes that their losses are ones for which they really can be compensated. Often this is not the case, either because it is impossible to pay them an adequate sum (section 8.3.3) or because it demeans them to try (section 6.6). The appropriate strategy for responding to these sorts of risks is "specific deterrence," prohibitions aimed at preventing occurrence of the harm in the first place rather than at trying to compensate people for it after the fact.[22] Modern regulatory practice, in conspicuous contrast to earlier common law remedies,

> attempts to prevent undesirable occurrences and thereby eliminate the necessity for compensating injured persons.... For example, the laws of nuisance that were developed to protect

22. In the former case the prohibition should be firm and absolute, whereas in the latter it need perhaps only be notional. Furthermore, if we opt for less than absolute "specific deterrence," it is especially important that such a choice be made through the political process in order to protect the dignity of those deprived, as I argue below.

> against infringements on property operate after an injury has
> taken place. In contrast, government control of pollution, to-
> day's regulatory counterpart to nuisance law, aims to prevent
> unwarranted substances from entering the air or water. [Morri-
> son and Noll 1980, 5]

Such a preoccupation with preventing harms rather than compensating for them seems curiously inefficient—it flagrantly ignores
"individual differences in tastes" and Pareto-optimal trades that can
arise from them (Calabresi 1970, 107)—until we realize that there are
some losses which are simply not compensatable.

Sometimes, of course, one person's noncompensatable loss can
be prevented only by imposing similar deprivations on others. That
presents us with a hard choice. But it is the sort of choice we are
quite accustomed to making through the political process. "Virtually all our political judgments ... are decisions regarding goals,
principles, and ideas—choices among unmeasurables" (Calabresi
1970, 98). And, in the case of the decision of who is to bear noncompensatable burdens, it is peculiarly appropriate that the choice
should be made through the political process. We must be concerned, first and foremost, to preserve the dignity of those who are
eventually asked to shoulder such losses. Were the demand to come
through market or quasi-market processes, people would be likely to
find the implicit monetarization underlying the decision demeaning
(cf. section 6.6 above). Were it to come instead through a political
process conspicuously embodying higher ideals, as in section 6.5.2
above, they might regard it as a noble sacrifice.

8.4.3. Choosing Collective Risks

Some of the political decisions that will be required concern risks
not just to isolated (albeit, ex ante, unidentifiable) individuals but
rather to society as a whole. Safety sometimes takes the character of
a public good, in that everyone must bear more or less the same
levels of risk (Lave 1968, 424–27). Something about such cases
seems to demand a different decision rule from that we are comfortable in using ordinarily. It seems to be wrong to allow the majority to
impose its risk preferences on the rest, even if those preferences are
perfectly well informed, stable, and so on. Instead, a society ought
to accept no greater a collective risk than its most risk-averse
member is prepared to bear, at least where risks of some really
catastrophic consequences are involved.

This argument is best made by reference to an example which,
although hypothetical, seems a reasonable analogue for many social
decisions. Imagine a team of four mountain-climbers out for a day's

expedition. It has taken longer to reach the summit than planned. Now they face a choice of two ways down the mountain: they could take a somewhat dangerous short cut that will get them home by dusk; or, alternatively, they could take a longer but much safer route. The latter would mean spending the night on the mountain which, since they have come unprepared, would be slightly uncomfortable. Suppose, further, that all four must come down together—their safety equipment, say, depends upon there being four of them. Hence they must arrive at some collective choice of path. Three vote for the faster route, one for the safer. Try as the others might, they cannot persuade him to change his vote. He is unimpressed by the offer of compensation if things go wrong: if he falls off the mountain, he will be dead. Furthermore, he is not being silly or superstitious in fearing the more dangerous route: everyone, let us say, agrees that the probability of an accident there is 5 percent. The only difference is that the others are prepared to accept that risk, while he is not. Under these conditions, it seems absolutely clear to me that the others ought to accede—grumblingly, perhaps—to his demand and take the slower but safer path down.[23] Majority rule seems to have no place in this sort of risk decision.

That conclusion depends crucially on the fact that everyone has to bear the same risk. Were there a way for the coward to make his own way down the mountain while the others went on ahead, we would not allow him to dictate their decision. Many social risk decisions, however, share this "public good" property. Maybe someone fearful of occupational hazards or toxic chemicals can change jobs or move away from Love Canal, but the risk of nuclear war or climate change must be the same for everyone everywhere. There is no opting out or moving away. We must make a single, collective determination of the risk we will all bear identically. And if my example is persuasive, that means that we must give the most risk-averse a virtual veto over such decisions.

The conclusion also depends upon the assumption that the recalcitrant climber's veto is based on a plausible assessment of real risks. Were he instead a crank, refusing to take the faster way down merely because he superstitiously feared passing through an old

23. The "principle of reciprocal risk" is ambiguous on just this crucial point. On one reading, it might require precisely the result I favor: the three cannot impose greater risks on the one than the one imposes on them. But on another rather more standard reading, the right to impose reciprocal risks would yield just the opposite result, viz., that people can impose any risks on others so long as they are willing for the others to impose similar risks on them (Fried 1970, 188, 185; Fletcher 1972). Since the three would be more than happy for the one to take a 5 percent chance with their lives under similar circumstances, they might therefore be said to be entitled to take that risk with his life now.

Indian burial ground, we would have little hesitation in ignoring his demands. In telling the tale, I stipulated that everyone agrees on the same 5 percent probability of accidents. But universal agreement on the chances of disaster is not strictly necessary. Surely it would be enough that the reluctant climber's estimate not be totally groundless. Precisely how to specify that requirement—for climbers, much less for policymakers—is difficult. Still, I think we want to distinguish between risk aversion predicated on a fear of Sitting Bull's ghost, which we feel no need to respect, and that based on plausible but unproven assessments of risk, which we cannot dismiss so casually.

A final special feature of my example is that it involves the risk of a really awful outcome—falling off the mountain. Were the possible consequences of the risky course less severe (merely a twisted ankle, say) and the certain consequences of the safe course more severe (catching a bad cold), then it may not be nearly so clear that the coward should get to veto the majority choice. Perhaps we give the reluctant climber a veto in my original story for roughly the same reason we guarantee vested rights for ordinary political minorities—in order to prevent tyrannical majorities from imposing severe deprivations on a minority contrary to its intensely held preferences or moral rights (Barry 1979b; Fried 1970, 191–93).[24] This may make the example look less exciting, collapsing it into more familiar moral categories, but it hardly deprives it of practical significance. Many social decisions similarly pose risks of really horrid outcomes analogous to falling off the mountainside, and there too the most risk-averse should enjoy a veto over these risky policy developments.

For an example of a collective risk decision which seems sensibly left to the most risk-averse, consider the problem of antibiotic additives to animal feeds. Over 40 percent of the antibacterials produced in the U.S. are used for nonhuman purposes. Low doses added to animal feeds can, by preventing disease, help livestock and poultry gain weight rapidly. This practice, however, poses two sorts of risks to humans. The first and arguably lesser risk is of cancer from consuming meat from animals fed DES, etc. The second and larger risk is that such uses of antibiotics might contribute to the development of resistant strains of bacteria which attack humans as well as animals. The U.S. National Academy of Sciences committee convened to study these dangers concluded:

24. My hunch is that the crucial thing about these cases is that the losses are noncompensatable. Certainly we do not think that one's legal rights, for example, should be allowed to be cashed in for money (Okun 1975, chap. 1).

1. the case against the use of antibiotics in feeds had been "neither proven nor disproven";
2. although there may be a real danger here, "the research necessary to establish and measure a definite risk has not been conducted"; and
3. it is "not possible to conduct a feasible, comprehensive epidemiological study of the effects on human health." [Marshall 1980, 376]

And, as the U.S. Congress Office of Technology Assessment (1979, 10) emphasizes, "Once significant effects on human and animal health do become widely observable and quantifiable, it may be too late to address the problem." Thus, the NAS committee recommends that, since there are theoretically well-founded fears which cannot be disproven, antibiotics should cease being added to animal feed.

This is precisely the recommendation which follows from my discussion here of collective risks. Risks of cancer from eating DES-contaminated meat are "private" ones—anyone wanting to avoid them could simply refuse to eat the flesh of animals fed such additives or, insofar as feed histories were uncertain, abstain from eating meat altogether. There is, however, nothing any particular individual could do to avoid the risks of drug-resistant bacteria. This is truly a collective risk which all must share equally. There is no agreement as to the probabilities, as in the mountaineering example; but neither is there any basis for confidence in dismissing these dangers. Under these conditions, it seems proper to respect the preferences of the risk-averse, at least until we can prove their fears to be groundless.

9 Uncertainty as an Excuse for Myopia

When our policies have effects stretching over a long period of time, we tend to weight consequences falling far in the future much less heavily than those we must face immediately. The most poignant examples concern the disposal of toxic chemicals and radioactive wastes. We typically take great care to assure their isolation for the near future, while happily accepting the very real possibility that in the long term they might well escape and endanger human life.[1]

In many ways, this myopia is eminently understandable. Politically, the unborn are naturally disenfranchised, the interests of future generations being taken into account only through the sympathetic impulses of current voters (Rawls 1972, sec. 45). Psychologically, we discount even our own future interests, feeling less empathy with future selves the further removed they are from us (Mill 1848, bk. 5, chap. 11, sec. 10; Parfit 1976, 99). The tendency to downgrade future interests is, therefore, natural and understandable. The question here is whether it is also morally justifiable.

Officially, both economists and philosophers have long seemed to suggest that it is not. Most economists concur with Ramsey (1928, 543) in saying that to "discount later

This chapter is reprinted, with additions and revisions, from Robert E. Goodin, "Uncertainty as an Excuse for Cheating Our Children," *Policy Sciences* 10 (1978): 25–43, by permission of the publisher, Elsevier Scientific Publishing Company, Amsterdam.

   1. "Of the fifty-seven million tons of hazardous industrial chemical wastes produced annually in the United States, more than ninety percent are disposed of improperly," creating nonnegligible probabilities of release some time in the future (Anon. 1981, 584). Simulations of the movements of radioactive wastes, discussed in section 10.2.2 below, suggest similar risks there.

enjoyments in comparison with earlier ones... is ethically inde-fensible and arises merely from the weakness of the imagnation." Pigou (1932, pt. I, chap. 2, sec. 3) calls it a defect of the "tele-scopic faculty," and Harrod (1948, 40) blasts "pure time pref-erence" as "a polite expression for rapacity and the conquest of reason by passion."[2] To philosophers, for their part, "it seems clear that the time at which a man exists cannot affect the value of his happiness from a universal point of view" (Sidgwick 1874, bk. 4, chap. 1). And Rawls (1972, sec. 45) endorses Sidgwick's judgment on this score.

That generous principle established, however, both economists and philosophers promptly find ample practical excuses for violating it. My discussion will focus mainly on the notion of "uncertainty," which figures especially prominently among philosophers as well as among economists themselves. In section 9.5 I shall turn to examine the shortcomings of another even more orthodox economic excuse for shortchanging the future, couched in terms of "opportunity costs."

9.1. Uncertainty as an Excuse

"The interests of posterity must concern a utilitarian," Sidgwick (1874, bk. 4, chap. 1) writes, "except in so far as the effects of his actions on posterity—and even on the existence of human beings to be affected—must necessarily be more *uncertain.*" Pigou (1932, pt. I, chap. 2, sec. 7) strikes a similar theme:

> Nobody ... holds that the state should force its citizens to act as though so much objective wealth now and in the future were of exactly equal importance. In view of the *uncertainty* of produc-tive developments, to say nothing of the mortality of nations and eventually of the human race itself, this would not, even in the extremest theory, be sound policy.

This argument recurs in the writings of various contemporary economists and philosophers. In his famous paper "On Optimising the Rate of Saving," Sen (1961, 483) includes "the *uncertainty* as-sociated with the future" as "one of the reasons for preferring a unit of present consumption to the same in the future." Rawls (1972, sec.

---

2. A few economists, overwhelmed by the tenets of consumer sovereignty, are willing to let people discount the future—their own, or that of their successors—at any rate they please (Eckstein 1957, 75; 1961, 454, 459; Marglin 1963, 97). But some-one who accords a low priority to events far in the future, merely because they are far in the future, is very likely to take a very different view of them when they occur. Social decisions should, as I argued in chapter 3 above, be based on those latter judgments rather than upon mistaken ex ante anticipations of what those judgments will turn out to be.

45) comments, with an offhandedness which is revealing, "Of course, a present or near future advantage may be counted more heavily on account of its greater *certainty* or probability." In like fashion, Hart (1979, 80) mentions that we may want to "discount somewhat the value of the later satisfaction because of its *uncertainty*."

Far from being confined to the realm of pure theory, these arguments and conclusions also figure prominently in much applied research. Passmore (1974, 85), assessing "man's responsibility for nature," argues that "the *uncertainty* of the harms we are hoping to prevent would, in general, entitle us to ignore them." And Hitch and McKean (1960, 208), in their immensely influential application of economic principles to defense policy, refer to "the existence of risk and *uncertainty* about the gains and costs" as being "in the typical military case [the] quantitatively more important reason for discounting future costs and benefits."

The italics in all these quotations are my own, but the emphases are clearly those of the authors themselves. Uncertainty is the theme running through their arguments. We are advised to pay special heed to the duties arising out of our "special relationships" with our families and our friends and our contemporaries merely because, knowing more of the details of their situations, we are able to direct our aid in such a way as to prove most useful. Distant peoples—both in time and in space—are to be ignored merely because we are so much less certain of their circumstances and, hence, of how to help them.

To appreciate how very weak the moral force attaching to this proposition really is, consider the following mundane case. High snowdrifts have kept grandfather from arriving in time for Christmas dinner, and nobody can recall whether or not he likes turkey. Surely no one would suggest that, in light of this uncertainty, those present should feel free to finish the bird themselves. The decent thing to do is, no doubt, to set his portion aside for him.

The analogy is somewhat inappropriate, of course, insofar as it ignores the irreversibilities—the "now or never" character of the choices—that are posed by questions of intergenerational justice. The family can always come back to the turkey at a later sitting should Gramps not want it, whereas earlier generations cannot return to enjoy what they have saved in vain for future ones. But notice that the irreversibilities work both ways. Just as earlier generations cannot consume what they needlessly saved for their heirs, so too later ones cannot enjoy what earlier ones used up. The situations of the two parties are perfectly symmetrical in this respect. Preferring either over the other must be based on nothing more than a blind bias in favor of certain groups or certain time slices.

The impact of uncertainty is more pragmatic than principled. It does nothing to lift our obligations to future generations, but it does much to raise doubts about how they might best be discharged (Routley and Routley 1978). The only reason uncertainty about the future matters is that with uncertainty comes the risk of waste. Suppose the Christmas celebrants were unsure of grandpa's taste for sprouts, which are perfectly dreadful reheated. Then their choice is between finishing them all at the main sitting or keeping some warm for grandpa, knowing that if he declines them they will be fit only for Fido. Those gathered around the table are certain of their desires for sprouts. While there is a chance that grandpa might be just as keen, there is also a chance that he is not, in which case they will be wasted if saved. The goal of minimizing the risks of waste then dictates a preference for satisfying current demand over uncertain future desires.

Philosophers are comfortable dealing in terms of these loose "verbal" formulations. Economists, for their part, prefer the formalisms of decision theory. There policy options are evaluated according to their "expected utility," i.e., the sum of pleasures derived from all their various possible outcomes, each discounted by the improbability of its occurring. "Uncertainty," in these terms, means that we are not sure what those probabilities are; and, as Parfit (1981, 9) says, "We ought to discount those predictions which are more likely to be false." If we suffer only slight uncertainty, and we can still assign probabilities with some confidence, we might proceed much as before. But if our uncertainty is great, and we have very little confidence in our probability assessments, then that must be reflected in a further discounting of the expected utility of highly uncertain outcomes. On the assumption that we are always likely to be less certain of distant events than of proximate ones, this formalism similarly biases our decisions in favor of our neighbors in time as well as in space.

9.2. Ignoring versus Discounting Uncertain Futures

Under certain circumstances, such logic might suggest that consideration of future consequences drop out of our reckoning altogether. Where distant futures are concerned, desirable and undesirable possibilities might be treated as mutually canceling. There are two ways to make this argument. The "rule of insufficient reason" suggests that, if we are very uncertain of the true probabilities of alternative outcomes, we should treat them *as if* they were equally likely. The more popular approach uses the "law of large numbers" to infer that, since any action will have a great many consequences in distant futures which are largely independent of one another, the very good and the very bad outcomes actually *will* occur with equal frequency. If we assume that every awfully bad outcome is (or is expected to be) perfectly matched by an awfully good one, the consequences of our actions for distant futures will be (or will be expected to be) mutually canceling and should therefore be ignored when deciding our present course of action. Such arguments are popular with both philosophers and economists. Smart (1973, 64–65), contemplating the standard ethical hypothetical of the man trying to decide whether to seduce his neighbor's wife, concludes,

> The man need not consider the possibility that one of his remote descendants, if he seduces the woman, will be a great benefactor of the human race. Such a possibility is not all that improbable, considering the very likely vast number of descendants after a good many generations, but it is no more probable than the possibility that one of his descendants will do great harm to the human race, or that one of the descendants from a more legitimate union would benefit the human race. It seems plausible that the long-term probable benefits and costs of his alternative actions are likely to be negligible or to cancel one another out.

Economists similarly argue that, while it is reasonable for individuals to be risk-averse, there is no reason for society as a whole to be: for every project that turns out much worse than expected, there will be one turning out much better than expected (Arrow 1966; Baumol 1970, 281; Little and Mirrlees 1974, sec. 15.4).

Notice, however, that the argument for ignoring distant futures presupposes *symmetrical* distributions of possible payoffs. That is to say, it presupposes that for every outcome with a cost of $-x$, if it occurs, there is a corresponding possibility of an outcome with a benefit of $+x$, if it occurs. If the distribution of possible payoffs is at all asymmetrical, if there is a single "unmatched" possibility, then the argument for ignoring future consequences fails.

Imagine, for example, a worker in the mid-nineteenth-century Pennsylvania oil fields being offered a well-paid job hauling nitroglycerine. The behavior of this chemical, only recently discovered, is absolutely unpredictable—there is no way of estimating the probability of its exploding at any given moment. Such uncertainty, some would suppose, calls into play the rule of insufficient reason, telling the worker to presume that the nitro is equally likely to explode in his hands as not. The argument sketched above suggests that this, in turn, implies that the worker should forget such worries and go for the certain prospect of a well-paid job. But the rational laborer would surely notice that, while the probability of the two outcomes may be the same, the payoffs are far from it: if the nitro explodes in his hands, he loses far more than he would gain if he manages to get safely to the blasting site and collect his wage.

Or, again, imagine the ruler of a peasant society where everyone exists at the margin of subsistence. Were peasants to employ more innovative methods of cultivation, they could increase average crop yields in average years. Sometimes the yields would be well above this average, sometimes well below. The "law of large numbers" advises the ruler that such fluctuations will go in one direction as often as the other; and since they balance one another, he should ignore them in deciding whether to impose these innovations on peasants. But the ruler would rightly resist this advice. Although good years and bad may be equally frequent, their utilities are no-wise symmetrical. In a bare subsistence setting, a bad year means mass starvation whereas a good year just means a little extra to eat.

The sort of symmetry which is required to ignore the future with a clear conscience is probably relatively rare. Cases such as the disposal of toxic chemicals or radioactive wastes suggest so, at least. There are uncertainties aplenty about the long-term futures of such storage systems. But there is virtually no symmetry in the payoffs attached to the alternative possible outcomes: the best we can hope is that the wastes cause us no further trouble; the uncertainty surrounds only the myriad of possible ways they might return to poison us. Thus it would be unforgivable to use such uncertainties as an excuse for ignoring the long-term dangers and just dumping the wastes at sea or in insecure landfills. Since the worst and best possible outcomes seem not to balance one another, we must not allow possible futures to cancel each other out of our decision calculus.

Typically, then, uncertainty does not excuse us in ignoring the future altogether. But it might still allow us to discount it. Future consequences are always taken into account, only weighted less heavily the longer they will take to appear. And dangers which will not arise for a long time—such as leaks of toxic chemicals or radioactive wastes—will still be virtually ignored. Hence it is important to examine carefully the more modest argument for merely discounting the future in light of uncertainty.

9.3. Sources of Uncertainty

There are various types of uncertainty which are commonly said to justify discounting the claims of the future. First, we discount distant futures more heavily because we are more uncertain that we—or anybody—will be alive to experience whatever pains or pleasures that moment might hold. Second, we discount distant futures more heavily because we are more uncertain of what preferences might prevail at that time. Third, we discount further futures more heavily because we are more uncertain of what the ramifications of our actions might be by that time, and, fourth, of what technologies might be available by then to deal with them.[3] While these four uncertainties obviously interact, they are in principle distinct influences demanding separate consideration.

9.3.1. Uncertain Existence

Imagine a pathogen which would cause a horrible illness, but only after an incubation period of two hundred years. Who would worry? By then, everyone will have died of something else anyway. The background risk of death provides one of the most powerful motives for an individual to discount distant future payoffs in his own decision-making. How much he should discount them depends upon how far they are in the future and how long he expects to live. For an average middle-aged American male circa 1961, the appropriate discount rate would have been something on the order of 0.4 percent per year (Eckstein 1961, 457).

The relevance of this to public policy may be thought somewhat doubtful. It is argued, for example, that "although individuals are mortal, society is not," and hence that risk-of-death discounting has no place in social decision-making (Dasgupta and Pearce 1972, 139; Eckstein 1961, 459).[4] But surely societies—and, in the atomic age especially, the human species itself—may be mortal. The relevant

3. Notice that in all four cases we are "discounting" strictly on account of uncertainty. Temporal distance is involved only indirectly—only insofar as it is contingently related to increases in that uncertainty. That correlation is, of course, far from perfect. Hence, considerations of uncertainty do not warrant time-discounting in anything like its ordinary form of a firmly fixed, flat-rate discount of r percent per year (Stokey and Zeckhauser 1978, 173; Parfit 1981, 9).

4. To put the question another way: if social decision-makers are prepared to accept time horizons growing out of people's chances of dying, why should they not similarly accept time horizons growing out of the chances of people's moving away? Burton, et al. (1978, 96) tell the story of a Missouri Valley real estate developer who, when queried about the flood risk to his new apartment building, replied, "There isn't any risk; I expect to sell this building before the next flood season." Burton, et al. (1978, 130) conclude that, "given the increasing mobility of societies, the time horizon for an individual moving from farm to city or from one part of a city to another may be very short—e.g., less than 10 years. In that case the homeowner might regard a flood with a recurrence interval of once a century as having only a very small chance of occurring during his limited tenure.... For the community, however, the recurrence of such an event must be inevitable." This must count as further evidence of the need for a social time horizon which is longer than individual ones.

time scale may be much greater than that appropriate for natural individuals. Still, many public policy payoffs—costs of improper toxic chemical or radioactive waste disposal, for example—might fall far enough in the future for even very low discount rates to have some real relevance.

Philosophers might try to preempt such considerations by arguing that it is our duty to assure continuity of our species, if not our particular society, and that it is immoral to predicate social planning on the assumption that this duty will be breached. Despite the undeniable intuitive appeal of such a duty, it has yet to find a very firm moral basis. Couching the argument in terms of the interests—much less the rights—of potential people is contentious, at best (Sikora and Barry 1978). And, if we seek a justification outside the terms of human interests, it seems difficult to get beyond merely reporting a sense of "cosmic impertinence" (Barry 1977, 284).

Far the most effective rejoinder to the "uncertain existence" argument, applied to either the individual or the species, is that we simply must plan on the assumption of continuing existence in the absence of firm evidence to the contrary. For the individual, Olson and Bailey (1981, 10) discuss how in this way "uncertainty about the date of one's death can increase . . . [one's] provision for the future, because it can create an incentive to save more to provide undiminished consumption in the event of an unexpectedly long life." For societies and species, the same logic applies even more powerfully. The individual can be certain of expiring some time in, say, the next hundred fifty years. The society or species, while it might expire at any moment, might also go on forever. In the absence of conclusive evidence to the contrary, the obligation is to plan as if it will.

9.3.2.   Uncertain Tastes

A second sort of uncertainty surrounds the preferences of unknown people and, especially, of unknowable unborn generations. "We cannot be certain that posterity will need what we save—or on the other side that it will not need what we should not think of saving" (Passmore 1974, 98). Uncertainty about future tastes is one of the most standard excuses for discounting payoffs that fall far in the future (Rawls 1972, sec. 45; Dobb 1960, 13; Little and Mirrlees 1974, sec. 15.1; Haveman 1977, 365–66; Barry 1977, 274). And, within limits, it should be taken seriously. We have all heard quite enough of missionaries (or their contemporary equivalents in foreign aid missions) who demand sacrifices of their own people for the benefit of savages who, owing to superstition or sloth or plain good sense, then reject the benefices. On a more personal level, we must all know some aged aunt who never lets anyone sit on "the good sofa"—the one she is "saving for the children"—little realizing that they will, by the time of the bequest, have such refined sensibilities as to be unable to abide it even in their attic.

We can know these were needless sacrifices only in hindsight, of course. Ex ante, there was some chance that others would appreciate the sacrifices. But there was also a chance that they would not. While the losses entailed in the sacrifices are certain, the gains are problematic. On simple grounds of minimizing the risk of waste, the sacrifice seems inadvisable, ceteris paribus.

These conclusions hold, however, only within certain narrow limits hidden beneath that ceteris paribus clause. One of the more important ones is that the benefits, should they obtain, be of roughly the same magnitude as the sacrifices required to produce them. The aged aunt would, presumably, take as much pleasure in lounging on the sofa as the children could ever be expected to receive; so the certainty of her loss against the uncertainty of their gain settles the matter. But consider the case of famine relief. This decision, too, is plagued with uncertainties from the point of view of the individual contributor—the Red Cross volunteer may pocket his donation, the food may arrive too late or too spoiled, or it may never reach those most in need. These risks are well worth running, however, since the sacrifice of the well-fed is so slight compared with the potential benefits to the starving.[5]

Furthermore, tastes may not be all that variable. Even economists concede that "the unpredictability of consumers' tastes is often exaggerated as a source of uncertainty" (Little and Mirrlees 1974, 307). And this is especially true when it comes to basic necessities (Barry 1977, 274; Kavka 1978, 189; Routley and Routley 1978; Dasgupta and Heal 1979, 255–56). One may well wonder whether others will share one's tastes for Victorian furniture or "Christian" attire

5. Zeckhauser (1969) shows that a rational individual, knowing his preferences are susceptible to change, should sacrifice a certain increment of consumption of goods he currently desires to insure against the possibility that he might later come to desire goods which he now eschews and which would otherwise be unattainable at that time. Zeckhauser's model works with zero present demand and the possibility of a positive future demand for the good in question; but his "insurance against changing preferences" model can be generalized as saying that such sacrifices might be rational whenever future desires threaten to be stronger than current ones. (How much to sacrifice depends on several factors—the subjective probability of preference change, the magnitude of probable differences between present and future desires, taste for risks, etc.) The argument that changing tastes will allow us to discount the future works only in the converse case, i.e., if future desires are expected to be less strong (or, at most, no stronger) than current ones.

or electronic gadgets. But no one can seriously doubt that they will share similar tastes for good health, respect, and affection, along with food, clothing, and shelter in some form or another. Those desires are somehow special: they flow from immutable biological and psychological imperatives; they are, and shall remain, basic to anything else one might desire to be or to do.[6]

Chemical and radioactive wastes seem to transgress both these limits badly. The possible gains for present generations from creating them—much less cutting corners in safeguarding them—are rarely likely to be anywhere near commensurable with the possible gains to future generations from eschewing them. There are few gains that can compete with the avoidance of mass poisoning, which is what future generations are facing should storage systems fail. Furthermore, the desire to avoid such poisoning is hardly an idiosyncrasy of presently fashionable tastes.

9.3.3.   Uncertain Effects

Deciding how to "evaluate uncertainty regarding future effects," even "assuming no change in tastes from one generation to the next," is the second of what economists regard as the "two fundamental issues" in this area (Haveman 1977, 365). In addition to wondering what the tastes of future generations might be, we are also left wondering what the actual impact of our interventions on them might be. Short-term consequences of our actions might be clear enough, but very long causal chains can become very unclear and unpredictable. Thus there is the genuine worry that "our well-intentioned sacrifices will have the long-term effect of making the situation of posterity worse than it would otherwise be" (Passmore 1974, 98).

Various responses are possible here, however. One is, quite simply, that the claim is false. Often we are more—not less—certain of the long-term than the short-term consequences of our actions (Parfit 1981, 9). Recall that the great complaint with classical economics was that its laws told us what to expect "in the long run," after new equilibrium had been established, without predicting what would happen in the interim.

6. The "need" and "primary good" formulations arguably amount to the same thing: what makes "primary goods" or "needs" instrumental toward any possible end in any possible world is that they are connected to something inherent in the nature of man, which, in turn, delimits what can count as a possible variation on our world.

Furthermore, notice that uncertainty about the long-term consequences of our actions does not extinguish our obligation to future generations. Instead, it "remains latent" and will be activated whenever relevant information does become available (Barry 1977, 274). And whereas we must passively await information about future tastes, we can and should actively seek out information about the future effects of our action. Market consultants may regard anticipating the tastes of the unborn as an impossible feat, but trying to predict the ultimate consequences of our actions is not nearly so obviously a waste of effort. Here decision-makers can rightly be blamed if they waste a research opportunity which, if seized, would have prevented much future misery. Such ignorance, like other constraints of one's own making, can hardly serve as an excuse, as section 7.1 has shown. The more catastrophic the possible outcomes of a contemplated course of action, the stronger this research imperative. This follows straightforwardly from the expected utility calculus itself: the more costly a disaster would be, the more it is worth to find out whether it will really occur and to avoid it (Olson 1977). The application to problems of storing toxic chemicals or radioactive wastes is particularly striking. Since the catastrophe in question—mass poisoning—is of sizable proportions, it is worth a major investment to make sure it does not occur.

9.3.4.   Uncertain Technologies

Economists commonly claim there is no point planning too far into the future in the face of uncertain technologies (Dobb 1960, 13; Little and Mirrlees 1974, sec. 15.1; Dasgupta and Heal 1979, chap. 13). Indeed, their formal models of "resource depletion under technological uncertainty" (Dasgupta and Stiglitz 1981) show that under some plausible conditions rational agents, anticipating technological breakthroughs, may perversely consume more of an exhaustible resource the less there is left of it.

Apologists for nuclear power openly evoke such technological uncertainties to excuse their radioactive residues. First, we might find better disposal techniques. As Atomic Energy Commission spokesmen emphasized at the 1972 OECD-IAEA Symposium on the Management of Radioactive wastes, "consideration of long-term disposal options for high-level wastes is not limited by the level of current technology," and "decades are available to develop permanent disposal methods" (J. H. Rubin, in OECD-IAEA 1973, 36; cf. F. K. Pittman, quoted in Hollocher 1975, 220–21). A 1978 report to the Interagency Review Group on Nuclear Waste Management similarly conceded "numerous limitations to our knowledge" but argued that "such gaps in our current knowledge need not rule out successful underground containment" because, inter alia, "active R&D programs focused at filling knowledge gaps currently are underway or planned and our understanding of the relevant hydrogeology, geochemistry, rock mechanics, and risk assessment should increase rapidly over coming years" (U.S. IRG 1978, 11–12). Even if we do not discover better ways to store the wastes, we can always hope that "science can develop a cure for the untoward biological side effects of the environmental insult" by developing "a safe and simple method of immunizing against cancer" and by reducing "the risk of genetic abnormality . . . by amniotic analysis and therapeutic abortion" (Weinberg 1972a, 217).

Barry (1977, 275) is right to scorn "this Micawberish attitude of expecting something to turn up" because, of course, there are no grounds for expecting any *particular* thing to turn up. We may be able to predict the aggregate level of technological innovation from the level and distribution of research investments. Any particular breakthrough must, however, be fundamentally unpredictable. The prospect of technological advance cannot, therefore, provide any guarantee that future generations will be spared the evil consequences of our actions.

It can, nevertheless, provide the comfort of uncertainty, which might be almost as good. While we cannot be sure that future generations will be spared our evil side-effects, neither can we be sure that they will have to suffer them. The greater our uncertainty of the outcome, this argument holds, the nearer we should come to dropping the entire matter from our decision calculus. This comforting conclusion rests, however, on a gross misspecification of the situation. What is conveniently lost is this crucial fact: we are certain that, in the absence of technological breakthroughs, our descendants will suffer from the consequences of our present actions. Such uncertainties as exist surround only their capacity to ameliorate harm which we know would otherwise occur. The greater *that* uncertainty, the more inadvisable the contemplated course of action. Thus, the British Royal Commission on Environmental Pollution was quite right to conclude that "it would be irresponsible and morally wrong to commit future generations to the consequences of fission power on a massive scale unless it had been demonstrated beyond reasonable doubt that at least one method exists for the safe isolation of these wastes for the indefinite future" (Flowers 1976, para. 181). And a similar conclusion could be offered regarding toxic chemical wastes.

9.4.   The Implications of Profound
Uncertainty

Uncertainty implies neither that we may blithely ignore nor that we may heavily discount the distant future. Limits have been found to any such conclusions even within the familiar expected utility calculus, which generally tends toward that implication. A more fundamental challenge will call into question the application of expected utility reasoning to such problems at all.

Let us distinguish two different levels of uncertainty. With the *modest* form, the uncertainties surround our probability estimates. With the *profound* form, we are not even certain of our specification of the set of the possible. So far, discussion has focused on modest uncertainties. The further in the future an event falls, the less sure we are of its chances of occurring or of people's reactions to it if it does. We have no doubts about what could conceivably happen. We fear only being surprised by what we did not "expect"—i.e., did not confidently regard as likely—so far ahead of time. In a deeper sense, we might be uncertain of the future because we cannot even imagine all that could possibly happen. We are prepared to be surprised not just by outcomes that we thought unlikely but, more fundamentally, by outcomes we had not thought about at all.

This distinction is important because the expected utility calculus is well equipped to deal only with modest uncertainties. It can handle uncertainty regarding the probabilities associated with various possible outcomes—by Bayesian guesswork, if nothing else. But the expected utility calculus must start with a full list of all the discrete outcomes that might conceivably occur (Shackle 1966). If we cannot draw up such a list—if we suffer from the more profound form of uncertainty—then we are lacking an absolutely essential prerequisite to the expected utility calculus in its ordinary form.

All we can do at this point is list such possibilities as we can foresee and assign them probabilities, and then create a residual "everything else" category and assign *it* a probability. Logically, that provides an exhaustive list of possibilities at last. But in practical terms, it does not really meet our needs. The trouble is that we have utterly no basis for assigning probabilities to this ragbag of possibilities so uncertain as even to defy complete description.[7] Not only is there no basis for confidence in such estimates—we also have grounds for *lacking* any confidence in them. This mode of presenting

7. Instead of trying to list everything that might happen and to specify what the payoff would be if it did, we might try collapsing the two steps into one. We might just define a probability function over a range of payoffs, without any pretense that any of them corresponds to possible outcomes in the real world. Then, however, we have even less basis for assigning the probabilities we do.

the possibilities has been shown to exacerbate greatly the difficulties people have, even at best of times, in assessing probabilities accurately. Fischhoff, et al. (1978) offer experimental evidence to show that people are grossly insensitive to, and wildly underestimate the probability of, things lumped together into an "everything else" category; and this is true even of "experts" who should, in principle, be able to compile for themselves the list of possibilities for themselves. Thus, when faced with profound uncertainties, we cannot use the expected utility calculus in the standard form and dare not use it in this revised form.

For an example to which I shall return in section 10.1.1, consider the Rasmussen (1975) nuclear reactor safety study. Its methodology was to construct elaborate "fault trees" describing sequences of events required for any particular accident to occur. From the probabilities of these contributory failures, the overall probability of a meltdown can be computed. But this methodology "*requires* essentially complete identification of all the elements of these families [of accidents with serious consequences]. Otherwise, one may omit an important event and, thus, a dominant contribution to the risk" (Kendall and Moglewer 1974, sec. 2. Cf. Lieberman 1976, 271–72; Fischhoff 1977; Fairley 1977, 334). Certain failure modes, such as mechanical defects, lend themselves well to such analysis. Assuming the plant is constructed strictly according to specifications, we could, at least in principle, deduce from the blueprint alone all the avenues by which mechanical failure might lead to a meltdown (cf. Kendall and Moglewer 1974, sec. 3.2). Other failure modes, however, are not amenable to fault tree analysis precisely because it is impossible, even in principle, to list all paths leading to failure—i.e., the more "profound" form of uncertainty prevails. Consider, for example, the danger of sabotage or human error: were we able to anticipate all paths that would-be saboteurs might take or all mistakes that operators might make, we could block them ahead of time and remove those risks, altogether. The main reason there is any risk of these sorts of failures at all is that we cannot anticipate how they might come about.[8]

Some of the most frightful dangers to mankind arise out of this sort of uncertainty. Schelling (1966, 94), for example, argues that "there is just no foreseeable route by which the United States and the Soviet Union could become engaged in a major nuclear war. This does not mean that a major nuclear war cannot occur. It only means that if it occurs it will result from a process that is not entirely foreseen." Surely this puts the point a little too strongly, for there

8. We may, of course, foresee some of the risks and simply decide that they are not worth protecting against.

are some scenarios by which we can imagine coming to nuclear blows. But insofar as we can anticipate the scenarios we can at least hope to plan in such a way as to avoid them or their worst consequences. What Schelling rightly emphasizes is that the greatest risks of really catastrophic nuclear exchanges arise from sequences which ex ante we could not (or at least did not) imagine to be possible ones.

This profound uncertainty often characterizes the hazards associated with new chemicals or organisms. "A possibility that weighs heavily on the minds of many who are worried about recombinant DNA research is that this research may lead to negative consequences for human health or for the environment which have not yet even been thought of" (Stich 1978, 194). The same is true of new chemicals, as evidenced by the early history of Freon and other fluorocarbons:

> Twenty years ago, the possibility that fluorocarbons, when released into the air, might destroy the protective layer of ozone in the earth's outer atmosphere was not suspected .... Today scientists are certain that fluorocarbons erode the ozone layer, but are not certain of the extent of ozone depletion that can be expected or of the effect of increased exposure to ultraviolet rays. [Cornell, et al. 1976, 469]

Profound uncertainty has, in this case, given way to more modest forms of uncertainty. What we once did not conceive of as among the possible outcomes we now see as clearly possible, and only wonder how probable.

The uncertainties associated with toxic chemical and radioactive waste disposal in particular, and with very distant futures in general, are likely to be of this more profound form. To refer back to the list of uncertainties developed in section 9.3, they all seem to fit into this more awkward category. Producing a complete list of all the scientific breakthroughs that are possible presents a special paradox—to know which are possible and which are not, we must already have made the breakthroughs in question! (See Popper 1957, vi–viii.) Anticipating the effects of our actions projected far into the future, we must worry once again that we cannot conceive of all the outcomes that might result: one of our major concerns with placing toxic chemical or radioactive wastes in carefully engineered storage sites is that there may be routes we simply cannot imagine by which they might escape; one of our major worries about dumping heavy metals into the oceans is that "there could be unexpected pathways back to man or effects on the natural world in the remote future" (Flowers 1976, para. 180); one of our major hesitations in letting radioactive wastes melt their way into the polar ice is that something—quite what we cannot now imagine—might go wrong and we might want to recover them (Kubo and Rose 1973). Even as regards anticipating the tastes of people in the future, the most difficult step lies in imagining and distinguishing all the possible objects of desire.

Distant futures thus pose profound uncertainties which undermine the expected utility calculus. With it goes the confident connection between uncertainty and the justifiability of shortchanging future generations. The expected utility calculus cheats our children, recall, in the sense that their interests are weighted less heavily (owing to the uncertainty of whether and how they will be affected) in that decision calculus. The weights we attach to various factors matter, in turn, only because we are going to make the decision by summing up the uncertainty-weighted payoffs of all possible outcomes of all the alternative options. This is precisely how the expected utility calculus proceeds, of course; but it is precisely this sort of procedure that profound uncertainty precludes. When we have no complete list of possible outcomes, there can be no adding up of sums at all, so discounted weights attached to various factors lose significance. In this way, profound uncertainty removes the mechanism by which the expected utility calculus cheats our children.

Other decision rules can, in contrast, operate effectively in conditions approximating profound uncertainty. There is no single rule that should be uniquely favored where the expected utility principle is ruled out. The three most widely discussed, however, are the following:

1. Wald's (1950) "maximin" rule, requiring that we choose that course of action with the best worst-possible consequences;
2. Savage's (1954) "minimax regret" rule, enjoining us to choose that course of action which minimizes the maximum regret you might suffer from choosing it; and
3. the Arrow-Hurwicz (1972) rule directing us to choose by means of a comparison based on an index combining the maximum and minimum payoffs possible under various courses of action.[9]

9. For a more complete description, see Luce and Raiffa (1957, chap. 13) or Dasgupta and Pearce (1972, chap. 8). Notice that all these rules operate only under conditions *approximating* profound uncertainty, since all require us to know *something* about the range of possibilities—i.e., what is the worst, worst and best, or most regrettable possible outcome. "Possible" bears emphasizing. Science fiction writers can always imagine some utterly implausible scenario by which anything can go badly wrong. Before such worries are allowed to enter into our calculations, however, there must be some reason to suppose that they are indeed "real" rather than merely "logical" possibilities. This amounts to a requirement that the scenario be backed either by "producible evidence" (Routley and Routley 1978) or at least by

All these rules characteristically deal in terms of possibilities rather than probabilities. Wald asks us to examine the worst possible outcome of each alternative, Savage the most regrettable, Arrow-Hurwicz the best and worst—regardless of the probability of these outcomes. It is quite conceivable that, with any of these rules, we would make a decision on the basis of costs and benefits of outcomes which might, if we were trying to assign probabilities, seem extremely unlikely to occur. But we are here admitting that we cannot sensibly assign probabilities. Possibility is all that matters.[10]

Unlike the expected utility calculus, all of these rules dictate equal consideration of the interests of present and future generations. They direct attention to the worst, best and worst, or most regrettable possible outcomes of each alternative whenever they might occur. If alternative A at its worst causes some suffering in five years and alternative B at its worst causes substantially more in five thousand, the maximin rule clearly indicates choice of A in spite of the deferred nature of B's threat. Similarly, if A at its best brings a little pleasure in five years and at its worst much suffering in five thousand, and B at best brings much pleasure in five thousand years and at worst a little suffering in five, the Arrow-Hurwicz rule would prefer B irrespective of the relatively immediate nature of its potential cost and the deferred nature of its potential benefits.

In assessing what are the worst, best and worst, or most regrettable possible outcomes, our judgments must reflect the values which would be assigned to outcomes by those who would experience them. Tastes of future generations once again become a crucial consideration, therefore. But whereas the expected utility calculus re-

---

some plausible theory showing how we would get there from the present situation. Rescher (1975, 3), consolidating recent philosophical work on "possible worlds and possible individuals," remarks that "the domain of unrealized possibility" must be analyzed in terms of "a rational construction proceeding from the domain of the actual."

10. Beckerman (1974, 127) voices a common concern: "There is always *some* risk of almost any catastrophe one cares to think about.... Life is full of risks, and rational, prudent behavior consists in weighing up the costs of insuring against the risks in question. The fallacy in the crude eco-doomster's risk argument, in other words, is that it overlooks the costs of avoiding risks." In expected utility terms, he might have a point: we might be better off taking our chances with the catastrophe, whose costs are discounted by its improbability, than paying the certain costs of insuring against it. Under the other decision rules, however, this point largely disappears. In order for Wald or Savage to suggest that we take our chances, the costs of insurance must exceed the (undiscounted) costs (or, for Savage, regrets) of the catastrophe! The Arrow-Hurwicz rule recommends such a course only if the savings from not buying insurance against catastrophes that do not occur (best outcome) are so great as to overshadow the costs of a catastrophe against which you are not insured that happens (worst outcome). That would mean either that the "catastrophe" is pretty trivial, or that the insurance is ludicrously expensive, or that your index assigns an incredible weight to the optimistic scenario.

quires us to anticipate what their tastes will probably be—and allows us to discount in light of the attendant uncertainties—these alternative decision rules require only that we consider what their tastes *might* be in the worst, best and worst, or most regrettable scenarios. In the case of toxic chemical or radioactive wastes, the worst scenario would be that the biggest possible leak occurs in a generation and in a place where people dislike such threats of poisoning as much as conceivably possible.[11]

9.5. Opportunity Costs as an Excuse for Discounting

Economists, in their more careful discussions, distinguish time-discounting per se from the sort of adjusting for risk and uncertainty discussed above (Henderson 1965, 63; Stokey & Zeckhauser 1978, 173). Naturally they would want to make those adjustments as well. But they find other reasons besides risk and uncertainty for discounting future payoffs, as indeed they must to justify the usual sort of discounting of them at a flat n percent per year.[12]

The classic economic justification for discounting is couched in terms of opportunity costs. Efficient allocation of resources requires that we invest in whichever course of action offers the highest rate of return. Expected future returns from an investment must be adjusted in light of what we could have gained from alternative investments, as reflected in interest rates. Thus, the argument goes, we should work compound interest calculations backward as a means of discounting the anticipated net gains from a project. Symbolically, this can be expressed as an injunction to maximize the sum $\Sigma W_t / (1 + n)^t$ where W_t is the social welfare of a generation living at the time t and n is the discount rate (Eckstein 1961, 460–63; Arrow

11. We also need to consider what the objective circumstances of future generations might possibly be. Both Arrow (1973b, 261) and Harsanyi (1975) argue that the maximum rule commits Rawls (1972) to a zero—or perhaps even a negative—rate of savings. Since future generations will be better off than the present one, the latter is the worst-off group whom maximin, in the Rawlsian application, protects. But that presupposes, quite without cause, that it is *impossible* for the future to be worse than the present. Surely maximin would have us focus upon the possibility of being the worst-off individual in the worst possible world, and among the possibilities we must envisage there is the chance of a future world where people generally are much worse off than presently.

12. Parfit (1981, 9) agrees that "we ought to discount those predictions which are more likely to be false," but points out that "predictions about the further future are not less likely to be true at a rate of n percent per year." So, too, with the diminishing marginal utility argument: if future generations will be better off than the present one, we should discount so as to avoid "redistributing income from a present that is relatively poor to a future relatively rich" (Arrow 1976, 122; cf. Baumol 1970, 285, and Page 1977, 151–52); but we cannot be sure that they will be better off at all, and even if they are it is unlikely to be by a flat n percent per year.

1966; 1976; Baumol 1970; Little and Mirrlees 1974, sec. 9.13; Page 1977, chap. 7).

Settling upon the correct discount rate is, of course, a great challenge. Judgment on specific projects can be enormously sensitive to the choice of rates, as has often been shown for water management projects (Hanke and Anwyll 1980). Energy choices seem similarly sensitive. Nuclear power plants seem superior to conventional ones only if we use discount rates low enough to allow the cheaper long-term operating costs of nuclear plants to overcome their higher short-term costs of construction, but high enough to trivialize the present value of the enormous costs of ultimately decommissioning the reactors, of storing their wastes, and of bearing their relatively more long-term health hazards.[13]

Economists have debated various strategies for choosing an appropriate discount rate. The problem with simply using whatever rate prevails in capital markets is that those rates also contain elements of risk premiums, which must somehow be factored out to reveal the "pure time discount." The government borrowing rate has, consequently, been commonly regarded as "the" risk-free interest rate. But even this imperfectly reflects the real rate of return on private investments which would be displaced by government projects, and there have been several attempts to measure these more directly (Prest and Turvey 1965; Dasgupta and Peace 1972, chap. 6). None of my principal objections to opportunity cost discounting, however, turns on the intricacies of these calculations.

My first objection builds on the simple observation that the discount rate has to be revised from time to time as opportunities, and the costs of forgoing them, shift. Arrow (1976, 125–27), for example, claims that the 10 percent discount rate urged by economists in the mid-1960s and endorsed by the U.S. Office of Management and Budget reflected an "unprecedentedly high rate" of technological progress over the two previous decades; and now that that rate has declined, Arrow argues, a lower discount rate is appropriate. Similarly in Britain, the Treasury test discount rate of 10 percent has now been reduced to a 5 to 7 percent range (Barnett 1978). Perhaps such constant readjustment of the discount rate is broadly consistent with its use in short-term calculations—if the period is sufficiently short and the world sufficiently stable, roughly the same rate might be expected to prevail throughout the period. But the necessity to readjust the rate renders this justification very inapplicable to long-

13. The Ford-MITRE Nuclear Energy Policy Study Group found that, even using an exceptionally high 9 percent discount rate, they had to ignore health and decommissioning costs in order to make nuclear power plants look competitive with coal-fired ones (Keeny 1977, chap. 3).

term discounting. Over many centuries, there is no telling what the true opportunity costs of investments today might be. Indeed, we cannot even be certain that a positive interest rate will always prevail: there might be some particularly dire patches during which an investment of $x in one year might bring a real return of only $x $-e$ the next.[14] In the face of these imponderables associated with distant futures, the opportunity cost argument for discounting must be confined strictly to near futures.

Changing interest rates particularly undermine Freeman's (1977) ingenious attempt at separating the efficiency and equity implications of discounting. The essence of his argument is that the logic of exponential growth works both ways. In reckoning the present value of a project, we discount future damages D according to the formula $P = D/(1 + n)^t$. Suppose the immediate benefits of the project exceed P, its discounted costs. Then we could still realize a net benefit even if we were to set aside a sum P now to compensate future generations for the harm we do them. This sum accumulates compound interest according to the formula $(1 + n)^t P$, so by the end of t years the fund will have grown to the sum D and will therefore just compensate future generations for the harms they will then experience. The crucial presumption in Freeman's argument, however, is that the rate n which was used in discounting future damages actually *will* prevail as the interest rate throughout the period. An amount sufficient to compensate future generations fully will be accumulated only if that rate (or some combination of rates with the same ultimate effect) does prevail. Unless Freeman can guarantee this—and I cannot imagine how he could, for a very long period—it is not necessarily true that the amount D could be provided, even if we wanted to do so.

My second objection is that the opportunity cost argument in its most powerful form applies only to a restricted class of economic goods, i.e., those which have a monetary equivalent. Discussions of discounting are always "couched in terms of discounting dollar flows." Even in ordinary public investment decisions "what happens in real terms is that real resources—land, labor, raw materials, plant and equipment, and so on—are diverted from one use to another" (Stokey and Zeckhauser 1978, 175, 170–71). All these can, however, be converted to monetary equivalents and discounted in those terms. Real problems arise only where this is not possible. "It is arguable," Stokey and Zeckhauser (1978, 175–76) concede,

14. Negative discount rates are unusual but not inconceivable. Stokey and Zeckhauser (1978, 175) offer various examples, concluding that, "in general, negative discount rates are applicable when people have no recourse but to rely on highly imperfect stores of value, that is, on commodities that are expected to deteriorate over time."

that ordinary discount rates are not appropriate for discounting flows that consist of intangibles such as pain and suffering, or improved health, or especially changes in the risk of death.... This issue is still very much up in the air. Some economists and analysts have in the past preferred not to discount such streams; others discount routinely at going rates. A few are beginning to think seriously about this enormously perplexing problem.

Koopmans faces this issue squarely in his presidential address to the American Economic Association. He starts with the honorable inclination to "make the present value of future human life independent of the time at which it is lived" (Koopmans 1979, 9). But in the end he sees that, so long as we put a price on human life, consistency requires that future lives be subjected to the same sort of discounting as money itself. "The reason for discounting future life years is precisely that they are being valued relative to dollars and, since a dollar in the future is discounted relative to a present dollar, so must a life year in the future be discounted relative to a present dollar" or a present life (Weinstein and Stason 1977, 720; Clark and Fleishman 1980, 21).

Surely that *is* the implication of establishing a monetary equivalent of human life. But that is at least as much an argument against putting a price on life as it is in favor of discounting future life years. Consider the implications of discounting future lives at even a modest 5 percent. We would have to be indifferent between a clinic that cured 10 patients of a disease immediately and a preventative health system costing as much that prevents 16 people from contracting the same disease in ten years' time. We should be willing to use a drug like DES to prevent pregnant women from miscarrying today even if it increases future miscarriages among their daughters, just so long as we do not induce more than 26 miscarriages in twenty years for every 10 we prevent today. Or, again, we should be indifferent between killing one person today with the sulphurous emissions from coal-fired power plants and killing 1,730 with the leaking wastes from nuclear power plants in two hundred years' time (Slovic and Fischhoff 1980, 141; Ramsay and Russell 1978). Insofar as we do not believe that sort of tradeoff is permissible, to that extent we are rejecting the notion of monetary equivalents for human lives, at least for some purposes. The opportunity cost argument demonstrates that a dollar tomorrow is worth less than a dollar today; and, by extension, anything convertible into dollars (and back again) is worth less tomorrow than today. But there are some things which cannot be assigned monetary equivalents, either because it degrades people and their cherished principles to do so (section 6.6) or else because people cannot be compensated in any way for their losses (section 8.3.3). Those things can be discounted only in their own terms, if at all.[15]

15. Under certain circumstances, "life years ... can be invested to yield more life years as dollars can be invested to yield more dollars" (cf. Weinstein and Stason 1977, 720)—e.g., by investing in research into life-saving technologies rather than installing life-saving devices now available. Some lives are thereby sacrificed in the short term but, if the research pays off, we may be able to save two lives in five years' time for every one the machine would have saved. Future lives saved by the machine must, therefore, be discounted in light of these opportunity costs. But the discount rate used must never exceed the "internal rate of return" on research itself, which limits not only the size of the discount rate but also the form of the discounting function. Research, although always cumulative, is unlikely to be as powerfully cumulative as the geometric progression implicit in compound interest/discount calculations. Scientific discoveries simply do not snowball in the way that suggests. The discounting of future lives must mimic the more modest, nongeometric form of the function describing returns on research investments. Nongeometric discounting may entail some intertemporal inconsistency, but so too may geometrical discounting once we take into account the pleasure people derive from anticipating future pleasures or recollecting ones past (Page 1977, 195).

Policies

10 The Ethics of Nuclear Power

One hardly needs initiation into the dark mysteries of nuclear physics to contribute usefully to the debate now widely raging over nuclear power. While many important empirical questions are still unresolved, these do not really lie at the center of the controversy. Instead, it is a debate about values. Survey research shows that, among both experts and the public at large, the disagreement between advocates and opponents of nuclear energy is less over what the benefits and risks are than over which are worth pursuing.[1] Philosophers need make no apologies upon joining such issues.

In any case, philosophers are unduly shy of empirical questions. It is, as I have argued in chapter 1, far better to address genuine policy issues in a genuine way than to resort to "desert island examples," disingenuously assuming away all the complexities that combined to make the issues problematic in the first place. Philosophers, it is often said,

This chapter is reprinted, with revisions and updated information, from Robert E. Goodin, "No Moral Nukes," *Ethics* 90 (1980): 417–49. ©Copyright 1980 by The University of Chicago.
    1. Duncan (1978, 19) sees the nuclear power controversy as following the general pattern of "a steady evolution in which problems are initially defined as scientific and technical, later as economic, and still later . . . as intrinsically social and political." Among American energy experts, surveys show that advocates and opponents of nuclear technology perceive the same risks and differ only in their assessment of whether they are worth running—of whether or not nuclear power would contribute to the "quality of life" (Otway and Fishbein 1976). Surveys of the general public in Austria and America similarly show that advocates of nuclear power want "economic and technological benefits," whereas opponents are more concerned to avoid "psychological risks" associated with fears of "technology out of control." These findings lead Otway, et al. (1978) to conclude that nuclear power is basically a "life style" issue.

have no special expertise in resolving empirical questions. Neither, I would add, do they suffer any special disabilities, save those which are self-imposed.

My discussion of the ethical problems surrounding nuclear power will focus upon three areas of substantive concern: risk assessment, distributive justice, and democratic theory. It concludes with a survey of some new decision rules suggested by the problem of nuclear energy. These are broadly applicable to any policy choice with similarly "low probability, high risk" characteristics.

10.1. Risk Assessment

Nuclear technology poses risks of several sorts. There are the "ordinary" risks in the fuel cycle—risks of mining and refining uranium, of transporting it to the reactor, of operating the reaction, and of removing, treating, transporting, and finally disposing of the leftover radioactive wastes. All these have parallels, but rarely strict equivalents, in any method of generating power. Serious as accidents at coal-fired plants can be, none could have such catastrophic consequences as seem to have followed from the 1957–58 Soviet nuclear mishap (Trabalka, et al. 1980). Nuclear power plants also pose more extraordinary risks—of sabotage, of theft of fissionable material, and of further proliferation of nuclear weapons. The task of assessing all these risks falls naturally into two parts. First I shall discuss techniques for estimating the extent of the risks. Then I shall turn to evaluating their acceptability (Otway and Phaner 1976).

10.1.1.   What Are the Risks, and How Do We Know?

In ordinary life we usually learn from past experience, using trial-and-error techniques both for estimating risks and for eliminating them. Sometimes it is said in defense of nuclear reactors that "thus far the safety record has been excellent. The 200 reactor-years of operation of U.S. commercial light-water reactors have had no demonstrable adverse effects on public health" (Keeny 1977, 213). All that this proves, however, is that the probability of a serious nuclear accident is unlikely to be much higher than 1 in 200. That is hardly reassuring, given the catastrophic consequences that might follow— $17 billion in property damage, 45,00 immediate fatalities, 100,000 delayed casualties, according to the Brookhaven Report WASH-740 (Green 1973; Shrader-Frechette 1980, 78). We would demand that the probability of that sort of accident be very tiny indeed. But, "because the probability is so small, there is no practical possibility of determining this failure rate directly" (Weinberg 1972a, 211). For example, the probability of a nuclear reactor accident is officially estimated at 10^{-7} accidents per reactor per year. For experience to prove those estimates correct, we would have to build 1,000 reactors and operate them for well over 10,000 years.

Trial and error, and learning by doing, are appropriate—either for the epistemic task of discovering what the risks are or for the adaptive task of overcoming them—only under the special conditions identified in chapter 2. These are conspicuously missing in the case of nuclear power. First, we must have good reasons for believing that the errors, if they occur, will be small—otherwise the lessons may prove far too costly. No doubt some nuclear mishaps will be modest. But for the same reasons that small accidents are possible, so too are large ones; and some of the errors resulting in the failure of nuclear reactor safeguards may be very costly indeed. This makes trial and error inappropriate in that setting (Häfle 1974). Second, errors must be immediately recognizable and correctable. The impact of radioactive emissions from operating reactors or leaking waste storage sites upon human populations or the natural environment may well be a "sleeper" effect that does not appear in time for us to revise our original policy accordingly. Finally, learning by doing is a flawed strategy because it is often unclear how to describe the salient features of what you have done in the past and hence what "lessons" to draw from the experience. Models building on "fuzzy set theory" show how complicated the decision problem becomes if the classification of events is in doubt as well as the probabilities of their occurrence: it is one thing to judge the probability of pulling a black ball out of the urn if you know you have already pulled out two blacks and one red; it is quite another if the last ball was reddish black, and you are not sure whether to count it as red or black (Nurmi 1979). Such problems in interpreting feedback, difficult even in the most leisurely scientific experiments, are especially acute in crisis situations. In the Three Mile Island accident, for example, technicians were getting wildly contradictory signals on their monitors—they were not sure whether the reactor was completely empty of coolant or was flooded with it. Not being sure what they had done, they could not know with any confidence what they should do next (Kemeny 1979, 27–33, 113–22).

Our estimates of reactor accident probabilities should, of course, be constantly revised in light of our experiences (Lewis 1975; 1978, 16; Flowers 1976, para. 274). So too should our operating procedures becomes more efficient with experience, as indeed they seem to have done (Joskow and Rozanski 1979). The question is not whether, having made errors, we should try to learn something from them. It is, instead, whether we should invite such errors in hopes of learning from them—whether, in other words, we should *count* on these trial-and-error and learning-by-doing processes. In the absence of any guarantees that our errors would be small, immediately recognizable, and correctable, I argue we should not.

If experience is an inadequate teacher, we might turn instead to more formal experiments. There have been, for example, "loss of fluid tests" taking a one-fiftieth-scale reactor critical to see how it behaves. The trouble with this approach lies, obviously, in generalizing up to the behavior of full-scale reactors. "Unless one is willing to build a full-scale prototype, and test it under the precise conditions which will be encountered in practice, there is always the uncertainty of extrapolating to new and untried circumstances" (Weinberg 1972a, 211).

This leaves us with little option but to try to surmise nuclear risks through elaborate mathematical models (Häfle 1974). Such exercises are always problematic. Typically, parameters can be estimated and variables related in many different ways, as reflected in the several alternative models of future energy demand (Manne, et al. 1979). Even the simple process of writing the computer program for so complicated a set of itneractions leaves much room for error. Five American reactors had to be shut down owing to an error in the computer program used to evaluate how well their emergency cooling systems would stand up to earthquake stresses (Lanouette 1979a).

The most comprehensive attempt at assessing nuclear safety in this way, the Rasmussen (1975) *Reactor Safety Study,* analyzed "fault trees" to calculate the probability of a "major" leak of radiation (one causing more than 1,000 fatalities) to be equivalent to that of a meteor landing on a large city. The Nuclear Regulatory Commission has since admitted that this much-touted conclusion is an inaccurate summary of the report's findings (Lewis 1975; 1978; Carter 1978; Lanouette 1979b). Widespread criticism has, however, raised doubts about the Rasmussen methodology as well as the summary of its findings (Kendall and Moglewer 1974; Lieberman 1976). Some problems, such as those concerning the treatment of "common mode failures" and the statistical techniques employed, may be correctable in principle (Lewis 1978) but not in practice (Levi 1981). Others are more fundamental. These include, for example, problems in mixing very different types of probability judgments, based on diverse types and qualities of evidence, in determining one composite probability statistic for each branch of the fault tree (Hansson 1979).

Perhaps the most fundamental flaw in such mathematical models is that they require us to list all possible sources of error. Only after we have sketched in all the possible branches of the fault tree can we go about assessing overall probabilities of an accident. Often this is not possible, as section 9.4 has argued. Maybe this would not matter much if, as Rasmussen (1975) and Lewis (1978, 14) claim, we were sure that all *significant* branches had been explored—i.e., that none of the others would double the overall estimate of the probability of an accident. But, alas, "it is clear that the unexpected hazards are not necessarily only the small ones" (Flowers 1976, para. 175). To argue anecdotally, recall the comment of a former Nuclear Regulatory Commission project manager: "What really spooked us about Three Mile Island is that you had a loss of coolant accident—the most severe—from a sequence of events that should never have caused one. It's made us reassess our whole approach to analyzing accidents" (David Jaffe, quoted in Lanouette 1979c, 681; cf. Weinberg 1979, 98). Such unanticipated chains can easily pose hazards that totally overshadow those associated with the chains we can foresee.[2]

The dominant source of risks that defy mapping ex ante in fault trees is "the human factor." The saboteur, explicitly excluded from consideration in Rasmussen (1975), presents a particularly dramatic example: if we could anticipate all the ways he might enter a reactor, we could in principle block all his entry points and foil his plan (cf. section 9.4 above). More mundane examples of human error of the sort that abound in the "nugget file" (Lanouette 1979b) pose much the same problem for fault trees. Who, in constructing a mathematical model, could have guessed that technicians would plug a leaky coolant pipe with a basketball or connect a radioactive waste storage tank to the plant's drinking water system or carry a lighted candle into electrical cable housing at Browns Ferry? (See Flowers 1976, paras. 174–75; Keeny 1977, 227–29; Fairley 1977, 334.) Of course, the human factor can work both ways: "Operators . . . might make matters much better during an accident, in ways that are intrinsically hard to analyze," such as the useful improvisation by Browns Ferry technicians during their fire (Lewis 1978, 13, 26). But current nuclear

2. Fairley (1977, 334–35), criticizing the use of fault trees to estimate the risks of marine transportation of liquefied natural gas, emphasizes that "the estimates of probabilities made for identifiable and analyzed sources have to be considered *together with* the probability of an accident arising from all other sources," and the latter may utterly overshadow the former. He illustrates with an example from poker. We can use the laws of probability to analyze the chances of a royal flush's appearing through a fair deal: 1 in 649,740. To this, we must add "the chance that it arises from cheating." Although that defies systematic analysis, Fairley suggests a probability estimate of 1 in 10,000. The overall probability of seeing a royal flush in the real world is, thus, 1/649,740 plus 1/10,000, or just over 1/10,000. The unanalyzable path dominates the probability estimate.

reactor safety standards are wrong to count on things' turning out this way. "They concentrated on equipment, assuming that the presence of operators could only improve the situation," whereas at Three Mile Island, in contrast, "the major factor that turned this incident into a serious accident was inappropriate operator error" (Kemeny 1979, 8–9, 11). This should hardly come as a surprise, given all the organizational (Wolf 1980), psychological (Otway and Misenta 1980), and cultural (Roberts, et al. 1980) factors leading humans to err and preventing them from coping successfully with the emergencies that result from their errors. Whether mathematical models overestimate the risks or underestimate them, the real point is that, because they cannot account for the human factor adequately, they are bound to estimate the risks badly. We can place no great faith in such error-prone techniques for estimating risks.

The conclusion is that, with nuclear power plants, we would be living not merely with risk but also with *irresolvable uncertainties*. In most cases, we cannot assign probabilities to outcomes on the basis of either objective data or even plausible scientific theories.[3] We could, of course, fall back upon subjective probability estimates, constantly corrected in light of experience. As I have already said, however, experience is likely to prove a poor guide for error correction. And, in any case, subjective probability estimates are subject to the well-known distortions discussed in section 8.1.1 above. The overall conclusions must be that "individuals are poor probability assessors and perhaps more important, that they underestimate their poorness by assessing probabilities too tightly" (Zeckhauser 1975, 445). In psychological laboratory experiments, people were asked to assess a 98 percent confidence interval; instead of 2 percent of true values coming as "surprises" (i.e., falling outside the stated interval), something between 20 and 50 percent did so (Lichtenstein, et al. 1977). And experts are as prey to this tendency to overconfidence as laymen: the peer review of the Rasmussen (1975) report concludes, "We are unable to define whether the overall probability of a core melt . . . is high or low, but we are certain that the error bands are understated" (Lewis 1978, vi). When we know that subjective probability estimates are distorted in these ways, it is simply irrational to rely upon them (Elster 1979a). Naturally we would like to resolve these uncertainties if we could. But if we cannot, we need not be dismayed. There *are* techniques, discussed in section 9.4, for making decisions in the face of irreconcilable uncertainties. Since

3. Either we have no plausible theories or we have too many of them. And, as Føllesdal (1979, 405) wryly remarks, "Where we have several competing theories, which give different predictions, all these theories should be regarded with suspicion and we should be prepared for a risk that is higher than what is predicted by any of the theories."

we cannot specify all the possible ways for a nuclear disaster to happen, much less fix reliable probabilities (objective, theoretical, or subjective) for each of them, we had better fall back upon these less familiar techniques.

10.1.2. What Risks Are Acceptable?

Arguments over what level of risk is *socially* acceptable always seem to be cast in terms of what risks *individuals* are willing to bear (Pearce 1981, 182).[4] Advocates of nuclear power point with glee to the fact that people voluntarily assume risks much greater than those apparently associated with nuclear technology—when crossing a busy road or driving several miles, for example. They insist that if people are willing to accept those greater risks, they should surely be willing to accept the lesser risks of nuclear technology (Starr 1969; Rasmussen 1975, chaps. 6, 7; Flowers 1976, paras. 168–77; Parker 1978, para. 10.29–34; Rothschild 1978).[5]

In this form, the argument is totally fallacious. The risks are cumulative. If I am presently engaging in activities carrying a 5 percent risk of death, far from indicating my willingness to do anything else with a 5 percent or less chance of getting me killed, that fact makes me all the more reluctant to do anything else that would raise my risks to 6 percent (Weinstein, et al. 1980; Pearce 1981, 185). What other risks I voluntarily run are not, therefore, indicative of what new risks I will accept. What other risks I run involuntarily are even less so. The standard practice of using "natural background" levels of radiation as a benchmark for judging how much more radiation may be introduced into the environment is utter nonsense (cf. Weinberg 1979, 107–8). Even if people have reconciled themselves

4. Economists sometimes argue that, while it is reasonable for individuals to be averse to risk-taking, there is no reason for society as a whole to mirror those sentiments. For every project turning out much worse than expected, there will be another turning out much better than expected; and, if we assume that many risky ventures are under way concurrently, the law of large numbers assures that these variations will all balance out. Thus, society (as distinct from individual entrepreneurs) runs no real risks, so it would be irrational for society as a whole to be averse to "risky" ventures. But, as I have argued in section 9.2 above, this presupposes a payoff structure that is symmetrical, admitting of both worse-than-expected and better-than-expected results. In the case of nuclear power, this seems to be missing. What unexpected windfall might conceivably balance out the giant costs of a meltdown's breaching containment walls? It seems extraordinarily likely that all the good that can ever come from nuclear power can be anticipated ahead of time, leaving only the evil to surprise us.

5. Although it is perfectly legitimate to impute "revealed" risk preferences to people on the basis of their other behavior, we obviously have no moral right to hold them to those preferences. Maybe they are just being silly and inconsistent when they now balk at risks considerably smaller than others they have already accepted happily. But simple inconsistency on people's part does not remove whatever moral reasons we had for respecting their preferences in the first place.

to suffering this inevitable background radiation, that is no reason to suppose that they would be willing to take double the dose, which is what we are really contemplating when asking them to subject themselves to as much again from a manmade source.[6]

There is something superficially puzzling about the way in which people happily run some large risks but balk at others which are much smaller. A large part of the solution lies in comparing the benefit-risk ratios of each of these activities—obviously people will run bigger risks for bigger benefits, although the relationship is hardly linear. It is especially important, in this process, to compare the benefit-risk ratios of alternative ways of securing the *same* benefit. People may be willing to run the relatively large risks entailed in driving because there are no other ways (or, at any rate, no much less risky ways) of getting where they need to go. And the reason people balk at nuclear reactor risks, which are arguably much smaller, may well be that there *do* seem to be other less risky ways to achieve roughly the same benefits. The relevant question in assessing the acceptability of nuclear risks is, then, whether by shifting to nuclear power we can eliminate more risks than we incur.

Some suggest this is the case, at least when nuclear power is compared with that from conventional sources. The burning of fossil fuels releases into the atmosphere vast quantities of CO_2 which threaten serious alterations in the global climate (Flowers 1976, para. 192; Keeny 1977, chap. 6; Woodwell 1978; Weinberg, et al. 1979, chaps. 3, 11). Emissions of SO_2 and NO_x from coal-fired plants aggravate heart and lung and chronic respiratory disease, leading in some cases to premature death—although it should be emphasized that these emissions can be reduced substantially, at a cost, "by the use of lime scrubbers alone or in conjunction with low-sulfur coal or by the use of other new technologies, such as fluidized bed combustion" (Keeny 1977, 196; cf. Squires 1970 and Weinberg, et al. 1979, chaps. 3, 11). McBride and associates (1978) conclude that the airborne effluent of coal power plants has a greater radiological impact, too, than "routine emissions" from nuclear installations. When we take into account *all* the risks (including those of mining, building

6. Similar illogic pervades the report of the British Health and Safety Executive on the interacting hazards associated with petroleum storage tanks, a methane gas terminal, and oil refineries on the small (9 miles by 2½ miles), inhabited Canvey Island. The HSE calculates that the annual fatality risk to Canvey residents from these activities is 5.3 in 10,000 at present, and could be reduced to 1.4 in 10,000 through various improvements. The HSE argues that this compares favorably with other risks Britons run, e.g., a 1.3 in 10,000 chance of a fatal traffic accident (Locke, et al. 1978, 25, 15). But, as objectors at the Public Inquiry were quick to point out, Canvey Islanders run those other risks, too. The question is not one of consistency—whether they are willing to run the same sorts of risks they have already accepted before. Rather, the question concerns the acceptability of *doubling* their fatality risks (Ward 1981).

the plant, operating it, etc.), it is sometimes argued that the number of deaths that must be expected with coal, oil, or renewable sources of energy might exceed the expected fatalities from nuclear power.[7]

These studies suffer certain common shortcomings. Casual phrases such as "routine emissions" and "expected fatalities" hide a great disparity in the confidence of our judgments. We pretty well know how many lives are lost each year in coal mines or construction accidents, but are much less certain of the number that might die in a nuclear accident. Furthermore, calculations of "expected fatalities" hide great disparities in the profiles of possible accidents. An expected fatality of one person per year might mean that there is one chance in ten of ten people's dying, or it might mean there is one chance in a million of a million's dying. Most accidents with coal, oil, or renewable sources are of the former type, whereas many of the risks of nuclear installations are of the latter. Since people are disproportionately averse to risks of large-scale catastrophes (Fischhoff, et al. 1978), the latter sorts of risks should be weighted especially heavily in social decision-making (Flowers 1976, para. 172). Simple "expected fatality" calculations (McBride, et al. 1978; Inhaber 1979; 1981; Weinberg, et al. 1979) fail to do so, thus inadequately reflecting people's real concerns with social risks. In addition, many of these studies tend to make very limited comparisons of only a few of the many possible energy alternatives. Some (Keeny 1977, chaps. 5, 6; McBride, et al. 1978; Weinberg, et al. 1979, chaps. 3, 11) just compare environmental and public health impacts of nuclear and coal-burning plants.[8] Even when assessing risks of "nonconventional" as well as conventional sources, these studies (Inhaber 1979; 1981; Weinberg, et al. 1979, chaps. 4, 12) focus upon risks *per unit* of power generated or per some fixed anticipated demand level. In this way, they overlook some of the most promising strategies for dealing with the energy crisis, i.e., of increasing the efficiency of energy usage and curtailing energy de-

7. This is the conclusion of the much-touted Inhaber (1979; 1981) study. Letters in subsequent issues of *Science* from Rein Lemberg and Richard Caputo (May 4, 1979, p. 454) and especially from John P. Holdren, Kirk R. Smith, and Gregory Morris (May 11, 1979, pp. 564–68) were, however, unusually devastating. As the latter concludes, "When the effects of major errors and inconsistencies . . . are removed, the [Inhaber 1979] *Science* article's conclusions change drastically: The difference between coal's health hazards and those of nuclear power shrinks, and the calculated hazards of the renewables fall to near or below those of nuclear."

8. Lovins (1977, 148), commenting on an earlier draft of Weinberg, et al. (1979), protests, "Those analysts who, like Dr. Weinberg, arbitrarily assume that a nuclear moratorium only means building big fossil-fueled power stations, are automatically barring themselves from examining any policy questions of real interest." Subsequent drafts have only partially overcome this objection. There is, in Weinberg, et al. (1979, chaps. 4, 12), a cost comparison between nuclear and solar energy systems. But environmental impact comparisons are limited to coal-burning and nuclear power plants (chaps. 3, 11).

mand (Lovins 1977; Barker 1978; Carter 1980; U.S. NAS 1978; Stobaugh and Yergin 1979). Even the Oak Ridge team admits that in its "low-energy demand scenario" solar energy proves least costly (Weinberg, et al. 1979). Cost-benefit or benefit-risk studies must compare *all* the available options, as few of these analyses have done.

All this emphasis upon what risks people are willing to accept might be misleading in still another way. Public policymakers cannot, as the judge chairing the Windscale inquiry supposed, simply ask themselves, "Are the public likely voluntarily to accept this risk?" (Parker 1978, para. 10.28), because the public are not being given a choice. Instead, such a question is asked only when public officials are about to make the choice and impose the decision—and the concomitant risks—upon the public. Involuntary risks of this sort must be treated differently from voluntary ones, such as driving or crossing the street or playing football. That does not necessarily mean we should ban the imposition of involuntary risks altogether: psychometric studies show that people are willing to accept voluntary risks about a thousand times greater than risks they would accept having imposed on them involuntarily (Starr 1969); and using these results, we can easily calculate "voluntary risk equivalents" by multiplying the costs of involuntary risks by a thousand. That makes the option of imposing such risks less attractive but, since you typically start with low levels of risk anyway in the case of nuclear power, these "adjusted" risk costs may still fall within tolerable limits for many people. The fact that nuclear risks tend to be involuntary is not enough, if this procedure is adopted, to disqualify that option automatically.

More leverage on the problem can be obtained by asking, as in chapter 8 above, whether there is really any reason to respect people's preferences for risks. There are some sorts of risks we would not allow people to run, even if they wanted to do so; and there are others we would not mind making people run, even if they did not want to do so. In the case of nuclear energy these considerations might argue either way, for ignoring "irrational" fears of nuclear reactors (Hohenemser, et al. 1977) or for ignoring reckless optimism about them. The latter seems more persuasive: Psychologists show that people start out with a healthy skepticism about new technologies (Fischhoff, et al. 1978), but that as they become familiar with them they dread their risks much less (Slovic and Fischhoff 1980, 130; Slovic, et al. 1981), probably because they make unwarranted inferences about their safety from a small sample of experiences (Tversky and Kahneman 1971; 1974). If we overrule people's risk preferences at all, then we should rule against rather than in favor of "low-probability/high-risk" technologies like nu-clear power.

10.2. Distributive Justice

Morally, our obligation is to render just treatment to natural individuals. Artificial constructs, such as "nation" or "generation," lack any formal status in such discussions. Nevertheless, they retain enormous practical significance because, for better or worse, they are the bases upon which distributions are made. Consequently, everyone sharing the same generational or national status will, ipso facto, share many of the same interests, too. Thus, "nations" and "generations" can serve as a kind of shorthand in my discussion of the implications of energy policy for distributive justice.

10.2.1. Justice between Nations

Were we selecting energy strategies strictly with regard to international distributive justice, we would be investing heavily in research into solar technologies. Solar energy is the resource distributed most equitably throughout the world, being most abundant in the least prosperous equatorial regions and least abundant in the richest countries of the North (Russett 1979). If ways could be found to tap this resource effectively, the poorest nations would realize most of the benefits. But the initiative in developing and spreading the technologies needed to do so must inevitably lie with the richer nations (Ashworth 1980).

One of the most interesting defenses of nuclear energy is, paradoxically, couched in similar terms of international distributive justice. Edward Teller (1978, 1–2) claims that "among the many hazards of energy . . . the one that is by far the biggest . . . is the maldistribution of energy throughout the world." In many nations, per capita energy consumption is less than a tenth that in the United States. Teller would "not want to say that energy and the standard of living are directly related." Nevertheless, "they do have something to do with each other, and if energy is really deficient then a decent standard of living is practically impossible." The Green Revolution—which Teller regards as the only way to feed the starving masses—is illustrative of this connection, depending as it does upon energy-intensive irrigation systems and nitrogen-based fertilizers. The crucial step in Teller's case for nuclear power is this: "For these poorer countries to develop, it is necessary to have energy in smaller packages—and that means, preferably, oil." These energy sources peculiarly appropriate to Third World development could be "freed up" if only the First World were to shift to nuclear power, which could effectively substitute for fossil fuels in a developed economy but not in a developing one.

This case for nuclear power rests, however, upon some implausible assumptions. The most dubious is that, if the First World reduced its consumption of oil, then that same amount of oil would be available to the Third World. Of course it would not. The Third World simply cannot exercise the same sort of "effective demand" (desire backed by money) for the fuel. Exploration for and extraction of oil from many fields (the North Sea, the North Slope of Alaska) are economic only because the First World is willing and able to pay so dearly for the oil. If the Third World alone were bidding for it, the oil would stay in the ground. The argument here resembles the argument that Americans should stop eating beef so that the vast quantity of grain going to fatten cows could go instead to Asians who are starving; all that would happen if Americans shifted their dietary habits would be a reduction in the amount of grain cultivated, since starving Asians are in no position to pay nearly so much (Christensen 1978).

We are saved from an utterly depressing conclusion by the fact that development does not depend upon energy nearly so heavily as Teller suggests. Energy-intensive development strategies are not the only, or perhaps even the best, ways for the Third World to develop. The Green Revolution is now widely questioned, and "appropriate technology" widely embraced (Sen 1960; Myrdal 1968, chap. 20). Thus we may well wonder whether the correlation between standard of living and energy consumption is not a historical artifact, proving merely that most of the now-developed countries did in fact pursue energy-intensive development paths rather than proving (as Teller's argument requires) that that is the only path available. The fact that the correlation disappears when we look at developed market economies alone suggests that alternative paths might be available (Mazur and Rosa 1974).

Whereas Teller would confine nuclear technology to the First World, a second argument for nuclear energy, also couched in terms of international distributive justice, would spread it widely. This argument points quite simply to the fact that very many Third World nations want nuclear reactors desperately badly. Justice requires the "haves" to share the goods of the world (defined as those things people desire) with the "have-nots." This principle seems to be captured admirably in the language of Article IV of the Non-proliferation Treaty, obliging all parties to facilitate the right of all other parties "to participate in the fullest possible exchange of equipment, materials and scientific and technological information for the peaceful uses of nuclear energy."

Why Argentina, Brazil, Bangladesh, Korea, Taiwan, and the Philippines are so anxious to have nuclear reactors is, according to the classical liberal principles still governing international law, very much their own business. Certainly fission power promises no economic advantages for such countries. As the World Bank reasoned in refusing to make further loans for nuclear projects in very poor countries, "Without national electricity-transmission systems or the possession of modern electrical appliances to plug into them, . . . it makes no economic sense to go for ambitious generating stations— especially fission-power plants" (Breach 1978, 85). But perhaps Third World countries realize that nuclear reactors would be bad investments and desire them instead strictly as status symbols. Who, then, is to say what price one should pay for one's pride? Afghanistan's economy might be infinitely stronger were she to merge with Russia, but who is to say that she is wrong to try to retain her independence?

More plausibly, Third World nations may want nuclear power as a step toward—and as cover for—developing nuclear weapons capabilities. Once they have nuclear reactors, "many nations would be only a step or two from nuclear weapons competence," small plutonium separation plants being both technologically simple and relatively cheap (Keeny 1977, 272–73, 279). Thus, the British Royal Commission on Environmental Pollution concludes, "The spread of nuclear power will inevitably facilitate the spread of the ability to make nuclear weapons" (Flowers 1976, para. 167. Cf. Wohlstetter 1976–77; Wohlstetter, et al. 1976; Lovins 1977, chap. 11; 1980; Lovins, et al. 1980). Actual nuclear weapons acquisition may, for political reasons, lag somewhat behind acquisition of the capacity, as seems to have happened in recent years (Farley 1976, 148; Keeny 1977, chap. 9). But this is, on any reckoning, a most precarious situation.

Frightening and undesirable as nuclear proliferation undoubtedly is, we have also to face up to the serious question of distributive justice posed by the monopoly by developed nations of nuclear arms and the advantages they afford in the international balance of power. Falk (1976, 303) asks, "If we're prepared to use nuclear weapons . . ., why shouldn't the same option be permitted to all those other nations that have other goals in the world?" And, to speak pragmatically, the more we try to keep nuclear technology from the Third World—by forbidding reprocessing, for example— the more they will try to get it (Rose and Lester 1978). Pragmatism and justice alike seem to indicate that, if anyone is to have a nuclear capacity, then everyone should—and eventually will. If we cannot live with that result, then we must commit ourselves to a world in which no one has a nuclear capacity.

10.2.2.   Justice between Generations

Most energy options seem to have strong implications for inter-generational distributions. Conventional burners use up irreplace-able natural resources—coal and oil—and emit CO_2 which may alter the global climate, more likely in the next century than in this (Weinberg, et al. 1979, chaps. 3, 11). With nuclear energy, the challenge is disposal of radioactive wastes (Routley and Routley 1978; Kneese 1973). In the process of generating energy, we also create isotopes which will continue to pose serious hazards for a very long time—the half-life of plutonium-239 is 24,000 years, that of neptunium-237 is 2,130,000 years, that of iodine-129 is 16 million years, and so on. We have little choice but to leave this inheritance to our successors. The only hope is to store these radioactive wastes in such a way as to protect future generations from their effects.[9]

The method currently dominating American, British, Canadian, and Swedish planning is to embed the wastes in glass or ceramics, encapsulate that in a three-layed metal capsule, and deposit the capsule in deep rock (U.S. IRG 1978; Johansson and Steen 1978; 1979; Kubo and Rose 1973). Through the centuries, each of these three barriers is increasingly likely to be breached. Even nuclear apologists (Cohen 1977, 25) concede that the cannisters will corrode after only a few hundred years, leaving the glass exposed. Water can leach the radioactive isotopes from the glass, all the more rapidly if it crumbles, as some suggest it might. The only remaining hope is that geologic barriers will prevent ground water from carrying dissolved wastes up to the human environment. In one simulation, de Marsily and associates (1977) find that, under the best possible conditions, in 1.7 million years iodine-129 will reach the human environment in concentrations 5.3 times the international standards currently in

9. The best protection for future generations would appear to come through ac-tinide separation and incineration in either a modified light-water or fast-breeder reactor. This done, "the wastes would closely approach the 'non-toxic' level in 1000 years" (Kubo and Rose 1973, 1208), and "it is conceivable that engineered storage could be provided that would contain the fission products effectively for periods up to 1000 years" (Flowers 1976, para. 384). There are, however, unresolved "scientific and engineering problems" with this process sufficiently severe to lead the British Royal Commission on Environmental Pollution to conclude somewhat tentatively that "it would probably not be right to delay the programme of vitrification in the hope that the [actinide separation] process might eventually be developed" (Flowers 1976, para. 388; cf. U.S. GAO 1979, 4).

force; under the worst circumstances, it will reach us in only 10,700 years at 28 times the currently acceptable dose. The Swedish simulation is slightly more encouraging: in their baseline model, the maximum individual dose to the most exposed future group of people is within internationally accepted limits; but a sensitivity analysis, using altered parameters which cannot be ruled out at the present state of knowledge, shows that the most exposed group could receive ten times the acceptable dose of plutonium-239 (Johansson and Steen 1978; 1979). In addition to these risks associated with ordinary geologic forces, we must also consider cataclysmic events. The U.S. Environmental Protection Agency (1979, 124) calculates that we must, statistically, expect a meteorite impact sufficient to release 20 percent of the stored wastes directly into the air every 10^{11} years. Long as that seems, it is less than three half-lives for plutonium-239 (i.e., we still have more than an eighth of the original mass remaining), and it is less than two for neptunium-237 (i.e., we have more than a quarter left). Thus, it seems that the best ideas anyone has for disposing radioactive wastes carries very real possibilities of irradiating future generations.

Several jurisdictions have attempted to address these concerns by outlawing nuclear power plants unless operators specify how and where highly radioactive wastes will be stored with "absolute" safety, to borrow the phrasing of the Swedish Nuclear Stipulation Act of 1977. But will operators "have shown" this merely by demonstrating that "some experts believe that the specified conditions can be fulfilled in the future"—or must they also offer experimental evidence (or even a full-scale mock-up) proving these experts correct? Will "absolute" safety have been demonstrated if operators show that "nobody should, within the next 1000 years, be exposed to radiation doses not accepted today"—or must they show that no one will be exposed to these (or even lower) doses all the while the isotopes are decaying? Swedish decision-makers, by accepting a minimalist interpretation of each of these requirements, have substantially circumvented their Nuclear Stipulation Act and the protection it offers to future generations (Johansson and Steen 1979).

Justifications for discounting the interests of future generations in such ways have been discussed and dismissed in chapter 9 above. Uncertainties about future effects or tastes or technologies cannot excuse recklessness with radioactive wastes. Neither can the opportunity costs of alternative investments or the unwarranted assumption that people will be better off in the future than at present. Furthermore, the sort of decision rule within which discounting itself proceeds—viz., expected utility reckonings such as underlie cost-benefit and benefit-risk analysis—is inappropriate in the case of nuclear waste management. Just as it is impossible to list all the things that might go wrong in the operation of nuclear reactors (cf. section 10.1.1 above), so too is it impossible to imagine all the ways nuclear waste storage chambers might leak radiation into the biosphere. Since we cannot list all the possible outcomes, and we should not rely upon distorted subjective probabilities, we must not use the expected utility techniques or discounting practices predicated upon them. We must instead turn to decision rules, introduced in section 9.4 above and discussed further in section 10.4 below. None of these allows discounting the interests of future generations in the same way as does expected utility analysis.

10.3. Democratic Theory

A democratic society is characterized both by its way of making decisions and by the kinds of decisions it makes. In a democracy there is widespread public participation in policymaking. But, while majorities rule, they do not rule just as they please—no society that wantonly infringes certain especially cherished rights and liberties of its citizens can qualify as a democracy, however its rules are made. The nuclear state seems to violate democratic tenets in both respects.

10.3.1. Expert Decision-Making versus Public Participation

The choice of energy strategies clearly involves expert assessments at several points. Often, however, experts disagree; and sometimes disagreements are "transscientific" rather than merely scientific, raising questions which science cannot decide, either because crucial experiments cannot be performed or because the problems are undisciplined or because the judgments required are moral or aesthetic (Weinberg 1972a). In this impasse, we might give way to ordinary democratic inclinations and let the decisions be made by a vote of everyone who would be affected by them. Even if scientific evidence cannot settle such disputes, however, such evidence as is available should at least be brought to bear upon them. The public, alas, is sadly lacking in such information. Perhaps they might acquire more if they had any real chance of using it, i.e., if the issue really were in their hands. But the relatively low levels of sophistication displayed by the Swiss and Austrians in the course of their nuclear referenda do not hold out much hope of this (Hirsch and Nowotny 1977).

Doubtless this is partly due to the grievous shortcomings of official "public information" campaigns, there as elsewhere. Sometimes they amount to frank exercises in pronuclear propaganda, often conjoined with attempts at cooptation and intimidation (Nelkin and Pollak 1981, chap. 12). Rothschild (1978) goes so far as to suggest that when asking people whether they are willing to bear nuclear risks, we should draw attention to the various other much larger risks they run daily. And the chairman of the British Windscale inquiry, ostensibly an impartial assessment of the evidence on nuclear safety, revealingly described its purpose as to "reassure" the local community (Parker 1978, para. 15.3). Even where there seems to be a genuine attempt at communicating scientific information to the public, as in Sweden, the result is often only increased confusion (Nelkin 1977, 95; Nelkin and Pollak 1977). This may be because political issues are mixed with technical ones (Pearce, et al. 1979, 49), or because of the inherent difficulties in communicating highly uncertain scientific knowledge (Meltsner 1979, 354). Equally likely, it might be the result of the effective manipulative ploy of "information overload," wherein people are given so much information all at once that they are then willing to accept any framework they are offered to make sense of it (Goodin 1980, 58–61).

More effective confrontations between experts and representatives of the public come in more adversarial contexts. While these are clearly inappropriate for settling scientific issues, they are perfectly suited to settling "transscientific" ones (Weinberg 1972a) and especially to evoking suppressed information (Pearce, et al. 1979, 56–57). Purely advisory hearings, such as the British system of public inquiries and analogous American administrative hearings, probably provide the least useful sort of forum for such disputations. Basically, such institutions are designed merely to defuse opposition—to draw its sting in settings where it will not impinge on the real decision-making process.[10] American public interest groups have found much more promising opportunities for input into energy policymaking through lobbying Congress and executive agencies and, like their German counterparts, through litigation (McFarland 1976; Nelkin and Pollak 1981, chap. 11). Alternatively, the interests of the public might be represented by competing scientists in "sci-

10. Nelkin and Fallows (1978, 297), commenting on purely advisory hearings in America, conclude, "If agencies, in the name of efficiency, have the ultimate discretion to shape the nature of dissent and to determine the influence of opposing views, public participation becomes an exercise in impotence. If token participation does result in the acceptance of agency decisions, the price may be a subtle but pernicious undermining of the democratic process." No doubt these procedures could be improved: appointment of an impartial inspector (or a balanced team of them) is among the more crucial reforms required in British public inquiries, judging from the shameless biases in Parker's (1978) report of Windscale findings (Breach 1978, chaps. 1, 9; Pearce, et al. 1979). But those alone can never suffice.

ence courts" (Mazur 1977). Thorough peer review might be a preliminary step in that direction (Johansson and Steen 1978; Lewis 1978).

All this has the public being represented, rather than participating directly, in nuclear decision-making. There is a further problem of what "representation" means—much less how it can be guaranteed—in such situations. Clearly it cannot be a matter of representing mass opinion, which is too ill informed to be allowed to settle the issues directly. Neither can it be a matter of asking people to set the ends and letting the representatives choose the means. In transscientific issues "ends and means are hardly separable" (Weinberg 1972a, 209). Neither, finally, can we rely upon ordinary electoral checks, with representatives pursuing whatever policies they please subject to the threat that constituents will turn them out if they do not like the results. Where policies have sleeper effects (especially ones extending over several generations, as with nuclear wastes), people will not come to realize the evils of the policy in a direct, personal way until it is much too late to "turn the rascals out."

If firm guarantees that representatives will promote constituents' interests are impossible, we can at least insist upon certain procedures for making and justifying decisions which increase the chances that all interests will be given fair consideration. The simple fact that an American federal agency now must go through the process of preparing an environmental impact statement forces it to consider factors in making a decision which it would otherwise have neglected (Majone 1979). It has been suggested that the British require similar submissions in connection with the siting of nuclear installations (Breach 1978). Alternatively, submission of a cost-benefit or benefit-risk assessment might be required (Hansson 1979; Pearce 1979). The principal justification for this is, significantly, not that these procedures yield the right results so much as that they evoke the right considerations. Pearce (1979) explicitly argues the advantages of cost-benefit *formats* in drawing out all relevant factors, without setting much store by the bottom-line cost-benefit balancing. Hansson (1979, 4) argues even more emphatically that, while "matters of scientific fact speak *against* a belief in formal decision-making" in ways canvassed in section 10.1.1, "matters of ethics speak *for* it." By formalizing decision procedures, we force ourselves to take into account all sorts of morally significant considerations (such as the interests of people distant from us in time and space) which we would inevitably overlook when using more informal procedures.

Formalizing decision procedures may help assure that people's interests are protected, but they themselves are still unable to participate directly in making nuclear (or, indeed, any other high-technology) policy. There are, of course, ways to help increase the scope for public participation in technological decision-making (Nelkin 1977; Pearce, et al. 1979). Insofar as the incompatibility between democracy and technology can be reduced, it obviously should be. But this search for new mechanisms for democratic control of technology is, in an important way, misleading. It suggests that, where democracy is inconsistent with the requirements of technological decision-making, it is necessarily democracy which will have to give way. The contrary seems more plausible. We not only are concerned to achieve the optimal solution—we also want to achieve it in the right way. If the "best" solution to our energy problems is one which precludes any real public participation in decision-making, then that might not be the best policy after all. We are, at least at the margin, prepared to trade off efficiency of outcomes in order to allow more democratic participation in selecting them. And, if technological decisions cannot be made democratically, then perhaps they should not be made at all.

One of the strongest arguments against nuclear and other high-technology energy options is that they are inherently centralized and nonparticipatory. Once we have embarked on a "hard-energy path," its own internal logic dictates most of the subsequent choices, leaving little room for further public choice. Perhaps the most striking current example concerns siting of radioactive waste disposal facilities. The U.S. General Accounting Office (1979, 12), in an otherwise eminently sensible report, offers the following proposal:

> Because nuclear problems are such highly emotional issues and becoming even more so, as evidenced by the States that have indicated an unwillingness to permit nuclear waste disposal within their boundaries, it may be impossible to get the public and political support necessary for a State to accept nuclear waste. Ultimately, if State approval for waste repository sites cannot be obtained within an established time, the Federal Government might have to mandate selections. While such action would not be easy it may be necessary if the waste problem is to be solved in a reasonable time. [Cf. Lee 1980.]

The issue I would focus upon is not federal versus states' rights but is instead whether decision-makers will respect democratic decisions at whatever level of government. Here they cannot afford to do so: having embarked upon the nuclear course, they cannot now allow popular opposition to prevent safe disposal of its lethal by-products. One of the strongest arguments in favor of solar and other "soft-energy paths" is that they, in contrast, are inherently "decentralized" and "participatory" (Lovins 1977; Orr 1979; Brunner 1980).[11]

10.3.2. Civil Liberties

In an early and influential article, Alvin Weinberg (1972b), sometime director of Oak Ridge, described nuclear energy as a "Faustian bargain." On the one hand, we get a virtually inexhaustible source of clean and cheap energy. The price, on the other hand, is that we must design stable social institutions capable of operating the plants without incident and especially of tending their lethal waste products virtually forever. Weinberg phrased it invitingly as a challenge to which we should rise—as a demand for a collective undertaking that we will all behave responsibly for the rest of human history. It could equally well be construed sinisterly as a threat of unprecedented proportions to civil liberties—as an excuse for "garrison state" institutions capable of guaranteeing absolutely that we will all behave.

The fear is that nuclear plants will be operated by a technocratic elite, self-selected and self-perpetuating and largely beyond the bounds of ordinary political accountability. Weinberg actually suggests that we "place the generation of nuclear electricity in the hands of special nuclear generating consortia—*possibly although not necessarily governmental*—that would be responsible for the secure and safe generation of nuclear electricity into perpetuity .... A special nuclear corps—perhaps analogous to airline pilots—may be required to man the ultimate nuclear enterprise" (Weinberg, et al. 1979, 83, emphasis added; cf. Weinberg 1979, 104). Already operators of nuclear installations are given extraordinary powers, in vetting employees, to investigate the background and activities not only of employees but also of their families and even of their friends. The installations themselves are armed camps policed by forces that are virtually a law unto themselves. The U.K. Atomic Energy (Special Constables) Act of 1976 created a special armed force to guard nuclear installations, making it answerable not to the Home Office (as are ordinary police) but to the U.K. Atomic Energy Authority. Justice, the British section of the International Commission of Jurists, complains that this constitutionally unique arrangement

11. Perelman (1980, 395) foresees roughly the same outcome but describes it more pejoratively as "feudalism." Whether "political decentralization" and a "quasi-steady-state economy" is accompanied, as he suggests, by "wealth and power ... largely based on land holdings" and "social stratification by caste or class" depends, obviously, upon what collective arrangements the society makes for distribution and redistribution. These are, in principle, independent of energy choices. Furthermore, it is hard to see why such a decentralized system should need mechanisms for instilling social cohesion, much less why Perelman's "theocracy" is the only such mechanism available to do it.

"conflicts with all our traditions of civilian and politically accountable policing" (quoted in Breach 1978, 69).

Weinberg and associates (1979, 83) hope that, "by keeping the corps relatively small, one minimizes the chance that necessary security measures would intrude on the rest of society." In principle, the problem of on-site security certainly "should be manageable." After all, nuclear facilities "can be isolated or screened and protected in a way that other targets of terrorists (airports, Olympic stadia, public figures, and international meetings) inherently cannot" (Farley 1976, 148–49). But the security record of nuclear facilities is not, in fact, very impressive. The *Barrier Technology Handbook* (Sandia Laboratories 1977) lists a multitude of ways present security systems might be breached, either by thieves or by terrorists. And already we have found evidence—circumstantial, but sufficient to convince the CIA—that ninety-four kilograms of the "special nuclear material" appearing as "material unaccounted for" on the records of the Apollo, Pennsylvania, NUMEC facility for 1965–66 were diverted to Israel for bomb-building (U.S. Congress 1978, 138). A 1977 report by the U.S. Congress's Office of Technology Assessment concludes that a squad of seven to fifteen people would be enough to present a credible threat to a reactor; and, assuming none of them were previously known to the police, there is no assurance that this level of conspiracy could be detected ahead of time. The same report also concludes that a small group of people, none with access to classified literature, could construct a rudimentary nuclear bomb. "Reactor-grade" plutonium makes a perfectly good bomb, as the 1977 test detonation in the Nevada desert demonstrates. "Though extremely inefficient in nuclear terms, such a device would still cause much damage and would create immediate radiation which would be lethal over a range of several hundred meters as well as dispersing radioactive material over a wide area" (Flowers 1976, para. 324. Cf. Wohlstetter 1976–77, and Lovins 1980).[12]

The only hope for shielding the public from the "civil liberties fallout" from nuclear power plants would seem to be to improve on-site security immensely. This might be made easier by concentrating all the nuclear fuel cycle at a few sites in self-contained "nuclear parks" (Weinberg 1979, 100–102; Weinberg, et al. 1979, chaps. 4, 12; Burwell, et al. 1979). The British Royal Commission on Environmental Pollution, however, "were informed by the utilities" that "the grouping of plutonium production plant and fast reactors onto a few integrated sites or 'nuclear parks,' and the provision of a

12. Substantial skepticism surrounds the sort of technological fixes Parker (1978, chap. 7) was counting on to render stolen plutonium useless to terrorists (Conroy 1978, chap. 6; Keeny 1977, chap. 9).

sufficient armed force at a power station to prevent it being taken over by terrorists, would be uneconomic" (Flowers 1976, para. 312).

The judge chairing the Windscale inquiry, reflecting upon threats of nuclear subversion, reluctantly concludes, "I can see no solution at all. If the sort of activities under consideration are to be checked, innocent people are certain to be subjected to surveillance, if only to find out whether they are innocent or not. Equally certainly, friends and relatives will be subject to distasteful and embarrassing enquiries." Parker's (1978, paras. 7.24–25) next paragraph even more disquietingly suggests the stifling of legitimate dissent:

> I do not for a moment suggest that any of the objectors before me were motivated by a desire to harm this country, but it is plainly possible that the aim of doing harm can be pursued under the outward guise of furthering such a worthy aim as the protection of civil liberties. A campaign to lessen surveillance, ostensibly to preserve civil liberties, could therefore be mounted by people whose aim was not the preservation of such liberties but increased opportunity to further their own destructive ends.

Against the background of official pronouncements such as these, the fears of civil libertarians can hardly be dismissed as unduly alarmist (Ayres 1975; Flood and Grove-White 1976).

A particularly striking feature of Weinberg's Faustian bargain is that it is never subject to renegotiation. The need to guard nuclear waste disposal sites, protecting against accidental incursion as well as sabotage and theft, persists long after the day of the fission reactor has passed. So, too, will the security measures required to protect those sites, and any infringement of civil liberties those measures might entail. The benefits to be obtained from nuclear power are clustered in a mere instant in the incredibly long time scale implied by the decay rates of the radioactive wastes thereby created; the costs necessarily persist throughout the almost-eternal period.

10.4. Alternative Decision Rules

In these various ways, nuclear power poses some very special problems, rendering the ordinary utilitarian decision rule (maxmimize expected utility) an unreliable guide. But, while special, these circumstances are by no means unique to the case of nuclear power. The various modifications in and alternatives to the expected utility rule suggested by that case will apply, mutatis mutandis, to many other "low-probability/high-risk" social decisions as well.

10.4.1. Keep the Options Open
         (Reversibility)

Gross uncertainty about the future in general, and about energy futures in particular, recommends strategies preserving our future range of options. "Open-ended planning" would require that "any choice made now must be made in such a way that it has the certainty of an associated negating choice attached to it: a later generation, or the same generation at a later date, can reverse the choice and return to the original situation" (Pearce, et al. 1979, 26). The U.K. Department of Energy's *Energy Policy* review (1978) argues that energy choices "should not prematurely close options." And that Department's Deputy Secretary testified at Windscale of the need to "establish a wide range of energy options and maintain a flexible energy strategy which can be reviewed and adjusted if necessary in light of subsequent developments" (quoted in Breach 1978, 27–28). Such suggestions perfectly parallel Barry's (1978, 243; 1977, 275) analysis of the demands of intergenerational justice "that the overall range of opportunities open to successor generations should not be narrowed."

Keeping options open does not, of course, entail refusing to make any choices at all. Once we have chosen one path, it will always be costly to shift over to some other; but, provided that the cost is not absolutely prohibitive, the shift is at least possible. This is all that "keeping options open" requires. Thus we may, consistently with that rule, pursue certain options provided our policy is *reversible*— provided we can backtrack if necessary. Such considerations must be superimposed on ordinary expected utility calculations, which overproduce irreversible outcomes because they systematically understate the value of having options in a world where preferences and circumstances change in unpredictable ways (Fisher, et al. 1972; Arrow and Fisher 1974; Henry 1974).

Reversibility criteria enter nuclear policy debates at various points. First is in the implementation of the nuclear option. As regards the storage of radioactive wastes, for example, Rochlin (1978) recommends "reversibility" as one of two "social criteria" to be used in selecting sites and techniques. It is better to place radioactive wastes in deep rock deposits, where we can recover them if something goes wrong and they begin leaking, than to put them where we cannot get them back (letting them melt their way into the polar ice or slide between continental plates in the deep seabed, or shooting them off into deep space).

Second, the reversibility criterion is used in choosing between nuclear and nonnuclear options. Elster (1979a) supposes that this

makes fossil fuels preferable to nuclear power. Both risk catastrophic consequences: CO_2 discharges from coal or oil-burning
plants that alter the global climate in the one case; proliferation of
nuclear arms in the other. The "hothouse" effect could, however,
be reversed. If it really does happen—which is far from certain—
then by stopping burning fossil fuels we can gradually reverse the
damage to the climate. This is a slow process and perhaps less certain
of success than Elster supposes (cf. Pearce, et al. 1979, 26), but at
least reversibility may be possible here. Nuclear weapons proliferation, in contrast, seems more nearly irreversible. Once nations have
the technical knowledge required to build nuclear weapons, they
have it forever. Nuclear reactors and their by-products themselves
impose irreversible obligations. As the Oak Ridge team (Weinberg,
et al. 1979, 79) concedes, "One cannot simply abandon a nuclear reactor the way one can abandon a coal-fired plant." It is instead an
"unforgiving" technology which, as Kneese (1973) worries, "will
impose a burden of continuous monitoring and sophisticated management of a dangerous material, essentially forever. The penalty of
not bearing this burden may be unparalleled disaster. This irreversible burden would be imposed even if nuclear fission were used only
for a few decades, a mere instant in the pertinent time scales."

While we must always pay special attention to the dangers of irreversible outcomes, which *are* underweighted in ordinary decision
rules, any strict application of the "keep the options open" rule is
not only inadvisable but impossible. Economists suggest we discount options that are irreversible merely by something like 13 percent, representing the values of the options they foreclose (Henry
1974). Indeed, in some cases irreversibility might actually be a
virtue—there are some options that should be closed forever. One
example might be the option to initiate a nuclear war. "Peaceful nuclear programs" are sometimes defended on the grounds that "they
constitute a hedge against failure of nonproliferation efforts, an assurance that countries which try the nonproliferation option will not
be permanently disadvantaged if it fails" (Farley 1976, 160; cf.
Keeny 1977, chap. 9). But keeping the nuclear weapon option open
in this way would be utterly indefensible if we ever could find a way
of closing it irrevocably for everyone. Similarly, if we found an absolutely certain method of disposing of nuclear wastes, we would
prefer to be rid of them permanently and irreversibly rather than
keep them where we (along with saboteurs, thieves, and careless
miners) can get at them. Even in the absence of such a discovery, we
must weigh the advantages of retrievability against its "additional
problems with respect to flooding, water absorption, radioactive gas
effluents," and so on. On balance, we might be persuaded by the

"safety advantages in sealing the storage chambers as soon as they are full" (U.S. IRG 1978, 18).

Besides, keeping all options as open as before is a practical—and perhaps a logical—impossibility. "As the same issues come around again for the second, third and nth time they do so in a context slightly altered by the previous minimal choices to which they have been subjected" (Schilling 1961, 44). For example, consider President Truman's 1949 decision to "explore the technical feasibility" of the H-bomb. That option was favored because, at the time, it "seemed to close off the least number of future alternatives." But notice that, after that minimalist decision, several old options were either unavailable or radically altered: there could be no question of "unilateral renunciation" any longer; and "international control" discussions had to be cast instead in terms of agreements not to test H-bombs. "In place of an agreement on a device which no one knew how to make, agreement would now have to be made with regard to a device which one side knew how to make and the other, presumably, did not" (Schilling 1961, 24, 44). Thus, even minimal decisions close or recast options.

Keeping all options open is also impossible in energy policy because, there too, some options can be preserved only by closing off others. "Hard" and "soft" energy paths are "mutually exclusive" insofar as "commitments to the first . . . foreclose the second," as Lovins (1977, 26, 59–60) argues they do. The construction of capital intensive nuclear power plants in general and reprocessing plants in particular, although justified in terms of keeping options open, may actually foreclose them: given the immense investment, we will inevitably be stuck with using such plants once we have built them (Breach 1978). If some options can be kept open only by closing off others, we must look closely at the likely costs and benefits of each. It would be foolhardy to keep the second, third, and fourth-best options open if the price were foreclosing the first best.

10.4.2.   Compare the Alternatives

If we cannot keep all the options open, and are forced to make some irrevocable commitments, we should at least do so on the basis of a full survey of the advantages and disadvantages of all available alternatives. This principle of comparing the alternatives is fairly obvious and widely practiced, as when various authors routinely compare costs, benefits, and risks arising from different energy strategies (Lovins 1977; McBride, et al. 1978; U.S. NAS 1978; Inhaber 1979; 1981; Weinberg, et al. 1979). Such a principle also clearly underlies their criticisms of each other, for failing to make *comprehensive* comparisons between all the available alternatives.

Alongside these very ordinary and perfectly acceptable applications of the "compare the alternatives" principle, we also find another far less acceptable one. This assesses the riskiness of a policy in terms of the *increment* of risk it adds to those preexisting in the status quo, rather than in terms of the absolute value of the risk associated with the policy. Føllesdal's (1979, 441) paper on recombinant DNA research, for example, argues that we need not fear a "mad scientist's" using these new techniques to unleash a deadly virus on the world, not because that could not happen, but rather because there are already enough devastatingly lethal viral and chemical agents available to any given mad scientist to do the job. The "added risk" entailed in offering him one more way to destroy all life on earth is effectively zero, although of course the absolute risk of his doing so is frighteningly high. Similarly, the British public inquiry into the concentration of hazardous activities (petroleum storage, oil refining, a methane gas terminal) on Canvey Island concluded that "the risk of an accident involving 10 or more fatalities stands at 11 chances in 10,000 a year, or nearly ten times more than the risk of an individual being killed in a motor accident." The inspector deemed this risk "too great" in absolute terms. But, using "risk-added" logic, he could find no real objection to one more oil refinery that "would be responsible for only 0.15 [more] chances in 10,000 a year in the area most affected" (Ward 1981, paras. 220–21).

A similar principle emerges at various points in the nuclear energy debate. It is suggested, for example, that when setting standards for an acceptable nuclear waste disposal system, the radiation hazard to future generations need not be eliminated altogether but only reduced to where it is "comparable to the cumulative risk to all future generations from the original uranium resources from which the radioactive wastes were derived, assuming these . . . were unmined" (Cochran and Rotow 1979; cf. Weinberg 1979, 94).[13] Even if we cannot provide that limited sort of guarantee, we might use risk-added reasoning to proceed anyway. We might have been willing to forgo nuclear energy "if that action would protect future societies forever. But [we] would be in no position to control the choices of future societies"; and, so long as someone will contaminate the environment of distant generations anyway, we might as well be the ones (Zeckhauser 1975, 439). The risk-added argument is also used by the Oak Ridge team (Weinberg, et al. 1979, 56) to brush aside concern with the proliferation of nuclear weapons: "We believe that the ef-

13. All this, of course, presupposes the validity of some "hazard index" for rendering commensurable the threats of the various different isotopes involved. This has proven a highly contentious undertaking.

fect of a moratorium [on nuclear power] adopted only by the United States would be marginal...because reactors would be available from other countries" (cf. Conroy 1978, 59–60; Rose and Lester 1978).

Wohlstetter aptly replies that "to argue...that such restrictions would be irrelevant because there are other ways to get a bomb is like opposing inoculation for smallpox because one might also die of bubonic plague. Better to suggest protection against the plague" (quoted in Conroy 1978, 57). That the status quo contains other ways for nuclear weapons to spread or for people to be poisoned or irradiated is a criticism of the status quo rather than a defense of policies only modestly increasing its risks. The general flaw of the risk-added approach is that it adopts the status quo as a baseline. True benefit-risk analysis acknowledges no baseline. We must compare the benefit-risk profiles of *all* alternatives, the status quo being just one option among many.

Finally, we can question the moral relevance of how bad one's alternative opportunities might be. Would we really feel comfortable buying up a bankrupt farmer's land at bargain basement prices just because we know there are no other bidders or, as a spokesman for Dow Chemical suggests, subjecting workers to asbestos just because they would be exposed to equally hazardous carcinogens anywhere else they worked (P. J. Ghering, quoted in Nemetz and Vining 1981, 130; cf. Maugh 1978)? Would we not have a moral duty to pay the farmer a "fair" price and offer workers a "decent" working environment, even if the market did not force us to do so? The recent U.S. Supreme Court decision on the drug Laetrile, thought by some to cure cancer, offers an interesting case in point. Those taking the drug are dying of cancer anyway—their "alternatives" are grim indeed. Still, we object to other people's taking advantage of their sadly restricted opportunity set to peddle drugs which have never been shown to be either safe or effective. The fact that cancer victims have little to lose is beside the point—the law's protection extends even to the terminally ill.[14] Judging from this case, we do seem to feel that certain things should or should not be done, whatever the competing alternatives look like. The injunction to "compare competing alternatives" might have distinctly limited applicability if many cases fit into this category.

14. The appeals court had "held that 'the safety and effectiveness terms used in the statute have no reasonable application to terminally ill cancer patients.' Since those patients, by definition, would 'die of cancer regardless of what may be done,' the court concluded that there were no realistic standards against which to measure the safety and effectiveness of a drug for that class of individuals. The Court of Appeals therefore...permit[ted] the use of Laetrile by cancer patients certified as terminally ill." The U.S. Supreme Court, in *U.S. et al.* v. *Rutherford et al.*, overturned that ruling (Marshall 1979, 551 ff.).

10.4.3. Protect the Vulnerable

To build on the last point, a further rule might require that we give those who are most vulnerable special protection. Someone may be vulnerable *to* particular others, whose actions strongly and directly affect him; or he may, like the cancer victim or bankrupt farmer, simply be vulnerable *tout court,* in that he has such a severely restricted opportunity set that he is put at the mercy of others in general.

Protecting the vulnerable might, in the context of energy choices, mean many things. Some try to justify America's quest for "energy independence" in these terms, wrongly conflating "vulnerability" with "*inter*-dependence" when it really is an aspect of "*unilateral* dependence." Others might use this principle to justify judging the acceptability of radiation hazards by reference to the dose risked by the "most exposed group." The most striking application, however, seems to be to future generations, who are particularly vulnerable to the effects of our energy choices. They would, for example, be strongly and directly affected by our decision to leave them with the radioactive wastes from our nuclear power plants; and, once we have made that decision, they have very little choice but to live with it.

Intergenerational transactions are singularly one-way affairs. Later generations are extraordinarily vulnerable to the choices of earlier ones, but forebears are largely immune to the choices of their successors. This absence of reciprocal relations would, on Hobbesian or Humean accounts, imply that we have no moral obligations toward future generations (Barry 1978). But, on other understandings, such asymmetrical power relations are the very stuff of moral obligations: those in a position of dominance have a special obligation to protect those dependent upon them. Such codes clearly underlie the patronal arrangements of peasant societies (Scott 1976), codes of professional ethics (B. Williams 1978, 56; Goodin 1981), and loving relationships (Wilson 1978) in our own societies. Within the family the very fact that children are dependent upon their parents gives them rights against their parents. Were we to extend such a principle to policy decisions more generally, we would have to cease discounting the interests of vulnerable future generations. Instead, we would have to count their suffering (e.g., from leaky nuclear waste dumps) at least on a par with our own pains and pleasures.

10.4.4. Maximize the Minimum
Payoff

A related rule—"maximin," or maximize the minimum payoff—is sometimes recommended, but on epistemic rather than ethical grounds. This rule compares the "worst possible outcomes" of all alternative policies, selecting that policy with the least unbearable consequence should worse come to worst.[15] This decision rule, or something very much like it, is forced upon us wherever any of the three crucial steps in performing the expected utility calculus is impossible. That procedure requires (1) that we list all the possible outcomes; (2) that we then set a value on each of them; and (3) that we set a probability on each. One or more of these steps is often infeasible. As section 10.1.1 shows, it is often impossible to list all the possible scenarios and outcomes, especially where the "human factor" is involved (as in the operation or sabotage of a nuclear reactor). Furthermore, it is typically difficult to get reliable probability estimates: objective statistics are unavailable; theories are lacking or are too numerous; and subjective estimates are unreliable. Finally, it might be difficult even to get a good indicator of the value (or cost) of each of the consequences. Such problems might motivate our reluctance in section 10.1.2 to let people run any risks they want—we just do not believe they fully appreciate the pains of the possible outcomes. (See chapters 3 and 8 above.)

Where any of these steps cannot be performed, the expected utility (or cost-benefit or benefit-risk calculations based on it) cannot be performed. We must rely instead on one of the three decision rules discussed in chapter 9 which can function under such conditions: the Wald (1950) "maximin" (maximize the minimum payoff) rule, nicely captured in Føllesdal's (1979, 406) suggestion that where we have wildly varying probability estimates we should "estimate the probability of the worst consequences to be 1, and act accordingly"; Savage's (1954) "minimax regret" rule, requiring us to choose the course of action which minimizes the regret we might suffer; or Arrow and Hurwicz's (1972) suggestion—adopted by the Swedish Energy Commission for assessing nuclear reactors (Elster 1979a)—to choose policies on the basis of a weighted combination of the best-possible and worst-possible outcomes under each policy option. If, as Elster (1979a) argues is the case with alternative energy strategies, all alternatives have roughly the same best-possible outcomes, then the Arrow-Hurwicz rule reduces to Wald's, and we need worry only about maximizing the minimum possible payoff.

Popular resistance to untried technologies with the potential for causing large-scale catastrophes—usually dismissed as rationally groundless risk aversion—might be a wholly rational response to ir-

15. There is a difference between "maximin" and "protecting the vulnerable": the former implies avoiding the worst state of the world all around, whereas the latter implies avoiding the worst consequences possible for certain target groups. It is, of course, possible to build a similar distributive focus into maximin—as does Rawls (1972), for example—but it is important to realize that we *are* building something more into the rule when we do that.

resolvable uncertainties. Such uncertainties clearly plague energy choices and render expected utility calculations impossible. The British Department of Energy considers this an argument in *favor* of the nuclear option, saying that "our energy strategy should be robust, producing minimum regret whatever course future events take" (quoted in Breach 1978, 28). Apparently the most regrettable outcome they—like most advocates of nuclear power (e.g., Bethe 1976)—could imagine is running short of energy. The consequences of that may, however, be less horrible than are commonly supposed: among developed market economies, there is virtually no correlation between per capita energy consumption and a wide range of indicators of social well-being (Mazur and Rosa 1974; Nader and Beckerman 1978). More regrettable outcomes can easily be imagined, ranging from alteration of the world climate (by burning hydrocarbons) to genetic mutations or nuclear weapon proliferation (resulting from nuclear power). Perhaps none of these things will happen in the immediate future. But it is one of the virtues of these alternative decision rules that they consider future interests on a par with present ones, unlike the expected utility calculus.[16] On balance, it would seem that both nuclear and conventional fossil-fuel power plants are disqualified on this criterion in favor of energy conservation, combined with a range of "alternative" (solar, wind, wave, geothermal, etc.) strategies.

10.4.5.   Maximize Sustainable Benefits

Another rule would direct us to opt for the policy producing the highest level of net benefits which can be *sustained* indefinitely. This contrasts with the directive of ordinary expected utility maximization, viz., to go for the highest total payoff without regard to its distribution interpersonally or intertemporally. Utility maximization looks only to the total sum of benefits and is indifferent to whether they come in a steady stream or all bunched in one period. Considerations of intergenerational equity would demand instead that each

16. Such calculations are, as section 9.4 above notes, sensitive to the vagaries of tastes of future generations. We must value outcomes in terms of the preferences of those who will actually experience them, as chapter 3 above has argued. Thus, in applying "maximin," for example, we must imagine the worst possible outcome under each policy alternative happening to the individual who is as sensitive to that outcome as he might possibly be. I think the upshot for energy choices is identical with or without this refinement: imagine as big an energy glutton as you will, his suffering from energy deprivation cannot conceivably be as large as the suffering of the most intense ban-the-bomber from nuclear war. Similarly, a risk-lover in this generation may regret that his forebears were so risk-averse; but his regret can hardly match that of a risk-hater who lives downstream in time from risk-takers.

generation be guaranteed at least as many benefits as the last, insofar as possible; and one generation may justly enjoy certain benefits only if those advantages can be sustained for subsequent generations as well (Page 1977; Mueller 1974).[17] Following the "maximize sustainable benefits" rule would strongly encourage current decision-makers to think in maximin terms also, since the lowest possible payoff is one the initial generation must suffer, too.

As applied to questions of energy policy, the rule of maximizing sustainable benefits decisively favors renewable sources (solar, geothermal, wind, wave, etc.) over utilization of scarce natural resources (oil, coal). Uranium falls into the category of scarce resources: "The amount of uranium available to the United States at costs that can be afforded in an LWR [light-water reactor] is usually estimated to be 3×10^6 tons. Thus, prima facie, we would have enough uranium to support about 25,000 reactor-years of LWRs—say 800 reactors for 30 years" (Weinberg, et al. 1979, 82). With the fast breeder reactor, of course, the supply of fissionable plutonium could be rendered virtually inexhaustible, transforming nuclear energy into a sustainable benefit. Then the question would become simply which strategy, among those yielding sustainable benefits, yields maximal ones. But in a deeper sense, the benefits of nuclear energy might never be sustainable, even with the fast breeder. The benefits must, remember, be calculated net of costs, which will be increasing throughout time if the arguments in this chapter are correct. Even if the energy flow remains constant, the benefits of nuclear power, net of those constantly increasing costs, will be steadily diminishing.

10.4.6. Harm Avoidance

In all the previous discussion, harms and benefits have been treated as symmetrical. To avoid a harm is to produce a benefit. We are indifferent between two plans, one generating positive benefits valued at X and the other avoiding costs of X which we would otherwise have had to suffer. Avoiding a harm of a certain magnitude is just as desirable as (and, indeed, arguably equivalent to)

17. In the absence of time-discounting, even the goal of maximizing utility would lead to the same results. The case for broad equality of holdings intergenerationally perfectly parallels that for a broad equality of holdings interpersonally, building on the assumptions of diminishing marginal utility and rough similarity of tastes for certain basic commodities. Likewise, maximizing undiscounted utility usually—although not always—prohibits destruction of "interest-bearing resources... like crop species, fish species, draft animal species, topsoil, genetic variation, etc." The total utility to be derived from such goods is usually maximized by skimming off the interest and leaving the capital intact, which, once again, amounts to extracting the maximum sustainable yield from the resources in question (M. Williams 1978, 170).

producing a benefit of the same size. The "harm avoidance" principle denies this symmetry, arguing instead that it is much worse to create costs than it is just to fail to produce equally large benefits. Initially, we might be inclined to run this together with the more familiar "act/omission" doctrine. But, as I have argued in section 1.2.2 above, the "harm avoidance" principle not only is distinct from but is also part of what really underlies the appeal of that spurious doctrine.

Although the "harm avoidance" principle is not yet central to the nuclear power debate, it does figure importantly in discussions of, for example, the seeding of hurricanes (Howard, et al. 1972). Applying the principle to the problem of energy choices would, I think, argue strongly in favor of "alternative" and "renewable" energy sources (solar, geothermal, wind, wave, etc.), combined with strenuous efforts at energy conservation, in preference to either nuclear or fossil-fuel generation of power. The worst that can be said against the alternative, renewable sources is that they may yield rather less energy, i.e., that they produce fewer benefits. Both nuclear and oil or coal-fired plants, in contrast, run real risks of causing considerable harm. If we weight the harms much more heavily than the benefits forgone, as the "harm avoidance" principle directs, both nuclear and conventional power plants will appear much less advantageous than reliance upon solar, geothermal, wind, or wave power combined with energy conservation programs.

10.5. Conclusion

In this chapter, methodological conclusions and substantive ones are intermixed. The larger point is that they should be. Theories are best criticized through extended analysis of some issue of genuine social concern, and policy debates are themselves upgraded by theoretical reflections. Plausible abstractions time and again have to be qualified in their application to the peculiar problems associated with nuclear power. When the full extent of the revisions becomes apparent, it is clear that this is not just part of the natural process of bending generalizations to fit particular cases. Conventional understandings of ethics and public policy must themselves be revised, at least for an important class of cases displaying properties analogous to those of nuclear energy. Likewise, many problems with nuclear power which we might pooh-pooh if seeing them in isolation look far more ominous in the context of the theoretical whole. Simple confrontation with the facts, of course, goes far toward undermining confidence in nuclear energy—the more you read about the possibility of sabotage or proliferation or leaking waste containers or restricted civil liberties, the more justifiably worried you become. What makes nuclear power more worrying still is that it presents problems with which our decision processes are unsuited to cope: ordinary social decision processes contain certain presuppositions about the nature of the problems to which they will be applied; with nuclear power, the risks are too uncertain, and the possible consequences too enormous in their magnitude and too extraordinary in their character, for the decision to be processed in the ordinary ways. When we shift to decision techniques which are appropriate to such extraordinary problems, it seems that there are indeed "no moral nukes."

11 The Priority of Defense

Providing for the defense of the nation has long been among the first priorities of government. Logically, defense is one of the "defining activities" of a nation-state, and historically defense ministries are among the first a new nation establishes (Rose 1976). Philosophically, defense has always enjoyed pride of place among legitimate state activities. Even laissez-faire philosophers, who would allow the state to do little else, are nonetheless anxious that it safeguard citizens against external attack (Smith 1776; Humboldt 1854; Nozick 1974, chap. 2). In practical political terms, "defense" has long been a powerful word with which to conjure. The Federalist could find no stronger argument for the new American Constitution than to say it enhanced "the common defense" (Hamilton 1787). And even in our own day military budgets seem largely immune from careful scrutiny, as evidenced by booming defense allocations in both Reagan's America and Thatcher's Britain at a time when other budgets are being savaged brutally.[1]

1. Russett (1970, 27) observes that "Congress's success in cutting the military budgets presented to it is unimpressive even when compared with the experience of Tudor parliaments and Henry VIII.... Once the executive branch has reached agreement on its defense request from Congress, not once in the past quarter-century has the legislature voted down a major weapons system proposal. It has always provided virtually everything asked of it, and sometimes more." The rash of defense budget-cutting in the early 1970s was, in retrospect, clearly an aberration owing to the special circumstances of the reaction to the Vietnamese war. Indeed, it may have reflected little more than old interservice rivalries being carried over into Congressional battles (Kanter 1972; Laurance 1976). Abroad, Kandell (1980) reports that "among many nonissues in the presidential campaign in France, defense spending surely ranks alongside the preservation of historical monuments, the declining purity of the French language and the merits of this year's Beaujolais.... [There is] no political resistance to a

The claims of national defense thus do seem to enjoy some sort of priority. There are, however, various senses of "priority." This chapter explores which type of priority defense claims over competing considerations in public policymaking, the extent to which such claims are honored, and the reasons why. I shall also ask whether those reasons are good ones or not. The conclusion of this chapter is that the priority we accord defense is based on an explicable but unjustifiable error.

One of the most interesting features of this error is that it is typically tacit. Explicit priority claims are inevitably put to the test and, when they are, their implausibility simply becomes too glaring. There are, however, little-noticed methods of according considerations such as defense a kind of tacit priority. Such disjunctions between our words and our deeds are common (Deutscher 1966). Some principles figure as absolutes in our rhetoric but are compromised regularly in our actions; others are denied any special status in our rhetoric but are accorded it in our actions. On the one side come cases involving the taking of human life: it is utterly indecent to *admit* that we are willing to sacrifice one person's life for another's idle amusements, but that is precisely what we do every time we spend public money building a sports center instead of straightening out dangerous curves in roads (cf. section 6.6). On the other side, I suggest, come cases like defense. In practice if not in principle, defense projects seem curiously immune to kinds of criticisms which are commonly raised—and often reckoned to be decisive—against nondefense projects.

11.1. Varieties of Priority Claims

Talk of establishing "priorities" among competing claims comes quite naturally. "At first blush, this appears to be a commendable and systematic way to tackle the problem" of policy choice (Hitch and McKean 1960, 122). Upon closer examination, however, what it means to accord an item a high priority turns out to be unclear. Here I shall distinguish three types of priority. The first two are relatively familiar, and each has been claimed for national defense from time to time. The first, while conspicuously flawed, sometimes still seems to operate sub rosa. The second, although obviously legitimate, is far less compelling. The most interesting sort of priority rule is the third,

---

budget that increases its defense spending by about 5 percent for 1981. The parliamentary record in recent years makes no mention of defense bills getting bogged down in committee hearings. Rarely has an opposition legislator here questioned the price tag on a new missile or jet fighter. . . . No Communist or Socialist politician has yet proposed to President Valéry Giscard d'Estaing that with unemployment reaching post-war record levels and inflation at 14 percent the military budget should be trimmed in favor of social expenditures."

which, although commonly employed with respect to defense matters, has heretofore attracted altogether too little discussion.

11.1.1. Lexicographical Priority

The strongest sort of priority rule is a lexicographical ordering (Rawls 1972, sec. 8; Zeckhauser and Shaefer 1968). If there is any difference whatsoever between alternatives on the lexicographically prior value, they are ranked on that basis alone. Only when alternatives are indistinguishable on that basis are other subsidiary values even considered.

Sometimes it is suggested that national defense should be accorded this kind of priority. Perhaps the most dramatic recent instance came in Kennedy's Inaugural promise to "pay any price, bear any burden" to defend freedom throughout the world. But according to Huntington (1961, 199), it always had been quite common for "statesmen and experts concerned with security problems" to assume that "the requirements of security were absolute and that the only legitimate limit on their fulfillment was the physical capacity of the economy. They balanced the 'requirements' of security against economic capacity rather than against requirements derived from legitimate but competing purposes of government and society." Or, as Morgenstern (1959, 201) puts it, "The defense we need is the defense we can afford." The maximization they have in view is subject to a constraint—the total physical capacity of the economy—but it is not subject to competing claims from the domestic sector.

It seems slightly preposterous that anything, defense included, should ever enjoy this sort of absolute priority. Critics have seized upon this as among the most vulnerable aspects of Rawls's (1972) theory. Obsessive concern with the worst thing that might happen—putting safety lexicographically prior to all else—would mean that no improvement (however large) in employment prospects should ever induce anyone to board an airplane to fly from New York to Chicago so long as there is any chance (however slight) of the plane's crashing (Harsanyi 1975). The "difference principle" growing out of this would imply that no gain (however large) for the second-worst-off individual should ever induce us to impose a sacrifice (however small) on the worst-off (Sen 1974). Neither proposition is particularly plausible, at least not in ordinary sorts of cases.

This general implausibility of lexicographical orderings is only magnified in the more practical context of budgetary decision-making. Giving any one item lexicographical priority there would mean committing all our resources to that item and none whatsoever to any others, which is obviously absurd (Hitch and McKean 1960, 122). Certainly that is not how we treat defense in drawing up the national budget. While defense spending is undeniably high and growing, it does after all claim only about a quarter of the total U.S. federal budget and something around 5 percent of GNP. This would seem to constitute prima facie proof that defense is not given this kind of priority. It looks much more as if we are trying to balance a "Great Equation" in which both civilian and military claims are treated as legitimate competitors for scarce national resources (Huntington 1961, chap. 4).

That evidence may be less conclusive than is ordinarily supposed, however. Defenders of any kind of lexicographical priority rule are generally quite sensitive to the fact that, with such rules, "unless the earlier principles have but a limited application and establish requirements which can be fulfilled, later principles will never come into play" (Rawls 1972, 43). They are, accordingly, careful that lexicographically prior claims should be ones which are easily satisfied. Thus, Rawls (1972, sec. 8) feels comfortable in giving his "equal liberty" principle lexicographical priority because he is confident that he has defined *liberty* narrowly enough to leave his subsidiary principle plenty to do.

Likewise, those who would give defense lexicographical priority over all other public policy demands do so on the assumption that an *adequate* defense can be mustered without devoting the entire national budget to the cause. In Congressional hearings, for example, Representative Vinson coupled what looks to be a lexicographical priority rule with an important qualifier: "I think the Government's first obligation is its defense.... Nothing comes ahead of insuring the people of the nation that they can be protected as far as possible by an Army, a Navy, and an Air Force *of adequate strength*" (quoted in Schilling 1962, 117, emphasis added). Similarly, former Secretary of Defense Robert McNamara testified, "When I took office in January 1961, President Kennedy instructed me to: (1) Develop the force structure *necessary to meet our military requirements* without regard to arbitrary budget ceilings. (2) Procure and operate this force at the lowest possible cost."[2] Or, again, the

2. Quoted in Crecine and Fischer (1973, 199, emphasis added). Whether or not he lived up to this task is, of course, debatable. Murdock (1974, 100) observes that, "after taking office, McNamara quickly established a new level of defense expenditures. Supplemental appropriations to Eisenhower's FY 1962 budget . . . raised it from $44.9 billion to $50.7 billion. In the following years, the total defense budget did not vary from this figure by more than $1 billion—2% of the total defense budget—prior to the Vietnam buildup.... This is not the kind of behavior one would expect of an administration that promised there would be no 'arbitrary' economic constraints and that the expenditure level would be determined by military needs."

Brookings report on defense policy for "the next ten years" concludes similarly that "the nation can only protect itself and its interests abroad if it is willing to spend *what is necessary* to maintain a credible military posture" (Blechman 1976, 128, emphasis added). The italicized phrases in all the above quotations seem to point to a "requirements approach" to defense, the "essence" of which "is that there are certain absolute needs, stated in terms of military hardware and manpower, which must be met regardless of cost, if the security of the United States is to be guaranteed in some absolute sense" (Enthoven and Rowen 1961, 375). The implication for lexicographical priority models is that there are thresholds of defense "adequacy" below which the nation must never fall—but, correlatively, above which additional efforts are superfluous. That means we can give defense absolute budgetary priority and still have money left over for other desirable social objectives. If defense gets only about 5 percent of GNP, that may be because that is all it takes to provide an adequate defense—the lexicographically prior claim having been met, we have gone on to other lower-level considerations.

Needless to say, this reply is not particularly persuasive. Perhaps if we already have a fivefold overkill capacity, a few more warheads would not make us any more secure: we have enough already. More generally, however, it is nonsense to talk of "absolute" or "bare minimum" defense "needs" (Enthoven and Rowen 1961, 376; Murdock 1974, 13, 70–71). There will always be a military project somewhere on which the marginal tax dollar could be spent with positive—if only infinitesimal—returns in terms of improved national defense (Hitch and McKean 1960, 46–48, 122–23). Thus, the "adequacy" move fails to save the lexicographical priority rule from illogicality. What is ultimately more interesting, however, is that it ever was attempted in the first place. The fact that it was must count as impressive evidence of people's inclination to cling to a model of lexicographical priority for defense even in spite of its prima facie implausibility.[3]

3. Furthermore, the lexicographical priority model might still exert some influence on the practical level even though—and, indeed, all the more because—the adequacy move has failed. Murdock (1974, 72) reports that "the very ambiguity of these defense goals [national security, deterrence, etc.]—in a period where the need for defense seems paramount—results in making the purchase of defense 'means' relatively open-ended. Because there is no way of relating each additional purchase to goal accomplishment, it is tacitly assumed that each purchase does add to the nation's security. To date, there has been little reduction in these additional purchases for there has been no definition of what constitutes a sufficiency of defense." Tobin (1966, 60) explicitly argues, "We are too rich a country to keep our defenses at the margin of taking very serious risks with our very survival.... The U.S. has no private uses of resources so compelling that they justify keeping the Western World in such a precarious position that any reduction in the budget will gravely threaten the security."

11.1.2. Weighting Priority

Another much more modest sense of "priority" is best illustrated through budgetary decision-making. Assigning an item high budgetary priority merely means that it weighs heavily in our reckonings. Saying that it has "top" priority just means that it weighs more heavily than anything else. But those things which are "higher" priorities in this sense do not trump lower-priority ones in any automatic fashion, as in lexicographical priority rules. Here we are always considering all factors simultaneously, and there is always the chance that several lower-priority considerations might conspire to defeat a higher-priority one.[4]

With this sort of priority rule, the question ceases to be *whether* various considerations should receive priority. All social goals deserve *some* priority in this sense. The crucial question instead is *how much* priority they deserve. Notice that this apparently modest weighting priority rule can degenerate into the more tyrannical lexicographical rule if one factor carries an infinitely greater weight than all others. And even in less extreme cases, outcomes can be biased heavily by giving one factor a very great weight relative to others.

Defense obviously carries a very heavy weight, in these terms. But, to judge from budgetary allocations, it does not seem that it is accorded an unreasonably high priority. Figures vary from country to country and period to period. But, from Reconstruction days forward, America has never committed more than 12.6 percent of its peacetime GNP to paying for defense or past wars. The figure dwindled steadily from 11.2 percent in 1955 to 5.7 percent in 1975, only to rise again in recent years (Schultze 1976, 326, 328). Abroad, the highest-spending NATO allies seem to commit only about half as much of their GNPs to defense (Russett 1970, 104). Whether this is too high or too low depends, naturally, upon circumstances. As Enthoven and Smith (1971, 203) say, "There is no discernible 'optimum percentage of GNP' for defense spending. If it were really necessary, the United States could probably spend half of its GNP on defense for a sustained period of time. Under other circumstances, 5 percent might be wasteful." But if we look just at orders

4. It may not be particularly appropriate to talk about "priorities" in such a context at all. "If one thinks about the use of an extra dollar or of the next half-hour of his time, it is sensible to ask, 'What is the most urgent—the first-priority—item?' If one is deciding what to do with a budget or the next eight hours, however, he ordinarily faces a problem of *allocation,* not of setting priorities. A list of priorities does not face the problem or help solve it" (Hitch and McKean 1960, 123; cf. Enthoven and Rowen 1961, 377–78). Nevertheless, discussion of budgetary allocations commonly *are* couched in terms of priorities. Indeed, the Brookings Institution's annual counterbudget takes as its title *Setting National Priorities.*

of magnitude, not attempting any fine-grained judgment, this level of priority of defense does not seem outlandish.

11.1.3. Exclusionary Priority

There the story would end, were it not for the third sort of priority rule. This one is rather more subtle and certainly less familiar than either of the previous two. It works by providing what Raz (1975) calls "exclusionary reasons." To say that a goal or value has high priority, in this sense, is to say that when contemplating it we should exclude from consideration a range of other goals or values that might have provided countervailing reasons for action. The classic case of the drowning child provides a good example. When we see a child drowning in a shallow pool, we have no business even in *thinking* about the fact that we will muddy our clothes saving him. It is not just that the stronger claims of the child *outweigh* the weaker claims arising out of our laundry bills; rather, the claims of the child *exclude* the latter considerations. Those should not even be allowed into the balance.

Judgments about the comparative exclusionary priority enjoyed by different values or goals can take two forms. Sometimes, one value or goal enjoys exclusionary priority *over* another. Then the former value is immune to counterclaims arising out of the latter. That is the case in the drowning-child example: saving lives enjoys exclusionary priority over keeping clean. Similarly, "needs" are ordinarily thought to enjoy exclusionary priority over—i.e., to exclude from consideration claims arising out of—"mere wants" (Braybrooke 1968). This, of course, is just another way of saying that the one value (saving lives, meeting needs) enjoys lexicographical priority over the other (keeping clean, satisfying mere preferences).

A more interesting and distinctive form of this type of priority is when one value or goal enjoys *more* exclusionary priority *than* another. This happens when value A excludes a wider range of counterclaims than does value B. If B is vulnerable to countervailing considerations arising out of values C, D, and E, from which A is immune, then we can say that A has "more" or "a higher" exclusionary priority than B. This is the sense in which I think national defense enjoys suspiciously high exclusionary priority: defense activities enjoy a curious kind of immunity from a wide range of criticisms commonly lodged and often thought telling against civilian undertakings.

Evidence of this priority is more behavioral than verbal. Explicit acknowledgments come only in the form of clauses exempting the military from the requirements of laws on occupational safety, hours and wages, environmental protection, and so on. Even academic commentators rarely recognize the phenomenon. To my knowledge, the only other writer noticing it is Weisskopf (1980). He finds it "not surprising" that so many people fear civilian nuclear power programs, but adds:

> What is surprising, however, and most depressing is that the public and most of the interested scientists rarely discuss a related danger, far greater and more imminent than any resulting from nuclear power production. It is the danger of nuclear war. There are more than 50,000 nuclear warheads now deployed and ready.... An unintentional accidental detonation of a nuclear weapon is much more probable and it would cause many more immediate and long-term fatalities than the most catastrophic reactor accident.... We are justly worried about human error and design failures in nuclear reactors. But what about human errors and design errors in our strategic planning, in the conduct of our political affairs and in the handling of our nuclear weapons? Aren't these much more subject to wrong decisions, irrational actions and accidents? The public distrusts the industrial experts. Why does it trust the military and political experts who have not performed too well in the past?... Certainly it is reasonable to be concerned about nuclear reactors. But to worry about them while ignoring the vastly greater problem of nuclear weapons is like sitting in an airplane with a growing crack in the wing, and worrying only about a leak in the heating system.

Perhaps this is slightly unfair. People *are* concerned, although perhaps insufficiently so, both about all-out nuclear war and also about "broken arrows" (accidents involving nuclear warheads).[5] But it is true that even here concern is curiously blinkered. Public inquiries following the explosion in a Titan II missile silo in Damascus, Arkansas, in September 1980 focused narrowly on the safety of the "outdated" Titan II delivery system. The real source of the danger—the nuclear warhead that was thrown clear in the blast—is generally neglected. Apparently no one is willing to ask any larger

---

5. The two most notorious cases are the inadvertent dropping of four H-bombs near Polmares, Spain, in 1966—requiring a $50 million clean-up operation and shipment of 1,100 tons of plutonium-contaminated soil to American dumps—and a similar incident at Thule, Greenland, in 1968. Perhaps the most dangerous broken arrow of all, however, was the 1962 crash of a nuclear-armed B-52 near Goldsboro, North Carolina. "A hunk of core uranium was never recovered." Furthermore, "five of six safety interlocks were set off by the fall: 'A single switch prevented the 24-megaton bomb (800 times the Hiroshima model) from exploding'" (Ralph Lapp, quoted in Scobie 1981). Altogether, the Pentagon acknowledges thirty-two such accidents between 1950 and 1968, "when the Air Force stopped flying nuclear-armed bombers on military alert" (Halloran 1981).

questions about the policy of nuclear retaliation that imposes these standing risks of accidental irradiation on the populations supposedly being "protected."

For a more systematic demonstration of the power of defense to exclude considerations which bear—sometimes decisively—on civilian projects, consider the following pairs of "matched" military and civilian operations.

1. Stratospheric flight. The Concorde SST, because it flies much higher than other commercial jets, emits exhausts which threaten irreparable damage to the ozone layer shielding the earth from the ultraviolet rays of the sun. Many thought that reason enough to ban such flights, at least pending further study. But, of course, military jets have been doing the same for many years now, as defenders of the Concorde were quick to remind the U.S. Secretary of Transportation and appeals court (Coleman 1976). Nobody quite knows what the effects of those flights have been—sufficiently sensitive instruments are not in place to take the needed measurements. Given the frequency of the military incursions into the stratosphere, however, it seems highly likely that much more damage will be done by them than by the marginal two Concorde flights daily scheduled between Europe and America.

2. Operation of nuclear reactors. Many people oppose civilian nuclear power programs because they doubt the safety of nuclear reactors. There are risks—probably small, but essentially unquantifiable—of large-scale accidents, releasing large amounts of radiation into the environment. And there are much larger risks of routine low-level radioactive emissions, whose impact on human health is radically uncertain. The same, however, is true of nuclear reactors used by the military to produce weapons-grade plutonium. The worst nuclear accident to date seems, in fact, to have come in the course of the Soviet bomb-building program (Trabalka, et al. 1980).

3. Storage of radioactive wastes. We have yet to find any absolutely reliable method for disposing of the radioactive waste products from nuclear reactors. Many think that this evil inheritance we will be leaving to future generations is reason enough to declare a moratorium on the use of civilian nuclear reactors (Flowers 1976, paras. 181, 338). But, again, the military has been doing the same for some time. "Over the last 30 years the Federal Government has generated a vast quantity of high-level and transuranic contaminated wastes from its military weapons and research and development programs. The volume of these wastes exceeds 20 million cubic feet—enough to cover four highway lanes with 10 inches of waste for almost 100 miles" (U.S. GAO 1979, 1). Furthermore, the military "experience with the storage of high-level liquid waste has not been encouraging. From 1958 to 1974, eighteen leaks, totaling 429,400 gallons, were detected at Richland [Washington].... Considering that the Richland site contains ... facilities spread over more than five square miles so badly contaminated that the land may never be cleaned up, immobilization of the waste in place might be the most practical alternative.... Whether these wastes really can be sealed off for hundreds of thousands of years and the land be removed from man's use for this period is far from clear" (Keeny 1977, 250–51). Advocates of civilian nuclear energy argue that, given the fact of such massive problems in disposing of military radioactive wastes, the question of radwaste disposal is not whether but merely how much. Since we will have to make provision for all these military wastes anyway, we might as well add those of a civilian nuclear power program as well.

4. *Toxic chemicals and lethal bacteria.* Many oppose recombinant DNA experiments on the grounds that scientists, fiddling around with this basic unit of life, run the risk of creating organisms which are at once indestructible and devastatingly lethal to the human life form. Once again, however, the military have long done something very similar in chemical and biological warfare laboratories. Defenders of recombinant DNA argue that, given the stock of lethal agents already available to any "mad scientist" out to destroy all human life, we would hardly be adding to their power or to our risks by allowing recombinant DNA experiments to proceed (Føllesdal 1979). Similarly, those exercised by the threat of leaking toxic chemical wastes seem curiously insensitive to the threat of leaking chemical warfare weapons. The Army concedes that "there are 'defective' nerve and blister gas munitions stored in Alabama, Arkansas, Colorado, Kentucky, Oregon and Utah—some of which leaked, creating 'mild' symptoms for some people" (Wilson 1981). But so far there has been no public furor even mildly equivalent to that which met the Love Canal leaks. Quite the contrary: "When, in December of 1969, the army decided to transfer nerve gas from Okinawa to the Umatilla Army Depot in Hermiston, Oregon, ... residents of Hermiston were 95% in favor of the transfer, despite the warning that the fuses on the gas bombs deteriorate with age, but that the gas does not" (Slovic and Fischhoff 1980, 130).

It is curious and regrettable that in so many of these cases military decisions have effectively preempted civilian ones. What is even more curious, however, is the extraordinary exclusionary priority exercised by defense claims. Objections which are regarded as compelling when lodged against civilian projects have never even been raised against their military counterparts. Interveners saw Concorde's threat to the environment as sufficiently grave to justify violation of commercial treaty obligations with two of America's principal allies, Britain and France. Yet they never for a moment suggested cessation of military operations in the stratosphere, which are more frequent and hence objectively more dangerous to the environment. Risks associated with the operation of nuclear reactors or with the disposal of their wastes are sufficient to turn many against this source of civilian energy, even if they are otherwise persuaded of its economic advantages. Only a few of them, however, are willing to extend the argument to closing down nuclear activities of the military as well. Opponents of recombinant DNA experiments seem curiously content with the 1969 American ratification of the Geneva protocol renouncing first-strike use of chemical or biological weapons. That protocol allows signatories to continue both research and development on and stockpiling of CBW weapons; and, in fact, the U.S. continues to store 42,000 tons of such materials, with a further build-up in view. Arguments against research into and storage of civilian recombinant DNA materials are, for some reason, not applied to research into and storage of military CBW materials.[6]

This tendency to overlook defense horrors is not easily explained away. Conspiracy theorists might point to the power of the military-industrial complex, which would render any protests ineffectual and therefore (following the "law of anticipated consequences") preclude them altogether. But that does not explain why various antiwar politicians, whose reputations depend upon their repeated attacks on the military, fail to take up the battle on these fronts.

Others might reply that the accidental effects of military activities are properly regarded as secondary considerations when the direct, intended uses of the weapons are so horrific. But if, as seems to be the case, we can get no agreement on the legitimacy of using these weapons in the situations for which they are intended, then surely it would be reasonable to examine these secondary considerations. We might be able to show that the unintended effects of the weapons threaten to be so intolerable that we should dispense with them, whether or not it would be legitimate to use them as planned should the occasion arise.

Yet another explanation might point to the fact that the military

6. *Newsweek* (Atlantic Edition), March 10, 1980, p. 17. So far as recombinant DNA research itself is concerned, the U.S. Department of Defense has endorsed the National Institute of Health guidelines. Thus, there are some grounds for hoping that CBW research relying on these techniques will be subject to the same safeguards as civilian research. But there are grounds for doubting even that: the Department of Defense has already, on at least one occasion, applied for exemption from those requirements in the name of national security (Wade 1980, 271). And, in any event, there are no such externally imposed safeguards on CBW research using other techniques which may be equally dangerous.

activities in question got under way before their civilian counter-parts. In some cases, the problems were initially thought to be already solved, or at least solvable. This is true of radioactive waste management.[7] In other cases, the hazards of military activities were only recently discovered. Military jets had been whipping around the upper atmosphere for years before it occurred to anyone that such flights might damage the ozone layer. All that might explain why the objections were not raised initially. None of it, however, explains why, once the dangers have been perceived or the putative solutions shown to be unsatisfactory, we do not hear the same objections being lodged against military flights or nuclear waste as against analogous civilian hazards.

The only plausible explanation for this pattern of behavior is, I conclude, that defense activities are accorded a high exclusionary priority, exempting them from a wide range of criticisms deemed proper and possibly compelling as applied to civilian activities. It is far from obvious how this priority could be justified. If those criticisms carry as much weight as ordinarily thought when brought to bear on civilian activities, then there is a prima facie case for at least *considering* them in relation to strictly analogous military ones.

In the end, of course, we may decide that it is proper to continue military projects while curtailing civilian ones, since defense goals carry greater weight. But usually a lower weighting priority would hardly mean ceasing the civilian activity altogether, while allowing the defense version to proceed at the same levels as before. Take, for example, the case of stratospheric flight. As a crude guide, let us suppose that the relative weighting of defense to environmental goals is about seven to one, the figure implied by recent U.S. federal budgets (Schultze 1976). Other things being equal, that weighting would seem to imply that we ought to allow one civilian flight in the stratosphere for every seven military ones. By those standards, Concorde's schedule hardly seems unreasonable; or, by the same token, if Concorde's is unreasonable, then the military's is very much more so. The larger point, however, is not that bringing these neglected considerations to bear will necessarily be decisive in re-directing military activities, but only that there is a prima facie case for at least considering them.

7. "In its first two decades, the Nation's nuclear weapons program concentrated on producing nuclear materials for weapons and other defense-related activities. Little budget or management attention was given to addressing permanent disposal of the resulting nuclear wastes. The Atomic Energy Commission believed the disposal problem was technically solvable and could be addressed at some future time. As a result, decisions on nuclear waste management were based on short-term expediency rather than long-term management" (U.S. GAO 1979, 3).

11.2. Arguments from Analogies

The most powerful yet dubious method of giving defense considerations priority treatment is one which works tacitly. Since much of its power lies in its being an unstated rule, we should hardly expect to find explicit arguments in its favor. The more appropriate way to defend such practices is indirectly, through allusions and analogies. Here I shall examine four such analogies, showing that none of them really justifies the practice of according defense such great exclusionary priority.

11.2.1. Defense as a Primary Good

Frequently national defense is analyzed, after the fashion of Rawls's primary goods (1972, sec. 15), as an indispensable prerequisite to everything else the nation might do. Defense of the nation is said to be analogous to an individual's quest for food and shelter. These are not particularly noble goals, for the nation or the individual, either—people who pursue these goals alone lead very impoverished lives indeed. What makes these goals so important is simply their urgency (Scanlon 1975). All other more exalted goals come to naught unless survival needs are met first. Thus, it is argued, it is entirely proper that defense claims should enjoy an absolute priority over all the nation's other projects, since all others are logically dependent upon the survival of the state.

This all depends, however, upon just how possessive we are about our projects. If it makes all the difference to a person that *he* be the one to accomplish the goal in question, then certainly he must stay alive to do so. But those who are more concerned with the goals themselves than with claiming credit for accomplishing them will see that the goals can be accomplished even after their death—and, if their death inspires others, perhaps even because of their death. So too are social policies only loosely linked to the continuation of any particular regime. Policies begun under one government often continue under their successors, even when the succession was far from smooth. De Gaulle's new constitution for the French Fifth Republic "did not repudiate spending commitments embodied in the social security legislation of previous French regimes"; and "the Federal Republic of Germany still pays benefits to the families of soldiers who fought for the Third Reich" (Rose and Peters 1979, 115, 263). There has been no thorough study of the extent of policy continuity in successor states, but it seems likely to prove very great. If so, the continued existence of the regime—or perhaps even of government itself—is not a necessary precondition for the continuation of all sorts of desirable social policies.

Furthermore, it is not only permissible but desirable to trade primary goods off for other goods under certain circumstances. National defense is said to be equivalent to health and wealth for an individual: whatever else the nation wants to do, it must first secure itself against attack, just as for individuals safeguarding health and accumulating wealth are crucial preconditions for achievement of their more particular goals. But if the only reason you want money is for what it will buy you, then it surely is ludicrous to insist that you should forever amass more of it without spending any. Similarly with health: an aspiring ski-jumper should jealously safeguard his health in preparation for that physically demanding activity; but it would be absurd to insist that he not jump, on the grounds that it is dangerous activity, if the only reason he had been protecting his health had been to prepare him for jumping.

Likewise in the case of national defense, nations amass power in the international system not for its own sake but rather to pursue their "ideals." It is, therefore, folly to criticize them for "squandering" power when they use it in pursuit of those ideals (Stebbing 1944; Hoffman 1959). Or, as Aquinas put it more prosaically, if the highest aim of the captain were to preserve his ship, he would keep it in port forever (Goodin 1980, 149). The "primary good" analogy suggests that the value of defense is strictly derivative—it is desirable only as a precondition for pursuing other desirable goals. If so, those other goals must occasionally be allowed to override defense claims.

The conclusion must be that it is obviously wrong, on the "primary good" model, to allow defense lexicographical priority, enabling it to trump all other goals. It would be equally wrong to allow defense very great exclusionary priority, exempting it from counterclaims arising out of those other more basic goals. Defense should, of course, carry a heavy weight in social decisions if the primary good model is accurate. Given this, it may frequently outweigh certain other goals. But it would be blatantly wrong to build this result in right from the start by exempting defense from challenges arising from those other goals. The difference is between "characteristically" and "necessarily"—between "usually" and "always"—overriding other goals. Even if defense usually (or even almost always) prevails, we should preserve a form of decision rule that allows for those occasional instances wherein defense claims themselves might be overridden.

11.2.2.   Defense as Insurance

Both generals and congressmen fondly refer to military prepared-
ness as "an insurance premium on democracy" (Schilling 1962, 13;
cf. Taylor 1974). On this analogy, shortchanging national defense
amounts to simple recklessness, akin to that of a parent with several
dependents letting his life insurance lapse. Maybe he will get lucky
and nothing will happen, but it is simply irresponsible to run the risk.

Notice that insurance works by compensating victims for their
losses. Under ideal circumstances, insurance would provide full
compensation, restoring the victim to his antecedent state of well-
being. In that case, he should be indifferent between suffering the
harm and collecting on his insurance, or being spared the harm and
denied the payoff on his insurance policy. No one would suppose the
same is true of defense. We are far from indifferent between being
attacked and defended and not being attacked at all.

Some insurance schemes, too, fail to realize that ideal. There are,
section 8.3.3 above has argued, some harms for which we simply
cannot be compensated fully. We scorn our insurance agent's offerings not just because the sums ($5,000 for loss of one eye or limb,
$20,000 for two of a kind, etc.) are ludicrously inadequate, but rather
because *no* sum can adequately compensate for loss of sight, and so
on. Against such risks, no insurance coverage can ever be complete;
hence, we will never be indifferent to these things happening to us.
Perhaps defense is akin to these cases of imperfect insurance.

Even this revised analogy, however, will not generate any very
high priority for defense preparations. Where insurance is
imperfect—where no compensation could ever restore our
losses—we do not generally commit everything we have to insurance premiums nonetheless, supposing more is always better
even if it can never be enough. Rather, we usually tend to insure
only minimally, if at all. Recall the example, discussed in section
8.3.3, of a woman facing breast cancer: it is perfectly reasonable that
she should spend a lot of money preventing it from happening, but
only a little arranging for insurance compensation if it does, because
the money will not restore her breast. Likewise, few people carry
very much insurance against blindness. Certainly blindness would
change their lives dramatically, but not in ways that money could
help much to avoid or to overcome. Where compensation is impossible, insurance can no longer be justified *as* insurance. Thus,
even if national defense were analogous to insurance, the analogy
would imply no more than that a moderately high weight be given to
it in social decisions. Nothing so strong as lexicographic or high
exclusionary priority would be warranted.

11.2.3. Defense as Security

While both insurance and defense provide the same good—peace of mind—they do so in very different ways. Insurance policies, even imperfect ones, afford such peace of mind as they do by compensating the victim. Defense creates peace of mind rather by preventing the untoward event in the first place. "The defense budget," writes Warner Schilling (1962, 13), is "very much unlike life insurance," because "the amount purchased of the latter normally has no influence on the health of the insured. In contrast, the kind of armament a nation carries may have a most significant influence on the course of its public life."

This suggests the further analogy of "defense as security." When I hand over the deed to my house as "security" on my mortgage, the point is not just that, should I default, my banker will be able to sell off the property and thus recoup his loss. That, too, of course is true. But the real point of handing over the deed is to guarantee that I do not default rather than to compensate my creditors if I do. Similarly, when a ship's mate "secures" the cargo on deck during a storm, he is not arranging compensation in case it blows overboard; rather, he is arranging the cargo in such a way as to guarantee that does not happen. On this analogy, defense secures the nation just as the deed to my house secures my loan: with someone else holding the title to my property, I am not likely to miss my payments; similarly, with an impressive military machine we are not likely to be attacked.[8]

The security analogy does seem to capture the essential logic underlying national defense. "National security" was, indeed, a catch-phrase adopted quite self-consciously by politicians planning America's place in the postwar world. As early as 1945, State Department officials were commenting upon how "the abstract noun 'security' has acquired a very concrete significance for us." And the import of the term, then as in the present analysis, was to emphasize the distinction between preventing enemy attacks ("security") and merely defending against them when and if they occur. This point, stressed in Navy Secretary James Forrestal's 1945 congressional testimony, was enthusiastically endorsed by senators present (Yergin 1978, 194–95).

The security analogy justifies giving defense considerations some

---

8. This presents security arrangements as essentially a way of reducing uncertainty. But, of course, there must be something more involved. After all, one way of "settling things" would be to attack your opponent and get it over with; another would be to know with absolute certainty that he will attack you within the hour. Neither would be particularly satisfactory solutions, although both eliminate the uncertainty. The real point of security arrangements is to reduce the probabilities of undesirable outcomes rather than just resolving the uncertainties one way or another.

sort of priority. People are generally averse to risks, and their aversion generally increases with the size of the stakes (Arrow 1971, chaps. 1, 3). Maybe they will make small loans without demanding that they be secured; but the larger the stakes, the more likely they are to demand better security for the loan. If national security can be portrayed as a high-stakes issue, then the very great aversion people feel toward taking risks in such situations will justify giving security requirements a high priority.

At most, however, this will be a high weighting priority. More dramatic forms—lexicographic or high exclusionary priority—could be justified only if we displayed *absolute* aversion to the sorts of risks which defense preparations remove. In fact, we do no such thing. Certainly when making a large loan we display considerable risk aversion, insofar as we demand good security for it. But for our risk aversion to be absolute, we would have to refuse to make any large unsecured loan however big a rate of return it promises. Intuitively, it seems there must be some rate of return (100%? 1000%?) sufficiently fantastic that we would be prepared to take the chance without any security. Hence our risk aversion is less than absolute. Security weighs heavily but not absolutely in our calculations where large stakes are at risk (Harsanyi 1975).

Even if we gave security absolute priority, however, that would not translate automatically into a similarly absolute priority for defense preparations. Military expenditures do not translate automatically into security. At the outset of this section, I observed that defense preparations, unlike insurance premiums, actually alter the probability of the occurrence of untoward events. The "defense as security" analogy presupposes that the larger a nation's defense effort, the lower the probability of its suffering losses. That is plausible enough in "games against nature"—securing against a storm does indeed decrease our likely losses, for example. Something rather different, however, is involved in national defense: "We have to make decisions . . . . . in the face of the fact that our opponent will try to nullify our efforts by his own decisions" (Morgenstern 1959, 193). The arms-race dynamic suggests that each side tries to match or best the effort of its opponents.[9] At best, the balance is restored with each side possessing an ever-more-lethal arsenal; at worst, an imbalance leads one side to attack the other (Richardson 1960). In neither case has the extra defense effort really contributed to security for either side.[10] At the very outset of the Cold War, General

9. Ostrom (1977) finds that arms-racing is not *all* that underlies U.S. defense spending. But in his more complete "reactive linkage" model (Ostrom 1978), Soviet expenditures turn out to be second only to U.S. battle deaths as determinants of the U.S. defense budget.

10. In the absence of arms-control agreements, defensive moves are inter-

George Marshall warned President Truman that "we should not plunge into war preparations which would bring about the very thing we are taking steps to prevent" (quoted in Schilling 1962, 244). And Robert McNamara similarly recommended against the antiballistic missile system in 1967 on the grounds that "all that we would accomplish by deploying ABM systems against one another would be to increase greatly our respective defense expenditures, without any gain in real security for either side" (quoted in Murdock 1974, 133). Security and defense expenditures are, thus, separable issues, and giving the one priority does not imply giving it to the other likewise.

11.2.4.   Defense and the Logic of Safety First

"The prudent decisionmaker," Enthoven (1963) says, "will keep asking himself, 'Would the outcome be acceptable if the worst possible happened, i.e., if all the pessimistic estimates were borne out?'" There are two arguments for such supercaution. One builds on the "game of strategy" analogy just introduced. It is often said that defense preparations form part of a zero-sum game of international politics, wherein one side's losses are the other's gains and vice versa. The standard response to such a situation is to play a maximin strategy. Each player, knowing his worst enemy will be making the next move, should choose whichever alternative has the best minimum payoff for him, since (given it is a zero-sum game) he knows that the outcome he likes least is the one his opponent will like best (Schelling 1963; Wohlstetter 1964, 131).

This zero-sum analogy, however, captures only part of the reality of international diplomacy. Most games there are far from being purely zero-sum contests. Indeed, that they are not is presupposed in some of our most central notions in strategic thinking:

> "Deterrence," for example, is meaningless in a zero-sum context. So is "surrender"; so are most limited-war strategies; and so are notions like "accidental war," escalation, preemptive war, and "brinkmanship." And of course so are nearly all alliance relationships, arms-race phenomena, and arms control. The fact that war hurts—that not all the losses of war are

changeable with offensive ones in the arms-racing logic. But where there are "limitations on offensive weapons systems but not on defensive systems," Rothenberg (1967, 91) finds that "one could easily predict that deterrence against central nuclear war will be enhanced . . . .: only extreme inadvertent exacerbation of political tensions would seem likely to make an attack worth considering." The Russians do indeed seem "interested in reducing the absolute level of damage through a limitation on offensive weapons and a mutual build-up of defensive weapons" (Murdock 1974, 134–35), but the Americans will have none of it.

recoverable—makes war itself a dramatically nonzero-sum activity. [Schelling 1967, 106]

In all these cases, the interests of one side partially coincide with those of its enemies, flatly contradicting the zero-sum model.

Another more plausible argument for using the maximin rule in relation to defense planning treats defense as an instance of the sort of "profound uncertainty" discussed in chapters 9 and 10 above. Just as we cannot anticipate all the possible ways a saboteur might attack a nuclear reactor, so too are we unable to anticipate all possible aggressive moves against the nation as a whole. If we cannot exhaustively list possibilities, it does not pay to think in terms of probabilities; and we should fall back on other sorts of decision rules, such as maximin. George Kennan (quoted in Yergin 1978, 403) applies a similar logic to the problem of defense planning:

It is safer and easier to cease to attempt to analyze the probabilities involved in your enemy's processes or to calculate his weaknesses. It seems safer to give him the credit of every doubt in matters of strength, and to credit him indiscriminately with *all* aggressive designs, even when some of them are mutually contradictory.

There are various objections to using the maximin rule in defense planning, most of them proving more telling against the zero-sum justification than against that couched in terms of profound uncertainty.[11] Even if we were to accept that the maximin rule should be applied, however, its practical implications are far from obvious. Usually that rule is said to demand that we keep a military establishment strong enough to repel the strongest possible attack from our strongest possible enemy—i.e., that we should give defense lexicographical priority over everything else. But that would be the correct inference only if being conquered is the worst possible outcome we can imagine. Surely it is not. The *very* worst outcome—the one against which maximin insists that we must protect at all costs—is surely the possibility that deployment of nuclear defenses might lead to an exchange of warheads leaving the earth virtually unfit for human life as we know it (U.S. Congress OTA 1980). The maximin rule would, therefore, favor arms limitation

11. Schlesinger (1968, 366), for example, complains of "increasing political fluidity," making us unsure of who our enemies will be when: if we don't know who our enemy is, we cannot maximinimize against him. Hitch (1964, 17) complains that the maximin rule "is too conservative and forfeits opportunities to exploit enemy mistakes, or what we know about his predilections." And Enthoven (1963) worries that focusing on the worst case might make us believe that an adequate defense is impossibly expensive, and hence lead us to protect inadequately (or not at all) against more modest threats which we could afford to meet.

over the unlimited armament implied in any rule giving military preparations any sort of strong priority.[12]

11.3. The Temporal Bias of Defense

At most, these analogies might justify giving defense a moderately high weighting priority in our social decisions. None of them justifies giving defense either of the more extreme forms of lexicographical or exclusionary priority. Yet section 11.1.3 has shown that defense does seem to enjoy high levels of exclusionary priority—defense projects appear to be exempt from a wide range of powerful criticisms ordinarily raised against strictly analogous civilian projects. To explain this, we must examine the temporal biases contained in the notion of "defense."

The anomalies discussed in section 11.1.3 differ in various ways. But they generally have one thing in common: the considerations which bore heavily on civilian projects but not at all on military ones were considerations of long-term consequences.[13] Depletion of the ozone layer, even if it does result from stratospheric flights, will not become a serious problem until sometime next century. Even if radioactive waste containers begin leaking the moment they are deposited below ground, it will take hundreds of years for the wastes to make their way back to contaminate the human environment. With nuclear reactor or CBW operations, the hazards may be objectively more immediate—if anything goes wrong, people are in imminent danger. But these risks might be bearable for people who look only a few years ahead, becoming intolerable only if we take a longer view and ask about the probability of a serious accident sometime over the course of the next decade or two.[14]

12. Maximin may still sanction acquisition of some weapons, but these will be fewer and of a different character than those which would be acquired if armament were given lexicographical priority over all other goals in the national budget. The most acceptable worst possible outcomes might, for example, emerge from a strategy of acquiring "arms suitable for deterrence but ill-suited for attack." As McGuire (1965, 29) observes, "The ultimate in . . . insurance against war by mistake is reached when both sides positively prefer being attacked by the opponent to attacking the opponent first."

13. There is further evidence of this temporal bias in the way we choose to finance defense expenditures. "The costs may be entirely in the form of current benefits forgone or, if the nation's resource base is eroded, they may be paid largely by future generations." Examining U.S. expenditure patterns, Russett (1970, 128, 144) finds that "proportionately . . . investment is much harder hit by an expansion of the military establishment than is consumption. . . . According to some rough estimates, the marginal productivity of capital in the United States is between 20 and 25 percent . . . . Hence if [as statistics suggest] an extra billion dollars of defense in one year reduced investment by \$292 million, thenceforth the level of output in the economy would be *permanently* diminished by on the order of \$65 million per year."

14. It does not sound so bad to say we run a 1/7000 chance of an accident this year. But if we run the same risk every year for a decade, the chances of an accident

There is something built into the notion of "defense" that helps explain—if not justify—this systematic exclusion of long-term considerations from defense planning. Normally we regard "national defense" and "national security" as harmless euphemisms that put a friendlier face on our war-making apparatus. There is, however, one important side effect of this way of talking: "defense" forces us to think in all-or-nothing terms. Such stark categories are inappropriate in more ordinary discussions of war-making, where winning or losing is typically a relative thing. Few fights are to the finish. More often, wars are "instrumental" struggles or, indeed, such norm-governed forms of "antagonism" that they more nearly resemble family fights (Speier 1941). A loser might sue for peace on more or less favorable terms: although he has lost, he might get off lightly; he can hope to return to fight another day. This flexibility is almost entirely missing from the notion of "defense." Protecting the integrity of a nation is akin to protecting the integrity of a virgin: once lost, it is lost totally and forever. This, in turn, makes national defense unlike ordinary social goals. If economic planners fail one year they can always redeem themselves next year. With national defense, understood as an all-or-nothing proposition, we will have no such opportunity to recoup our losses next year. Unless we defend ourselves this year, we will not enjoy a next.[15]

Under these conditions, it makes sense to give a kind of absolute priority to the present demands of defense. It does no good to protect against threats—even, perhaps, greater threats—in the future if you cannot provide adequate protection against present dangers. Failing to defend against these, you will not even survive to face the future challenges. The principle of "first things first" must rule. The future must defer to the present. It may not be appropriate to give defense lexicographical priority over everything else, since there might be some social goals for which we would willingly risk (and maybe even sacrifice) the nation itself. But we can, on this analysis, categorically rule out one whole class of countervailing considerations—generically characterized as long-term future hazards. There is no point protecting our distant futures unless we can be confident of surviving into them.

---

sometime during that decade are 1/700; and, for two decades, 1/350. That starts sounding frightening, but only if we are willing to look at the risk in the relatively long term.

15. Yergin (1978, 196), discussing the concept of "national security," offers a parallel analysis: "Virtually every development in the world is perceived to be potentially crucial. An adverse turn of events anywhere endangers the United States. Problems in foreign nations are viewed as urgent and immediate threats. Thus, desirable foreign policy goals are translated into issues of national survival, and the range of threats become limitless."

This, I think, *explains* the kind of exclusionary priority given to defense claims. It would *justify* such priority, of course, only if defense really were an all-or-nothing proposition. This seems most doubtful, deriving such superficial plausibility as it enjoys from a linguistic trick. Such tricks are both common and persuasive, at least in the short term. But once we see through them, they lose their power (Goodin 1980, chap. 3). The trick exposed, it now seems that the "first things first" principle does not really justify the temporal bias of defense decision-making or the exclusion of considerations of future hazards that grows out of it.

Conclusions

12 Lessons Learned

Countless other issues could no doubt profit from intensive examinations such as the previous chapters have given nuclear power and national defense. But perhaps those two extended examples are sufficient to make my most basic point. Above all else, I hope that this book has demonstrated to students of public policy the advantages of a theoretical approach to their subject, and to students of ethics the advantages of real rather than artificial examples. It is, of course, perfectly proper that theoretical points be surrounded by a fair bit of institutionalist stage-setting—provided that is not an end in itself. And stripped-down examples can, as in chapters 3 and 8, help isolate morally important features of complicated policy puzzles—provided we exercise great caution in applying simple lessons in a world of complex realities.

In arguing these points, I have offered few precepts and many examples. That may seem odd. The opposite balance usually predominates in books centrally concerned to make such fundamentally methodological points. But here argumentation by example is inevitable. Policy analysis—in this mode even more than in Wildavsky's (1979)—is an art and craft rather than a rigidly codified or codifiable discipline.

12.1. Ethics

Methodology aside, this book has also advocated certain substantive positions in ethics and politics. As an exercise in applied ethics, this book has been in quest of a *really* credible form of utilitarianism. The flaws with that doctrine cannot be ignored. Neither, however, should they be exaggerated. The classic example is, perhaps, the problem of interpersonal utility comparisons. Long regarded as dealing utilitarianism a knock-out blow, this problem can now be seen as a phantasm created by crude forms of logical positivism that linger only among economists. Refusal to make such comparisons is indefensible both in theory and in practice. It is simply indecent for policymakers to try to avoid such considerations when reflecting upon the distribution of benefits and burdens between citizens, nations, and generations.

Other problems with utilitarianism, although genuine, need not spook us into a headlong flight to an equally absurd Kantian extreme. The whole *Philosophy & Public Affairs* program seems dedicated to showing that rights-based theories can, with sufficient twisting and turning, yield reasonable answers to policy puzzles. And so they can. But, of course, the twisting and turning is itself a confession of failure. Theories requiring contortions to come up with the right answer are much less persuasive than ones yielding similar results effortlessly.

As Bernard Williams (1973, 90) says, it is wrong to suggest that the material consequences of our actions count for everything, morally speaking, and it is equally absurd to suggest that they count for nothing. Plausible policy prescriptions can come only from cultivating the middle ground between utilitarianism and Kantianism. Having despaired of the implausibility of recent efforts at working back from Kant, I have pursued instead the less fashionable strategy of searching for guidance in the shadow of utilitarianism.

One of the most important revisions here suggested in classical utilitarianism is recognition of the fact that people have feelings as well as interests. Chapters 5 and 6 have shown that people have self-conceptions and seriously held moral principles that demand special protection. A more utilitarian way of putting the point might be to say that people have interests in their feelings—but that only goes to show how easy it is to obscure the real force of this point. Self-respect is not just one more aspect of people's utility to be promoted, nor is it even just the aspect to which people themselves attach paramount importance. Rather, respecting people, their self-image, and their dignity is what provides the whole *raison d'être* for utilitarian and contractarian schemes for respecting their preferences; and policymakers must therefore always give dignity and self-respect precedence over preferences and choices in cases of conflict. Similarly, treating people's seriously held principles as just another preference destroys whatever it is that makes them special for people.

Here I have also loosened the long-established connection between utilitarianism and consumer sovereignty. There is no reason for policymakers to defer to people themselves as the best—much less the only—judges of their own true interests. Often this is simply because policy issues are complex and people's understandings limited. People sometimes run unwarranted risks, to use an example from chapter 8, merely because they misjudge the probabilities of the hazards involved; or, if they know the statistics, they are psychologically incapable of conjuring up a clear and vivid image of themselves suffering the accident. More fundamentally, however, we can discount people's preferences (as in chapter 3) because people are poor predictors of their own future preferences. People's preferences change, largely in response to their own past experiences, and in ways which usually are predicted best by less interested parties. Public officials, choosing policies with distant payoffs, should therefore feel free to substitute their own predictions of people's future preferences for those of the people themselves. While freeing them from the slavish obedience to citizen preferences which characterizes ordinary utilitarian prescriptions, this revised standard is still very much in the same preference-regarding spirit, for what justifies policymakers in substituting their own judgment is the prediction that citizens' future preferences will thereby be better served.

Some crude forms of utilitarianism truly are prone to disaster, for either individuals or whole societies. Under such decision rules, uncertainty is allowed to sanction recklessness and thereby to invite disaster. Furthermore, through their indifference to distributions, such rules actually *welcome* substantial disasters for some people, just so long as losses will be counterbalanced by gains to other people or in other periods. These shameful features have been largely removed from the form of utilitarianism advocated here. Chapter 9 has broken any easy connection between uncertainty and recklessness. Chapter 5 has, through the notion of dignity, introduced broadly egalitarian distributional constraints reinforcing those arising naturally through diminishing marginal utility. And, in any case, chapters 9 and 10 have shown that the sort of probabilistic knowledge required for confidence in the "averaging out" strategy is lacking in important classes of policy choices. So utilitarianism, suitably reformulated, need not spell disaster either for isolated individuals or for societies as a whole.

12.2. Politics and Policymaking

The political message of this book is that we should not be shy of social planning. There is no need to proceed incrementally. Indeed, as chapter 2 has shown, there is no point in doing so in the absence of some theoretical foundations; and, given such theory, we can proceed to plan on that basis. Depending on what those theories dictate, our policy interventions may be large or small scale, long or short term, adaptive or irreversible. In perfectly general terms, none of these types has any absolute advantages over its opposite. Everything depends on the circumstances of the case at hand. Our plans might always go awry, as their underlying theories turn out to have been wrong or incomplete. But even then such planning is preferable to the irresponsibly atheoretical incrementalism that just tries a little policy change and waits to see what happens.

Classically, the greatest danger to effective planning is "suboptimization." If we maximize over a limited subset of goals and options, those others which we have neglected are bound to be shortchanged. This danger should make us especially suspicious of any excuses tending to restrict the political agenda. Pleas of "impossibility" must, as chapter 7 has argued, be examined carefully to see wherein the impossibility resides—to see whether it is truly objective or an impossibility of one's own making. We must, as chapter 8 has shown, look carefully behind talk of "luck" to make sure redistribution really is morally unwarranted. And we must be especially careful not to fall for any tacit priority rule such as chapter 11 shows shields defense policies from a wide range of legitimate countervailing considerations. Upon examination, of course, the excuses might prove to be valid—the impossibility genuine, the risks fair, the priority deserved—and there will be no danger of suboptimization in respecting them. But we must always be wary.

Another threat to effective social planning, revealed in chapter 4, lies in trying to plan too tightly. Desirable as it is to set goals across the full range of social concerns, it is obvious folly for planners to try prescribing rigidly from the center precisely how these goals are to be pursued. Loose laws, specifying broad goals but leaving the choice of means to those more directly concerned, are preferable on both practical and moral grounds. Instead of relying on "command-and-control" techniques, plans should depend for their enforcement upon incentives—moral incentives (as in chapter 6) where possible, and material ones (such as pollution taxes, as in chapter 4, or risk taxes, as in chapter 8) where necessary.

The sort of sociopolitical institution best suited to these requirements seems to be "market socialism," as described by Lange (1936–37) and approximated in Yugoslavia. There, the central plan is shaped by and enforced through interactions in a quasi-market. And there is some chance for seriously held moral principles to guide people's macropolitical choices regarding the broad structure of their society, uncontaminated by mundane concerns which are confined to the quasi-market.

In practice, there may well be political obstacles to all these proposals. Politicians ruled by "the will to power" naturally try to dictate means as well as ends, as chapter 4 has observed. And planners might well threaten to overstep the charter, given them in chapter 3, to override people's present preferences in order better to serve their future preferences. Ultimately, however, these power plays can pose a real threat only so long as they can hide behind principled rhetoric. They can plausibly pretend to be in the public interest only so long as our choice is seen merely to be among the undisciplined market, blind incrementalism, and authoritarian central planning. But once we see that there is a further alternative—that policymakers can be activist without being overbearing—we can and inevitably will use the ordinary mechanisms of democratic accountability to hold them to that course.

References

Aaron, H. J. 1975. Cautionary notes on the experiment. In Pechman and Timpane 1975, pp. 88–114.

Abel, R. L. 1973. A comparative theory of dispute institutions in society. *Law and Society Review* 8: 217–347.

Abell, P. 1977. The many faces of power and liberty. *Sociology* 11: 3–14.

Abey-Wickrama, I.; A'Brook, M. F.; Gationi, F. E. G.; and Herridge, C. F. 1969. Mental hospital admissions and aircraft noise. *Lancet* 7633: 1275–79.

Ackerman, B. A., and Hassler, P. 1981. *Clean air/dirty coal.* New Haven: Yale University Press.

Acton, H. B. 1963. Negative utilitarianism. *Proceedings of the Aristotelian Society (Supplement)* 37: 83–94.

Aigler, R. W. 1922. Legislation in vague or general terms. *Michigan Law Review* 21: 831–51.

Allison, G. T. 1971. *Essence of decision.* Boston: Little Brown.

Anderson, C. W. 1979. The place of principles in policy analysis. *American Political Science Review* 73: 711–23.

Anderson, M. 1964. *The federal bulldozer.* Cambridge: MIT Press.

Angino, E. E. 1977. High-level and long-lived radioactive waste disposal. *Science* 198: 885–90.

Anon. 1980. Compensating victims of occupational disease. *Harvard Law Review* 93: 916–37.

Anon. 1981. Allocating the costs of hazardous waste disposal. *Harvard Law Review* 94: 584–604.

Anscombe, G. E. M. 1957. Does Oxford philosophy corrupt the youth? *The Listener* 57: 267, 271.

———. 1970. War and murder. In *War and Morality,* ed. R. A. Wasserstrom, pp. 42–53. Belmont Calif.: Wadsworth.

Arnould, R. J., and Grabowski, H. 1981. Auto safety regulation: an analysis of market failure. *Bell Journal of Economics* 12: 27–48.

Arrow, K. J. 1963. *Social choice and individual values.* 2d ed. New Haven: Yale University Press.

————. 1966. Discounting and public investment criteria. In *Water research,* ed. A. V. Kneese and S. C. Smith, pp. 13–32. Baltimore: Johns Hopkins University Press.

————. 1967. The place of moral obligation in preference systems. In *Human values and economic policy,* ed. S. Hook, pp. 117–19. New York: New York University Press.

————. 1971. *Essays in the theory of risk-bearing.* Chicago: Markham.

————. 1972. Gifts and exchanges. *Philosophy & Public Affairs* 1: 343–62.

————. 1973a. Social responsibility and economic efficiency. *Public Policy* 21: 303–17.

————. 1973b. Some ordinalist-utilitarian notes on Rawls. *Journal of Philosophy* 70: 245–63.

————. 1976. The rate of discount for long-term public investment. In Ashley, Rudman, and Whipple 1976, pp. 113–40.

————, and Fisher, A. C. 1974. Environmental preservation, uncertainty and irreversibility. *Quarterly Journal of Economics* 88: 312–19.

————, and Hurwicz, L. 1972. An optimality criterion for decision-making under ignorance. In *Uncertainty and expectations in economics,* ed. C. F. Carter and J. L. Ford, pp. 1–11. Oxford: Blackwell.

Ashley, H.; Rudman, R. L.; and Whipple, C., eds. 1976. *Energy and the environment.* New York: Pergamon.

Ashworth, J. 1980. Technology diffusion through foreign assistance: making renewable energy sources available to the world's poor. *Policy Science* 11: 241–61.

Aubert, V. 1959. Chance in social affairs. *Inquiry* 2: 1–24.

Austin, J. L. 1956–57. A plea for excuses. *Proceedings of the Aristotelian Society* 57: 1–30.

Averch, H. A.; Koehler, J. E.; and Denton, F. H. 1971. *The matrix of policy in the Philippines.* Princeton: Princeton University Press.

Axelrod, R. 1977. The place of policy analysis in political science: the medical metaphor. *American Journal of Political Science* 21: 430–32.

Ayres, R. W. 1975. Policing plutonium: the civil liberties fallout. *Harvard Civil Rights/Civil Liberties Law Review* 10: 369–443.

Bacon, R., and Eltis, W. 1976. *Britain's economic problem.* London: Macmillan.

Bardach, E. 1978. Reason, responsibility and the new social regulation. In *American politics and public policy,* ed. W. D. Burnham and M. W. Weinberg, pp. 364–90. Cambridge: MIT Press.

Barker, R. J. S. 1978. "Alternative" energy: some recent contributions to decision making. *Political Quarterly* 49: 86–92.

Barlow, R.; Brazer, H. E.; and Morgan, J. N. 1966. *Economic behavior of the affluent.* Washington, D.C.: Brookings.

Barnes, B. A. 1977. Discarded operations: surgical innovation by trial and error. In *Costs, risks and benefits of surgery,* ed. J. P. Bunker, B.A.

Barnes, and F. Mosteller, pp. 109–24. New York: Oxford University Press.

Barnett, J.   1978.   Written answer: test discount rate. *Hansard* 947: columns 147–48.

Barry, B.   1965.   *Political argument*. London: Routledge & Kegan Paul.

———.   1977.   Justice between generations. In *Law, morality and society*, ed. P. M. S. Hacker and J. Raz, pp. 268–84. Oxford: Clarendon Press.

———.   1978.   Circumstances of justice and future generations. In Sikora and Barry 1978, pp. 204–48.

———.   1979a.   And who is my neighbor? *Yale Law Journal* 88: 629–58.

———.   1979b.   Is democracy special? In Laslett and Fishkin 1979, pp. 155–96.

———.   1979c.   On editing *Ethics*. *Ethics* 90: 1–6.

———.   1980.   Editorial. *Ethics* 90: 317–18.

———.   1983.   *Rich nations and poor nations*. New York: Cambridge University Press (forthcoming).

Barth, F.   1967.   Economic spheres in Darfur. In *Themes in economic anthropology*, ed. R. Firth, pp. 149–74. London: Tavistock.

Batson, C. D.; Coke, J. S.; Jasnoski, M. L.; and Hanson, M.   1978.   Buying kindness: effect of an extrinsic incentive for helping on perceived altruism. *Personality and Social Psychology Bulletin* 4: 86–91.

Baumol, W. J.   1968.   Entrepreneurship and economic theory. *American Economic Review (Papers & Proceedings)* 58: 64–71.

———.   1970.   On the discount rate for public projects. In Haveman and Margolis 1970, pp. 273–90.

Bayles, M. D.   1971.   Legal principles, rules and standards. In *Legal reasoning*, ed. H. Hubien, pp. 223–28. Brussels: Émile Bruylant.

Becker, G. S.   1974.   A theory of social interactions. *Journal of Political Economy* 82: 1063–94.

———.   1976a.   Altruism, egoism and genetic fitness: economics and sociobiology. *Journal of Economic Literature* 14: 817–26.

———.   1976b.   *The economic approach to human behavior*. Chicago: University of Chicago Press.

Beckerman, W. A.   1974.   *In defence of economic growth*. London: Jonathan Cape.

Beitz, C. R.   1979.   *Political theory and international relations*. Princeton: Princeton University Press.

Bellow, S.   1970.   *Mr. Sammler's planet*. Harmondsworth: Penguin.

Bendix, R.   1964.   The extension of citizenship to the lower classes. In *Nation-building and citizenship*, pp. 74–104. New York: Wiley.

Benn, S. I.   1971.   Privacy, freedom and respect for persons. In *Nomos XII: Privacy*, ed. J. R. Pennock and J. W. Chapman, pp. 1–26. New York: Atherton.

———.   1978.   The rationality of political man. *American Journal of Sociology* 83: 1271–76.

———.   1979.   The problematic rationality of political participation. In Laslett and Fishkin 1979, pp. 291–312.

Bennett, J.   1966.   Whatever the consequences. *Analysis* 26: 83–102.

Bentham, J.   1787.   Panopticon. In *Works*, ed. J. Bowring, vol. 4, pp. 37–172. Edinburgh: W. Tait, 1843.

———.   1789.   *An introductoin to the principles of morals and legislation*, ed. J. H. Burns and H. L. A. Hart. London: Athlone Press, University of London, 1970.

———.   1824.   *The handbook of political fallacies*, ed. H. A. Larabee. New York: Harper, 1952.

———.   1827.   Rationale of judicial evidence. In *Works*, ed. J. Bowring, vols. 6 and 7. Edinburgh: W. Tait, 1843.

Bergson, A.   1967.   Market socialism revisited. *Journal of Political Economy* 75: 655–73.

Bernardo, R. M.   1971.   *The theory of moral incentives in Cuba*. University, Ala.: University of Alabama Press.

Bethe, H. A.   1976.   The necessity of fission power. *Scientific American* 234 [January]: 21–31.

Bickel, A. M.   1975.   *The morality of consent*. New Haven: Yale University Press.

Black, M.   1958.   The analysis of rules. *Theoria* 24: 107–36.

Blackstone, W.   1785.   *Commentaries on the laws of England*. Oxford: Clarendon Press.

Blechman, B. M.   1976.   Toward a new consensus in U.S. defense policy. In Owen and Schultze 1976, pp. 59–128.

Bloch, M., ed.   1975.   *Political language and oratory in traditional society*. London: Academic Press.

Blumberg, P.   1968.   *Industrial democracy*. London: Constable.

Bohannan, P.   1955.   Some principles of exchange and investment among the Tiv. *American Anthropologist* 57: 60–70.

———, and Dalton, G., eds.   1962.   *Markets in Africa*. Evanston, Ill.: Northwestern University Press.

Bourdieu, P.   1977.   *Outline of a theory of practice*, trans. R. Nice. Cambridge: Cambridge University Press.

Brand, M.   1971.   The language of not doing. *American Philosophical Quarterly* 8: 45–53.

Brandt, R. B.   1972.   Utilitarianism and the rules of war. *Philosophy & Public Affairs* 1: 145–65.

Braybrooke, D.   1968.   Let needs diminish that preferences may prosper. *American Philosophical Quarterly Monographs* 1: 86–107.

———.   1978.   Stages on the way to ultimate political philosophy. Paper read at American Political Science Association Conference, September 1978, New York, N.Y.

———, and Lindblom, C. E.   1963.   *A strategy of decision*. New York: Free Press.

Breach, I.   1978.   *Windscale fallout*. Harmondsworth: Penguin.

Break, G. F.   1957.   Income taxes and incentives to work. *American Economic Review* 47: 529–49.

Breyer, S.   1979.   Analyzing regulatory failure: mismatches, less restrictive alternatives, and reform. *Harvard Law Review* 92: 549–609.

Bricker, P. 1980. Prudence. *Journal of Philosophy* 77: 381–401.

Broder, D. S. 1980. *Changing of the guard.* New York: Simon & Schuster.

Bronfenbrenner, M. 1971. *Income distribution theory.* New York: Aldine-Atherton.

Brooks, M. P. 1965. The Community Action Program as a setting for applied research. *Journal of Social Issues* 21: 29–40.

Broome, J. 1978. Trying to value a life. *Journal of Public Economics* 9: 91–100.

Brown, C. V. 1980. *Taxation and the incentive to work.* Oxford: Oxford University Press.

Brown, P. G., and Shue, H., eds. 1981. *Boundaries: national autonomy and its limits.* Totowa, N.J.: Rowman & Littlefield.

Brunner, R. D. 1980. Decentralized energy policies. *Public Policy* 28: 71–91.

Buchanan, J. M. 1970. In defense of caveat emptor. *University of Chicago Law Review* 38: 64–73.

Burton, I.; Kates, R. W.; and White, G. F. 1978. *The environment as hazard.* New York: Oxford University Press.

Burwell, C. C.; Ohanian, M. J.; and Weinberg, A. M. 1979. A siting policy for an acceptable nuclear future. *Science* 204: 1043–51.

Caiden, N., and Wildavsky, A. 1974. *Planning and budgeting in poor countries.* New York: Wiley.

Calabresi, G. 1970. *The costs of accidents.* New Haven:Yale University Press.

———, and Bobbitt, P. 1978. *Tragic choices.* New York: Norton.

Cameron, J. R. 1981. Moral rules as expressive symbols. *Mind* 90: 224–42.

Campbell, D. T. 1969. Reforms as experiments. *American Psychologist* 24: 409–29.

———. 1970. Considering the case against experimental evaluation of social innovations. *Administrative Science Quarterly* 15: 110–13.

Carens, J. H. 1981. *Equality, moral incentives, and the market.* Chicago: University of Chicago Press.

Carlyle, T. 1890. Rights and mights. In *Chartism,* pp. 30–39. Chicago: Belford, Clarke.

Carter, L. J. 1978. NRC panel renders mixed verdict on Rasmussen reactor safety study. *Science* 201: 1196–97.

———. 1980. Academy energy report stresses conservation. *Science* 207: 385–86.

Christensen, C. 1978. World hunger: a structural approach. *International Organization* 32: 745–74.

Christie, G. C. 1968. The model of principles. *Duke Law Journal* 1968: 649–69.

Clark, M. J., and Fleishman, A. B. 1980. Cost benefit analysis: a review of basic principles and a bibliography. In *The application of cost benefit analysis to the radiological protection of the public: a consultative document*, pp. 17–75. Harwell, Didcot: U.K. National Radiological Protection Board.

Clecak, P.   1969.   Moral and material incentives. *Socialist Register* 1969: 101–35.

Cochran, T. B., and Rotow, D.   1979.   Radioactive waste management criteria. Mimeo., Natural Resources Defense Council, Washington, D.C.

Coddington, A.   1974.   Re-thinking economic policy. *Political Quarterly* 45: 426–38.

Cohen, B. L.   1977.   The disposal of radioactive wastes from fission reactors. *Scientific American* 236 [June]: 21–31.

Cohen, M.; Nagel, T.; and Scanlon, T., eds.   1974a.   *Rights and wrongs of abortion.* Princeton: Princeton University Press.

———; ———; and ———.   1974b.   *War and moral responsibility.* Princeton: Princeton University Press.

———; ———; and ———.   1977.   *Equality and preferential treatment.* Princeton: Princeton University Press.

Coleman, J. S.   1975.   Problems of conceptualization and measurement in studying policy impacts. In *Public policy evaluation,* ed. K. M. Dolbeare, pp. 19–40. Beverly Hills, Calif.: Sage.

Coleman, W. T., Jr.   1976.   *The Secretary's decision on Concorde supersonic transport.* Washington, D.C.: U.S. Department of Transportation.

Collard, D.   1978.   *Altruism and economy.* London: Martin Robertson.

Connolly, W.   1974.   *The terms of political discourse.* Lexington, Mass.: D.C. Heath.

Conroy, C.   1978.   *What choice Windscale?* London: Friends of the Earth.

Cook, P. J., and Graham, D. A.   1977.   The demand for insurance and protection: the case of irreplaceable commodities. *Quarterly Journal of Economics* 91: 143–56.

Cornell, N. W.; Noll, R. G.; and Weingast, B.   1976.   Safety regulation. In Owen and Schultze 1976, pp. 457–504.

Cornfield, J.   1977.   Carcinogenic risk assessment. *Science* 198: 693–99.

Cornford, F. M.   1908.   *Microcosmographia academica.* Cambridge: Bowes & Bowes.

Cowherd, R. G.   1977.   *Political economists and the English Poor Laws.* Athens: Ohio University Press.

Crecine, J. P., and Fischer, G. W.   1973.   On resource allocation processes in the U.S. Department of Defense. *Political Science Annual* 4: 181–236.

Culyer, A. J.   1971.   Merit goods and the welfare economics of coercion. *Public Finance* 26: 546–72.

———.   1973.   *Quids* without *quos*—a praxelogical approach. In *The economics of charity,* pp. 33–61. London: Institute of Economic Affairs.

Cummings, R., and Norton, V.   1974.   The economics of environmental protection: comment. *American Economic Review* 64: 1021–24.

Curley, E. M.   1976.   Excusing rape. *Philosophy & Public Affairs* 5: 325–60.

Dahl, R.   1979.   Procedural democracy. In Laslett and Fishkin 1979, pp. 97–133.

Darwell, S. L.   1977.   Two kinds of respect. *Ethics* 88: 36–49.

Dasgupta, A. K., and Pearce, D. W.   1972.   *Cost-benefit analysis*. London: Macmillan.

Dasgupta, P. S., and Heal, G. M.   1979.   *Economic theory and exhaustible resources*. Cambridge: Cambridge University Press.

———, and Stiglitz, J.   1981.   Resource depletion under technological uncertainty. *Econometrica* 49: 85–104.

Davidson, D.   1983.   Interpersonal comparisons of utility. In Elster and Hylland 1983.

Davis, N.   1980.   The priority of avoiding harm. In *Killing and letting die*, ed. B. Steinbock, pp. 172–214. Englewood Cliffs, N.J.: Prentice-Hall.

Day, J. P.   1977.   Fairness and fortune. *Ratio* 19: 70–84.

Deci, E. L.   1975.   *Intrinsic motivation*. New York: Plenum Press.

Derrett, J. D. M.   1961.   The administration of Hindu law by the British. *Comparative Studies in History and Society* 4: 10–52.

———.   1963.   Justice, equity, and good conscience. In *Changing law in developing countries*, ed. J. N. D. Anderson, pp. 114–53. London: Allen & Unwin.

Derthick, M.   1975.   *Uncontrollable spending for social services grants*. Washington, D.C.: Brookings.

Deutsch, K. W.   1972.   The contribution of experiments within the framework of political theory. In *Experimentation and simulation in political science*, ed. J. A. Laponce and P. Smoker, pp. 19–35. Toronto: University of Toronto Press.

Deutscher, I.   1966.   Words and deeds: social science and social policy. *Social Problems* 13: 235–54.

Dickinson, J.   1927.   *Administrative justice and the supremacy of law in the United States*. Cambridge: Harvard University Press.

Di Quattro, A.   1978.   Alienation and justice in the market. *American Political Science Review* 72: 871–87.

Dobb, M.   1960.   *An essay on economic growth and planning*. New York: Monthly Review Press.

Douglas, M.   1966.   *Purity and danger*. London: Routledge & Kegan Paul.

———.   1968.   Pollution. In *International encyclopedia of the social sciences*, ed. D. L. Sills, vol. 12, pp. 336–42. London: Collier-Macmillan.

———, and Isherwood, B.   1978.   *The world of goods*. Harmondsworth: Penguin.

Downs, A.   1957.   *An economic theory of democracy*. New York: Harper.

———.   1972.   Ups and downs with ecology—the "issue attention cycle." *Public Interest* 28: 38–50.

Duesenberry, J. S.   1949.   *Income, savings and the theory of consumer behavior*. Cambridge: Harvard University Press.

Duncan, O. D.   1978.   Sociologists should reconsider nuclear energy. *Social Forces* 57: 1–22.

Durkheim, É. 1915. *Elementary forms of religious life*, trans. J. W. Swain. London: Allen & Unwin.

Dworkin, G. 1971. Paternalism. In *Morality and the law*, ed. R. A. Wasserstrom, pp. 107–26. Belmont, Calif.: Wadsworth.

Dworkin, R. M. 1977. *Taking rights seriously*. London: Duckworth.

———. 1981. What is equality? *Philosophy & Public Affairs* 10: 185–246, 283–85.

Eckstein, O. 1957. Investment criteria for economic development and the theory of intertemporal welfare economics. *Quarterly Journal of Economics* 71: 56–85.

———. 1961. A survey of the theory of public expenditure criteria. In *Public finances: needs, sources and utilization*, pp. 439–94. Princeton: Princeton University Press for National Bureau of Economic Research.

Eisner, R., and Strotz, R. H. 1961. Flight insurance and the theory of choice. *Journal of Political Economy* 69: 355–68.

Elster, J. 1977. Ulysses and the Sirens: a theory of imperfect rationality. *Social Science Information* 16: 469–526.

———. 1978. *Logic and society*. London: Wiley.

———. 1979a. Risk, uncertainty and nuclear power. *Social Science Information* 18: 371–400.

———. 1979b. *Ulysses and the Sirens: studies in rationality and irrationality*. Cambridge: Cambridge University Press.

———, and Hylland, A., eds. 1983. *Foundations of social choice theory*. Cambridge: Cambridge University Press.

Enthoven, A. C. 1963. Defense and disarmament: economic analysis in the Department of Defense. *American Economic Review (Papers & Proceedings)* 53: 413–23.

———, and Rowen, H. 1961. Defense planning and organization. In *Public finances: needs, sources, and utilization*, pp. 365–420. Princeton: Princeton University Press for National Bureau of Economic Research.

———, and Smith, K. W. 1971. *How much is enough? Shaping the defense program, 1961–1969*. New York: Harper & Row.

Etzioni, A. 1967. Mixed scanning. *Public Administration Review* 27: 385–92.

———, and Remp, R. 1973. *Technological shortcuts to social change*. New York: Russell Sage.

Eulau, H. 1977. The place of policy analysis: the interventionist synthesis. *American Journal of Political Science* 21: 419–23.

Fairley, W. B. 1977. Evaluating the "small" probablility of a catastrophic accident from the marine transportation of liquefied natural gas. In *Statistics and public policy*, ed. W. B. Fairley and F. Mosteller, pp. 331–54. Reading, Mass.: Addison-Wesley.

Falk, R. 1976. A non-nuclear future: rejecting the Faustian bargain. *Nation* 222: 301–5.

Farley, P. J. 1976. Nuclear proliferation. In Owen and Schultze 1976, pp. 129–65.

Feaver, D. B. 1976. Last bar to SST gone. *Washington Post*, 20 May 1976, pp. A1, A6.

Feinberg, J. 1970. Problematic responsibility in law and morals. In *Doing and deserving,* pp. 25–37. Princeton: Princeton University Press.

———. 1973. *Social philosophy.* Englewood Cliffs, N.J.: Prentice-Hall.

———. 1980. *Rights, justice and the bounds of liberty.* Princeton: Princeton University Press.

Ferber, R., and Hirsch, W. Z. 1978. Social experimentation and economic policy: a survey. *Journal of Economic Literature* 16: 1379–1414.

Findlay, J. N. 1961. *Values and intentions.* London: Allen & Unwin.

Fiorina, M. P. 1981. *Retrospective voting in American national elections.* New Haven: Yale University Press.

Fischhoff, B. 1977. Cost-benefit and the art of motorcycle maintenance. *Policy Sciences* 8: 177–202

———; Slovic, P.; Lichtenstein, S.; Read, S.; and Combs, B. 1978. How safe is safe enough? A psychometric study of attitudes towards technological risks and benefits. *Policy Sciences* 9: 127–52.

Fisher, A. C.; Krutilla, J. V.; and Cicchetti, C. J. 1972. The economics of environmental protection: a theoretical and empirical analysis. *American Economic Review* 62: 605–19.

———; ———; and ———. 1974. The economics of environmental preservation: further discussion. *American Economic Review* 64: 1030–39.

Fitzgerald, P. S. 1967. Acting and refraining. *Analysis* 27: 133–39.

Flathman, R. E. 1972. *Political obligation.* New York: Atheneum.

———. 1976. *The practice of rights.* Cambridge: Cambridge University Press.

Fletcher, G. P. 1972. Fairness and utility in tort theory. *Harvard Law Review* 85: 537–73.

Flood, M., and Grove-White, R. 1976. *Nuclear prospects: a comment on the individual, the state and nuclear power.* London: Friends of the Earth.

Flowers, B., chairman. 1976. *Nuclear power and the environment.* Royal Commission on Environmental Pollution, 6th report. Cmnd. 6618. London: HMSO.

Foot, P. 1978. *Virtues and vices.* Oxford: Blackwell.

Freeman, A. M. III. 1977. Equity, efficiency and discounting: the reasons for discounting intergenerational effects. *Futures* 9: 375–76.

Freund, E. 1921. The use of indefinite terms in statutes. *Yale Law Journal* 30: 437–55.

Fried, C. 1964. Moral causation. *Harvard Law Review* 77: 1258–70.

———. 1969. The value of life. *Harvard Law Review* 82: 1415–37.

———. 1970. *An anatomy of values.* Cambridge: Harvard University Press.

———. 1978. *Right and wrong.* Cambridge: Harvard University Press.

Friedel, R., and Servos, J. W. 1977. The saccharin flap of '07. *Washington Post,* 27 March 1977, p. C5.

Friedman, M. 1953. Comments on monetary policy. In *Essays in positive economics,* pp. 263–73. Chicago: University of Chicago Press.

————. 1977. Nobel lecture: inflation and unemployment. *Journal of Political Economy* 85: 451–72.

Friendly, H. J. 1962. *The federal administrative agencies.* Cambridge: Harvard University Press.

Frohlich, N. 1974. Self-interest or altruism, what difference? *Journal of Conflict Resolution* 18: 55–73.

Fuller, L. L. 1964. *The morality of law.* New Haven: Yale University Press.

Føllesdal, D. 1979. Some ethical aspects of recombinant DNA research. *Social Science Information* 18: 401–19.

Galanter, M. 1968. The displacement of traditional law in modern India. *Journal of Social Issues* 24: 65–91.

————. 1974. Why the "haves" come out ahead: speculations on the limits of legal change. *Law and Society Review* 9: 95–160.

Galbraith, J. K. 1975. *Money.* London: André Deutsch.

Gauthier, D. 1977. The social contrast as ideology. *Philosophy & Public Affairs* 6: 130–64.

Geertz, C. 1977. The judging of nations. *Archives Européennes de Sociologie* 18: 245–61.

Georgescu-Roegen, N. 1967. *Analytical economics.* Cambridge: Harvard University Press.

————. 1971. *The entropy law and the economic process.* Cambridge: Harvard University Press.

Gert, B., and Culver, C. M. 1976. Paternalistic behavior. *Philosophy & Public Affairs* 6: 45–57.

Ginzburg, E., and Solow, R. M. 1974. Some lessons of the 1960s. In *The Great Society,* ed. Ginzburg and Solow, pp. 211–20. New York: Basic Books.

Glover, J. 1977. *Causing death and saving lives.* Harmondsworth: Penguin.

Gluckman, M. 1955. *The judicial process among the Bartose of Northern Rhodesia.* Manchester: Manchester University Press.

Goffman, E. 1968. *Asylums.* Harmondsworth: Penguin.

Goldfarb, R. S. 1975. Learning in government programs and the usefulness of cost-benefit analysis: lessons from manpower and urban renewal history. *Policy Sciences* 6: 281–99.

Goodin, R. E. 1975. Cross-cutting cleavages and social conflict. *British Journal of Political Science* 5:516–19.

————. 1976. *The politics of rational man.* London: Wiley.

————. 1977. Ethical perspectives on political excuses. *Policy and Politics* 5: 71–78.

————. 1979. The development-rights tradeoff: some unwarranted economic and political assumptions. *Universal Human Rights* 1: 31–42.

————. 1980. *Manipulatory politics.* New Haven: Yale University Press.

————. 1981. Review of A. H. Goldman, *Moral foundations of professional ethics. Ethics* 92: 137–40.

————. 1982. Banana time in British politics. *Political Studies* 30: 42–58.
————. 1983. Laundering preferences. In Elster and Hylland 1983.
————, and Roberts, K. W. S. 1975. The ethical voter. *American Political Science Review* 69: 926–28.
Gramlich, E. M., and Koshel, P. P. 1975. *Educational performance contracting*. Washington, D.C.: Brookings.
Green, H. P. 1973. Nuclear power: risk, liability and indemnity. *Michigan Law Review* 71: 479–510.
Green, O. H. 1980. Killing and letting die. *American Philosophical Quarterly* 17: 195–204.
Greenberg, D.; Moffitt, D.; and Friedmann, J. 1981. Underreporting and experimental effects on work effort: evidence from the Gary income maintenance experiment. *Review of Economics and Statistics* 63: 581–89.
van Gunsteren, H. 1978. Notes on a theory of citizenship. In *Democracy, consensus and social contract,* ed. P. Birnbaum, J. Lively, and G. Parry, pp. 9–36. London: Sage.
Häfle, W. 1974. Hypotheticality: the new challenges and the pathfinder role of nuclear energy. *Minerva* 12: 303–22.
Haksar, V. 1979. *Equality, liberty and perfectionism*. Oxford: Clarendon Press.
Halloran, R. 1981. U.S. study discloses 5 accidents with nuclear arms in '50s, '60s. *International Herald-Tribune,* 27 May 1981, p. 3.
Hamilton, A. 1787. Federalist # 23. In *The Federalist,* ed. J. E. Cooke, pp. 146–51. Middletown, Conn.: Wesleyan University Press, 1961.
————. 1788. Federalist #84. In *The Federalist,* ed. J. E. Cooke, pp. 575–87. Middletown, Conn.: Wesleyan University Press, 1961.
Hampshire, S., ed. 1978. *Public and private morality*. Cambridge: Cambridge University Press.
Hanke, S. H., and Anwyll, J. B. 1980. On the discount rate controversy. *Public Policy* 28: 171–84.
Hansson, B. 1979. Can we ever hope to have a formal model for rational behaviour? Mimeo., Department of Philosophy, University of Lund, Sweden.
Hare, R. M. 1951. Freedom of the will. *Proceedings of the Aristotelian Society (Supplement)* 25: 201–16.
————. 1963. *Freedom and reason*. Oxford: Clarendon Press.
————. 1972. Rules of war and moral reasoning. *Philosophy & Public Affairs* 1: 166–81.
————. 1972–73. Principles. *Proceedings of the Aristotelian Society* 73: 1–18.
————. 1981. *Moral Training*. Oxford: Clarendon Press.
Harrod, R. 1948. *Towards a dynamic economics*. London: Macmillan.
Harsanyi, J. C. 1955. Cardinal welfare, individualistic ethics and interpersonal comparisons of utility. *Journal of Political Economy* 63: 309–21.
————. 1969. Rational-choice models of political behavior vs. functionalist and conformist theories. *World Politics* 21: 513–38.

————. 1975. Can the maximin principle serve as a basis for morality? *American Political Science Review* 69: 594–60.

————. 1977. *Rational behavior and bargaining equilibrium in games and social situations.* Cambridge: Cambridge University Press.

Hart, H. L. A. 1955. Are there any natural rights? *Philosophical Review* 64: 175–91.

————. 1961. *The concept of law.* Oxford: Clarendon Press.

————. 1979. Between utility and rights. In *The idea of freedom,* ed. A. Ryan, pp. 77–98. Oxford: Clarendon Press.

————, and Honoré, A. M. 1959. *Causation in the law.* Oxford: Clarendon Press.

Hart, H. M., Jr., and Sacks, A. M. 1958. *The legal process.* Tentative ed. Mimeo., Harvard Law School.

Hatry, H. P. 1980. Pitfalls of evaluation. In *Pitfalls of analysis,* ed. G. Majone and E. S. Quade, pp. 159–78. London: Wiley.

Haveman, R. H. 1977. The economic evaluation of long-run uncertainties. *Futures* 9: 365–74.

————, and Margolis, J., eds. 1970. *Public expenditures and policy analysis.* Chicago: Markham.

Hayek, F. A. 1944. *The road to serfdom.* London: Routledge.

————. 1960. *The constitution of liberty.* London: Routledge & Kegan Paul.

————. 1973. *Rules and order.* Chicago: University of Chicago Press.

————. 1976. *The mirage of social justice.* Chicago: University of Chicago Press.

Heal, G. M. 1973. *The theory of economic planning.* Amsterdam: North-Holland.

Heclo, H. 1972. Review essay: policy analysis. *British Journal of Political Science* 2: 83–108.

————, and Wildavsky, A. 1974. *The private government of public money.* London: Macmillan.

Heller, J. 1979. *Good as gold.* London: Jonathan Cape.

Henderson, P. D. 1965. Notes on public investment criteria in the United Kingdom. *Bulletin of the Oxford University Institute of Economics and Statistics* 27: 55–92.

Henry, C. 1974. Investment decisions under uncertainty: the "irreversibility" effect. *American Economic Review* 64: 1006–12.

Hill, T. E., Jr. 1973. Servility and self-respect. *Monist* 57: 87–104.

————. 1979. Symbolic protest and calculated silence. *Philosophy & Public Affairs* 9: 83–102.

Hirsch, F. 1976. *Social limits to growth.* Cambridge: Harvard University Press.

Hirsch, H., and Nowotny, H. 1977. Information and opposition in Austrian nuclear energy policy. *Minerva* 15: 316–34.

Hirschman, A. O. 1977. *The passions and the interests.* Princeton: Princeton University Press.

Hitch, C. J. 1964. Analysis for Air Force decisions. In *Analysis for mili-*

tary decisions, ed. E. S. Quade, pp. 13–23. Chicago: Rand McNally.

———, and McKean, R. N.   1960.   *The economics of defense in the nuclear age.* Cambridge: Harvard University Press.

Hobbes, T.   1651.   *Leviathan,* ed. M. Oakeshott. Oxford: Blackwell, 1946.

Hochman, H. M., and Rogers, J. D.   1969.   Pareto optimal redistribution. *American Economic Review* 59: 542–57.

Hodgson, D. H.   1967.   *The consequences of utilitarianism.* Oxford: Clarendon Press.

Hodson, J. D.   1977.   The principle of paternalism. *American Philosophical Quarterly* 14: 61–69.

Hoffman, S. H.   1959.   International relations: the long road to theory. *World Politics* 11: 346–77.

Hofstadter, R.   1948.   *The American political tradition.* New York: Knopf.

Hohenemser, C.; Kasperson, R.; and Kates, R.   1977.   The distrust of nuclear power. *Science* 196: 25–34.

Holdsworth, W.   1956.   *A history of English law.* 7th ed. London: Methuen.

Hollocher, T. C.   1975.   Storage and disposal of high level radioactive wastes. In *The nuclear fuel cycle,* ed. Union of Concerned Scientists, pp. 219–75. Cambridge: MIT Press.

Honderich, T.   1980.   Our omissions and their violence. In *Violence for equality,* pp. 58–100. Harmondsworth: Penguin.

Honoré, A. M.   1962.   Social justice. *McGill Law Journal* 8: 78.

Hospers, J.   1961.   *Human conduct.* New York: Harcourt, Brace.

Howard, R. A.; Matheson, J. E.; and North, D. W.   1972.   The decision to seed hurricanes. *Science* 176: 1191–1202.

Hubbart, W. N., Jr.   1973.   Preclinical problems of new drug development. In *Regulating new drugs,* ed. R. L. Landau, pp. 35–51. Chicago: Center for Policy Study, University of Chicago.

Hughes, G.   1958.   Criminal omissions. *Yale Law Journal* 67: 590–637.

———.   1968.   Rules, policy and decisionmaking. *Yale Law Journal* 77: 411–39.

Huitt, R. K.   1968.   Political feasibility. In *Political science and public policy,* ed. A. Ranney, pp. 263–76. Chicago: Markham.

von Humboldt, W.   1854.   *The limits of state action,* trans. and ed. J. W. Burrow. Cambridge: Cambridge University Press, 1969.

Hume, D.   1739.   *A treatise of human nature.* London: John Noon.

———.   1760.   Of the independence of Parliament. In *Essays, literary, moral and political.* London: A. Millar.

———.   1777.   *An enquiry concerning the principles of morals.* London: T. Cadell.

Huntington, S. P.   1961.   *The common defense.* New York: Columbia University Press.

Husak, D. N.   1981.   Paternalism and autonomy. *Philosophy & Public Affairs* 10: 27–46.

Hutcheson, F. 1738. An inquiry concerning moral good and evil. In *British moralists, 1650–1800,* ed. D. D. Raphael, vol. 1, pp. 261–99. Oxford: Clarendon Press, 1969.

Inhaber, H. 1979. Risk with energy from conventional and nonconventional sources. *Science* 203: 718–23.

———. 1981. The risk of producing energy. *Proceedings of the Royal Society of London* A376: 121–31.

Jackson, E. J., and Mukerjee, T. 1974. Human adjustment to the earthquake hazard of San Francisco, California. In *Natural hazards,* ed. G. F. White, pp. 160–66. New York: Oxford University Press.

Jackson, J. 1789. Speech in the House of Representatives, 8 June 1789. In *A second Federalist,* ed. C. S. Hyneman and G. W. Carey, pp. 261–63. New York: Appleton-Century-Crofts, 1967.

Jencks, C., et al. 1972. *Inequality.* New York: Basic Books.

Jevons, W. S. 1911. *The theory of political economy.* 4th ed. London: Macmillan.

———. 1933. *Economic equality in the cooperative commonwealth.* London: Methuen.

Johansson, T. B., and Steen, P. 1978. *Radioactive waste from nuclear power plants: facing the Ringhals-3 decision.* Swedish Ministry of Industry. DsI 1978:36. Stockholm: Liber Förlag.

———, and ———. 1979. The 1978 Swedish decision on nuclear waste. *Bulletin of the Atomic Scientists* 35: 38–42.

Joskow, P. L., and Rozanski, G. A. 1979. The effects of learning by doing on nuclear plant operating reliability. *Review of Economics and Statistics* 61: 161–68.

Kadish, S. 1957. Methodology and criteria in due process adjudication: a survey and criticism. *Yale Law Journal* 66: 319–63.

Kahn, A. E. 1966. The tyranny of small decisions. *Kyklos* 19: 23–47.

Kahneman, D., and Tversky, A. 1979. Prospect theory: an analysis of decision under risk. *Econometrica* 47: 263–91.

Kandell, J. 1980. It's hard to get an argument over defense spending in France. *Washington Post,* 27 December 1980, p. A 14.

Kant, I. 1785. *Foundations of the metaphysics of morals,* trans. L. W. Beck. Chicago: University of Chicago Press, 1949.

Kanter, A. 1972. Congress and the defense budget, 1960–70. *American Political Science Review* 66: 129–43.

Kavka, G. 1978. The futurity problem. In Sikora and Barry 1978, pp. 186–203.

Kecskemeti, P. 1951. The "policy sciences": aspiration and outlook. *World Politics* 4: 520–35.

Keeny, S. M., Jr., chairman. 1977. *Nuclear power: issues and choices.* Report of the Nuclear Energy Policy Study Group, Ford Foundation and MITRE Corporation. Cambridge, Mass.: Ballinger.

Kemeny, J. G., chairman. 1979. *The need for change: the legacy of TMI.* Report of the President's Committee on the Accident at Three Mile Island. Washington, D.C.: GPO.

Kendall, H., and Moglewer, S. 1974. *Preliminary review of the AEC reactor safety study.* San Francisco and Cambridge, Mass.: Sierra Club and Union of Concerned Scientists.

King, M. L., Jr.   1964.   Letter from a Birmingham jail. In *Why we can't wait.* New York: Signet.

Kirchheimer, O.   1961.   *Political justice.* Princeton: Princeton University Press.

Kirzner, I. M.   1973.   *Competition and entrepreneurship.* Chicago: University of Chicago Press.

Kneese, A. V.   1973.   The Faustian bargain. *Resources,* no. 44.

———, and Schultze, C. L.   1975.   *Pollution, prices and public policy.* Washington, D.C.: Brookings.

Kolta, G. B.   1977.   Catastrophe theory: the emperor has no clothes. *Science* 196: 287, 350–51.

Koopmans, T. C.   1979.   Economics among the sciences. *American Economic Review* 69: 1–13.

Kryter, K. D.   1966.   Psychological reactions to aircraft noise. *Science* 151: 1346–55.

Kubo, A. S., and Rose, D. J.   1973.   Disposal of nuclear wastes. *Science* 182: 1205–11.

Kunreuther, H.   1968.   The case for comprehensive disaster insurance. *Journal of Law and Economics* 11: 133–63.

———, et al.   1978.   *Disaster insurance protection: public policy lessons.* New York: Wiley.

Lane, R. E.   1978.   Autonomy, felicity, futility: the effects of the market economy on political personality. *Journal of Politics* 40: 2–24.

Lange, O.   1936–37.   On the economic theory of socialism. *Review of Economic Studies* 4: 53–71, 123–42.

Lanouette, W. J.   1979a..   A faulty computer program—and a possible nuclear disaster. *National Journal* no. 14, pp. 556–59.

———.   1979b.   NRC disavows methods and findings of reactor safety study. *National Journal* no. 17, pp. 676–87.

———.   1979c.   Nuclear power—an uncertain future grows dimmer still. *National Journal* no. 4, p. 153.

Laslett, P., and Fishkin, J., eds.   1979.   *Philosophy, politics and society.* 5th series. Oxford: Blackwell.

Laurance, E. J.   1976.   The changing role of Congress in defense policymaking. *Journal of Conflict Resolution* 20: 213–53.

Lave, L. B.   1968.   Safety in transport: the role of government. *Law and Contemporary Problems* 11: 512–35.

Lee, K. N.   1980.   A federalist strategy for nuclear waste management. *Science* 208: 679–84.

Leontief, W.   1971.   Theoretical assumptions and nonobserved facts. *American Economic Review* 61: 1–7.

Lerner, D., and Lasswell, H. D., eds.   1951.   *The policy sciences.* Stanford: Stanford University Press.

Levi, I.   1981.   Assessing accident risks in U.S. commercial nuclear power plants: scientific methods and the Rasmussen Report. *Social Research* 48: 395–408.

Lewis, G. C. 1852. *A treatise on the methods of observation and reasoning in politics.* London: Parker.

Lewis, H. W., chairman. 1975. Report to the American Physical Society by the Study Group on Light-Water Reactor Safety. *Review of Modern Physics* 47 (Supplement 1): S1-S124.

———, chairman. 1978. *Risk Assessment Review Group Report to the U.S. Nuclear Regulatory Commission.* NUREG/CO-0400. Washington, D.C.: GPO.

Lichtenstein, S.; Fischhoff, B.; and Phillips, L. D. 1977. Calibration of probabilities: the state of the art. In *Decision making and change in human affairs,* ed. H. Jungermann and G. de Zeeuw. Amsterdam: D. Reidel.

Lieberman, B. 1969. Combining individual preferences into a social choice. In *Game theory in the behavioral sciences,* ed. I. R. Buchler and H. G. Nutini, pp. 95–116. Pittsburgh: University of Pittsburgh Press.

Lieberman, G. J. 1976. Fault-tree analysis as an example of risk methodology. In Ashley, Rudman, and Whipple 1976, pp. 247–76.

Liebow, E. 1967. *Tally's corner.* Boston: Little Brown.

Lightman, E. S. 1981. Continuity in social policy behaviours: the case of voluntary blood donorship. *Journal of Social Policy* 10: 53–79.

Lindblom, C. E. 1977. *Politics and markets.* New York: Basic Books.

———, and Cohen, D. K. 1979. *Usable knowledge.* New Haven: Yale University Press.

Lindsay, A. D. 1924. The organization of labour in the Army in France during the war and its lessons. *Economic Journal* 34: 69–82.

Lipsey, R. G., and Lancaster, K. 1956. The general theory of second best. *Review of Economic Studies* 24: 11–33.

Lipsky, M. 1980. *Street level bureaucracy.* New York: Russell Sage.

Lipton, M. 1968. The theory of the optimising peasant. *Journal of Development Studies* 4: 327–51.

Little, I. M. D. 1957. *A critique of welfare economics.* 2d ed. Oxford: Clarendon Press.

———, and Mirrlees, J. A. 1974. *Project appraisal and planning for developing countries.* New York: Basic Books.

Llewellyn, K. M., and Hoebel, E. A. 1941. *The Cheyenne way.* Norman: Oklahoma University Press.

Locke, J. 1690. *Second treatise of government,* ed. J. W. Gough. Oxford: Blackwell, 1946.

Locke, J. H.; Dunster, H. J.; and Pittom, L. A. 1978. *Canvey: summary of an investigation of potential hazards in the Canvey Island/Thurrock area.* U.K. Health and Safety Executive. London: HMSO.

Lovins, A. B. 1977. *Soft energy paths.* Harmondsworth: Penguin.

———. 1980. Nuclear weapons and power-reactor plutonium. *Nature* 283: 817–23.

———; Lovins, L. H.; and Ross, L. 1980. Nuclear power and nuclear bombs. *Foreign Affairs* 58: 1137–77.

Luce, R. D., and Raiffa, H. 1957. *Games and decisions.* New York: Wiley.

Lynn, L. E., Jr.   1980.   *Designing public policy*. Santa Monica, Calif.: Goodyear.

Lyons, D.   1965.   *Forms and limits of utilitarianism*. Oxford: Clarendon Press.

McBride, J. P.; Moore, R. E.; Witherspoon, J. P.; and Blanco, R. E.   1978. Radiological impact of airborne effluents from coal and nuclear plants. *Science* 202: 1045–51.

McCloskey, D. N.   1976.   English open fields as behavior towards risk. *Research in Economic History* 1: 124–70.

MacEwan, A.   1975a.   Ideology, socialist development and power in Cuba. *Politics and Society* 5: 67–82.

————.   1975b.   Incentives, equality and power in revolutionary Cuba. *Socialist Revolution* 20: 117–30.

McFarland, A. S.   1976.   *Public interest lobbies: decision making on energy*. Washington, D.C.: American Enterprise Institute.

McGuire, M. C.   1965.   *Secrecy and the arms race*. Cambridge: Harvard University Press.

MacIntyre, A.   1968.   Egoism and altruism. In *Encyclopedia of Philosophy,* ed. P. Edwards, vol. 2, pp. 462–66. London: Collier-Macmillan.

McKean, R. M., ed.   1967.   *Issues in defense economics*. New York: National Bureau of Economic Research.

McLean, A. E. M.   1981.   Assessment and evaluation of risks to health from chemicals. *Proceedings of the Royal Society of London* A376: 51–64.

MacRae, D., Jr.   1976.   *The social function of social science*. New Haven: Yale University Press.

————, and Wilde, J. A.   1979.   *Policy analysis for public decisions*. North Scituate, Mass.: Duxbury Press.

Mabbott, J. D.   1939.   Punishment. *Mind* 48: 152–67.

————.   1967.   *The state and the citizen*. London: Hutchinson.

Madison, J.   1787.   Speech of 7 August 1787. In *Notes of debates in the Federal Convention of 1787,* ed. A. Koch, pp. 403–4. New York: Norton, 1969.

Maine, H. S.   1871.   *Village-communities in the East and West*. London: John Murray.

Majone, G.   1975.   The notion of political feasibility. *European Journal of Political Research* 3: 259–74.

————.   1979.   Process and outcome in regulatory decision-making. *American Behavioral Scientist* 22: 561–84.

de Man, H.   1828.   The social inferiority complex of the working class. In *The psychology of socialism,* trans. E. and C. Paul, chap. 2. London: Allen & Unwin.

Manne, A. S.; Richels, R. G.; and Weyant, J. P.   1979.   Energy policy modeling: a survey. *Operations Research* 27: 1–36.

March, J. G.   1972.   Model bias in social action. *Review of Educational Research* 42: 413–29.

Marglin, S. A.   1963.   The social rate of discount and the optimal rate of investment. *Quarterly Journal of Economics* 77: 95–111.

Margolis, H. 1981. A new model of rational choice. *Ethics* 91: 265–79.

Marris, P., and Rein, M. 1967. *Dilemmas of social reform.* New York: Atherton Press.

Marshall, E. 1980. Antibiotics in the barnyard. *Science* 208: 376–79.

Marshall, T. 1979. *U.S. et al.* v. *Rutherford et al.* 442 U.S. 544.

Marshall, T. H. 1963. Citizenship and social class. In *Sociology at the crossroads,* pp. 67–127. London: Heinemann.

de Marsily, C.; Ledoux, E.; Barbreau, A.; and Margat, J. 1977. Nuclear waste disposal: can the geologist guarantee isolation? *Science* 196: 519–27.

Martin, J. N. 1979. The concept of the irreplaceable. *Environmental Ethics* 1: 31–48.

Marx, K. 1844. Economic and philosophic manuscripts of 1844. In *The Marx-Engels reader,* ed. R. C. Tucker, pp. 52–103. New York: Norton, 1972.

———, and Engels, F. 1848. Manifesto of the Communist Party. In *The Marx-Engels reader,* ed. R. C. Tucker, pp. 331–62. New York: Norton, 1972.

Maugh, T. H. 1978. Chemical carcinogens: how dangerous are low doses? *Science* 202: 37–41.

Mazrui, A. 1979. The cross of humiliation. *The Listener* 102: 656–60.

Mazur, A. 1977. Science courts. *Minerva* 11: 243–62.

———, and Rosa, E. 1974. Energy and lifestyle. *Science* 186: 607–10.

Mazzini, J. 1912. *The duties of man and other essays.* London: Dutton.

Melden, A. I., ed. 1958. *Essays in moral philosophy.* Seattle: University of Washington Press.

Meltsner, A. J. 1972. Political feasibility and policy analysis. *Public Administration Review* 32: 859–67.

———. 1979. The communication of scientific information to the wider public: the case of seismology in California. *Minerva* 17: 331–54.

Merton, R. K. 1946. *Mass persuasion.* New York: Harper.

———. 1949. *Social theory and social structure.* Glencoe, Ill.: Free Press.

———. 1973. Technical and moral dimensions of policy research. In *Sociology of science,* pp. 70–98. Chicago: University of Chicago Press.

Mew, P. 1975. Doubts about moral principles. *Inquiry* 18:289–308.

Michelman, F. I. 1977. Formal and associational aims in procedural due process. In *Nomos XVIII: due process,* ed. J. R. Pennock and J. W. Chapman, pp. 126–71. New York: New York University Press.

Mill, J. 1828. *Essay on government.* London: J. Innes.

Mill, J. S. 1848. *Principles of political economy.* London: Parker & Son.

———. 1859. *On liberty.* London: Parker & Son.

———. 1861. *Considerations on representative government.* London: Parker, Son & Bourn.

———. 1863. *Utilitarianism.* London: Parker & Son.

———. 1869. *The subjection of women.* London: Longmans Green, Reades & Dyer.

Mishan, E. J. 1969. *Cost-benefit analysis.* Amsterdam: North-Holland.
————. 1971. Evaluation of life and limb: a theoretical approach. *Journal of Political Economy* 79: 687–705.
Montefiore, A. 1958. "Ought" and "can." *Philosophical Quarterly* 8: 24–40.
Montesquieu, C. L. de. 1748. *The spirit of the laws,* trans. T. Nugent. New York: Macmillan, 1949.
Moore, B., Jr. 1970. *Reflections on the causes of human misery.* Boston: Beacon Press.
Morgenstern, O. 1959. *The question of national defense.* New York: Random House.
Morillo, C. R. 1976. As sure as shooting. *Philosophy* 51: 80–89.
Morley, J. 1874. *On compromise.* London: Watts.
Morrison, A. B., and Noll, R. G., chairmen. 1980. *Government and the regulation of corporate and individual decisions in the eighties.* Report of a Panel of the President's Commission for a National Agenda for the Eighties. Washington, D.C.: GPO.
Mortimore, G., ed. 1971. *Weakness of will.* London: Macmillan.
Mosteller, F., and Nogee, P. 1951. An experimental measurement of utility. *Journal of Political Economy* 59: 371–404.
Moynihan, D. P. 1973. Politics as the art of the impossible. In *Coping,* pp. 248–58. New York: Random House.
Mueller, D. C. 1974. Intergenerational justice and the social discount rate. *Theory and Decision* 5: 263–73.
Murdock, C. A. 1974. *Defense policy formation.* Albany: State University of New York Press.
Myerson, M., and Banfield, E. C. 1955. *Politics, planning and the public interest.* Glencoe, Ill.; Free Press.
Myrdal, G. 1968. *Asian drama.* New York: Pantheon.
Nader, L., and Beckerman, S. 1978. Energy as it relates to the quality and style of life. *Annual Review of Energy* 3: 1–28.
Nagel, T. 1970. *The possibility of altruism.* Oxford: Clarendon Press.
———— 1972. War and massacre. *Philosophy & Public Affairs* 1: 123–44.
Nelkin, D. 1977. *Technological decisions and democracy: European experiments in public participation.* London: Sage.
————, and Fallows, S. 1978. The evolution of the nuclear power debate: the role of public participation. *Annual Review of Energy* 3: 275–312.
————, and Pollak, M. 1977. The politics of participation and the nuclear debate in Sweden, The Netherlands and Austria. *Public Policy* 25: 333–57.
————, and ————. 1981. *The atom beseiged: extraparliamentary dissent in France and Germany.* Cambridge: MIT Press.
Nell, O. 1975. Lifeboat earth. *Philosophy & Public Affairs* 4: 273–92.
Nemetz, P. N., and Vining, A. R. 1981. The biology-policy' interface. *Policy Sciences* 13: 125–38.
Nichols, A. L., and Zeckhauser, R. 1977. Government comes to the

workplace: an assessment of OSHA. *Public Interest* 49: 36–69.

Notz, W. W. 1975. Work motivation and negative effects of extrinsic rewards. *American Psychologist* 30: 884–91.

Novitz, D. 1980. Of fact and fancy. *American Philosophical Quarterly* 17: 143–49.

Nozick, R. 1974. *Anarchy, state and utopia.* Oxford: Blackwell.

Nurmi, H. 1979. Modelling uncertainty in political decision-making. In *Models of political economy,* ed. P. Whiteley, pp. 291–318. London: Sage.

O'Neill, O. 1979. Begetting, bearing and rearing. In *Having children,* ed. O'Neill and W. Ruddick, pp. 25–38. New York: Oxford University Press.

Okrent, D. 1981. Industrial risks. *Proceedings of the Royal Society of London* A376: 133–49.

————, and Whipple, C. 1977. An approach to societal risk acceptance criteria and risk management. UCLA-ENG-7746. Mimeo., School of Engineering and Applied Science, University of California at Los Angeles.

Okun, A. M. 1975. *Equality and efficiency: the big tradeoff.* Washington, D.C.: Brookings.

Olson, M., Jr. 1965. *The logic of collective action.* Cambridge: Harvard University Press.

————. 1976. On Boulding's conception of integrative systems. In *Frontiers in social theory,* ed. M. Pfaff, pp. 57–86. Amsterdam: North-Holland.

————. 1977. Ignorance and uncertainty. Paper presented to Biennial Meeting of the Philosophy of Science Association, 1977, New York, N.Y.

————, and Bailey, M. J. 1981. Positive time preference. *Journal of Political Economy* 89: 1–25.

Opler, M. E., and Hoijer, H. 1940. The raid and war-path language of the Chirichua Apache. *American Anthropologist* 42: 617–34.

Organization for Economic Cooperation and Development (OECD), and International Atomic Energy Agency (IAEA). 1973. *Symposium on the management of radioactive wastes for fuel reprocessing.* Paris: OECD.

Orr, D. W. 1979. U.S. energy policy and the political economy of participation. *Journal of Politics* 41: 1027–56.

Ostrom, C. W., Jr. 1977. Evaluating alternative foreign policy decision-making models: an empirical test between arms race model and organizational politics model. *Journal of Conflict Resolution* 21: 235–66.

————. 1978. A reactive linkage model of the U.S. defense expenditure policymaking process. *American Political Science Review* 72: 941–57.

Otway, H. J., and Fishbein, M. 1976. The determinants of attitude formation: an application to nuclear energy. RM-76-80. Mimeo, International Institute for Applied Systems Analysis, Laxenburg, Austria.

————; Maurer, D.; and Thomas, K. 1978. Nuclear power: the question of public acceptance. *Futures* 10: 109–18.

————, and Misenta, R. 1980. Some human performance paradoxes of nuclear operations. *Futures* 12: 340–57.

————, and Phaner, P. D. 1976. Risk assessment. *Futures* 8: 122–34.

Owen, H., and Schultze, C. L., eds.   1976.   *Setting national priorities: the next ten years.* Washington, D.C.: Brookings.

Page, T.   1977.   *Conservation and economic efficiency.* Baltimore: Johns Hopkins University Press.

Papanek, H.   1973.   Purdah: separate worlds and symbolic shelter. *Comparative Studies in History and Society* 15: 289–325.

Parfit, D.   1973.   Later selves and moral principles. In *Philosophy and personal relations,* ed. A. Montefiore, pp. 137–69. London: Routledge & Kegan Paul.

———.   1976.   Lewis, Perry and what matters. In Rorty 1976, pp. 91–108.

———.   1981.   An attack on the social discount rate. *QQ: Report from the Center for Philosophy & Public Policy, University of Maryland* 1, no. 1: 8–11.

Parker, R., inspector.   1978.   *The Windscale Inquiry.* London: HMSO.

Partridge, P. H.   1968.   Freedom. In *Encyclopedia of philosophy,* ed. P. Edwards, vol. 3, pp. 221–25. London: Collier-Macmillan.

Passmore, J.   1974.   *Man's responsibility for nature.* London: Duckworth.

Pateman, C.   1970.   *Participation and democratic theory.* Cambridge: Cambridge University Press.

———.   1979. . *The problem of political obligation.* London: Wiley.

———.   1980.   Women and consent. *Political Theory* 8: 149–68.

Pearce, D. W.   1979.   Costs and benefits of nuclear futures. In *Biological implications of an expanded nuclear power programme,* ed. K. Mellanby. London: Institute of Biology.

———   1981.   Risk assessment: use and misuse. *Proceedings of the Royal Society of London* A376: 181–92.

———; Edwards, L.; and Beuret, G.   1979.   *Decision making for energy futures: a case study of the Windscale Inquiry.* London: Macmillan.

Pechman, J. A., and Timpane, P. M., eds.   1975.   *Work incentives and income guarantees.* Washington, D.C.: Brookings.

Peltzman, S.   1973.   An evaluation of consumer protection legislation: the 1972 drug amendments. *Journal of Political Economy* 81: 1049–91.

Perelman, L. J.   1980.   Speculations on the transition to sustainable energy. *Ethics* 90: 392–416.

Peston, M.   1967.   Changing utility functions. In *Essays in mathematical economics,* ed. M. Shubik, pp. 233–36. Princeton: Princeton University Press.

Philbrook, C.   1953.   "Realism" in policy espousal. *American Economic Review* 43: 864–59.

Phillips, D. Z.   1976.   Forty years on: anti-naturalism, and problems of social experiment and piecemeal social reform. *Inquiry* 19: 403–25.

Pico della Mirandola, G.   1948.   Oration on the dignity of man. In *The Renaissance philosophy of man,* ed. E. Cassirer, P. O. Kristeller, and J. H. Randall, Jr., trans. E. L. Forbes. Chicago: University of Chicago Press.

Pigou, A. C.   1932.   *The economics of welfare.* 4th ed. London: Macmillan.

———. 1935. *Economics in practice*. London: Macmillan.

———. 1951. Some aspects of economic welfare. *American Economic Review* 41: 287–302.

Pitkin, H. 1972. *The concept of representation*. Berkeley: University of California Press.

Pitt-Rivers, J. 1968. Honor. In *International encyclopedia of the social sciences*, ed. D. L. Sills, vol. 6, pp. 503–11. London: Collier-Macmillan.

Popkin, S. L. 1979. *The rational peasant*. Berkeley: University of California Press.

Popper, K. 1945. *The open society and its enemies*. London: Routledge & Kegan Paul.

———. 1957. *The poverty of historicism*. London: Routledge & Kegan Paul.

Posner, R. A. 1972. *Economic analysis of law*. Boston: Little Brown.

Pound, R. 1919. The administrative application of legal standards. In *Separation of powers and the independent agencies,* ed. Legislative Reference Service, U.S. Library of Congress, pp. 17–37. Document 91-49. 91st Congress, 1st Session. Washington, D.C.: GPO, 1970.

Prest, A. R., and Turvey, R. 1965. Cost-benefit analysis: a survey. *Economic Journal* 75: 685–705.

Pringle, M. L. K., and Fiddes, D. O. 1970. *The challenge of thalidomide*. London: Longman.

Ramsay, W., and Russell, M. 1978. Time-adjusted health impacts from electricity generation. *Public Policy* 26: 387–403.

Ramsey, F. P. 1928. A mathematic theory of savings. *Economic Journal* 38: 543–59.

Randolph, L. L. and S. H. 1965. Barristers and Brahmans in India: legal cultures and social change. *Comparative Studies in History and Society* 8: 24–49.

Ransom, R. L., and Sutch, R. 1977. *One kind of freedom: the economic consequences of emancipation*. Cambridge: Cambridge University Press.

Rapaport, A., and Wallsten, T. S. 1972. Individual decision behavior. *Annual Review of Psychology* 23: 131–76.

Rasmussen, N. C., chairman. 1975. *Reactor safety study: an assessment of accident risks in U.S. commercial nuclear power plants*. U.S. Nuclear Regulatory Commission. WASH-1400 (NUREG-75/014). Washington, D.C.: GPO.

Rawls, J. 1955. Two concepts of rules. *Philosophical Review* 64: 3–32.

———. 1957. Outline of a decision procedure for ethics. *Philosophical Review* 66: 177–97.

———. 1963. The sense of justice. *Philosophical Review* 72: 281–305.

———. 1972. *A theory of justice*. Oxford: Clarendon Press.

———. 1975. Fairness to goodness. *Philosophical Review* 84: 536–54.

———. 1977. The basic structure as subject. *American Philosophical Quarterly* 14: 159–65.

Raz, J. 1970. *The concept of a legal system*. Oxford: Clarendon Press.

———. 1975. *Practical reason and norms*. London: Hutchinson.

———. 1978. Professor Dworkin's theory of rights. *Political Studies* 26: 123–37.

Rees, W. J. 1953. Moral rules and the analysis of ought. *Philosophical Review* 62: 23–40.

Rein, M. 1976. *Social science and public policy*. Harmondsworth: Penguin.

———, and Miller, S. M. 1970. The demonstration as a strategy of social change. In Rein, *Social policy*, pp. 138–52. New York: Random House.

Rescher, N. 1975. *A theory of possibility*. Pittsburgh: University of Pittsburgh Press.

Richards, D. A. J. 1971. *A theory of reasons for action*. Oxford: Clarendon Press.

Richardson, L. F. 1960. *Arms and insecurity*. Pittsburgh: Boxwood Press.

Riecken, H. W., and Boruch, R. F., eds. 1974. *Social experimentation*. New York: Academic Press.

Riker, W. H. 1962. *The theory of political coalitions*. New Haven: Yale University Press.

———, and Ordeshook, P. C. 1968. A theory of the calculus of voting. *American Political Science Review* 62: 25–42.

———, and ———. 1973. *An introduction to positive political theory*. Englewood Cliffs, N.J.: Prentice-Hall.

Riskin, C. 1975. Maoism and motivation: work incentives in China. In *China's uninterrupted revolution*, ed. V. Nee and J. Peck. New York: Pantheon.

Rivlin, A. M. 1971. *Systematic thinking for social action*. Washington, D.C.: Brookings.

———. 1974. How can experiments be more useful? *American Economic Review (Papers & Proceedings)* 64: 346–54.

Robbins, L. 1932. *An essay on the nature and significance of economic science*. London: Macmillan.

———. 1938. Interpersonal comparisons of utility. *Economic Journal* 48: 635–41.

Roberts, J. M.; Golder, T. V.; and Chick, G. E. 1980. Judgment, oversight and skill: a cultural analysis of P-3 pilot errors. *Human Organization* 39: 5–22.

Rochlin, G. I. 1978. Nuclear waste disposal: two social criteria. *Science* 195: 23–31.

Rodda, M. 1967. *Noise and society*. Edinburgh: Oliver & Boyd.

Rogin, M. P. 1971. Liberal society and the Indian question. *Politics and Society* 1: 269–312.

Rorty, A. O., ed. 1976. *The identities of persons*. Berkeley: University of California Press.

Rose, D. J., and Lester, R. K. 1978. Nuclear power, nuclear weapons and international stability. *Scientific American* 238 [April]: 45–57.

Rose, R. 1974. Coping with urban change. In *The management of urban change in Britain and Germany*, ed. Rose, pp. 5–25. London: Sage.

———. 1976.   On the priorities of government: a developmental analysis of public policies. *European Journal of Political Research* 4: 247–89.

———, and Peters, B. G.   1979.   *Can government go bankrupt?* London: Macmillan.

Ross, W. D.   1930.   *The right and the good.* Oxford: Clarendon Press.

Roth, J. A.   1963.   *Timetables.* Indianapolis: Bobbs-Merrill.

Roth, P.   1971.   *Our gang.* London: Jonathan Cape.

Rothenberg, J.   1967.   The deployment of defensive weapons systems and the structure of deterrence. In McKean 1967, pp. 67–104.

Rothschild, V.   1978.   Risk. *The Listener* 100: 715–18.

Roumasset, J. A.   1976.   *Rice and risk.* Amsterdam: North-Holland.

Rousseau, J.-J.   1755.   *Discourse on inequality,* ed. L. G. Crocker. New York: Simon & Schuster, 1967.

———. 1762a. *Émile.* London: Dent, 1950.

———. 1762b. *Social contract,* trans. M. Cranston. Harmondsworth: Penguin, 1968.

Routley, R. and V.   1978.   Nuclear energy and obligations to the future. *Inquiry* 21: 133–79.

Russett, B. M.   1970.   *What price vigilance?* New Haven: Yale University Press.

———. 1978.   The marginal utility of income transfers to the Third World. *International Organization* 32: 913–28.

———. 1979.   World energy demand and world security. *Policy Sciences* 11: 187–202.

Ryle, G.   1958.   On forgetting the difference between right and wrong. In Melden 1958, pp. 147–59.

Salamon, L. M.   1979.   The time dimension in policy evaluation: the case of New Deal land-reform experiments. *Public Policy* 27: 129–83.

Samuelson, P. A.   1950.   The evaluation of real national income. *Oxford Economic Papers* 2: 1–29.

Sandia Laboratories.   1977.   *Barrier technology handbook.* U.S. Department of Energy, Security and Surveillance Division. Washington, D.C.: Department of Energy.

Santayana, G.   1953.   *My host the world.* London: Crescent Press.

Savage, L. J.   1954.   *The foundations of statistics.* New York: Wiley.

Sawyer, J.   1966.   The altruism scale: a measure of cooperative, individualistic and competitive interpersonal orientation. *American Journal of Sociology* 71: 407–16.

Scanlon, T. M.   1975.   Preference and urgency. *Journal of Philosophy* 72: 655–69.

Scheingold, S. A.   1974.   *The politics of rights.* New Haven: Yale University Press.

Schelling, T. C.   1963.   *The strategy of conflict.* New York: Oxford University Press.

———. 1966.   *Arms and influence.* New Haven: Yale University Press.

———. 1967.   The strategy of inflicting costs. In McKean 1967, pp. 105–27.

―――. 1968. The life you save may be your own. In *Problems in public expenditure analysis,* ed. S. B. Chase, Jr., pp. 127–62. Washington, D.C.: Brookings.

―――. 1981. Economic reasoning and the ethics of policy. *Public Interest* 63: 37–61.

Schilling, W. R. 1961. The H bomb decision: how to decide without actually choosing. *Political Science Quarterly* 76: 24–46.

―――. 1962. The politics of national defense: fiscal 1950. In Schilling, P. Y. Hammond, and G. H. Snyder, *Strategy, politics and defense budgets,* pp. 1–266. New York: Columbia University Press.

Schiltz, M. E. 1970. *Public attitudes toward social security, 1935–65.* U.S. Department of Health, Education, and Welfare, Social Security Administration, Office of Research and Statistics. Report 33. Washington, D.C.: GPO.

Schlesinger, J. R. 1968. The changing environment for systems analysis. In *Systems analysis and policy planning: applications in defense,* ed. E. S. Quade and W. I. Boucher, pp. 364–87. New York: North-Holland.

Schulman, P. R. 1975. Nonincremental policy-making. *American Political Science Review* 69: 1345–70.

―――. 1980. *Large-scale policy making.* New York: Elsevier.

Schultze, C. L. 1968. *The politics and economics of public spending.* Washington, D.C.: Brookings.

―――. 1970. The role of incentives, penalties and rewards in attaining effective policy. In Haveman and Margolis 1970, pp. 145–72.

―――. 1976. Federal spending: past, present and future. In Owen and Schultze 1976, pp. 323–69.

―――. 1977. *The public use of private interest.* Washington, D.C.: Brookings.

Schumpeter, J. A. 1950. *Capitalism, socialism and democracy.* 3d ed. New York: Harper & Row.

Schweinhart, L. J., and Weikart, D. P. 1980. *Young children grow up.* Ypsilanti, Mich.: High/Scope Press.

Scobie, W. 1981. U.S. rehearses "nuke" accident. *Observer* (London), 19 April 1981, p. 8.

Scott, J. C. 1976. *The moral economy of the peasant.* New Haven: Yale University Press.

Scott, R. H. 1972. Avarice, altruism and second party preferences. *Quarterly Journal of Economics* 86: 1–18.

Sears, D. O.; Lau, R. R.; Taylor, T. R.; and Allen, H. M., Jr. 1980. Self-interest vs. symbolic politics in policy attitudes and Presidential voting. *American Political Science Review* 74: 670–84.

Sen, A. K. 1957. A note on Tinbergen on the optimum rate of saving. *Economic Journal* 67: 745–48.

―――. 1960. *Choice of techniques.* Oxford: Blackwell.

―――. 1961. On optimising the rate of saving. *Economic Journal* 71: 470–98.

―――. 1966. Labour allocation in a cooperative enterprise. *Review of Economic Studies* 33: 361–71.

———. 1970. *Collective choice and social welfare.* San Francisco: Holden-Day.

———. 1972. Control areas and accounting prices: an approach to economic evaluation. *Economic Journal* 82: 486–501.

———. 1973. *On economic inequality.* Oxford: Clarendon Press.

———. 1974. Rawls versus Bentham: an axiomatic examination of the pure distribution problem. *Theory and Decision* 4: 301–10.

———. 1975. *Employment, technology and development.* Oxford: Clarendon Press.

———. 1977. Rational fools: a critique of the behavioral foundations of economic theory. *Philosophy & Public Affairs* 6: 317–44.

———. 1979. The welfare basis of real income comparisons: a survey. *Journal of Economic Literature* 17: 1–45.

Sennett, R., and Cobb, J.   1972.   *The hidden injuries of class.* Cambridge: Cambridge University Press.

Shackle, G. L. S.   1966.   Policy, poetry and success. *Economic Journal* 76: 755–67.

Shapiro, D. L.   1965.   The choice of rulemaking or adjudication in the development of administrative policy. *Harvard Law Review* 78: 921–72.

Shrader-Frechette, K. S.   1980.   *Nuclear power and public policy.* Dordrecht, Holland: D. Reidel.

Shrauger, J. S., and Schoeneman, T. J.   1979.   Symbolic interactionist view of self-concept: through the looking glass darkly. *Psychological Bulletin* 86: 549–73.

Shue, H.   1978.   Torture. *Philosophy & Public Affairs* 7: 124–43.

———. 1980.   *Basic rights.* Princeton: Princeton University Press.

Shue, V.   1980.   *Peasant China in transition.* Berkeley: University of California Press.

Sidgwick, H.   1874.   *The methods of ethics.* London: Macmillan.

———. 1897.   *Elements of politics.* London: Macmillan.

Siegenthaler, U., and Oeschager, H.   1978.   Predicting future atmospheric carbon dioxide levels. *Science* 199: 388–95.

Sikora, R. I., and Barry, B., eds.   1978.   *Obligations to future generations.* Philadelphia: Temple University Press.

Simmel, G.   1907.   *The philosophy of money,* trans. T. B. Bottomore and D. Frisby. London: Routledge & Kegan Paul. 1978.

Singer, M. G.   1958.   Moral rules and principles. In Melden 1958, pp. 160–97.

Singer, P.   1973.   Altruism and commerce: a defence of Titmuss against Arrow. *Philosophy & Public Affairs* 2: 312–20.

———. 1979.   *Practical ethics.* Cambridge: Cambridge University Press.

Skinner, B. F.   1971.   *Beyond freedom and dignity.* Harmondsworth: Penguin.

Slovic, P., and Fischhoff, B.   1980.   How safe is safe enough? In *Risk and chance,* ed. J. Dowie and P. Lefrere, pp. 121–47. Milton Keynes: Open University Press.

———; ———; and Lichtenstein, S.   1981.   Perceived risk: psychological factors and social implications. *Proceedings of the Royal Society of London* A376:17–34.

———; Kunreuther, H.; and White, G. F.   1974.   Decision processes, rationality and adjustment to natural hazards. In *Natural hazards,* ed. G. F. White, pp. 187–205. New York: Oxford University Press.

Smart, J. J. C.   1973.   An outline of a system of utilitarian ethics. In Smart and B. Williams, *Utilitarianism, for and against,* pp. 3–74. Cambridge: Cambridge University Press.

Smith, A.   1776.   *The wealth of nations.* London: W. Strahan & T. Cadell.

———.   1790.   *The theory of the moral sentiments.* 6th ed. London: A. Strahan and T. Cadell.

Smith, R. S.   1974.   The feasibility of an "injury tax" approach to occupational safety. *Law and Contemporary Problems* 38: 730–44.

Smith, V. L.   1978.   Psychology and economics: discussion. *American Economic Review (Papers & Proceedings)* 68: 76–77.

Sorokin, P. A., and Merton, R. K.   1937.   Social time. *American Journal of Sociology* 42: 615–29.

Speier, H.   1941.   The social types of war. *American Journal of Sociology* 46: 445–54.

Spiegelberg, H.   1970.   Human dignity: a challenge to contemporary philosophy. In *Human dignity: this century and next,* ed. R. Gotesky and E. Laszlo, pp. 38–64. New York: Gordon & Breach.

Squires, A. M.   1970.   Clean power from coal. *Science* 169: 821–28.

Starr, C.   1969.   Social benefits vs. technological risks. *Science* 165: 1232–38.

Staw, B. M.   1975.   *Intrinsic and extrinsic motivation.* Morristown, N.J.: General Learning Press.

Stebbing, L. S.   1944.   *Ideals and illusions.* London: Watts.

Stich, S. P.   1978.   The recombinant DNA debate. *Philosophy & Public Affairs* 7: 187–205.

Stigler, G. J., and Becker, G. S.   1977.   De gustibus non est disputandum. *American Economic Review* 67: 76–90.

Stobaugh, R., and Yergin, D., eds.   1979.   *Energy future.* Report of the Energy Project at the Harvard Business School. New York: Random House.

Stokey, E., and Zeckhauser, R.   1978.   *A primer for policy analysis.* New York: Norton.

Stone, D. A.   1978.   The deserving sick: income-maintenance policy towards the ill and disabled. *Policy Sciences* 10: 133–35.

Strawson, P. F.   1974.   *Freedom and resentment and other essays.* London: Methuen.

Sugden, R.   1982.   Hard luck stories: the problem of the uninsured in a laissez-faire society. *Journal of Social Policy* 11 (forthcoming).

Swalm, R. O.   1966.   Utility theory—insights into risk taking. *Harvard Business Review* 44, no. 6: 123–38.

Tamerin, J. S., and Resnick, H. L. P.   1972.   Risk taking by individual option—case study: cigarette smoking. In *Perspectives on benefit-risk decision making.* Washington, D.C.: National Academy of Engineering.

Taney, R. B.   1857.   *Scott v. Sanford.* 60 U.S. (19 Howard) 393.

Taylor, M.   1976.   *Anarchy and cooperation.* London: Wiley.

Taylor, M.D.   1974.   The legitimate claims of national security. *Foreign Affairs* 52: 577–94.

Teller, E.   1978.   The many hazards of energy. Paper read to School of Nuclear Engineering, Purdue University, 11 April 1978, West Lafayette, Ind.

Ten, C. L.   1971.   Paternalism and morality. *Ratio* 13: 56–66.

Thomas, L.   1980.   Sexism and racism: some conceptual differences. *Ethics* 90: 239–50.

Thompson, J. J.   1971.   A defense of abortion. *Philosophy & Public Affairs* 1: 47–66.

———.   1973.   Preferential hiring. *Philosophy & Public Affairs* 2: 364–84.

Thompson, M.   1979.   *Rubbish theory.* Oxford: Clarendon Press.

Titmuss, R. M.   1971.   *The gift relationship.* London: Allen & Unwin.

Tobin, J.   1966.   *National economic policy.* New Haven: Yale University Press.

Trabalka, J. R.; Eyman, L. D.; and Auerbach, S. I.   1980.   Analysis of the 1957–58 Soviet nuclear accident. *Science* 209: 345–53.

Tullock, G.   1967.   *Toward a mathematics of politics.* Ann Arbor: University of Michigan Press.

Tversky, A., and Kahneman, D.   1971.   Belief in the law of small numbers. *Psychological Bulletin* 76: 105–10.

———, and ———.   1974.   Judgment under uncertainty: heuristics and biases. *Science* 185: 1124–31.

———, and ———.   1981.   Framing of decisions and the psychology of choice. *Science* 211: 453–58.

Ullman, W.   1975.   *Law and politics in the Middle Ages.* Ithaca, N.Y.: Cornell University Press.

U.K. Department of Energy.   1978.   *Energy Policy.* London: HMSO.

U.S. Congress. House. Committee on Insular and Interior Affairs, Subcommittee on Energy and the Environment.   1978.   *Accuracy of U.S. Nuclear Regulatory Commission testimony held 27 February 1978.* 95th Congress, 2d Session. Serial 95-29. Washington, D.C.: GPO.

U.S. Congress. Office of Technology Assessment (OTA).   1977.   *Nuclear proliferation and safeguards.* Washington, D.C.: GPO.

———.   1979.   *Drugs in livestock feed.* Washington, D.C.: GPO.

———.   1980.   *The effects of nuclear war.* Washington, D.C.: GPO.

U.S. Environmental Protection Agency (EPA), Office of Radiation Programs.   1979.   Impact assessment of high-level wastes. In U.S. Congress, House Committee on Interior and Insular Affairs, Subcommittee on Energy and the Environment, *Oversight hearings: nuclear waste management, 25–26 January 1979,* pp. 119–40. 96th Congress, 1st Session. Serial 96-1. Washington, D.C.: GPO.

U.S. General Accounting Office (GAO).   1979.   *The nation's nuclear waste: proposals for organization and siting.* Washington, D.C.: GAO.

U.S. Interagency Review Group on Nuclear Waste Management (IRG), Subgroup for Alternative Technology Strategies.   1978.   Isolation of radioactive wastes in geological repositories: status of scientific and technological knowledge. In U.S. Congress, House Committee on Interior and Insular Affairs, Subcommittee on Energy and the Environment, *Oversight hearing: Interagency Review Group on Nuclear Waste Management, 11 July 1978*, pp. 80–158. 95th Congress, 2d Session. Serial 95-35. Washington, D.C.: GPO.

U.S. National Academy of Sciences (NAS), Committee on Nuclear and Alternative Energy Systems, Demand and Conservation Panel. 1978. U.S. energy demand: some low energy futures. *Science* 200: 142–52.

Urmson, J. O. 1958. Saints and heroes. In Melden 1958, pp. 198–216.

Valavanis, S. 1958. The resolution of conflict when utilities interact. *Journal of Conflict Resolution* 2: 156–69.

Vanek, J., ed. 1975. *Self-management*. Harmondsworth: Penguin.

Veatch, R. M. 1980. Voluntary risks to health. *Journal of the American Medical Association* 243: 50–55.

Viner, J. 1972. *The role of providence in the social order*. Princeton: Princeton University Press.

Viscusi, W. K. 1978. Wealth effects and earnings premiums for job hazards. *Review of Economics and Statistics* 60: 408–16.

———. 1979. *Employment hazards*. Cambridge: Harvard University Press.

Vlastos, G. 1962. Justice and equality. In *Social justice*, ed. R. B. Brandt, pp. 31–72. Englewood Cliffs, N.J.: Prentice-Hall.

Wade, N. 1980. BW and recombinant DNA. *Science* 208: 271.

Wald, A. 1950. *Statistical decision functions*. New York: Wiley.

Walker, J. L. 1977. Setting the agenda in the U.S. Senate: a theory of problem selection. *British Journal of Political Science* 7: 423–46.

Walzer, M. 1971. World War II: why was this war different? *Philosophy & Public Affairs* 1: 3–21.

———. 1973. Political action: the problem of dirty hands. *Philosophy & Public Affairs* 2: 160–80.

———. 1980. The moral standing of states. *Philosophy & Public Affairs* 9: 209–29.

Ward, R., inspector. 1981. Re-opened exploratory inquiry into the desirability of revoking the planning permission granted to United Refineries Ltd. on 28 March 1973 for the construction of an oil refinery on Canvey Island. Mimeo., U.K. Department of the Environment, London.

Warnock, G. J. 1971. *The object of morality*. London: Methuen.

Warnock, M. 1960. *Ethics since 1900*. London: Oxford University Press.

Warren, E. 1957. Dissent. *Perez v. Brownell*. 356 U.S. 44.

Watkins, J. W. N. 1963. Negative utilitarianism. *Proceedings of the Aristotelian Society (Supplement)* 37: 95–114.

Webb, S. and B. 1932. *Methods of social study*. Cambridge: Cambridge University Press.

Wechsler, H. 1959. Toward neutral principles of constitutional law. *Harvard Law Review* 73: 26–35.

Weinberg, A. M. 1972a. Science and trans-science. *Minerva* 10: 209–22.

————. 1972b. Social institutions and nuclear energy. *Science* 177: 27–34.

————. 1979. Salvaging the atomic age. *Wilson Quarterly* 3, no. 3: 88–115.

————, et al. 1979. *Economic and environmental impacts of a U.S. nuclear moratorium, 1985–2010.* 2d ed. Institute for Energy Analysis, Oak Ridge Associated Universities. Cambridge: MIT Press.

Weinstein, M. C.; Shepard, D. S.; and Pliskin, J. S. 1980. The economic value of changing mortality probabilities: a decision-theoretic approach. *Quarterly Journal of Economics* 94: 373–96.

————, and Stason, W. B. 1977. Foundations of cost-effectiveness analysis for health and medical practices. *New England Journal of Medicine* 296: 716–21.

Weiss, R. S., and Rein, M. 1970. The evaluation of broad-aim programs. *Administrative Science Quarterly* 15: 97–109.

Weisskopf, V. F. 1980. Editorial: the overwhelming priority. *Bulletin of the Atomic Scientists* 36, no. 2: 1.

von Weiszäcker, C. C. 1971. Notes on endogenous change of tastes. *Journal of Economic Theory* 3: 345–72.

Whyte, W. F. 1943. *Street corner society.* Chicago: University of Chicago Press.

Wicksteed, P. H. 1933. *The common sense of political economy.* London: Routledge.

Wildavsky, A. 1966. The political economy of efficiency. *Public Administration Review* 26: 292–310.

————. 1979. *Speaking the truth to power.* Boston: Little Brown.

————. 1980. Richer is safer. *Public Interest* 60: 23–39.

Williams, B. A. O. 1962. The idea of equality. In *Philosophy, politics and society,* ed. P. Laslett and W. G. Runciman, 2d series, pp. 110–31. Oxford: Blackwell.

————. 1973. A critique of utilitarianism. In J. J. C. Smart and Williams, *Utilitarianism, for and against,* pp. 75–150. Cambridge: Cambridge University Press.

————. 1976a. Persons, character and morality. In Rorty 1976, pp. 197–216.

————. 1976b. Utilitarianism and moral self-indulgence. In *Contemporary British philosophy,* ed. H. D. Lewis, 4th series, pp. 306–21. London: Allen & Unwin.

————. 1978. Politics and moral character. In Hampshire 1978, pp. 55–74.

Williams, G. L. 1945–46. Language and the law. *Law Quarterly Review* 61: 71–86, 179–95, 293–303, 384–406; and 62: 387–406.

Williams, M. B. 1978. Discounting versus maximum sustainable yield. In Sikora and Barry 1978, pp. 169–85.

Wilson, G. C. 1981. Disposal of poison chemical weapons seen costing Pentagon billions. *Washington Post,* 15 March 1981, p. A5.

Wilson, J. Q. 1981. "Policy intellectuals" and public policy. *Public Interest* 64: 31–46.

ı, J. R. S. 1978. In one another's power. *Ethics* 88: 299–315.

tetter, A. 1964. Analysis and design of conflict systems. In *'ysis for military decision,* ed. E. S. Quade, pp. 103–48. Chicago: d McNally.

-. 1976–77. Spreading the bomb without quite breaking the rules. *ign Policy* 25: 88–96, 145–79.

·; Brown, T. A.; Jones, G.; McGarvey, D.; Rowen, H.; Taylor, V.; Wohlstetter, R. 1976. *Moving toward life in a nuclear armed d.* Los Angeles: Pan Heuristics. Reprinted (abridged) as: The mili- potential of civilian nuclear energy. *Minerva* 15 [1977]: 387–538.

C. P., Jr. 1980. The accident at Three Mile Island: social science spectives. *Policy Studies Review Annual* 4: 371–76.

-. 1981. Ethics and policy analysis. In *Public duties,* ed. J. L. ishman, L. Liebman, and M. H. Moore, pp. 131–41. Cambridge: Har- rd University Press.

.lstonecraft, M. 1790. *A vindication of the rights of women,* ed. C. H. Post. New York: Norton, 1975.

oodward, B., and Bernstein, C. 1976. *The final days.* London: Secker & Warburg.

oodward, C. V. 1955. *The strange career of Jim Crow.* New York: Oxford University Press.

·oodwell, G. M. 1978. The carbon dioxide question. *Scientific American* 238 [January]: 34–43.

Wootton, B. 1945. *Freedom under planning.* Chapel Hill: University of North Carolina Press.

Wortman, P. M. 1981. Randomized clinical trials. In *Methods for evaluating health services,* ed. Wortman, pp. 41–60. Beverly Hills, Calif.: Sage.

von Wright, G. H. 1963. *Norm and action.* London: Routledge & Kegan Paul.

Yergin, D. 1978. *Shattered peace.* London: André Deutsch.

Zeckhauser, R. 1969. Resource allocation with probabilistic individual preferences. *American Economic Review (Papers & Proceedings)* 59: 546–52.

———. 1973. Coverage for catastrophic illness. *Public Policy* 21: 149–72.

———. 1975. Procedures for valuing lives. *Public Policy* 23: 419–64.

———, and Shaefer, E. 1968. Public policy and normative economic theory. In *The study of policy formation,* ed. R. A. Bauer and K. Gergen, pp. 27–102. New York: Free Press.

Zeeman, E. C. 1976. Catastrophe theory. *Scientific American* 234 [April]: 65–83.

Zelizer, V. A. 1978. Human values and the market: the case of life in- surance and death in 19th century America. *American Journal of Sociology* 84: 591–610.

Zolberg, A. 1972. Moments of madness. *Politics and Society* 2: 183–208.

Index